REMOVING REFORMATION GLASSES

VIEWING ROMANS BIBLICALLY, NOT THROUGH
THE LENS OF A THEOLOGICAL SYSTEM

JAMES S. HOLLANDSWORTH

HOLLYPUBLISHING

Copyright © 2024 by James S. Hollandsworth

All rights reserved.

No part of this book may be reproduced in any form or by any electronic or mechanical means, including information storage and retrieval systems, without written permission from the author, except for the use of brief quotations in critical reviews or articles.

Unless otherwise indicated, the Bible version used in this publication is the *New King James Version®*. Copyright © 1982 by Thomas Nelson. Used by permission. All rights reserved.

Scripture quotations marked HCSB are taken from the *Holman Christian Standard Bible®*, Used by Permission HCSB ©1999,2000,2002,2003,2009 Holman Bible Publishers. Holman Christian Standard Bible®, Holman CSB®, and HCSB® are federally registered trademarks of Holman Bible Publishers.

Scripture quotations taken from the (NASB®) *New American Standard Bible®*, Copyright © 1960, 1971, 1977, 1995, 2020 by The Lockman Foundation. Used by permission. All rights reserved. www.lockman.org

Scripture quotations marked (ESV) are from The ESV® Bible (*The Holy Bible, English Standard Version®*), © 2001 by Crossway, a publishing ministry of Good News Publishers. Used by permission. All rights reserved.

Scripture quotations marked (YLT) are taken from the 1898 *Young's Literal Translation of the Holy Bible* by J.N. Young, (Author of the Young's Analytical Concordance), public domain.

ISBN-13: 979-8-9869721-8-3

Printed in the United States of America

DEDICATION

To my dear wife Leslie.
We met forty years ago and what an adventure!
Thanks for being my soulmate and greatest supporter.
With all my love.

To my seven children and their spouses:
Katie and Adam
Josh and Maria
Phil and Jess
Rachel and Jon
Anna and Andrew
Beth and Bray
Sarah and Chris

And to my nine grandchildren (thus far):
Jackson
Liam
Jayden
Denver
Holland
Nathan
Brooklynne
Taylor
Eden

*I have no greater joy
than to hear that my children walk in truth.
3 John 4*

I love you all!
Dad/Papa

ACKNOWLEDGMENTS

I am truly thankful for godly friends who are committed to the truth of God's Word and not bound by tradition. Several read this book before publication, either in its entirety or in large part, and gave valuable input as to how to improve the manuscript, both grammatically and theologically. A hearty "thank you" goes to:

Keith Call
Arlen Chitwood
David Crain, Sr.
Tracy Daniels
Lindell Dillon
Leslie Hollandsworth
Carole Knobil
Jason Perry
Josh Phillips
Todd Tjepkema

I sincerely appreciate your contribution to this book!

A special "thank you" goes to Pastor Tracy Daniels and the good people of Faith Baptist Church in Chattanooga, for hosting the annual Bible conference where biblical truths are preached, taught, and discussed around meal times, year after year. I have personally been a part of this conference for thirteen years, and it is always a highlight of my year. Pastor Tracy and all the church folk are always so welcoming and gracious to make us comfortable and feed us well too! May the Lord reward you for being so hospitable.

CONTENTS

Foreword by Arlen Chitwood	ix
1. What Are Reformation Glasses?	1
2. Justified by Faith-Filled Works Part 1	11
In Hebrews	
3. Justified by Faith-Filled Works Part 2	32
In Galatians	
4. Justified by Faith-Filled Works Part 3	44
In James	
5. The Romans Road to Salvation Misnomer	59
Romans 1:1-17	
6. Exchanging Glory for Shame	75
Romans 1:18-32	
7. Eternal Life for Doing Good?	91
Romans 2:1-24	
8. The Righteous Requirements of the Law	106
Romans 2:25-29	
9. The Mystery of the Oracles	121
Romans 3:1-20	
10. Soul-Salvation by Grace Through Faith	136
Romans 3:21-4:8	
11. His Resurrection for Our Righteous Living	152
Romans 4:9-25	
12. Rejoicing in Hope of Glory	164
Romans 5:1-11	
13. Grace Wins!	181
Romans 5:12-21	
14. Buried in Death, Risen in Life	195
Romans 6:1-14	
15. Who's Your Master?	210
Romans 6:15-23	
16. The Deadening Effects of Legalism	220
Romans 7	
17. How to Have Victory Over Sinning	234
Romans 8:1-11	
18. The Revealing of God's Glorified Sons	245
Romans 8:12-19	

19. Birth of a New Age *Romans 8:19-25*	260
20. Promises for Firstborn Sons *Romans 8:26-39*	275
21. Has Israel Been Replaced? *Romans 9:1-3*	289
22. Israel's Future Restoration and Global Impact *Romans 9:4-13*	306
23. Vessels of Mercy Prepared for Glory *Romans 9:14-33*	322
24. The Word of Faith Is Near You *Romans 10*	334
25. Israel's Time-Out *Romans 11:1-15*	351
26. Israel Will Be Saved and All Mankind Too *Romans 11:16-36*	365
27. Metamorphosis Culminating in Glory *Romans 12:1-2*	381
28. Get Off Your High Horse *Romans 12:3-8*	393
29. Rules for Revolutionizing Home and Church *Romans 12:9-21*	407
30. Obeying Government and Loving Mankind *Romans 13*	420
31. Every Knee Shall Bow *Romans 14*	433
32. Glorifying God With One Mind and Voice *Romans 15*	449
33. Crushing the Devil *Romans 16:1-24*	466
34. The Fellowship of the Mystery *Romans 16:25-27*	480
Addendum 1: Eternal Is Not Forever	489
Addendum 2: Four Degrees of Salvation	505
Endnotes	523
Also by James S. Hollandsworth	537

FOREWORD BY ARLEN CHITWOOD

This book, *Removing Reformation Glasses*, is NOT about the Reformation per se. Rather, it is about HOW things emanating from the Reformation have governed or heavily influenced theology — mainly soteriology (the doctrine of *salvation*) — in Christian circles and the Church at large for the past five hundred years. And a main way that this has been done is through the reformers' heavy emphasis on one of the Pauline epistles, the Book of Romans.

In this respect, *Removing Reformation Glasses*, a commentary on Romans, shows from the very book looked to by the reformers time and again EXACTLY what has been done.

To begin, let's consider two questions regarding the Reformation and soteriological teachings down through the years, bringing us to the present day and time:

1. Is Christendom today, half a millennium removed from the beginning of the Reformation (seen beginning through actions of Martin Luther in 1517 at Wittenberg), better off because of the Reformation?
2. Or, is the opposite true instead? Does an almost completely leavened Christendom in today's world, with its numerous schisms and factions, owe its decadent state, in no small part, to what began in 1517 at Wittenberg?

And, to address those two questions, let's move on to the evolution of Reformation thought over a five-hundred-year period, the Book of Romans, and this commentary on Romans.

A PERSONAL WORD

But, before we look at the different aspects of soteriology (not only in "past" time, but "present," and "future" time), I want to say several things about myself, the author of this book, and hopefully you the reader as well.

There are a couple of things in this book that I would not agree with. And the author, conversely, of course, would not agree with my position on these things as well. But, nonetheless, he has graciously asked me to write this foreword, and I did not hesitate to consent.

Having read the draft of this book, I realized the importance of the information contained therein. And I wanted to see this material placed in the hands of interested individuals.

Then, with that in mind, I not only didn't hesitate to write this foreword, but I wanted to write it.

Now, you may think our doing this, with certain differences between us, as somewhat strange.

But, not so! The opposite would, instead, be true. That is to say, it would, instead, be strange if the author of the book and I did agree on everything in the book.

Allow me to explain, and maybe you can learn what I learned over sixty years ago.

In the fall of 1958 (I was twenty-five years old and studying for the ministry), I found myself sitting under the ministry of a pastor-teacher in the true sense of the word (A. Edwin Wilson) — where I remained for the next four years, and indirectly for a number of succeeding years.

This is the man who taught me the basics of practically everything that I've taught over the years.

And this is the man who taught me something about what I'm doing at the present time — writing the foreword for a book, with the author and I seeing several things in the book in a different light.

A. Edwin Wilson made this statement one time, perhaps more than once:

> If you ever find two Christians who believe exactly the same thing about everything in the Bible, you can know one thing for certain. You can know that one of them is not studying.

The author of this book and I have no problems with any of this. We see so many things alike, particularly regarding the complete soteriological (salvation) message — salvation not only "past," but "present," and "future" as well. And the "present" and "future" aspects of this complete soteriological message *have to do with the central message of Scripture, which is the central message that you will find in the Book of Romans and in this commentary on Romans.*

As well, the author of this book is not afraid to proclaim what he sees being taught from Scripture, regardless of many not seeing the matter after the same manner at all.

And THAT'S the approach you will find in this book!

I like this! It is quite refreshing to see, particularly coming from someone with a good Biblical background, acquired over time and study, who knows what he is talking about.

And in connection with the preceding, the author and I would have little to no differences in his overall approach to the main subject matter of this book, set forth in the title, *Removing Reformation Glasses*.

Now, with that behind us, let's move on to the evolution of Reformation thought over a five-hundred-year period, the Book of Romans, and this commentary on Romans.

And, doing this, let's state something about the Book of Romans up front:

SALVATION IN THE BOOK OF ROMANS

- The Book of Romans, in complete alignment and agreement with the central message of Scripture as a whole, deals with the salvation message in a "present" respect (an on-going process of salvation, dependent on an

individual having already been saved), NOT in a "past" respect (i.e., NOT relative to salvation by grace through faith).
- In that respect, individuals looking to Romans for Scripture to use in evangelistic work among the unsaved are looking at the wrong book.
- On the other hand, individuals looking to Romans for Scripture to use when dealing with the saved are looking at the right book.
- Romans, as elsewhere in the Pauline and General epistles, deals with the "present" aspect of salvation with a view to the "future," with a view to the realization of salvation/deliverance in the Messianic Era (i.e., occupying a position as co-heir with Christ in His millennial kingdom, as He rules the nations of this present earth with a rod of iron).

THE NEGATIVE INFLUENCE OF REFORMATION THOUGHT

And, what has Reformation thought over the past five hundred years done to this salvation message seen time and again throughout the Book of Romans, among the other epistles?

Reformation thought, through reading salvation by grace through faith into numerous passages in Romans, among like passages in other epistles — passages which deal NOT with the "past" aspect of salvation BUT with "present" and "future" aspects — has NOT ONLY misconstrued and corrupted the simple message of salvation by grace BUT has covered up and done away with the true message.

Reformation thought has progressively, negatively influenced generation after generation of Christians down through the years, misleading them NOT ONLY on the salvation message in Romans BUT the central salvation message throughout the N.T. as a whole, not to mention the salvation message seen throughout the O.T. as well, beginning in Genesis.

This complete leavening process began in a gradual manner, becoming entrenched and accepted. Then, with time, it began to accelerate, becoming even more entrenched and accepted. And, with additional time, it became rampant, becoming almost universally entrenched and accepted, bringing us to the present day and time.

That's the way leaven works. And if you want to know WHY the Church exists in its present decadent state, seen in Matt. 13:33 and Rev. 3:17, look no farther than what was set in motion five hundred years ago.

You won't read about this in Church history books, for Church history books don't present the Reformation and its results from a correct understanding of Scripture. Rather, they present the matter through the only other means left.

THE "LEAVENING" OF CHRISTIANITY

A history of the Church throughout the dispensation can be seen two places in the N.T. One was given by Christ before the dispensation began, in the first four parables of Matt. 13; and the other was given by John after the dispensation had ended (yet future today), in Rev. 2, 3.

Both present a digression of the faith throughout the dispensation, NOT a progression. And the completion of this digression of the whole of the matter, the completion of this leavening process, could only have been fostered, in no small part, by Reformation thought throughout the closing five hundred years of the present dispensation.

And don't be misled into thinking that this type thing is limited to what is referred to as the reformed segment of Christendom today.

FAR from it!

The WHOLE of Christendom is shot through and through with this type leavening process, which, from a Biblical standpoint, is the worst type leavening process possible.

WHY is it the worst type?

Note what this leavening process does. It substitutes one message for another message, doing away with the correct message. And the correct message, invariably, has to do with the Word of the Kingdom, the direction toward which all Scripture moves, the coming kingdom of Christ.

In short, to use modern-day vernacular, this leavening process goes to the wellhead and shuts matters down at that point!

BUT, wait a minute!

The cry of the Reformation was sola fide, Latin for "faith alone." And many today, attempting to take matters either to or back to "faith alone" reference the reformers and sola fide.

That's all very true! BUT, what did the reformers do with their cry of sola fide when it came to correct Biblical understanding and interpretation, with its far-reaching effects?

THAT'S the issue!

A REFORMATION OUT OF THE REFORMATION

And, again, if an individual wants to see how all of this has played out over the past five hundred years, bringing the matter down into modern times, all he has to do is attend any Church of any denomination on any Sunday morning and listen for any mention or reference to the Word of the Kingdom.

Unless it is a very unusual Church, he will listen in vain.

And the word "unusual" brings up another issue about the Reformation which needs to be addressed, which might be looked upon as a Reformation out of the Reformation.

There were individuals reached with the sola fide message who, at different times in later years, began to restudy the reformers' emphasis solely on salvation by grace and their corresponding interpretation of Scripture.

These men began to see Scripture dealing with the simple salvation message, salvation by grace through faith, as the beginning point, NOT as an end in itself.

And certain results of these individuals' work can be seen several hundred years beyond the Reformation in the writings of men such as Robert Govett, G. H. Pember, or G. H. Lang (men from the 19th and 20th centuries).

And individuals today, writing and speaking on this subject owe a large debt to those who went before them.

And I'll leave further comments for the contents of this book.

Study the matter out. BUT, do so in the light of Scripture, NOT in the light of this book or any other book. You might even surprise yourself and learn a few things.

BUT, a warning!

You might learn some things that you didn't want to know, for "knowledge" and "a corresponding responsibility for that knowledge" go hand-in-hand.

Arlen L. Chitwood
Cottonwood, Arizona

CHAPTER 1
WHAT ARE REFORMATION GLASSES?

The title of this book is *Removing Reformation Glasses: Viewing Romans Biblically, Not Through the Lens of a Theological System.* Thus, this volume is a call to interpret the biblical book of Romans *as Paul intended, not as the Reformers taught.* That begs the question: What are Reformation glasses? What did the Reformers teach about salvation and justification that has clouded our understanding of Romans? This chapter will begin to unfold some of the errant ideas that came out of the Reformation, which have been accepted as "gospel truth," when in reality they are merely man's ideas. Subsequent chapters will add more details as we go along.

The sincere desire of diligent students of God's Word is to rightly divide (2 Tim. 2:15) — i.e., to correctly interpret — the Scriptures. With that goal in mind, I intend to exposit the book of Romans historically, grammatically, and contextually, apart from Reformation theology. That is a tall order, seeing that our ideas about salvation and justification for the past five hundred years have been driven largely by Reformation doctrines that have been handed down to us, generation by generation. What that means is that when studying Romans, most Christians unwittingly interpret concepts in the book through the lens of their Reformation heritage. But it is improper to interpret Scripture through the lens of one's theology. We must *let Scripture determine our theology*, not allow our theology to determine the meaning of Scripture. If we truly want to understand Romans as Paul intended, then we must rid ourselves of traditional theological baggage, which has become Christianity's "default mode."

THOSE WHO DENY PROTESTANT HERITAGE

Incidentally, many independent Baptist churches deny having a Reformation heritage or affiliation with Protestantism, for they never came out of the Roman Catholic church. These churches claim to be descended from an unbroken lineage of pre-denominational, "Baptistic" groups (e.g., Montanists, Novationists, Donatists, Paulicans, Albigenses, Waldenses, Anabaptists, etc.) that remained doctrinally pure, separated from Roman Catholicism through the centuries, dating back to the early church and the apostles.

Despite this heritage (a discussion of which is outside the scope of this book), the fact remains that virtually all modern Christians and churches have been impacted in large measure by Reformation doctrines that have been perpetuated, oftentimes unwittingly, by pastors who attended Bible college or seminary and were trained by professors who were impacted by Reformation doctrines somewhere along the line. Thus, error has crept in and become widespread, even in independent Baptist churches that claim to be immune from such error. Even if you do not believe you have a Reformation heritage, I would encourage you to read on to see how your traditional theology has been influenced by Reformation theology, nonetheless. We come now to an important question:

DID LUTHER RECLAIM CHRISTIANITY OR MUDDY THE WATERS?

Martin Luther is widely recognized as the father of the Protestant Reformation, who publicly challenged the doctrines of the Roman Catholic Church, starting in the year 1517. Luther's doctrine of *salvation*, commonly known as *justificatio sola fide* — the Latin term for *justification by faith alone* — teaches that reconciliation with God, resulting in forgiveness of sin, is by faith alone and not of works. Luther was reacting to the Roman Catholic doctrine of salvation, which requires observing the sacraments of the Church.

The Reformation is revered by multitudes of evangelical Christians, who assume it rescued the church of Jesus Christ from centuries of Roman Catholic darkness and offered a much-needed corrective on the critical doctrine of salvation. But is that all the Reformation accomplished? Unfortunately, no.

While Paul wrote the book of Romans — which includes his primary treatise on justification — nearly two thousand years ago, Luther reinterpreted the book five hundred years ago, unwittingly affecting generations thereafter. Although emphasizing *sole fide*, he reintroduced and popularized the unbiblical doctrines of salvation, justification and sanctification that had been largely taught by Augustine in the early fifth century. Consequently, Luther did irreparable damage to the Scriptural interpretation, particularly the critical doctrine of soteriology, which is the doctrine of salvation, based on the Greek word *soteria* for *salvation*. More specifically, as I will explain in subsequent chapters, I believe Luther muddied the waters on Paul's salvation teaching by making at least two errors: a) viewing *salvation* and *justification* as essentially synonymous, and b) viewing *salvation* and *sanctification* as inseparable and, therefore, singular.

Thus, it seems the Reformation was hijacked by the evil one, thereby confusing the doctrine of salvation all the more.

THE WAKE OF THE REFORMATION

Consequently, today we do not find a cohesive Christianity, moving forward in unity for the cause of Christ, preparing to become Christ's co-rulers in the next age. Rather, in the Reformation's wake we encounter a Christianity that is fractured, splintered, and divided, as literally thousands of Protestant denominations have sprouted, having varying beliefs. It's as if Pandora's box has been opened, and there's no turning back. Incidentally, the attention of Christians has been diverted from the most important things.

Regarding the doctrine of salvation there are now three basic "Protestant" views. Though they all claim that salvation is by *faith alone* — adhering to the *sola fide* of Luther's legacy — two of the views, nonetheless, add *works* either on the "front end" or "back end" of regeneration.

1. CALVINIST VIEW – HELD BY LUTHERAN/PRESBYTERIAN/REFORMED

While I certainly agree with Luther's basic tenet — that salvation is *received* by God's grace, through faith alone in Jesus Christ, for that is biblical (Eph. 2:8-9; 2 Tim. 1:8-9; Titus 3:5) — I heartily disagree with Luther's conclusion that salvation is *evidenced* by works — in other words, that "genuine" believers confirm their salvation by living righteously. That Lutheran doctrine was later systematized and labeled by John Calvin's followers as *perseverance* (the "P" of the Calvinist T-U-L-I-P acrostic), which is the default soteriological view held by those who embrace Lutheran and Reformed Protestant doctrines, but has also spread into non-Reformed churches (e.g., many Baptist, nondenominational, and independent groups). It teaches that believers will essentially live by faith, or they were never saved. Consequently, those who hold to this position claim that Christians cannot know if they have "final salvation" until they meet Jesus in judgment, for they do not know from day to day how they will live tomorrow or in the distant future. Thus, their lifestyle in the future may not confirm they were saved/justified in the past.

Needless to say, if works are a necessary *evidence* of or *confirmation* of one's salvation, then is this not essentially requiring works for salvation on the "back end"?

2. ARMINIAN VIEW – HELD BY WESLEYAN/METHODIST/HOLINESS

Another erroneous spin-off that was spawned by Reformation doctrines is the salvation view held by those who embrace the Wesleyan/Methodist tradition. They also claim to hold to *sole fide*, but their Arminian theology says that holy living is essential to continuing in salvation. Believers who live in sinfulness forfeit their salvation.

If works are necessary for *maintaining* one's salvation, then is this not essentially requiring works for salvation on the "front end"?

Ironically, many view Calvinist and Arminian salvation doctrine as opposites, but they are virtually the same, at least with respect to how one remains saved. Calvinism says salvation must be *evidenced* by works, or the person was never saved. Arminianism says salvation must be *maintained* by works, or the person will lose salvation.

Both of these views of salvation and justification are erroneous legacies of Martin Luther, John Knox, John Calvin, Ulrich Zwingli, et al., passed along and repackaged by others who came along thereafter, such as Jacob Arminius, John Wesley, Francis Asbury, Richard Watson, et al. Incidentally, the twentieth century Pentecostal/Charismatic and Holiness/Nazarene denominations also grew out of the Methodist/Arminian tradition, and they comprise a huge segment of Protestant Christianity.

3. FREE GRACE VIEW — HELD BY SOME INDEPENDENT BAPTIST/BRETHREN/ NONDENOMINATIONAL GROUPS

Many Christian churches and denominations insist their salvation doctrine has not been shaped by the Reformation, for they do not hold to either Calvinism or Arminianism. Typically, these are independent Baptist, Brethren, and nondenominational groups (including Calvary Chapel and Bible churches), which see theological problems with both systems of theology. They typically hold to a dispensational view of the Scriptures. Some in this camp have branded their soteriology "Free Grace," which is defined as follows:

> Free grace theology is a Christian soteriological view which holds that the only condition of salvation is faith, excluding good works and perseverance, holding to eternal security. Free Grace advocates believe that good works are not the condition to merit (as with Catholics), to maintain (as with Arminians), or to prove (as with most Calvinists) salvation, but rather are part of discipleship and the basis for receiving eternal rewards ... This soteriological view distinguishes between salvation and discipleship — the call to believe on Christ as Savior and receive His gift of eternal life, and the call to follow Christ and become an obedient disciple, respectively. Free grace theologians emphasize the absolute freeness of salvation and the possibility of full assurance that is not grounded

upon personal performance. Norman Geisler has divided this view into a moderate form and a more radical form. The moderate form being associated with Charles Ryrie, and the more strong form with Zane Hodges.[1]

I believe the first two systems of soteriology — Calvinism and Arminianism — are unbiblical legacies left by the Reformation. Unfortunately, these theologies have pervaded most of Protestant Christianity during the past five centuries, propagated primarily through Bible colleges and seminaries, and passed along to churches by their pastors who were trained in those institutions of higher learning. Although Free Grace advocates remain, they are comparatively small in number. I identify with Free Grace soteriology, generally speaking, because I believe it is biblical and allows Christians to interpret the Scriptures consistently.

A FOURTH VIEW OF SALVATION?

I was going to add a fourth category for those pastors and churches who insist they are neither Calvinist nor Arminian in soteriology, but also reject Free Grace theology, labeling it "easy believism" — a term that they use pejoratively. They think simple faith is too easy for salvation. There must be repentance or commitment to Christ or something of that nature involved. But the Bible is clear that salvation is by simple faith (Eph. 2:8-9; Acts 16:31), believing Jesus for eternal (age-lasting) life. (Note: Throughout this book I repeatedly refer to the word eternal as "age-lasting." To see an explanation for this, see the exposition of Rom. 2:7 in Chapter 7, the section titled, "Revealing the Secrets of Men").

By requiring repentance or commitment to Christ as a condition for salvation, those who teach this are essentially taking the Calvinist position on salvation. For if a "professing believer" later backslides and continues in sinning, the claim is made that the person did not truly commit to Christ or repent. Believers in churches of this type tend to doubt their salvation during times of continued sinning and spiritual defeat. They wonder: Did I repent enough? Was I genuine? Did I really commit to Christ? Thus, we are right back to the dilemma of works on the "back end" to confirm salvation. This causes theological confusion and doubt.

Tragically, pastors and evangelists who hold to this inconsistent paradigm often convince those who are spiritually defeated that they are actually unsaved. Manipulative invitations are sometimes given, and unwitting believers flood the aisles to get "really saved" — only to repeat the process the next time they are defeated. This does great damage to Christianity, not to mention what it does for individual Christians spiritually.

Can you see the serious problem with this position? Those who reject basic Free Grace soteriology have essentially embraced Calvinist salvation doctrine in some degree — whether they realize it or not — doctrine that was formed during and shortly after the Reformation. Here's the point: Many Baptist and nondenominational pastors and Christians insist they are not Calvinistic — sometimes vehemently — but hold to Calvinist *perseverance* doctrine nonetheless! Why can they not see their inconsistency? It is important to be honest with ourselves and with others regarding our theology and the ramifications of it.

MISINTERPRETING SCRIPTURE

As a result of the proliferation of errant soteriological systems, multitudes of Christians — including pastors and theologians — misinterpret Scripture according to their system. Others are confused as to which system is correct and tend to interpret passages inconsistently, oftentimes combining elements of contrasting systems. For example, I have personally heard many pastors insist they do not hold to Calvinism but, nevertheless, unwittingly and vigorously defend *perseverance* doctrine for salvation when interpreting certain passages of Scripture.

The conflating of two or more systems also results in misinterpretation of Scripture. For example, what does one do with passages such as 1 Cor. 6:9-10?

> **1 Cor. 6:9-10** Do you not know that the unrighteous will not inherit the kingdom of God? Do not be deceived. Neither fornicators, nor

idolaters, nor adulterers, nor homosexuals, nor sodomites, nor thieves, nor covetous, nor drunkards, nor revilers, nor extortioners will inherit the kingdom of God. (See also Gal. 5:16-25; Eph. 5:1-5).

Arminians say these are believers who lose their salvation. Calvinists say these are professing Christians who were never actually saved. Free Grace advocates say these are children of God who, because of their sinful behavior, will be disinherited from ruling with Christ in the Millennium, when they receive their verdict at the Judgment Seat of Christ — which I believe is the correct interpretation. But many pastors and theologians who know salvation is by grace through faith alone and who believe in "eternal security," nonetheless, are confused, because they have not firmly embraced Free Grace doctrine and, consequently, typically end up taking the Calvinist view of the text. I have seen this kind of thing happen repeatedly throughout the decades of my pastoral ministry, and I cannot help but think this is Satan's way of keeping Christians confused and doubting, not moving forward in victory, preparing to become co-rulers with Christ.

I am ashamed to admit I inconsistently interpreted Scripture in the earlier years of my pastoral ministry, trying to explain texts by applying my theology and making assumptions, rather than interpreting biblically, considering only the historical, grammatical context. But I quickly learned that proper, biblical interpretation often goes cross-grain with theological systems, and I was troubled by this. In fact, as the inconsistencies mounted, I considered both Calvinism and Arminianism as hermeneutical (interpretive) options. But in every case, they come up short. None of these post-Reformation soteriological systems offer any satisfactory assistance in biblical interpretation.

I now believe that is because they are incorrect. If so, then the evil one hijacked the Reformation, leaving generations of God's children confused and derailed, not able to properly interpret and apply the Scriptures, to the great detriment of Christianity. The urgent need of our day is to return to a proper understanding of the Bible — as Jesus and the apostles understood it — starting with the critical doctrine of salvation.

THE KINGDOM INHERITANCE PARADIGM

After many years of struggling to interpret the Scriptures correctly in my earlier pastoral ministry, one day I threw up my hands in frustration and asked the Lord for wisdom and divine help to interpret His Word correctly. He answered by showing me the importance of historical, grammatical interpretation, apart from theology. In time I noticed patterns developing, consistent with Free Grace soteriology and the kingdom inheritance paradigm (my term for it) for sanctification and discipleship, leading to reward. Rather than explaining here, I will unfold that paradigm throughout the book. Kingdom Inheritance doctrine goes hand-in-hand with Free Grace soteriology. I have diligently studied these doctrines for many years to learn what God has to say on the matter, and I have been working tirelessly to systematize this theology for those in the congregation God has entrusted to my care, and for my children, and for anyone who will take heed, both now and in future generations, until the Lord returns.

In this expositional study on the epistle of Romans I hope to make clear the kingdom inheritance paradigm for rightly dividing the entirety of Scripture. Since the Lord has led me to this system, inconsistencies in interpretation have faded away, and the Bible has become much more cohesive and understandable. I love my Lord Jesus Christ and His Word more than ever, now that I understand it (and Him) better than at any other period of my life.

THE VAST GROWTH OF PROTESTANT CHRISTIANITY

Experts report there may be as many as 1 billion *Protestant* Christians in the world, out of a total of 2.5 billion Christians (in the broadest sense of the term).[2] The total number of denominations is approaching 55,000, the overwhelming majority of which are Protestant.[3] Virtually all of the denominational mushrooming has happened since the Reformation.

The Reformation has obviously left a prolific legacy, not only numerically, but also theologically. Consequently, questioning Reformation doctrines is an overwhelming, uphill battle, because such a high percentage of Christians have been thoroughly indoctrinated in the Protestant legacy, even those who claim their religious group remained independent of Protestantism. Nevertheless, if we want to be biblical, we must *take off our Reformation glasses* and interpret the book of Romans as Paul — and ultimately *God* — intended.

Unfortunately, the tentacles of Reformation doctrine have so pervaded Christian theology in the past five hundred years that one can hardly find commentaries that interpret the book of Romans biblically, particularly with respect to the doctrine of justification. The ramifications for Christianity are astounding!

The first section of this book (Chapters 2-4) will demonstrate from all of the texts where the term *the just shall live by faith* is used, both Old Testament and New, that justification is not positional and legal — and, therefore, not soteriological — but rather conditional and behavioral — and, therefore, focused on sanctification. Following the first section, an exposition of Romans will begin, starting in Chapter 5.

CHAPTER 2
JUSTIFIED BY FAITH-FILLED WORKS PART 1
IN HEBREWS

The statement, *the just shall live by faith,* became Luther's mantra during the Reformation, and he essentially treated the term as synonymous with salvation, which I do not believe was Paul's original intent. Because *the just shall live by faith* is used early-on in Romans (1:17), we must define what it means and how it is used throughout the Scriptures, particularly in Paul's writings. To that end, in the next three chapters, I intend to review the four Scripture passages where the term *the just shall live by faith* is used, and in so doing, I hope to define *justification* biblically and demonstrate that in every case, the term is used in reference to those who are already believers. Paul uses it, *not* as a soteriological term, but as a sanctification term.

JUDGMENT ACCORDING TO WORKS

The future judgment of all mankind has been assigned to Jesus:

> **John 5:22** For the Father judges no one, but has committed all judgment to the Son.

Furthermore, every judgment is according to works.

The **Judgment Seat of Christ** is for church-age believers, those who have received the gift of eternal (age-lasting) life and will, therefore, be resurrected prior to the Tribulation:

> **1 Cor. 3:13** Each one's work will become clear; for the Day will declare it, because it will be revealed by fire; and the fire will test each one's work, of what sort it is.
> **14** If anyone's work which he has built on *it* endures, he will receive a reward.
> **15** If anyone's work is burned, he will suffer loss; but he himself will be saved, yet so as through fire.

The **Sheep and Goats Judgment** is for Gentile believers who survive the Tribulation:

> **Matt. 25:34-36** Then the King will say to those on His right hand, "Come, you blessed of My Father, inherit the kingdom prepared for you from the foundation of the world: for I was hungry and you gave Me food; I was thirsty and you gave Me drink; I was a stranger and you took Me in; I was naked and you clothed Me; I was sick and you visited Me; I was in prison and you came to Me.

The **Jewish Judgment Seat** is for all the Jews — those living and those who will be resurrected at the end of the Tribulation:

> **Ezek. 20:34** I will bring you out from the peoples and gather you out of the countries where you are scattered, with a mighty hand, with an outstretched arm, and with fury poured out.
> **35** And I will bring you into the wilderness of the peoples, and there I will plead My case with you face to face.
> **36** Just as I pleaded My case with your fathers in the wilderness of the land of Egypt, so I will plead My case with you," says the Lord GOD.
> **37-38** I will make you pass under the rod ... I will purge the rebels from among you, and those who transgress against Me; I will bring them out of the country where they dwell, but they shall not enter the land of Israel.

The **Great White Throne Judgment** is for Gentile unbelievers who will be resurrected after the Millennium:

> **Rev. 20:12** I saw the dead, small and great, standing before God, and books were opened. And another book was opened, which is *the Book of Life*. And the dead were judged according to their works, by the things which were written in the books.
>
> **15** And anyone not found written in the Book of Life was cast into the lake of fire.

Many assume that the names written in the Book of Life are those who have believed on Jesus for eternal (age-lasting) life. But that is a mere assumption — an incorrect one — that has been perpetuated through the centuries (more on this in Addendum 2). The text says those at the Great White Throne are judged *according to their works*. The Book of Life lists the names of those who have *lived righteously* and consequently will *not* be cast into the lake of fire.

IS JUSTIFICATION POSITIONAL AND LEGAL?

All of the judgments in the Scriptures are according to works. What this clearly demonstrates is that *how* people live is critically important, for it affects their future verdict in judgment. No one is exempt, for it applies to Jews and Gentiles, believers and unbelievers.

In God's eyes, all humans living on Earth today are either justified or not justified, based on how each one is currently living (i.e., their lifestyle, behavior). Those who have died are either justified or not justified, based on how they lived. Those God deems *justified* will not be judged (in a negative manner), while those He deems *not justified* will be judged.

The common, traditional understanding of justification handed down from the Reformation, teaches that at the point of salvation, when regeneration takes place, God declares His new child positionally and legally righteous. In other words, the believer is instantaneously credited with Christ's righteousness and, consequently, forgiven of all sins — past, present, and future. Furthermore, the common understanding is that certain theological terms are generally synonymous, referring essentially to the same thing. For example, *eternal life* is typically equated with *going to Heaven*, which is equated with *being saved*, which is equated with *being justified*. Other terms could possibly be added to this list also. It seems the practice of conflating these terms and the habit of using them interchangeably was initiated during the Reformation.

IS JUSTIFICATION BY FAITH ALONE?

For instance, Martin Luther coined the term *justification by faith alone*, which he used in a soteriological sense, and which he supposedly derived from the book of Romans. That term became the mantra for the Reformation. In fact, those who hold to Reformation theology today would instantly recognize *faith alone*, or the Latin version, *sola fide*, as one of their hallmarks. However, the term *faith alone* is never used by Paul, who supposedly taught it.

Paul used the words *alone* and *only* dozens of times in his epistles, but never in connection with *faith*. The reason is because Paul rarely talked about *initial* salvation in his epistles, including Romans, since those to whom he wrote were already believers. Thus, he virtually always spoke about *faith for sanctification*, believing God for the enablement to serve Him, which involves works. Sanctifying faith is *not* by faith alone. While initial salvation is certainly by faith alone, that is not the message of the book of Romans, in spite of what the Reformers taught.

Some may wonder why I use the term "initial salvation." Perhaps a conceptual parenthesis is needed for further explanation.

THE THREE TENSES OF SALVATION

For those who may be unaware, *salvation* has three tenses:

Past — I *have been* saved — referring to initial salvation of one's spirit (regeneration). To become saved in this manner, one must believe the gospel of grace by faith alone, that is, believing Christ's promise of eternal (age-lasting) life. (See Rom. 8:10, 16; Eph. 2:8-9; Titus 3:5).

Present — I *am being* saved — referring to ongoing salvation, otherwise known as soul-salvation, the saving of the soul, or sanctification, which is *not* automatic, but requires repeated choices to cooperate with God. (See Matt. 16:24-27; Phil. 2:12-13; Heb. 10:39; James 1:21).

Future — I *hope to be* saved — referring to the expectation of hearing the verdict "Well done!" at the Judgment Seat for those believers who are deemed *good* and *faithful*. Because their soul has been saved, Jesus will reward their faithfulness. (See Heb. 10:39; 1 Pet. 1:9; Matt. 16:24-27 — Jesus speaks to both the present and future aspects of salvation). Those whose soul is not saved will receive a negative verdict and negative rewards as recompense for their wrongdoing. (See Col. 3:23-25; 2 Cor. 5:10).

When studying Scripture, you can easily distinguish which tense of *salvation* the writer is referring to, based on the context. If the reference is to that which happened in the past, then initial salvation by faith alone in Jesus for eternal (age-lasting) life is in view. If a passage is talking about behavioral matters in the present, either good or bad, then salvation of the soul (sanctification) is the focus. Those texts that speak of glorification or reward in the future, at the Judgment Seat of Christ, are speaking of future salvation. Incidentally, while all Christians will be resurrected or raptured before the tribulation, not all Christians will be glorified, for glorification is a reward conferred only upon those who live righteously, by faith, as we shall see in later chapters.

With the above guide in mind, texts about salvation can be interpreted consistently and biblically. Probably ninety percent or more of the salvation usages in the Scriptures refer to either the present or future tenses. Only a very small percentage refer to the past aspect of salvation.

Those who have been influenced by the theology passed along

from the Reformation reject these tenses of salvation and interpret virtually all references to *salvation* in a singular, soteriological (and therefore, evangelistic) sense. Doing so distorts the doctrine of salvation. There are two theological considerations driving their singular interpretation of *salvation* in the Scriptures.

First, both Calvinism and Arminianism essentially synthesize the doctrines of salvation and sanctification. According to their system of theology, you can't have one without the other. They are mutually inclusive. If you have been saved, then you are positionally justified and, therefore, you are being sanctified. If you are not being sanctified, then you were never saved (or you have forfeited salvation). As pointed out in the previous chapter, this makes *works* the determining factor in initial salvation. Thus, *sola fide*, or *faith alone*, is a misnomer for describing the salvation doctrine as taught by those who have been influenced by traditional Reformation theology.

TRICHOTOMY VS. DICHOTOMY

Second, those who hold to the Reformation theological tradition typically do not see a distinction between the spirit and soul of man. They take the position that man is dichotomous, or two parts, body and soul — physical and metaphysical, or material and immaterial. Nevertheless, God's Word is quite clear that man is trichotomous, having three parts — spirit, soul, and body — and God has a purpose for each part:

> **1 Thess. 5:23** Now may the God of peace Himself sanctify you completely; and may your whole spirit, soul, and body be preserved blameless at the coming of our Lord Jesus Christ.

> **Heb. 4:12** For the word of God is living and powerful, and sharper than any two-edged sword, piercing even to the division of soul and spirit, and of joints and marrow, and is a discerner of the thoughts and intents of the heart.

The *spirit* aspect of our being is our interface with God. The *soul* is the seat of the mind (thoughts), emotions (feelings), and will (volition) — our interface with self and others. Of course, the *body* is our interface with the material world. A detailed discussion of these three aspects of man's being is outside the scope of this book. Curious readers are advised to read Watchman Nee's *The Spiritual Man* for much greater detail.[1] Clarence Larkin also has an interesting chart and explanation on "The Threefold Nature of Man" in his book, *Dispensational Truth*.[2]

If you are a child of God, then your spirit *has been* saved. But that does not mean your soul *is being* saved (sanctified). What many fail to realize, largely due to the Reformation's influence, is that the salvation of one's soul is not automatic. It is conditional, based on one's behavior. How many Christians will meet Jesus at the Judgment Seat, expecting to hear, "Well done!" — because they are saved and, presumably, positionally justified? Instead, they will hear, "You wicked and lazy servant," for having lived unrighteously.

In Luke 12 Jesus told the parable of the rich man who was very successful, to the point that he tore down his barns and built larger ones. He had the philosophy, "eat, drink, and be merry." Jesus called him a fool, for he had stored up treasure on earth and was not rich toward God. His soul was not saved for God, but merely for self. That night his soul was required of him; that is, he died and had to give an account to God. This passage is typically interpreted (in the Reformation tradition) as a man who died and went to Hell. However, in the context Jesus was talking to Old Testament Jewish believers about the importance of living for God and preparing for the coming Messianic age, rather than focusing on the here-and-now. Judgment day is coming for God's children. If your soul is being saved now by consistent decisions to depend on Jesus and live righteously, your soul will be deemed "saved" at the Bema and richly rewarded.

These concepts will be explained in much greater detail as this book continues. The important thing to understand at this juncture is that the Reformation's understanding of the doctrine of justification — as positional and legal, and essentially equated with salvation — has led to numerous interpretive errors, particularly in the book of Romans.

NO CONTRADICTION BETWEEN PAUL AND JAMES

Consistent with Paul's usage of the words *salvation* and *justification* in Romans, James — who also teaches about *sanctifying faith* — uses the term *justified by works, and not by faith only (alone)*:

> **Jas. 2:24** You see then that a man is justified by works, and not by faith only.

Luther thought there was a contradiction between the theology of Paul and James — but we know that's not the case. Both apostles are teaching believers about sanctifying faith, which involves works. Some who do not understand this simple interpretation try to explain the seeming contradiction between Paul and James by recognizing two levels of justification — positional and practical. In other words, believers are positionally and legally justified at the point of salvation, and they must throughout their Christian lives seek to be practically, experientially, behaviorally justified. What, then, is the purpose for practical, behavioral justification if the believer is already positionally, legally justified? If there are no serious ramifications to behavior at the Judgment Seat, then does not this view implicitly condone licentious living?

While I accepted this view for many years because of my traditional Christian education, it bothered me from time to time, because I could not reconcile all Scripture passages about justification to my position (which, by the way, is doing things backwards). Upon further study, I have come to realize that the passages on justification in the Scriptures have to do with practical, experiential, behavioral justification. I no longer see positional, legal justification as a Scriptural doctrine. Again, a full explanation is forthcoming.

IMPORTANT CLARIFICATION

Am I suggesting that salvation is *not* by faith alone? Absolutely not! A person is saved (past tense) by believing on Jesus for eternal (age-lasting) life, not of works.

Eph. 2:8-9 For by grace you have been saved through faith, and that not of yourselves; it is the gift of God, not of works, lest anyone should boast.

Titus 3:5 not by works of righteousness which we have done, but according to His mercy He saved us, through the washing of regeneration and renewing of the Holy Spirit,

2 Tim. 1:9 who has saved us and called us with a holy calling, not according to our works, but according to His own purpose and grace which was given to us in Christ Jesus before time began,

Salvation in the initial sense of regeneration is by God's grace, through faith alone. It is called the *gift* of God. But justification is *not* by faith alone, as we shall see. Consequently, justification is *not* equated with initial salvation, nor is it bestowed positionally at initial salvation. Martin Luther and the Reformers were the ones who taught that justification is equated with initial salvation, but that is incorrect.

BIBLICAL DESCRIPTION OF JUSTIFICATION

If justification is not positional or legal, then how is it to be described?

Justification is God's declaration that a person is *living* righteously — and therefore accepted by Him — at a given point in time. The opposite is God's declaration that a person is living sinfully — and therefore condemned by Him — at a given point in time. Incidentally, the word condemned does not mean "on their way to Hell." Condemned simply means "under God's judgment," i.e., under His wrath, as in Rom. 1.

By way of illustration, suppose God sees *Mr. So-and-So* and says, "That man is righteous, justified in my sight." But in the future, *Mr. So-and-So* backslides and turns away from the Lord. God's declaration changes from *justified* — and therefore *accepted* — to *unrighteous* — and therefore *condemned*, under God's judgment. The reason why all the future judgments in Scripture are based on *works* is because the basis for those judgments is man's *behavior* — whether or not he was justified in a practical, experiential sense — not man's *position*.

Taking this one step further, the Bible teaches *the just shall live by faith*. What does that mean? It does *not* mean that a person who has been saved will essentially always live in a righteous manner. The Calvinist doctrine of *perseverance* is incorrect, as mentioned in the previous chapter, for the Scriptures do *not* teach that children of God will essentially always live righteously. Multitudes of believers do not live righteously, yet the Bible considers them children of God, nonetheless. This truth is clearly taught in Rev. 2-3, in the letters to the seven churches. In that passage, rewards are promised for believers who are overcomers, those who live victoriously over sin. Not all believers are overcomers, only those who live righteously. Unfaithful believers of the church age are rebuked. Rev. 2-3 would make no sense if all believers are overcomers. This point will be illustrated more fully in subsequent chapters.

THE JUST SHALL LIVE BY FAITH

What, then, is the meaning of the biblical phrase, "the just shall live by faith?" It means that to live righteously, one must believe God. A continued righteous lifestyle requires continued belief. Those who are living righteously, by faith, are declared righteous by God — justified, at that point in time. Faith is the primary component in justification, but it's not the only component, because the just *live* by faith — and *living* involves *doing*, behavior. The book of James, ch. 2, also makes quite clear that *works* are involved in justification. But the key is that the works are *faith-filled.*

Paul is writing to the church at Rome and proclaiming the truth that *mere works of the law do not justify*, but rather result in God's condemnation (i.e., judgment). Believing God for producing faith-filled works is the only way to be declared righteous (justified) by God. Jesus, the righteous One, is the means by which we live righteously. We appropriate His righteousness through the Holy Spirit to live the Christ-life. That is one of the focal points in the book of Romans — chapters 6-8 — which flow out of chapters 2-5, which I do not believe are salvation-oriented, as we have been taught since the Reformation.

Romans is sanctification-oriented, intended to show the believing Jews that doing works of the law is not the means by which we are justified. We are justified by faith-filled dependence on Christ for living righteously.

GOD'S DEFINITION OF JUSTIFICATION

The Old Testament provides God's definition of justification that would have been in the minds of the first century Jews. The Old Testament did not teach positional, legal justification. God has always justified those who are *living* righteously. This is explained in Ezekiel's prophecy:

> **Ezek. 18:5-9** If a man is just and does what is lawful and right; if he has not eaten on the mountains (referring to offering sacrifices in the high places), nor lifted up his eyes to the idols of the house of Israel, nor defiled his neighbor's wife, nor approached a woman during her impurity; if he has not oppressed anyone, *but* has restored to the debtor his pledge; has robbed no one by violence, *but* has given his bread to the hungry and covered the naked with clothing; if he has not exacted usury nor taken any increase, *but* has withdrawn his hand from iniquity *and* executed true judgment between man and man; *if* he has walked in My statutes and kept My judgments faithfully—he *is* just; he shall surely live!" says the Lord GOD.

Those who believe God and live righteously are just (i.e., "justified" in God's eyes). Consequently, they are not judged by God; instead, He allows them to live. The passage continues:

> **Ezek. 18:10-13** If he begets a son *who is* a robber a shedder of blood, *who* does any of these *things* and does none of those *duties,* but has eaten on the mountains or defiled his neighbor's wife; if he has oppressed the poor and needy, robbed by violence, not restored the pledge, lifted his eyes to the idols, *or* committed abomination; if he has exacted usury or taken increase—shall he then live? He shall not

live! If he has done any of these abominations, he shall surely die; his blood shall be upon him.

The man described in vs. 5-9 is righteous, but his son, described in vs. 10-13, is unrighteous. Notice that God condemns the unrighteous one, pronouncing a sentence of death upon him, because he has not believed God and lived righteously; he is not just (i.e., justified in God's eyes). Nevertheless, there is hope, for God makes the wicked man a promise. He also makes the righteous man a promise:

Ezek. 18:21 If a wicked man turns from all his sins which he has committed, keeps all My statutes, and does what is lawful and right, he shall surely live; he shall not die.
22 None of the transgressions which he has committed shall be remembered against him; because of the righteousness which he has done, he shall live.
23 Do I have any pleasure at all that the wicked should die?" says the Lord GOD, "*and* not that he should turn from his ways and live?
24 But when a righteous man turns away from his righteousness and commits iniquity, and does according to all the abominations that the wicked *man* does, shall he live? All the righteousness which he has done shall not be remembered; because of the unfaithfulness of which he is guilty and the sin which he has committed, because of them he shall die.

God mercifully allows sinners to repent and turn to righteousness. On the flip side, those who are living righteously, but turn away from righteousness and begin living sinfully, will die. Verse 20 gives a good summary:

Ezek. 18:20 The soul who sins shall die. The son shall not bear the guilt of the father, nor the father bear the guilt of the son. The righteousness of the righteous shall be upon himself, and the wickedness of the wicked shall be upon himself.

JUSTIFICATION FOR THE GENTILES ALSO

God's principle of justification does not merely apply to the Jews — though God is prophesying to the Jews in Ezekiel. The principle applies in a much broader sense to all mankind.

Think of **Noah**, who was not Jewish. He lived before the Flood. God praises this man's lifestyle.

> **Gen. 6:9** Noah was a just man, perfect in his generations. Noah walked with God.

Noah was a Gentile who lived righteously. God declares that he is justified.

Another example is found in **Abimelech**. When Abraham and Sarah lived in Gerar for a time, near Gaza, Abraham lied and said that Sarah was his sister rather than his wife. He did that out of fear for his life. Thinking Sarah was "fair game," Abimelech, the ruler of that region, took Sarah for himself, so that God was about to kill him. Abimelech was not a Jew; he was a Gentile who lived righteously, but he appealed to God on that basis.

> **Gen. 20:4-6** But Abimelech had not come near her; and he said, "Lord, will You slay a righteous nation also? Did he not say to me, 'She is my sister?' ... In the integrity of my heart and innocence of my hands I have done this." And God said to him ... "Yes, I know that you did this in the integrity of your heart ... you shall live."

Perhaps **Melchizedek** could also be included (Gen. 14), whose name means "king of righteousness" (Heb. 7:1-4). He was also the "king of peace," who ruled over Salem, and functioned as priest of the Most High God. Granted, mystery surrounds this character, whom many believe was a Christophany, a pre-incarnate appearance of Christ, but we cannot be certain. If Melchizedek was human, then he was — and presumably, the citizens of his nation were — righteous before God.

Job is another Old Testament example. He was not Jewish either.

Job 1:1 There was a man in the land of Uz, whose name *was* Job; and that man was blameless and upright, and one who feared God and shunned evil.

God declared that Job was righteous, for he lived righteously. In the end of the book, God vindicated him after all of his suffering

The **Ninevites** — an entire Gentile city — repented of their wickedness, and God let them live.

Cornelius is a New Testament example. He was a Gentile, a Roman centurion. When Peter arrived, he exclaimed:

Acts 10:34-35 In truth I perceive that God shows no partiality. But in every nation whoever fears Him and works righteousness is accepted by Him.

What an astounding statement! God considered all of these people justified because they were *living righteously,* even though they were not Jews.

Of course, the principle applies to the Jews as well. Even before the time of Christ's arrival, God considered **Zacharias and Elizabeth** righteous based on their behavior.

Luke 1:5-6 There was in the days of Herod, the king of Judea, a certain priest named Zacharias ... His wife ... *was* Elizabeth. And they were both righteous before God, walking in all the commandments and ordinances of the Lord blameless.

Zacharias and Elizabeth were both justified in the eyes of God, and so was Noah and Abimelech and Job and the citizens of Nineveh after they repented, and even Cornelius — both Jews and Gentiles having one common denominator: they believed God and lived righteously. Interestingly, not one of those mentioned knew about Jesus or eternal life, yet God considered them justified because of their righteous behavior.

"THE JUST SHALL LIVE BY FAITH" IN HEBREWS

The term "the just shall live by faith" is used three times in the New Testament — Gal. 3:11, Rom. 1:17, and Heb. 10:38. In every case, the New Testament writers are quoting the lone Old Testament usage in Hab. 2:4.

In this chapter and the next two, each of the New Testament usages will be explored in depth to see how the phrase is being used contextually. Our study will begin with the final usage in the Scriptures, Heb. 10:

> **Heb. 10:38** Now the just shall live by faith; but if anyone draws back, My soul has no pleasure in him.

The closing verses of Heb. 10 flow into the context of ch. 11. Of course, in the original, there are no chapter or verse divisions. Those were added later for easier reading.

Heb. 11 is about great men and women who lived by faith in Old Testament times. The intent of this chapter is to challenge us to live by faith, "looking unto Jesus," which starts out ch. 12. Most of the verses in ch. 11 start with the words, "By faith..."

FAITH-FILLED WORKS

For just a moment, ignore those words "by faith" and think what God is saying verse after verse. He describes how certain people in Old Testament times *lived* for Him. Of course, *living* involves *doing* — thinking, feeling, making decisions, carrying out daily duties. In Heb. 11 God focuses on what these men and women *did* for Him. Noah built an ark, Abraham moved his family from Ur to Canaan land, Moses forsook Egypt to lead the Israelites, Rahab hid the spies, and so on. So without a doubt, works are involved in Heb. 11, but the overall point is that these folks carried out these works for God by *believing* Him. A summary of their deeds is given at the end of the chapter:

Heb. 11:33-34 who through faith subdued kingdoms, worked righteousness, obtained promises, stopped the mouths of lions, quenched the violence of fire, escaped the edge of the sword, out of weakness were made strong, became valiant in battle, turned to flight the armies of the aliens.

35 Women received their dead raised to life again. Others were tortured, not accepting deliverance, that they might obtain a better resurrection.

36 Still others had trial of mockings and scourgings, yes, and of chains and imprisonment.

37-38 They were stoned, they were sawn in two, were tempted, were slain with the sword. They wandered about in sheepskins and goatskins, being destitute, afflicted, tormented—of whom the world was not worthy.

Notice that examples are given from the entirety of human history, some from every age:

- Pre-flood (vs. 4-7) Abel, Enoch, Noah
- Pre-law (vs. 8-22) Abraham, Sarah, Isaac, Jacob, Joseph
- Mosaic law era (vs. 23-32) Moses and his parents, the Israelites, Rahab (a Gentile), Gideon, Barak, Samson, Jephthah, David, Samuel, the prophets

There is no doubt Heb. 11 is a survey of the things *done* for God by man. Again, *works* are involved, but in every case, the works are carried out *in faith*. Incidentally, notice those from the era of the Mosaic law in 11:23-32. Does the writer emphasize obedience *to the law* as their means of pleasing God? Absolutely not! Every one of these Bible heroes did these things *by faith*, and that is what pleased God. The emphasis of this chapter dovetails quite nicely with James 2:

Jas. 2:21 Was not Abraham our father justified by works when he offered Isaac his son on the altar?

25 Likewise, was not Rahab the harlot also justified by works when she received the messengers and sent *them* out another way?

Abraham was pre-law and Rahab was a Gentile, yet they both did things for God by faith, along with the numerous Jewish examples that are mentioned. Heb. 11 is the context in which "the just shall live by faith" is used at the end of ch. 10. The phrase is obviously not used in a soteriological sense, for the context does not allow that. These are matters of *sanctification*, to use New Testament terminology.

Notice now the context leading up to Heb. 11:

> **Heb. 10:34** For you had compassion on me in my chains, and joyfully accepted the plundering of your goods, knowing that you have a better and an enduring possession for yourselves in heaven.

The writer to the Hebrews remembers the great love shown to him by those to whom he is writing. They even suffered persecution, thus they can be assured of rewards awaiting in heaven.

> **Heb. 10:35** Therefore do not cast away your confidence, which has great reward.

Confidence is "boldness, frankness, outspokenness." It is the idea of confessing Christ unashamedly. If they continue in this confidence — confessing Christ boldly — they will be rewarded further.

> **Heb. 10:36** For you have need of endurance, so that after you have done the will of God, you may receive the promise:

What is this promise? If they endure, they will be rewarded, which is the theme of the book of Hebrews — *persevering unto reward*. Here's why:

> **Heb. 10:37** *For yet a little while, and He who is coming will come and will not tarry.*

Judgment is coming! That is the context of this quote from the Old Testament, which will be explained in a moment.

Heb. 10:38 *Now the just shall live by faith; but if anyone draws back, my soul has no pleasure in him.*

The just shall live by faith. Is this phrase used in the context of initial salvation, believing on Jesus for eternal life? No, the context is *doing* things for God, *in faith*, which is the point of ch. 11. The writer wants his readers, who are believers, to be inspired by the Old Testament "witnesses" that he names in ch. 11, men and women who obeyed God and did great exploits for him as they trusted Him. Notice the last phrase of 10:36 "so that after you have done the will of God you may receive the promise." Again, the promise is the assurance of reward for those who persevere.

Heb. 10:39 But we are not of those who draw back to perdition, but of those who believe to the saving of the soul.

SANCTIFICATION LEADING TO REWARD

The writer to the Hebrews is obviously speaking to New Testament believers about matters of sanctification — that is the context of the entire passage. Therefore, the *saving of the soul*, which will be more fully explained in Chapters 4 and 5, is not initial salvation (regeneration). It is sanctification unto reward, that is, inheritance at the Bema Seat of Christ.

But remarkably, the writer is using illustrations of people who lived in Old Testament times, long before Christ. Yet they believed God and did works of righteousness — both Jews and Gentiles — despite never receiving the promise of reward.

The promise of reward (becoming *sons to glory*, Heb. 2:10) is a New Testament, church-age promise for those who live righteously in this era and are deemed justified by Jesus at His Judgment Seat and thereby included as His bride and co-rulers. Old Testament-era believers did not have this same privilege.

Heb. 11:39-40 These, having obtained a good testimony through faith, did not receive the promise, God having provided something better for us, that they should not be made perfect apart from us.

Perfection in a biblical sense is maturity resulting in the status of firstborn son (see Heb. 12:5-8) and, ultimately, glorification at the Bema. These concepts will all be explained more fully in subsequent chapters.

> **Heb. 10:38** *Now the just shall live by faith; but if anyone draws back, my soul has no pleasure in him.*

Those who are justified (declared righteous) by God are those who are living by faith, that is, they are behaving righteously, in dependence on God. God is obviously pleased with them, for they are justified in His sight. On the other hand, God has no pleasure in those who draw back (i.e., believers who stop living righteously). They are *not* justified in His sight. Their works will consequently burn up at the Judgment Seat (see 1 Cor. 3:13-15), and they will not be rewarded.

> **Heb. 10:39** *But we are not of those who draw back to perdition, but of those who believe to the saving of the soul.*

Again, *to draw back* is for a believer to stop living righteously, by faith. Here again is an example of how Reformation theology has wrongly influenced the interpretation. Arminianism teaches that *to draw back* is to lose one's initial salvation. Calvinism, on the other hand, teaches that *to draw back* is to demonstrate one was never truly saved. Thus, these theological errors confuse believers, leading them to doubt their salvation, and causing them to get saved again and again, every time they fall back.

A pastor-friend of mine, Todd Tjepkema, writes:

> I have seen this idea of not really being saved used in counseling relationship issues. The person most at fault for sinning against the other, whether it be husband, wife, or child, uses it as kind of a "Get out of Jail Free" card. Rather than asking for forgiveness and working on changing the sinful behavior, they will claim that they must not have really been saved. So, they get saved, get re-baptized, everyone celebrates their conversion, and the person returns to the

relationship thinking they get a free do-over. I have even seen where that same person will get re-saved again in 4-5 years when the relationship goes south again.[3]

Those believers who make repeated choices to continue in sinning, and consequently draw back, are on the pathway to *perdition*, which is "ruin" or "destruction." They are literally self-destructing. In contrast, those who continue believing God to live uprightly are experiencing the saving of their soul, and they will be rewarded at the Bema — which is the end result for the just who live by faith. The audience to whom the writer to the Hebrews was speaking, were those who had chosen the path of righteousness, by faith, so they were not drawing back. His admonition was to be taken as a warning, and it should be a warning to all of God's children, regardless of the era.

Thus, Heb. 10-11 give clarification as to the meaning of *the just shall live by faith*. This phrase is first used in the Old Testament, which Heb. 10:38 quotes:

"THE JUST SHALL LIVE BY FAITH" IN HABAKKUK

> **Hab. 2:4** Behold the proud, his soul is not upright in him; but the just shall live by his faith.

In the context, God tells Habakkuk that destruction is coming upon Judah at the hand of the Chaldeans (Babylonians) because of Israel's sins (1:5-7). The Chaldeans have been appointed by God as His tool of judgment (1:12), because God is righteous and hates unrighteousness in His people (1:13). So God forewarns Habakkuk that judgment is coming (2:3) — *It will surely come, it will not tarry*. The reason is because (2:4), *the proud, his soul is not upright in him*. In other words, judgment is coming upon Israel because the people have become proud (i.e., self-sufficient, not living by faith) and, consequently, they have not been living uprightly. The writer to the Hebrews, by quoting Hab. 2:4, warns his readers that judgment is also coming upon the house of God (1 Pet. 4:17).

Does Habakkuk's prophecy about living by faith, as quoted in

Heb. 10-11, have anything to do with initial salvation or so-called positional righteousness? No, it is about how Israel is *behaving* and the judgment forthcoming upon the nation because they have not been behaving righteously.

The context of the initial Old Testament use of the term, *the just shall live by faith,* would have been on the minds of the Jews when the New Testament writers quoted it. They would have known that "the just shall live by faith" is about believing God and living righteously. That being the case, why should Christians today take up Martin Luther's soteriological mantra, *justification by faith alone? The just shall live by faith* is not about regeneration; it's about righteous living, out of a heart of faith.

Besides this passage in Hebrews, the just shall live by faith is quoted in two other places in the New Testament — Galatians and Romans — and, not surprisingly, Paul also uses the phrase in a sanctification sense. Those passages will be examined in the next two chapters.

Are *you* living by faith? Are *your* works for Jesus faith-filled? If God were to look upon at this moment and issue a verdict on your life, what would it be? Justified or *not* justified?

CHAPTER 3
JUSTIFIED BY FAITH-FILLED WORKS PART 2
IN GALATIANS

The traditional, Reformed model of justification claims that when a person is saved (i.e. regenerated), God justifies His new child *positionally* and *legally*. The righteousness of Christ is credited to that individual's account, and all of their sins are forgiven — past, present, and future. The child of God, therefore, stands righteous before God perpetually, for righteousness is based on one's position as "in Christ," not on behavior. This has led generations of pastors and theologians since the Reformation to essentially use the terms *saved* and *justified* interchangeably, as if they were essentially referring to the same thing.

POSITIONAL JUSTIFICATION LEADS TO PERSEVERANCE DOCTRINE

To be consistent, Reformation theology takes this one step further. If children of God are *positionally* righteous, then they will essentially *live* righteously, or else they were never truly saved (or, in the case of Arminian theology, they *forfeit* salvation). Thus, sanctification for genuine Christians will be ongoing automatically. How could it be otherwise? This conflating or synthesizing of *salvation* and *sanctification* is known as *perseverance* doctrine, which is Scripturally incorrect, even if it is consistent with Reformation doctrines.

POSITIONAL JUSTIFICATION IMPLICITLY CONDONES LICENTIOUS LIVING

Many Free Grace advocates who reject Calvinism and Arminianism are, nonetheless, inconsistent. On the one hand, they rightly reject *perseverance* doctrine as unscriptural, believing instead that salvation and sanctification are independent doctrines. Children of God can choose *not* to follow Jesus in discipleship, and they will suffer consequences for making that choice, but it doesn't jeopardize their salvation. On the other hand, those same Free Grace advocates have embraced the Reformation model of *positional* justification. But if justification is *positional*, so that believers are perpetually righteous — at least in a *legal* sense — then what is the purpose for the Judgment Seat of Christ? If a believer is considered perpetually righteous in the eyes of God, then why would God need to judge them? Does not the Reformation doctrine of positional justification implicitly condone licentious living rather than preparedness for meeting Jesus in judgment?

In the previous chapter, I began making the point that justification is not *positional*, but *behavioral* and, consequently, has nothing to do with initial salvation (regeneration). Granted, at salvation God forgives the sinner of *past* sins (Eph. 1:7), so that *at that point* the child of God is justified (declared righteous by God). But sins committed going forward are not automatically forgiven and, therefore, must be confessed, on the basis of 1 John 1:9. If children of God do not consistently confess sins but rather choose a lifestyle of sinfulness, God will declare them "unrighteous." This does not mean they were never saved or that they have forfeited their salvation. Rather, it means they will face Jesus in judgment and give an account for their works of unrighteousness. Their verdict will not be "justified" — *good and faithful* — but rather "not justified" — *wicked and lazy* (see the parable of the talents in Matt. 25:14-30).

POSITIONAL JUSTIFICATION VIEWS THE JUDGMENT SEAT AS AN AWARDS CEREMONY

The Reformation doctrine of positional/legal justification implicitly condones licentious living, because if children of God have already been declared righteous and their future sins forgiven, then what does it really matter how we live? This pervasive, errant doctrine is the reason why so many view the Judgment Seat of Christ as a mere awards ceremony, having no negative consequences. Most evangelical Christians have been taught that *all* believers will be rewarded, *all* will be the bride of Christ, and *all* will reign with Him. There will be some momentary regret at the Judgment Seat of Christ, but it will all be over quickly, for God will wipe all tears from our eyes (which is a misapplication of Rev. 21:4, a verse that applies to the New Heaven and New Earth, *not* to the Judgment Seat and the Millennium). They think everything will be hunky-dory for all children of God, failing to realize that God's Word warns of negative reward and urges believers to persevere unto reward. Is not the doctrine of positional justification largely to blame for this?

Children of God do not have positional righteousness, nor have we been credited with Christ's righteousness. Thankfully, we *do* have the provision of Jesus living within — and He is the righteous One! — but multitudes of believers never appropriate their provision and so they continue living in a worldly, unrighteous manner. A biblical understanding of the doctrine of justification is critical!

"THE JUST SHALL LIVE BY FAITH" IN GALATIANS

In the previous chapter we studied God's definition of justification in Ezek. 18 and examined one of the three New Testament usages of the term *the just shall live by faith* in Heb. 10. In this chapter we will look at the usage in Gal. 3.

> **Gal. 3:11** But that no one is justified by the law in the sight of God *is* evident, for *"the just shall live by faith."*

To determine how the term is being used in this verse, it is important to explore the context, which extends back into Gal. 2:

> **Gal. 2:11-12** Now when Peter had come to Antioch, I withstood him to his face, because he was to be blamed; for before certain men

came from James, he would eat with the Gentiles; but when they came, he withdrew and separated himself, fearing those who were of the circumcision.

13 And the rest of the Jews also played the hypocrite with him, so that even Barnabas was carried away with their hypocrisy.

WHY WAS PETER TO BE BLAMED?

Before representatives of the Jerusalem church visited the church in Antioch of Syria, Peter ate freely with the Gentiles. But when the Jewish leadership showed up, he separated from the Gentiles and would not eat with them. Peter's change of policy was driven by *fear* of the Jews. In fact, Peter's hypocritical behavior also impacted the other Jewish believers in the church, including Barnabas.

> **Gal. 2:14** But when I saw that they were not straightforward about the truth of the gospel, I said to Peter before *them* all, "If you, being a Jew, live in the manner of Gentiles and not as the Jews, why do you compel Gentiles to live as Jews?

Paul noticed that Peter was not being straightforward about the truth of the *gospel*. Paul is not referring to the gospel of grace by faith, but the gospel of the kingdom, the good news of kingdom inheritance. We know that, because the matter at hand is Peter's unwillingness to eat with the Gentiles in the presence of the Jews from Jerusalem. According to Gal. 2:13 Peter's lapse of faith resulted in hypocrisy, which is a sanctification matter.

> **Gal. 2:15-16** We *who are* Jews by nature, and not sinners of the Gentiles, knowing that a man is not justified by the <u>works of the law</u> but by faith in Jesus Christ, even we have believed in Christ Jesus, that we might be justified by faith in Christ and not by the <u>works of the law</u>; for by the <u>works of the law</u> no flesh shall be justified. (emphasis added)

Keep in mind, the word *justified* in the minds of the Jews (based on their knowledge of Ezek. 18) is the idea of being considered righteous by God. These Jewish believers are not thinking of *positional* righteousness, for that is nowhere found in the Old Testament. They are surely thinking of *behavioral* righteousness — obedience, lawful living.

JUSTIFICATION NOT BY WORKS OF THE LAW, BUT BY FAITH

Paul makes clear that being *justified*, or declared righteous, is not *by* (or *through*) *works of the law*. The Pharisees, for example, obeyed the Mosaic law, and so did the rich young ruler. They all thought they were justified (righteous) in God's eyes, but they failed to realize that merely keeping the law is *not* the means of being considered righteous.

The Pharisees, in particular, had bigger heart problems that Jesus dealt with in the Sermon on the Mount, because they were not obeying God *in faith*. By acting hypocritically, Peter was no different than the Pharisees. He was not obeying God by faith, even after being given the vision of the sheet from Heaven with clean and unclean animals and being commanded to slay and eat. The message was clear: "What God has cleansed you must not call common" (Acts 10:15). But instead of fearing God, Peter feared man and essentially conveyed the message that God is pleased with mere *works of the law* — rituals such as circumcision and dietary laws.

Following a mere list of rules is not pleasing to God. Anyone can do *that* and not be righteous in God's eyes. Think of the Pharisees and the rich, young ruler! Think of modern-day fundamentalists!

> **Gal. 2:17** But if, while we seek to be justified by Christ, we ourselves also are found sinners, *is* Christ therefore a minister of sin? Certainly not!

Those to whom Paul is speaking are already believers, having believed on Jesus for eternal (age-lasting) life. Paul has been proclaiming to these folks the good news (gospel) of the kingdom, the teaching that if you remain faithful to Jesus, confessing Him and persevering to the end, you will receive an inheritance in the coming kingdom. Along comes Peter who, out of fear when the Jews show up, reverts back to living in accordance with the Old Testament law instead of living in accordance to the law of Christ, being enabled by Jesus and His Holy Spirit to live righteously.

Peter forsakes the Christ-life of faith out of fear. He does not appropriate the eternal (age-lasting) life that resides within by depending on Jesus by faith. Paul rebukes him for this, for he is not only hurting himself by not living righteously, he is hurting many around him, keeping them from living righteously also. Paul points out that those who seek to be justified, declared righteous, while living legalistically (and therefore, sinfully), cannot expect Jesus to sanction their sinfulness and declare them righteous.

> **Gal. 2:18** For if I build again those things which I destroyed, I make myself a transgressor.

By reverting back to the Mosaic law, Peter is not depending on Jesus to live righteously. He is living sinfully and sending the wrong signal to everyone around him.

> **Gal. 2:19** For I through the law died to the law that I might live to God.
> 20 I have been crucified with Christ; it is no longer I who live, but Christ lives in me; and the *life* which I now live in the flesh I live by faith in the Son of God, who loved me and gave Himself for me.

JUSTIFICATION DEMONSTRATED TO BE PRACTICAL AND BEHAVIORAL

Clearly, this passage is about sanctification — believers living by faith as they depend on Christ who dwells within. *Justification* in this passage is not positional or legal. It is practical and behavioral, living righteously by depending on Jesus in faith. Peter isn't doing that; instead, he has reverted back to law-living, which is not faith-living, so Paul calls him out on it. Then Paul adds in v. 21, "if righteousness comes through the law, then Christ died in vain."

Continuing into Gal. 3, Paul continues the argument by asking how these post-Pentecost Gentiles had received the indwelling presence of the Holy Spirit.

> **Gal. 3:2** This only I want to learn from you: Did you receive the Spirit by the works of the law, or by the hearing of faith?

The implied answer is: *by the hearing of faith.* In fact, the answer is obvious, so Paul doesn't even bother to answer it — they had received the Holy Spirit by faith in Jesus. This is referring to their initial faith in Jesus, at which time the Holy Spirit took up residence. Paul continues with an important follow-up question:

> **Gal. 3:3** Are you so foolish? Having begun in the Spirit, are you now being made perfect by the flesh?

Having believed in Jesus for eternal (age-lasting) life by faith, are you now being made perfect (being sanctified unto maturity) by the flesh? Notice that Paul equates "flesh" with "works of the law."
Being made perfect is the pathway of reward, the heart of the *gospel of the kingdom* message that Paul had been preaching to these believing Gentiles.

> **Gal. 3:5** Therefore He who supplies the Spirit to you and works miracles among you, *does He do it* by the works of the law, or by the hearing of faith?

Paul wants to know if Jesus gives the enabling power of the Holy Spirit to those who are depending on Him by faith or to those who are doing the works of the law. Again, the answer is obvious. Jesus gives Spirit-enabling power for victory to those who come to Him in faith.

ABRAHAM'S SANCTIFYING FAITH

> **Gal. 3:6** just as Abraham *"believed God, and it was accounted to him for righteousness."*

Paul quotes Gen. 15:6, using Abraham as an example of a man who believed God and obeyed Him, and it was accounted to him for righteousness. Many claim that Paul is speaking of Abraham's initial salvation, but that is not correct. In the context of Gen. 15:6, Abraham believes that he will have many offspring, as God said. The way Paul quotes Gen. 15:6 in Gal. 3:6 helps us interpret how the quotation is used in Rom. 4 — also in an ongoing sanctification sense, *not* soteriological.

Gal. 3:7 Therefore know that *only* those who are of faith are sons of Abraham.

This is *not* saying that everyone who has believed on Jesus for eternal (age-lasting) life is considered Abraham's spiritual descendant. The context will not allow that interpretation! Paul is talking about matters of sanctification. Peter's lapse is the apostle's showcase illustration, demonstrating that a man is justified, *not* by keeping the works of the law, but by continually believing Jesus for victory, i.e., depending on His Holy Spirit who lives within.

Notice the phrase *sons of Abraham* in v. 7. The Greek word translated *sons* is *huios*. In this context, Paul is teaching that those who are living righteously, by faith, are mature and on the pathway of inheritance as firstborn sons. In Bible times, firstborn sons would receive a double portion of the father's inheritance. Thus, those mature believers who are living by faith and not according to the *works of the law* — or, in a modern context, a list of legalistic, hyper-separational "personal standards" — are like Abraham, who also lived by faith. God considered him a righteous man, not positionally or legally, but simply because Abraham *lived* righteously, by faith in what the Lord had said to him.

Those believers in Jesus Christ who go about their Christian lives *in faith* are sons of Abraham. They are mature, walking by faith, and therefore stand to receive an inheritance in New Jerusalem if they persevere, like Abraham, who looked for that city.

Gal. 3:8 And the Scripture, foreseeing that God would justify the

Gentiles by faith, preached the gospel to Abraham beforehand, saying, *"In you all the nations shall be blessed."*

9 So then those who *are* of faith are blessed with believing Abraham.

When God said to Abraham, "In you all the families of the earth shall be blessed" (Gen. 12:3), He was ultimately prophesying of the glorious truth that Gentiles can also walk by faith, obey the Lord, and be declared righteous by God behaviorally. It is not limited to Jews. The point is that God considers *anyone* who walks by faith to be justified (righteous) in His sight. Again, this is not positional or legal; the justification is practical. The context dictates this conclusion.

Gal. 3:10 For as many as are of the works of the law are under the curse; for it is written, *"Cursed is everyone who does not continue in all things which are written in the book of the law, to do them."*

Those who think that merely keeping the Mosaic law makes them righteous in God's eyes are cursed if they don't keep the whole law.

Deut. 27:26 Cursed is the one who does not confirm all the words of this law.

Jas. 2:10 For whoever shall keep the whole law, and yet stumble in one *point,* he is guilty of all.

The Old Testament law required that it be kept in its entirety. However, no one can keep it in its entirety, so those who attempt to be justified by merely keeping the law of Moses are doomed by it. (That is the same point Paul makes in Romans, as we shall see). They are unrighteous and will be judged by God accordingly. Again, this is not positional or legal; it is practical. Incidentally, that is why all the judgments are according to works.

THE PINNACLE OF PAUL'S ARGUMENT

We now come to Paul's key statement.

> **Gal. 3:11** But that no one is justified by the law in the sight of God *is* evident, for *"the just shall live by faith."*

God declares as justified those who are living by faith, not those who are trying to keep the rituals of the Mosaic law (or some other man-devised legal system). The capstone of the passage is found in vs. 13-14.

> **Gal. 3:13-14** Christ has redeemed us from the curse of the law, having become a curse for us ... that the blessing of Abraham might come upon the Gentiles in Christ Jesus, that we might receive the promise of the Spirit through faith.

Neither Jews nor Gentiles are bound to keep the law, which brings a curse to those who do not obey it fully. Thus, Jesus became the curse:

> **Col. 2:14** having wiped out the handwriting of requirements that was against us, which was contrary to us. And He has taken it out of the way, having nailed it to the cross.

According to Gal. 2:20, which is contextual, only those who are living by faith in Jesus are being sanctified and are deemed righteous. They are the ones who are appropriating their eternal (age-lasting) life through the indwelling Holy Spirit.

Gal. 3:14 emphasizes that this blessing is for the Gentiles too. The entire passage is about sanctification by faith in contradistinction to sanctification by attempting to keep the law of Moses. This is evident from Paul's showcase illustration of Peter refusing to eat with the Gentiles.

WHITE ROBES FOR THE RIGHTEOUS ACTS OF SAINTS

Justification is practical, and it is obtained and maintained by walking in faith, not according to the Mosaic law. In Gal. 2-3 Paul is *not* saying that justification is by faith alone (not of works). His point is that justification is not by *works of the law*, referring to keeping the Mosaic rituals or the "rules" of any system. From Gal. 3, Heb. 10-11, and James 2, which we will examine in the next chapter, the Scriptures are clear that justification (being declared righteous by God) *is* by works, but they must be faith-filled works! Without faith, it is impossible to please Him, Heb. 11:6.

What difference does this teaching make? Multitudes of Christians have been taught the Reformation doctrine of positional, legal justification, and they have been led to believe it is what happens at salvation, apart from works. But that is *not* what the Bible teaches! The Scriptural doctrine of justification is God declaring righteous those who are *living* righteously, and the concept is used in a sanctification sense, not a soteriological sense. *The just shall live by faith* simply means, "those whom God considers righteous are producing faith-filled works."

Because of the incorrect teaching handed down through the centuries since the Reformation, countless generations of Christians believe there is essentially nothing they need to do to prepare to meet Jesus at the Judgment Seat of Christ. Their verdict is expected to be "righteous," because they have been credited with Christ's righteousness. In fact, they believe all children of God will surely be rewarded, and it doesn't really matter how we live. That is a devilish lie that has kept the masses of Christianity in darkness, unprepared to receive a positive verdict and thereby qualify to become His bride and co-regents in the Millennium. What a tragedy!

Although we have the righteous One living within, and He is our *provision* to live righteously, *His righteousness is not our righteousness*. We will all be judged based on our own righteousness, or lack thereof — that is, how we live, behave — as we appropriate His righteousness for daily living. This is made clear in the book of Revelation.

Rev. 19:7 Let us be glad and rejoice and give Him glory, for the marriage of the Lamb has come, and His wife has made herself ready."

8 And to her it was granted to be arrayed in fine linen, clean and bright, for the fine linen is the righteous acts of the saints.

The white robes of righteousness are given as rewards for *the righteous acts of the saints*, not because Christians have been supposedly positionally justified. That doctrine is erroneous!

What about you? Are you preparing to be rewarded by Jesus? Are you being justified by faith?

CHAPTER 4
JUSTIFIED BY FAITH-FILLED WORKS PART 3
IN JAMES

James 2:14-26 is one of the most misunderstood passages in all the Bible. In fact, as a result of misinterpreting this text, many religious groups, such as Roman Catholicism and, ironically, even some Protestant denominations, teach that works are required for salvation. Other Protestant groups — including many Baptists — while adamantly insisting that salvation is by faith alone, nevertheless, interpret James 2 to mean that if a person claims to be a Christian but doesn't live as a Christian should, then that person was never saved in the first place. As already mentioned in previous chapters, this is known as the Calvinist doctrine of *perseverance*. These misinterpretations do great damage to the *gospel of grace*, leading to initial salvation, which is received by simple faith.

LUTHER'S MISINTERPRETATION OF JAMES AND ROMANS

Why is there such confusion over this text? Undoubtedly, it is in large part due to the teachings of Martin Luther, who saw a contradiction between James 2 and Rom. 3-4. Luther thought James was teaching salvation by works, whereas Paul was teaching the opposite, salvation by faith alone. This prompted Luther to brand the book of James an "epistle of straw." He was unable to reconcile the two epistles because of his own presuppositions, which led to misinterpretation. Luther believed justification to be positional and legal, and he essentially equated it with salvation, thus arriving at the conclusion that Paul teaches salvation by faith alone. Consequently, Paul is right and James is wrong, or so Luther thought. Ironically, Luther's interpretation of justification and salvation in both James and Romans was incorrect, which will be made clear as we go along.

Paul was combating the Judaizers, who were out in full force. Many think the Judaizers were Jews who attempted to convince Gentiles that the way to be *saved* was by observing the Mosaic law — but that is not an accurate description. The Judaizers were Jewish Christians who taught Gentile Christians that the way believers are sanctified — set apart unto holiness and righteousness before the Lord — is by keeping the Mosaic rituals, such as circumcision, dietary laws, feast days, sabbaths, etc. *Eerdman's Dictionary* says:

> In Galatians Paul does not attack Judaism as such, but those Jewish Christians who undertake missions to the Gentiles to urge them to live as Jews. Their argument is not that Gentiles must become Jews before becoming Christians; rather, they want all Christians to be Jewish Christians, to "live as Jews" while following Christ.[1]

Paul's point *in both Galatians and Romans* is that God considers as justified (righteous) those who are *living* the Christian life *by faith*, not by keeping a list of rules, like the Mosaic law. Consistent righteous living is one of the qualifications for kingdom inheritance, and thus a matter of works *after* salvation. Thus, Paul's argument is *not* soteriological either in Galatians or in Romans. But because Martin Luther assumed that it was, and thought Paul was teaching *positional* justification, he totally dismissed James' argument of justification by works as contrary to Paul's doctrine, and that led him to discount the book as meaningless.

The misinterpretations of Scripture that came out of the Reformation have been passed down for more than five centuries and have become normalized for evangelical Christianity. Anyone who teaches otherwise is branded as ignorant or, worse yet, heretical. Thus it is critical that Christianity return to the correct, early-church interpretation of Scripture. To that end, it is incumbent upon us to rightly divide the book of James, especially 2:14-26.

WHAT IS JAMES NOT TEACHING?

James is *not* teaching that a person becomes saved (regenerated) by faith plus works. In fact, James is not talking about matters of salvation — at least in the initial sense — at all. Consider his audience. James is writing to Christians, not unbelievers:

> **Jas. 1:2** <u>My brethren,</u> count it all joy when you fall into various trials,

> **Jas. 2:1** <u>My brethren,</u> do not hold the faith of our Lord Jesus Christ, *the Lord* of glory, with partiality.

> **Jas. 3:1** <u>My brethren,</u> let not many of you become teachers, knowing that we shall receive a stricter judgment.

> **Jas. 2:14** What *does it* profit, <u>my brethren,</u> if someone says he has faith but does not have works? (emphasis added)

In fact, James uses the word *brethren* fifteen times in the epistle! He assumes those in his audience are already children of God, his Christian brethren. Accordingly, James is not teaching unbelievers how to be regenerated. He is teaching believers how to live in a manner pleasing to God, how to walk in victory, living a sanctified life — seeing they have been scattered in the dispersion. Years ago I preached through the book of James and titled the series, "How to Behave When Away From Home."

WHAT IS JAMES TEACHING?

James challenges his Jewish Christian brethren to keep obeying God in faith and doing good works. They need this encouragement, because they have been scattered throughout the nations due to persecution. James doesn't want them to throw up their hands in despair and stop serving God. He urges them to continue doing faith-filled works of righteousness. We might say to a believer who is overwhelmed in trials, "Don't lose heart! Jesus wants you to carry on in victory, persevering unto reward!" To that end, James motivates them in 1:12:

> **Jas. 1:12** Blessed *is* the man who endures temptation [trials]; for when he has been approved, he will receive the crown of life which the Lord has promised to those who love Him.

The teaching of the epistle of James should be interpreted through the lens of this verse. As if to say, keep living righteously, producing faith-filled works, despite the overwhelming pressures of life bearing down upon you. If you persevere, you will be rewarded by Jesus! If you do not continue living righteously, producing faith-filled works, your soul will not be saved — which is a sanctification matter — and you will not be rewarded.

The key to rightly dividing the books of James and Galatians and Romans — and, for that matter, the entire New Testament — is understanding that the word *salvation* has at least two aspects of meaning, not merely one. Context determines which aspect is being discussed.

SALVATION OF ONE'S *SPIRIT* — IN THE *PAST*

Most tend to think that *salvation* usages in the New Testament are singular, that is, referring to the salvation of their spirit, when they believed Jesus for eternal (age-lasting) life and became a child of God (Rom. 8:16, *The Spirit Himself bears witness with our spirit that we are children of God*). Examples of this aspect of salvation — which occurred in the *past* — include Eph. 2:8-9; Titus 3:5; and 2 Tim. 1:9. Each of these verses emphasizes salvation by faith alone, not of works, which happened in the *past*. But this is only one aspect and, in fact, a mere fraction of all salvation usages in the Scriptures. Going forward in this book, I will refer to these salvation references as *initial salvation* or *regeneration*.

SAVING OF ONE'S *SOUL* – IN THE *PRESENT*

Whereas initial salvation of one's *spirit* occurs at a point in the past, and is based on faith, not works, the saving of one's *soul* is ongoing in the present, from the point of salvation until the rapture of the church. It is more commonly referred to as *sanctification* and involves righteous deeds. For example, James admonishes:

> **Jas. 1:21** Therefore lay aside all filthiness and overflow of wickedness, and receive with meekness the implanted word, which is able to <u>save your souls</u>. (emphasis added)
>
> 22 But be doers of the word, and not hearers only, deceiving yourselves.

Notice the soul becomes "saved" (i.e., sanctified) by doing things — laying aside sinful behavior, receiving God's Word, and living obediently. Jesus also spoke of "soul salvation" in Matt. 16:24-27 and John 12:24-25.

> **Matt. 16:24** Then Jesus said to His disciples, "If anyone desires to come after Me, let him deny himself, and take up his cross, and follow Me.
>
> 25 For whoever desires to save his life [Greek *psuche*, i.e., *soul*] will lose it, but whoever loses his life [*soul*] for My sake will find it.
>
> 26 For what profit is it to a man if he gains the whole world, and loses his own soul? Or what will a man give in exchange for his soul?
>
> 27 For the Son of Man will come in the glory of His Father with His angels, and then He will reward each according to his works.

> **John 12:24** Most assuredly, I say to you, unless a grain of wheat falls into the ground and dies, it remains alone; but if it dies, it produces much grain.
>
> 25 He who loves his life [i.e., *soul*] will lose it, and he who hates his life [i.e., *soul*] in this world will keep it for eternal life.

Some teach that these verses describe initial salvation, but how can that be, for works are involved? By understanding these saving/salvation verses as referring to *ongoing salvation of the soul*, which involves works, the passages are no longer confusing and the doctrine of initial salvation by grace through faith is not muddied.

Those believers whose soul becomes saved in this life to the point of maturity, will be rewarded at the Judgment Seat of Christ with inheritance in the next age. They will be chosen to serve as Christ's bride and co-rulers in New Jerusalem.

Thus, it is imperative to determine which aspect of salvation is being used in a particular passage in order to interpret that text correctly. This is critical for understanding the book of Romans biblically, not merely theologically, as the Reformers viewed it.

After that important introduction, we come at last to an exposition of James 2:14-26. In this text James gives:

THREE OBSTACLES TO THE SAVING OF ONE'S SOUL

James uses as his showcase illustrations two Old Testament-era believers who did faith-filled works for God — similar to what we find in Heb. 11. Those who believe God and live righteously carry out righteous works for Him. James speaks of Abraham offering Isaac on the altar (v. 21) and Rahab hiding the spies (v. 25). Those are the actions of people who are believing God and acting in faith. The first obstacle to this is:

1. BIG TALK, NO ACTION

> **Jas. 2:14** What *does it* profit, my brethren, if someone says he has faith but does not have works? Can faith save him?

You can *say* that you are walking by faith, but if you are not obedient, carrying out works of righteousness, then your faith is not saving you. Remember that James is talking to believers, so the *saving* in v. 14 is not salvation of the *spirit*, in the sense of *regeneration*. It is salvation of the *soul*, or *sanctification*, that results in reward at the Judgment Seat. Incidentally, that's how James uses the word *save* in the entire epistle, for he is talking to believers about the importance of remaining faithful in obedience to the Lord while they are away from home, so to speak.

So a good paraphrase of v. 14 could be worded as follows: "What good is it Christian, if you claim to be living by faith, but your life is lacking works of righteousness? Can that kind of faith save your soul? Is that kind of faith victorious? Will it result in reward at the Judgment Seat?"

James goes on to give an example of a big talker:

> **Jas. 2:15-16** If a brother or sister is naked and destitute of daily food, and one of you says to them, "Depart in peace, be warmed and filled," but you do not give them the things which are needed for the body, what *does it* profit?

Take a brother in Christ who obviously has tremendous financial needs. He is naked, that is, poorly clothed because of his poverty. Perhaps he has holes in his clothes — and he doesn't have enough food to eat. Despite knowing about his needs, you put your arm around him and smile and pray, asking God to meet his needs. Then you encourage him to depart in peace — "Have a great day, and keep trusting the Lord, brother, because He is able to provide!" But you do not minister to your brother's needs by giving money or other resources to help him — you merely talk. What good is that kind of faith?

> **Jas. 2:17** Thus also faith by itself, if it does not have works, is dead.

Claiming that you are living by faith, even though you are not carrying out righteous, faith-filled works, is dead (lifeless, powerless) faith. This ties in with what James says in the previous chapter:

> **Jas. 1:22** Be doers of the word, and not hearers only, deceiving yourselves.

If you send away the poor believer with a slap on the back and a nice little prayer, then where is the profit in that? In other words, what good is that kind of faith? Does big talk save your soul, preparing you to hear "Well done!" at the Judgment Seat? That leads to a second obstacle to soul-salvation.

2. WORKS DONE IN THE FLESH

> **Jas. 2:18** Someone will say, "You have faith, and I have works." Show me your faith without your works, and I will show you my faith by my works.

The first half of the verse is the obstacle; the last half of the verse is James' response. There are many believers who talk like this in our own circles of Christianity. The objection: "You have faith and I have works." These are Christians who are depending on self rather than the Spirit of God as they live the Christian life, doing works for the Lord. Some of these folks downplay the Spirit-filled life of victory; they may even poke fun at the deeper life crowd. They mock those who claim to live by faith as if they were impractical. This crowd, without realizing it, downplays dependence on God while promoting fleshly effort and works of the flesh rather than fruit of the Spirit. They would never say it this way, of course, but their actions show their true colors.

I met a man like this many years ago, at a conference overseas. He was a former pastor who did not agree with my teaching about the Spirit-filled life. I was preaching from Eph. 3:14-21, pointing out that when one surrenders to the Spirit, his/her life will then be characterized by strengthening in the inner man (divine enablement), faith-filled victory, and deeper love for God and others. He disagreed; he did not view those things as characteristics of a Spirit-filled Christian, but rather as the means by which a person becomes Spirit-filled. In other words, you must become strengthened in your inner man, live the Christ-life of victory, and have genuine love, in order to be filled with the Spirit. I could not convince him that those things are impossible for us to accomplish apart from the enabling power of God's Spirit, to whom we must surrender all.

Sad to say, this is the mentality of much of Christianity, thus it is appropriately called "struggle-theology." It reverses God's order from faith-filled, Spirit-enabled works to works done in one's own strength that supposedly demonstrate one has faith. It is the objection of James 2:18a, "You have faith and I have works." God condemns this way of thinking in the latter half of the verse, where James argues back: James 2:18b, "Show me your faith without your works, and I will show you my faith by my works." In other words, the biblical position is that righteous works will always characterize the child of God who is truly walking by faith, depending on God. That leads to a third obstacle to soul-salvation.

3. ASSUMING ORTHODOXY IS ENOUGH

> **Jas. 2:19** You believe that there is one God. You do well. Even the demons believe—and tremble!

The Jews were monotheistic — *Deut 6:4 Hear, O Israel: The LORD our God, the LORD is one!* Amidst all the idolatry around them, the Israelites who had scattered throughout Asia Minor, continued to believe in Jehovah God. James says to them, "You do well." Today, Christians say, "We believe in the blood atonement." Ah, Christian, you do well. "We believe in the virgin birth and the deity of Christ and His bodily resurrection." You do well. "We believe in the inerrant, inspired word of God." Again, you do well.

But it's not enough merely to be orthodox or fundamental in doctrine! Even demons are orthodox. They believe in one God; they know the doctrines of the Bible. That leads James to another point.

> **Jas. 2:20** But do you want to know, O foolish man, that faith without works is dead?

Orthodoxy and fundamental doctrine are important, but of themselves, they are insufficient. You will not be rewarded merely because you hold to right doctrine. That also goes for those who believe the doctrine of kingdom inheritance. The point is, if you don't act on right doctrine and become justified (declared righteous by God) through a life of faith-filled works, then you will not be rewarded and will be excluded from the ruling realm of His kingdom. Anything less is dead — lifeless, powerless, dead orthodoxy, vain and empty. That leads James to share:

TWO ILLUSTRATIONS OF OLD TESTAMENT-ERA BELIEVERS WHO PRODUCED FAITH-FILLED WORKS

ILLUSTRATION #1: ABRAHAM

> **Jas. 2:21** Was not Abraham our father justified by works when he offered Isaac his son on the altar?
> **22** Do you see that faith was working together with his works, and by works faith was made perfect?
> **23** And the Scripture was fulfilled which says, *"Abraham believed God, and it was accounted to him for righteousness."* And he was called the friend of God.
> **24** You see then that a man is justified by works, and not by faith only.

Imagine being promised by God that you will be a father of many nations, yet you are quite old and have no children. You would have to wonder — and so did Abraham and his wife Sarah, at least for a time. But in process of time they came to believe God completely. Then Isaac was born when Abraham was one hundred years old and Sarah was ninety. I can picture the rejoicing in their home, even at their old ages. Then imagine fifteen to twenty years later, when God commands Abraham to offer his promised son Isaac on the altar. Wouldn't most believers shrink away from such a command, doubting if it could really be true? But not Abraham; he obeys. As he is about to plunge in the knife, the angel of the Lord stops him, and God declares His obedient servant righteous.

That is the first illustration James uses of faith-filled works. Verse 22 says that Abraham's faith in offering Isaac worked together (i.e., his faith cooperated) with his works, and thereby he was made *perfect* (complete or mature). Throughout life Abraham had a struggling, growing faith with many setbacks – and don't we all! Nevertheless, God continued to work with His servant, bringing him along, rounding off the rough edges through trials and tests. God did this refining work throughout Abraham's entire life. The key is that Abraham submitted to God's working and grew into a mighty man of God. God works patiently with His children, to the extent that we cooperate with Him.

> **Phil. 2:12-13** Work out your own salvation with fear and trembling; for it is God who works in you both to will and to do for *His* good pleasure.

GOD'S PREPARATION OF SONS

In other words, cooperate with God as He seeks to save your soul. Let him do His maturing work in your life. Don't resist Him!

> **Heb. 12:5b-6** My son, do not despise the chastening of the LORD, nor be discouraged when you are rebuked by Him; for whom the LORD loves He chastens, and scourges every son whom He receives.
> **7** If you endure chastening, God deals with you as with sons; for what son is there whom a father does not chasten?
> **8** But if you are without chastening, of which all have become partakers, then you are illegitimate and not sons.

Chastening (from the Greek word *paideia*) is the entire process of child-training — including punishment, if necessary. Those who submit to God's chastening are His sons (Greek, *huios*). In this context, the writer is speaking of those believers who are maturing, on the pathway to becoming *sons to glory* . Those who do not submit are not mature sons. In fact, God refers to them as "illegitimate." Though they remain children (Greek *teknon*) of God, Heb. 12 teaches that God only chastens those who are on the pathway of maturing unto reward. Are you cooperating with God in His sanctifying and chastening work in your life? He is patiently working to bring you to maturity through trials and tribulations and tests over time.

If God had asked Abraham to offer Isaac much earlier, Abraham might not have been willing to do it. But God knows the right timing. When He asked, Abraham was ready — he did not struggle;

he was victorious. This man of God offered his son Isaac in complete obedience and faith toward God, and that obedience signified that his faith was now mature. Notice what James concludes in v. 23:

> **Jas. 2:23** And the Scripture was fulfilled which says, *"Abraham believed God, and it was accounted to him for righteousness."* And he was called the friend of God.

God said this of Abraham more than thirty years earlier, after God told Abraham that Eliezer of Damascus would not be his heir, but rather a son would come forth from his own body.

> **Gen. 15:6** And he believed in the LORD, and He accounted it to him for righteousness.

Abraham believed what God said and acted on it. Granted, he erred in the beginning by taking matters into his own hands and attempting to bring forth a son by his wife's handmaid, Hagar. Consequently, Ishmael became the son of his fleshliness. God told him another would come of Sarah, and that son (Isaac) would be the promised heir. When Abraham was mature enough to obey God and sacrifice his son at a much older age, he fulfilled what God said of him much earlier in his life — that he was a righteous man — and that characterized his entire life!

Keep in mind: None of this has anything to do with initial salvation or regeneration. This is the Old Testament equivalent of New Testament *soul-salvation*. It is sanctification unto reward. Abraham will be rewarded with a position of honor in the kingdom of the heavens, New Jerusalem, the city of reward, for Jesus said:

> **Matt. 8:11** Many will come from east and west, and sit down with Abraham, Isaac, and Jacob in the kingdom of heaven.

What an example of believing God and living righteously! James concludes the section on Abraham by saying:

> **Jas. 2:24** You see then that a man is justified by works, and not by faith only.

Then James gives us one more illustration:

ILLUSTRATION #2: RAHAB

> **Jas. 2:25** Likewise, was not Rahab the harlot also justified by works when she received the messengers and sent *them* out another way?

Rahab was known in the scriptures as a harlot — that was her earlier life. But she believed in Jehovah God, even before the spies showed up. She shares her testimony with the spies:

> **Josh. 2:9** (She) said to the men: "I know that the LORD has given you the land, that the terror of you has fallen on us, and that all the inhabitants of the land are fainthearted because of you.
> **10** For we have heard how the LORD dried up the water of the Red Sea for you when you came out of Egypt, and what you did to the two kings of the Amorites who *were* on the other side of the Jordan, Sihon and Og, whom you utterly destroyed.
> **11** And as soon as we heard *these things,* our hearts melted; neither did there remain any more courage in anyone because of you, for the LORD your God, He *is* God in heaven above and on earth beneath."

What a testimony! Rahab believed Jehovah long before the spies ever arrived. Thus, her obedience in sparing God's messengers was an act of faith. In other words, her actions — despite the dangers — were an outward display of faith in the God she had believed in previously. She (by faith) hid them, not fearing the consequences.

Rahab's trust in Jehovah God led her to claim the promises of Israel — the promise of victory over their enemies — the promise that the land was theirs to possess. Rahab believed this too, and that is why she boldly hid the spies. Her works were faith-filled and resulted in deliverance. Joshua spared her household, and Rahab was later married to a prince of Judah, through whom she became the great grandmother of King David and an ancestor of Jesus.

Notice again James' summary statement:

> **Jas. 2:24** You see then that a man is justified by works, and not by faith only.

God declares those believers justified (i.e., righteous) who are producing faith-filled works. They are the ones on the pathway of soul salvation and kingdom inheritance. They are avoiding the obstacles of:

1. Big talk
2. Works done in the flesh
3. Assuming orthodoxy is enough

Are *you* avoiding these obstacles and being justified by faith-filled works? James tells us why this is so important:

> **Jas. 2:26** For as the body without the spirit is dead, so faith without works is dead also.

Just as a body without breath is lifeless, so having faith in God without righteous deeds is dead, empty, and powerless. Is your faith dead or alive?

SUMMARIZING "THE JUST SHALL LIVE BY FAITH"

The first three chapters of this book demonstrate that justification is *not* positional and legal, as if it were some kind of righteous "standing" that God bestows on His children when they are regenerated. A correct understanding of justification begins in the Old Testament.

According to Ezek. 18, God considers a person to be just if they are *living* righteously, which means that justification is based on one's behavior. This is consistent with the first use of the term, *the just shall live by faith*, found in Hab. 2:4. The context describes those who are humble and obedient as living uprightly, by faith, in contradistinction to those who are prideful and disobedient, who are living wickedly. These ideas about justification would have been in the minds of the Jews of the first century.

Not surprisingly, the New Testament writers continue with the same understanding. Justification is not used in connection with initial salvation, or regeneration, as the Reformers taught. It is always used in contexts of ongoing salvation, or sanctification, regarding behavior. That is clear in Heb. 10-11, Gal. 2-3, and James 2. As we shall see, it is also clear in Romans. Should we expect Romans to be any different?

CHAPTER 5
THE ROMANS ROAD TO SALVATION MISNOMER
ROMANS 1:1-17

When I was a kid, growing up in an independent, fundamental church, virtually everyone taught and believed that salvation was received by praying to ask Jesus to come into your heart and be your Savior. Some claimed that repentance was necessary to being saved; others did not. But that particular detail flew over the heads of most. What was most important was "praying the prayer," which was considered essential for keeping evangelistic statistics as to who was saved and who was not. That being the case, most of the church's emphasis was on evangelism, and it was common in church to hear evangelistic sermons. "Soulwinning" night was just as important as a church service and was emphasized heavily, even to the point that folks were made to feel guilty if they did not go.

We were regularly reminded of the statistics — those who had prayed the prayer — and it gave us opportunity to "give glory to God," even though the church seemed to take a lot of the glory for itself, particularly the ones who had done the "soulwinning."

Those who prayed the prayer essentially received a "ticket to Heaven," and did not have to worry about going to Hell. The serious ones were later dunked in the baptismal tank, and in some Baptist churches this was expected of the person on the very same Sunday when their salvation happened or became known.

"THE ROMANS ROAD TO SALVATION"

The most common method of witnessing to the lost was to use the *Romans Road to Salvation*. Here are the basic bullet points:

1. Everyone is a sinner, and that includes you — Rom. 3:23 (*All have sinned and fall short of the glory of God*); Rom. 3:10 (*There is none righteous, no, not one*).
2. Because of sin, by default, all will die and spend eternity in Hell — Rom. 6:23a (*The wages of sin is death*).
3. But God sent Jesus to die and pay the price for man's sins — Rom. 5:8 (*God demonstrates His own love toward us, in that while we were still sinners, Christ died for us*).
4. Jesus wants to save you and give you eternal life so you can go to Heaven when you die — Rom. 6:23b (*The gift of God is eternal life in Christ Jesus our Lord*).
5. You can be saved by asking Jesus in your heart — Rom. 10:9, 13 (*If you confess with your mouth the Lord Jesus and believe in your heart that God has raised Him from the dead, you will be saved. For whoever calls on the name of the LORD shall be saved*).
6. [The person sharing the plan typically urges the sinner to pray to receive Christ, often suggesting the words to a prayer or encouraging the person to "repeat these words after me." If the unbeliever prays to receive Jesus, then he is taken to one final passage (to emphasize "eternal security")]:
7. Now that you are saved, you will go to Heaven when you die, not to Hell — Rom. 8:1a (*There is therefore now no condemnation to those who are in Christ Jesus*).
8. [Sometimes Rom. 8:38-39 is given to demonstrate that the new believer is secure in Jesus. (*Nothing shall be able to separate us from the love of God which is in Christ Jesus our Lord*)].

There's one big problem. The book of Romans is *not* about initial salvation, which means that none of these verses are intended for leading an unbeliever to faith in Jesus Christ. In fact, the so-called *Romans Road to Salvation* misuses all of these verses. That is because the book of Romans is not written to unbelievers, telling them how to be saved in an initial sense; it is written to believers, telling them how to be sanctified. John Niemela, who wrote the *Introduction* to Zane Hodges' commentary on Romans, says:

> This book focuses on issues concerning *believers*, a fact overlooked by those who use the so-called *Romans road* to inform unbelievers of the importance of believing in Christ. Paul would be shocked to learn that his message for believers would be construed as a message for unbelievers ... Contrary to what advocates of the so-called Romans Road would say, his epistle was not designed as an evangelistic tool.[1]

THE PROBLEM AT ROME – DIVISION AND DISUNITY

Paul writes to the church at Rome — to Christians, both Jewish and Gentile — telling them how to be sanctified, with the ultimate goal of unity amongst believers. Accordingly, when I preached through Romans in my church, I entitled the series: *The Gospel That Sanctifies and Unifies*.

In typical eastern style, Paul does not begin with the problem. Instead, he takes a more diplomatic approach so that his audience doesn't lose face, which is very important in the Middle Eastern and Mediterranean world of Paul's day. He drops a few hints in ch. 1 that there could be a problem, but he skips over the *nature* of the problem and goes right to the *solution* to the problem. Because we have western minds, we want to see the nature of the problem up front. However, Paul does not lay out the problem until ch. 15 (near the end of the book) — "the elephant in the room," so to speak — for which he has already provided the solution in the preceding chapters.

> **Rom. 15:5-6** Now may the God of patience and comfort grant you to be like-minded toward one another, according to Christ Jesus, that

you may with one mind *and* one mouth glorify the God and Father of our Lord Jesus Christ.

7 Therefore receive one another, just as Christ also received us, to the glory of God.

8-9 Now I say that Jesus Christ has become a servant to the circumcision for the truth of God, to confirm the promises *made* to the fathers, and that the Gentiles might glorify God for *His* mercy, as it is written: *"For this reason I will confess to You among the Gentiles, and sing to Your name."*

10 And again he says: *"Rejoice, O Gentiles, with His people!"*

11 And again: *"Praise the LORD, all you Gentiles! Laud Him, all you peoples!"*

12 And again, Isaiah says: *"There shall be a root of Jesse; and He who shall rise to reign over the Gentiles, in Him the Gentiles shall hope."*

The problem is that the believers at Rome are *not* like-minded; they are *not* of one accord, they are *not* unified. According to 16:17 this lack of unity has led to divisions and offenses, which is contrary to the Scriptures and poses some serious ramifications for the church:

15:6-7 — They are not glorifying God.
15:8-12 — Messiah's kingdom objectives are not being fulfilled.

CONSEQUENCE: GENTILES NOT BEING REACHED WITH THE GOSPEL

In other words, because of the disunity and divisions in Rome, the Gentiles in other parts of the world are not being reached with either the gospel of grace regarding initial salvation or the gospel of soul-salvation regarding kingdom inheritance. Thus, implied in this problem is that the ultimate goal of bringing many *sons to glory* — using a term from Heb. 2:10 — is not being accomplished.

The last phrase of 15:12 says, "in Him the Gentiles shall hope." The word *hope* is a kingdom inheritance term. It is the confident expectation, along with an attitude of pleasure or delight, that we will be rewarded by Jesus if we are living righteously. Paul uses the word *hope* twelve times in the book of Romans. When Gentiles are being reached for the glory of God with the kingdom inheritance message, then the Holy Spirit is bringing many *sons to glory* who have *hope* in the coming kingdom of Christ. They will be rewarded with the privilege of co-ruling with Him as His bride in the kingdom. Because of the disunity and divisions in Rome, that is not happening; the Gentiles are *not* being reached. Could it be that because of disunity and division *within* Christian churches today — not to mention *amongst* churches — the goal of reaching Gentiles and *sons to glory* is not being accomplished?

PUTTING AN END TO DISUNITY AND DIVISION IN THE CHURCH

Here I would like to add an important parenthesis for thought. How can churches put an end to disunity and division?

a) Believers must humble themselves before others. No one can force you to be humble; that is a decision of your own free will, but God promises that if you humble yourself before the Lord, He will exalt you (1 Pet. 5:6).

b) Believers must choose to live by the principles taught in Rom. 6-8 — walking in the Spirit rather than in the flesh. That means getting victory over sins in the life through the enabling power of the Holy Spirit.

(c) Believers must draw closer to one another through regular fellowship. This is one of the reasons that church attendance is so critical.

God commands us not to forsake assembling with one another. Yet, as a pastor for nearly three decades, I find that multitudes of Christians pursue other things on Sundays that take them away from assembling with God's people. There are always going to be competing interests for your time on Sunday. But you must make the choice to obey God and assemble with fellow believers. That is the only way we can grow unified in Christ-likeness as a body. Is that not the purpose for the church of Jesus Christ?

> **Eph. 4:11-13** He Himself gave some *to be* apostles, some prophets, some evangelists, and some pastors and teachers, for the equipping of the saints for the work of ministry, for the edifying of the body of

Christ, till we all come to the unity of the faith and of the knowledge of the Son of God, to a perfect man, to the measure of the stature of the fullness of Christ;

Unity in Christ-likeness is the goal of the church, for it demonstrates that the believers in a local assembly are putting selfish considerations aside, and they are growing together in holiness and love. Those are the churches that will be rewarded in the presence of Jesus. If you, as an individual believer, are striving for that same objective, you will be rewarded also.

Paul urges the believers at Rome to fix their disunity problem by applying the truths written in the epistle and by separating from those who refuse to unify.

Rom. 16:17 Now I urge you, brethren, note those who cause divisions and offenses, contrary to the doctrine which you learned, and avoid them.

Then, in a pragmatic application, he urges them to support his mission to Spain.

Rom. 15:24 Whenever I journey to Spain, I shall come to you. For I hope to see you on my journey, and to be helped on my way there by you, if first I may enjoy your *company* for a while.

Of course, the church will not help him, if they are plagued with disunity and division. They must fix their problem by applying the truths Paul has shared with them earlier in the book, then they will be inclined to support the outreach to the Gentiles in western Europe.

THE PURPOSE OF PAUL'S CALLING

What is causing the disunity and division? We know the answer from the historical context of the early church at Rome, but Paul hints at the problem in ch. 1:

> Rom. 1:1 Paul, a bondservant of Jesus Christ, called *to be* an apostle, separated to the gospel of God
> 1:2 which He promised before through His prophets in the Holy Scriptures,
> 1:3 concerning His Son Jesus Christ our Lord, who was born of the seed of David according to the flesh
> 1:4 *and* declared *to be* the Son of God with power according to the Spirit of holiness, by the resurrection from the dead.
> 1:5 Through Him we have received grace and apostleship for obedience to the faith among all nations for His name.

1:1a. Paul refers to himself as a *bondservant* or, literally, an *indentured slave* of Jesus. Why does he use that language with the Romans who view slaves contemptuously? Because that is the attitude they need to have with respect to Christ and others — humble and servant-oriented.

1:1b. The apostle declares that he has been *separated*, or set apart, *to the gospel* — the good news! He expounds on this in Gal. 1:

> **Gal. 1:15-17** But when it pleased God, who separated me from my mother's womb and called me through His grace, to reveal His Son in me, that I might preach Him among the Gentiles, I did not immediately confer with flesh and blood, nor did I go up to Jerusalem to those who were apostles before me; but I went to Arabia, and returned again to Damascus.

Separated from my mother's womb. The apostle was born for this purpose! Little did he realize it when persecuting the church of Jesus Christ, but after the Damascus road experience, he was confirmed in this calling by the Holy Spirit through Ananias (see Acts 9:10-20) and taught by the Lord in Arabia.

Separated to the gospel. What is this gospel? As will be made clear as we go along, this is the good news of kingdom inheritance for those believers whose soul is being saved. This particular focus of ministry consumed Paul for the rest of his life, particularly among the Gentiles, so they could learn how to become *sons to glory*.

1:2. This gospel was promised by the Old Testament prophets, but they knew very little about it. To them it was a mystery. Peter explains their perplexity in greater detail:

> **1 Pet. 1:8b-9** Though now you do not see Him, yet believing, you rejoice with joy inexpressible and full of glory, receiving the end of your faith—the salvation of your souls.
>
> **10-11** Of this salvation the prophets have inquired and searched carefully, who prophesied of the grace that would come to you, searching what, or what manner of time, the Spirit of Christ who was in them was indicating when He testified beforehand the sufferings of Christ and the glories that would follow.
>
> **12** To them it was revealed that, not to themselves, but to us they were ministering the things which now have been reported to you through those who have preached the gospel to you by the Holy Spirit sent from heaven—things which angels desire to look into.

The good news of the *salvation of the soul* was of great interest to the Old Testament prophets, and they searched it out diligently. Nevertheless, the fullness of this gospel was not given to them, and they realized it was but a mystery in their day, with more details to be revealed to a future generation. Even the angels are curious about this magnificent subject of the glories that will follow Messiah's sufferings! Arlen Chitwood writes:

> This "good news" had to do with the *mystery* revealed to Paul by the Lord (evidently after he had been taken to Arabia, then into heaven [II Cor. 12:1-7; Gal. 1:11-17]). It had to do with believing Jews and Gentiles being placed together in "the same body" as "fellowheirs ['joint-heirs']" (Eph. 3:1-11); and these Jewish and Gentile believers (Christians), together, possessed a "hope" relative to one day occupying positions of honor and glory with Christ in "his heavenly kingdom" (cf. Col. 1:25-28; II Tim. 4:17, 18; Titus 1:2; 2:11-13; 3:7).
>
> And Paul referred to *the good news* pertaining to this message as "my gospel" (Rom. 16:25), "our gospel" (II Cor. 4:3), "the glorious

gospel of Christ [lit., 'the gospel of the glory of Christ']" (II Cor. 4:4), "the gospel of God" (Rom. 1:1; II Cor. 11:7), "the gospel of Christ" (Rom. 1:16; Gal. 1:7), etc. Then, numerous times Paul simply used the word "gospel" alone to refer to this good news (Rom. 1:15; Gal. 1:6).[2]

1:3-4. This gospel concerns Jesus Christ, the Son of God, a physical descendent of King David, Who arose from the grave in great power and authority. The implication is that Jesus is God incarnate — the God-man. Of course, if anyone is going to believe the gospel of kingdom inheritance, they must first believe Jesus died and rose again, and that He offers eternal (age-lasting) life, all of which are foundational to the saving of the soul.

1:5a. It is this very Son of God who has given Paul *grace* (the enablement to fulfill his calling) and *apostleship* (the authority to carry it out). However, rather than using the singular pronoun "I," Paul uses "we" — *we have received grace and apostleship* — "a kind of 'modest' plural."[3]

1:5b. The purpose for grace and apostleship is *for obedience to the faith among all nations for His name*. Thus, the goal of the good news of kingdom inheritance is to urge believers from the Gentile nations to live in obedience to Jesus Christ so they will qualify to be rewarded as *sons to glory* at the Judgment Seat of Christ, equipped to co-rule with Jesus in His Messianic kingdom.

THE NATURE OF PAUL'S AUDIENCE

> **Rom. 1:6 among whom you also are the called of Jesus Christ;**
> **1:7 To all who are in Rome, beloved of God, called to be saints: grace to you and peace from God our Father and the Lord Jesus Christ.**
> **1:8 First, I thank my God through Jesus Christ for you all, that your faith is spoken of throughout the whole world.**

1:6-7a. The word *called* means to be invited. Many interpret this through a Calvinistic (Reformation) lens, teaching that these are the ones God has elected or called to (initial) salvation, but that is not how the word is used in the New Testament. Paul is writing to those who have already believed in Jesus as Messiah, so this calling is not to *initial* salvation. It is to *ongoing* salvation, which is sanctification. They are called to live righteously, as *saints — set apart ones*, for that is the means by which believers qualify to be rewarded.

Ironically, Paul uses the same word to refer to these disciples that he uses for himself in v. 1. Just as he had been *called* to apostleship, so they have been *called to be saints*. He obviously does not use the word *saints* in a positional sense, but in a conditional sense — those whose spiritual condition is set apart unto holiness. Not all believers live as saints, but Paul wants his readers to know that is God's expectation for them. Jesus said:

> **Matt. 22:14** Many are called, but few are chosen.

The "many" are God's children, all of whom have been called to holiness. The "few" are the faithful ones who take up His invitation, live set apart from sin and to God, and are, therefore, chosen by Him to become His bride and co-regents in the kingdom.

1:7b *Grace and peace.* These simple words convey deep and wonderful spiritual concepts. *Grace* is God's divine enablement to help us do what we are unable to do. God promises, "My grace is sufficient" (2 Cor. 12:9), and He "gives more grace" as needed (James 4:6). *Peace* is calmness of soul that knows no anxiety, because one is right with God and man. His peace "surpasses all understanding" (Phil. 4:7). We struggle to articulate peace because it is so elusive. What a tremendous dual blessing to bestow on fellow-believers!

1:8 *Your faith is spoken of throughout the whole world.* Is this not another confirming evidence that the apostle is writing to believers? It seems that everyone in the Roman Empire knew of the "faith reputation" of the church at Rome. Perhaps that is due to their steadfastness amidst persecution.

THE DESIRE OF PAUL'S HEART

> Rom. 1:9-10 For God is my witness, whom I serve with my spirit in the gospel of His Son, that without ceasing I make mention of you always in my prayers, making request if, by some means, now at last I may find a way in the will of God to come to you.
> 1:11-12 For I long to see you, that I may impart to you some spiritual gift, so that you may be established—that is, that I may be encouraged together with you by the mutual faith both of you and me.

Paul longs to visit these dear brethren at Rome. As of the time of his writing, he has never been to Rome, but he eagerly desires to go and proclaim the good news of kingdom inheritance. To that end, he prays for them regularly. He hopes to visit soon and minister to them spiritually, but he also expects to be blessed and encouraged by them in return. Genuine Christian fellowship is a "two-way street."

Most commentators believe Paul wrote this in the late AD 50s, when he was at Corinth (Hodges says AD 56-57).[4] But Paul doesn't actually make it to Rome until around AD 60. When he finally arrives, he is under house arrest and apparently never makes it to Spain. Paul is ultimately executed in Rome, and most think it was due to Nero's orders.

THE ROOT OF THE CHURCH'S PROBLEM

> Rom. 1:13 Now I do not want you to be unaware, brethren, that I often planned to come to you (but was hindered until now), that I might have some fruit among you also, just as among the other Gentiles.
> 1:14 I am a debtor both to Greeks and to barbarians, both to wise and to unwise.

1:15 So, as much as is in me, I am ready to preach the gospel to you who are in Rome also.

As mentioned earlier, Paul doesn't explicitly reveal the church's problem or the cause of it until ch. 15. However, he hints at the root cause in these verses. He mentions Gentiles, Greeks, barbarians, wise and unwise — and Jews in v. 16. Why does he use all these terms?

The root of the problem in the church at Rome is cultural prejudice. Notice the different groups that he mentions. Of course, Gentiles are all who are not Jews. But Paul also uses the term *Greeks* to distinguish from Gentiles in general. Some assume the six references to *Greeks* in the epistle are used as a synonym for Gentiles, but that is not correct. Paul uses the specific word *Greeks* for a reason.

Greeks (translated from the Greek word *hellen* in the New Testament) are not necessarily those from Greece. They are Gentiles who are Hellenized, regardless of nationality. In other words, they are sophisticated Gentiles — at least, in their own view — as if to say, they are Greco-Romans, implying a certain cultural distinction as intelligent pursuers of wisdom.

That is very likely one of the key reasons Paul doesn't share his burden to go to Spain and spread the gospel there or his need for financial support to make the trip. The Greco-Romans will have none of it, for they condescendingly view those living in Spain as barbarians, non-sophisticated Gentiles, unwise (or foolish) and certainly not Greeks in their way of thinking. In fact, to these Greeks, even the Jews are barbarians, because the Jews had been forced out of Rome by the emperor Claudius about a decade before this. Granted, many Jews had returned to Rome, but they continue to be viewed contemptuously (like slaves) by the Greco-Romans. Not to mention, the Jews have animosity toward the Gentiles of all stripes.

Thus, Paul faces major spiritual problems within the church at Rome — cultural baggage that results in prejudices against other people groups. What a terrible dilemma — believers who have hostility toward others of a different ethnic background. Is the twenty-first century church any different? What is needed is the very gospel message that Paul preaches! The apostle is eager to go and proclaim so he can have fruit at Rome also. In fact, he feels indebted to both Greeks and barbarians — and to the Jews, first and foremost (v. 16).

THE SOLUTION TO THE PROBLEM

> Rom. 1:16 **For I am not ashamed of the gospel of Christ, for it is the power of God to salvation for everyone who believes, for the Jew first and also for the Greek.**
> 1:17 **For in it the righteousness of God is revealed from faith to faith; as it is written, *"The just shall live by faith."***

1:16. *The gospel of Christ ... to salvation.* Paul gives the *solution* to the problem of division and disunity in the church at Rome without the church knowing the *nature* of their problem until ch. 15. In going after the *root* of the problem, he will preach the same gospel that he preached wherever he went.

This *gospel* is not the good news by which they had been initially saved (the gospel of grace by faith alone). It is the gospel of soul-salvation (sanctification unto maturity) that results in kingdom inheritance. It is the good news that those who live righteously and persevere will be rewarded at the Judgment Seat of Christ to become Christ's bride and co-rulers in the coming kingdom. Paul uses the word *gospel* thirteen times in the book, and he uses the word *salvation* four times — and always in this sense of the word!

How do we know this is the correct meaning? First, because Paul is talking to believers, *not* unbelievers. Second, because the word *believes* is an active present participle and should read: "the gospel ... is the power of God to salvation for everyone who *is believing.*" This is referring to believers (Christians, those who are already regenerated) continuing to believe for daily sanctification, the salvation of their soul.

1:17a. *The righteousness of God.* Third, we know this is the correct meaning because Paul's gospel of soul-salvation reveals the righteousness of God. He uses the word *righteous* eight times and the word *righteousness* thirty times in the epistle.

HOW IS GOD'S RIGHTEOUSNESS REVEALED?

When believers are living righteously and thereby qualifying as sons to glory to co-rule with Jesus in His coming kingdom, His righteousness is being revealed *now*, even in advance of that day when He will rule in righteousness. In other words, the process of soul-salvation, here and now, *anticipates* crowning and ruling at His judgment bar, and also *anticipates* His salvation of Israel and the nations. Psalm 98 gives a beautiful glimpses of God's righteousness being revealed in the next age, His millennial kingdom:

> **Ps. 98:1** Oh, sing to the LORD a new song! For He has done marvelous things; His right hand and His holy arm have gained Him the victory.
> 2 The LORD has made known His salvation; His righteousness He has revealed in the sight of the nations.
> 3 He has remembered His mercy and His faithfulness to the house of Israel; all the ends of the earth have seen the salvation of our God.
> 4 Shout joyfully to the LORD, all the earth; break forth in song, rejoice, and sing praises.

God's righteousness will be revealed when He ascends to the throne during His Messianic reign and rules in uprightness and justice and peace over all the nations. When that happens, His salvation will be known to all the nations, and they will sing forth His praise. In fact, all creation will praise Him:

> **Ps. 98:7** Let the sea roar, and all its fullness, the world and those who dwell in it;
> 8 Let the rivers clap *their* hands; let the hills be joyful together before the LORD,
> 9 For He is coming to judge the earth. With righteousness He shall judge the world, and the peoples with equity.

This is marvelous truth and explains why Christians who are living righteously have so much hope. They are rejoicing "in hope of the glory of God" (Rom. 5:2). The millennial King will bring His salvation to the entire Earth by ruling in righteousness, and all creation will worship Him!

One of the glorious benefits of initial salvation is that we now have the *provision* for living righteously, victorious over sin.

> **2 Cor. 5:21** For He (God the Father) made Him (Jesus Christ the Son) who knew no sin, to be sin for us, that we might become the righteousness of God in Him.

The verb *might become* is in the subjunctive mood, which is the Greek mood of potential. So this verse does not mean that those who believe on Jesus for eternal (age-lasting) life become *positionally* righteous and have Christ's righteousness credited to their account. It means those who believe on Jesus for eternal (age-lasting) life have the *potential* to live righteously. This is corroborated further by the use of the subjunctive mood in another verse in the same context:

> **2 Cor. 5:15** He died for all, that those who live should live no longer for themselves, but for Him who died for them and rose again.

Not all Christians live righteously, but they *should*, for they have the provision for righteous living and thus the potential (see Gal. 2:20). But the believer must appropriate the provision. In fact, in Rom. 5-8 Paul is going to outline the details of this potential and how a child of God can draw upon it to live righteously. When believers are living *"from faith to faith,"* that is, from *initial*, saving faith to *ongoing*, sanctifying faith, they are living righteously and thereby reflecting the righteous character of God.

1:17b. *The just shall live by faith.* Paul closes his first section by quoting Hab. 2:4, *"The just shall live by faith."* The *just* are those who are living righteously, as corroborated everywhere else in the Bible. They are producing faith-filled works.

GLORIOUS APPLICATION

Do not miss the important application of these opening verses of Romans. The gospel of soul-salvation leading to kingdom inheritance is the means by which disunity and divisions can be resolved. When believers start walking in righteousness, producing faith-filled works — in the power of the Holy Spirit — they will stop being selfish and prejudiced. They will unite with other believers and will no longer cause division in the church of Jesus Christ. They will glorify God by reaching others with the truth of God's righteousness, which can be theirs too. Those who don't live by faith, spurn God's righteousness, and God labels them *unrighteous*. We will see what happens to them in the next chapter.

Incidentally, v. 16 specifies that this gospel — which is powerful to save the soul (i.e., sanctify) — is "for the Jew first and also for the Greek." It's even for barbarians! That is why Paul claims in v. 14 he is a debtor to all men, regardless of cultural background or status. He must preach this good news to all — and so must we!

Anyone who has been saved initially can continue to be saved in an ongoing sanctification sense. That is why the *Romans Road to Salvation* method of witnessing is a misnomer. The verses typically used in the *Romans Road* are not referring to salvation in the initial sense of regeneration. They are referring to soul-salvation, sanctification unto reward.

How glorious to think that this gospel message is powerful enough to enable believers to live righteously, in a manner that pleases the Lord, so they can become kingdom inheritors. Are you on the pathway of sanctification that leads to reward?

CHAPTER 6
EXCHANGING GLORY FOR SHAME
ROMANS 1:18-32

Rom. 1:17 ends with a quote from Hab. 2:4b, *The just shall live by faith*. As noted in previous chapters, this is not a soteriological statement. Paul is not sharing the gospel of grace with unbelievers. He is sharing the gospel of kingdom inheritance with believers. Arlen Chitwood writes:

> There is really nothing about salvation by grace through faith in these first seventeen verses. The verses, among related issues, have to do with "the seed of David" (v. 3), declared to be "the Son of God with power ['sonship' has to do with rulership]" (v. 4), with "obedience to the faith" (v. 5), with the faith of Christians in Rome being "spoken of throughout the whole world" (v. 8), and with Paul's expressed desire to go to and proclaim this good news to the Christians in Rome, for a stated purpose — "that I might have some fruit among you also, even as among other Gentiles" (vv. 10, 13; cf. vv. 15, 16).[1]

These evidences indicate that Paul is writing to believers. In fact, Rom. 1 has two types of Christians in view:[2]

1. Those living righteously and unashamed vs. 16-17
2. Those living unrighteously and shamefully vs. 18-32

Chitwood sees this division as well:

> Romans chapter one has to do with two types of Christians in relation to the gospel ... The division of the chapter into two parts, with respect to two types of Christians, is seen at the end of verse seventeen, with verse eighteen beginning the second part of the chapter.[3]

God reveals something specific to each of these types of believers.

GOD'S RIGHTEOUSNESS REVEALED – TO THOSE LIVING RIGHTEOUSLY

Capping the first half of Rom. 1 are two classic verses that set the tone for the entire epistle and summarize what God is revealing to the first type of Christian:

> **Rom. 1:16 For I am not ashamed of the gospel of Christ, for it is the power of God to salvation for everyone who believes, for the Jew first and also for the Greek.**
> **1:17 For in it the righteousness of God is revealed from faith to faith; as it is written, "The just shall live by faith."**

Paul is unashamed of the gospel (good news) of kingdom inheritance, despite the persecution he is receiving from the Jews. He recognizes this gospel as powerful to save those who *are believing*. This is ongoing salvation, or sanctification, as explained earlier. It was — and still is — being offered to both Jews and Gentiles. In this particular gospel, God's righteousness is revealed — here and now — when believers are living by faith in the indwelling Christ, producing faith-filled works. Verses 16-17 could be paraphrased to read:

> I am not ashamed of the good news of soul-salvation through Christ, for He is God's powerful means of sanctifying those who are believing God and living by faith. When believers are living in this

manner, continuing from *initial,* regenerating faith to *ongoing,* sanctifying faith, God's righteousness is made known in this world. Those who are righteous in God's eyes are producing faith-filled works.

This gospel message is what the believers at Rome desperately need, for they are not unified and have divisions in the church, primarily driven by ethnic prejudices. They need to transcend above their spiritual problems by submitting to Christ and living uprightly.

GOD'S WRATH REVEALED — TO THOSE LIVING UNRIGHTEOUSLY

Paul then turns his attention to those believers who are choosing to continue in unrighteous behavior, and he gives a warning.

> **Rom. 1:18a For the wrath of God is revealed from heaven against all ungodliness and unrighteousness of men,**

Proponents of Reformation doctrines, particularly those who hold to Calvinist soteriology, cannot fathom that Paul continues to speak about believers in vs. 18ff. Notwithstanding, Paul is not changing his focus from *believers* in the first half of the chapter (vs. 1-17) to *unbelievers* in the second half (vs. 18-32). That would only distract from his message, leading the believers to think the apostle's message going forward no longer applies to them. The disunity and division would never become resolved. While the principles in the latter half of Rom. 1 certainly *apply* to all mankind, Paul's point is that God's wrath is provoked when *believers* are living in an unrighteous, ungodly manner.

"GNOSIS" AND "EPIGNOSIS"

In addition to the evidences from the first half of Rom. 1 (see above quote by Chitwood) — that Paul is addressing believers — he gives additional clues in the latter half of the chapter, using specific terminology that can only apply to Christians:

Rom. 1:28 They did not like to retain God in their *knowledge* ...

1:32 Who, *knowing* the righteous judgment of God, that those who practice such things are deserving of death ... (emphasis added)

The word *knowledge* is used in the noun form in v. 28 and in the verb form (*knowing*) in v. 32. The usual Greek word for *knowledge* is *gnosis*. But the Greek words used for *knowledge* in these verses are *epignosis* (for the noun) and *epiginosko* (for the verb). The prefix *epi* changes the meaning from rudimentary knowledge to full, experiential, mature knowledge. If I say that I know something about brick masonry because I read about it in a book, that would be *gnosis*. But a brick mason, who says he knows about brick masonry because he is employed in the trade and does that kind of work on a daily basis, knows far more about it than I do. He has *epignosis* — experiential, full, complete knowledge of brick masonry.

Applying this in a spiritual sense, in the context of Rom. 1:16-17, Paul refers to those who have *epignosis* regarding the gospel of kingdom inheritance that Paul has been preaching. They have full, experiential knowledge of matters of righteousness and sanctification and reward. That certainly cannot be said of unbelievers.

1 Cor. 2:14 The natural man does not receive the things of the Spirit of God, for they are foolishness to him; nor can he know *them*, because they are spiritually discerned.

Unbelievers (natural mankind) cannot begin to understand spiritual verities, for they are spiritually dead in trespasses and sins. They have not been regenerated and do not have the Holy Spirit living within. Thus, by the specific Greek words for *knowledge* that Paul uses in vs. 28 and 32, he can only be speaking about believers. More specifically, these are believers who have come into full, mature knowledge of the gospel that Paul has been preaching — the good news of soul-salvation (sanctification) unto maturity and the glorious prospect of being rewarded in Christ's coming kingdom, with the privilege of serving as His co-rulers.

THE CORRUPTING OF KINGDOM INHERITANCE TRUTH

Sadly, only a tiny percentage of Christians are aware of this message today, for very few churches preach these truths. As a result of the Reformation's influence, virtually nowhere is the gospel of kingdom inheritance taught any more, as it was during the early church era. Remarkably, Jesus predicted this in His parable of the leaven in the loaf.

> **Matt. 13:33** Another parable He spoke to them: "The kingdom of heaven is like leaven, which a woman took and hid in three measures of meal till it was all leavened."

This parable demonstrates how the kingdom inheritance message has fared over the course of the church age. It has been choked out by leaven, which is corruption or error, and Jesus warned of this happening. Consequently, very few believers even have familiarity with this teaching (*gnosis*), much less *epignosis*, or full, experiential, mature understanding. That prompted Paul to prophesy near the end of his ministry:

> **2 Tim. 3:1-5a, 7** But know this, that in the last days perilous times will come: for men will be lovers of themselves, lovers of money, boasters, proud, blasphemers, disobedient to parents, unthankful, unholy, unloving, unforgiving, slanderers, without self-control, brutal, despisers of good, traitors, headstrong, haughty, lovers of pleasure rather than lovers of God, having a form of godliness but denying its power ... always learning and never able to come to the knowledge of the truth.

Ironically, this is not intended as a description of the world, but of the church of Jesus Christ, *having a form of godliness but denying its power*. The church is *always learning and never able to come to the knowledge of the truth*. The word *knowledge* is *epignosis*, but Paul uses it in the negative. In other words, regarding the kingdom inheritance message, they do not even have *gnosis*, or basic knowledge of the gospel of soul-salvation and kingdom inheritance, much less *epignosis*, or full knowledge. God predicts the end of this in later verses:

> **2 Tim. 3:8b-9** These also resist the truth: men of corrupt minds, disapproved concerning the faith; but they will progress no further, for their folly will be manifest to all, as theirs also was.

What does God have to say about believers and churches that ignore the importance of sanctification and kingdom inheritance and turn to unrighteous living?

1. They resist the truth.
2. They have corrupt minds.
3. They are disapproved concerning the faith.

The Greek word translated *disapproved* is usually translated *disqualified* in the New Testament, meaning that those who live in this manner will be disqualified from reward and inheritance and glorification when they meet Jesus at the Judgment Seat of Christ. They will not be allowed into His Messianic ruling headquarters, New Jerusalem, but will be relegated to the relative darkness outside, which is the earthly realm of the kingdom. Their shame will be manifested to all, for they will not be glorified.

Notice the huge contrast between vs. 17 and 18:

> **1:17** For in it (the gospel of kingdom inheritance) the righteousness of God is revealed from faith to faith ...
>
> **1:18a** For the wrath of God is revealed from heaven against all ungodliness and unrighteousness of men ...

In v. 17 the righteousness of God is revealed in His salvation of those believers who are living righteously, by faith. In v. 18 the wrath of God is revealed in His judgment of those believers who are living unrighteously. While this certainly applies to mankind in general, Paul's emphasis, as we've already seen, is on believers in particular.

WHY DOES GOD REVEAL HIS WRATH?

Dutchman Jan Bonda asks:

> What would happen if there were no divine wrath? It would mean that God would simply let the people do whatever they wanted with this earth. Evil would continue and death would have the final say — with God's approval. God's wrath signifies that He does not approve; that he does not abandon the earth and all that lives to evil and death. He does not abandon the goal He has for His creation. That divine purpose is all-important. It is the deliverance of His creation from all that attempts to destroy it. God's wrath is an intrinsic part of this deliverance, that is, of His saving righteousness.[4]

1. GOD REVEALS HIS WRATH BECAUSE MEN SUPPRESS THE TRUTH.

> **Rom. 1:18 For the wrath of God is revealed from heaven against all ungodliness and unrighteousness of men, who suppress the truth in unrighteousness.**

Ungodliness and unrighteousness. These words are similar, but not identical. Zane Hodges (1932-2008) suggests that *ungodliness* refers to the "irreligious spirit of man" while *unrighteousness* emphasizes "the 'wrongness' of his conduct."[5] Plainly put, this is sinful behavior, typically accompanied by an "attitude." Sin begins in the heart.

To *suppress* means "to hold down or withhold." Believers hold down the truth of God's righteousness by living unrighteously.

Consider the immediate situation that Paul is addressing in this epistle. The believers at Rome have all received the same gospel of kingdom inheritance. Based on his usage of the word *epignosis*, it seems they have also understood it and lived it out experientially, at least for a time. While some have continued on the pathway of sanctification leading to inheritance, others have "spun out" and defected from the faith. The cares of this world and the deceitfulness of riches apparently lured them away, so that they slid down the slippery slope. That could happen to any believer who does not persevere in righteousness. As a result, the church at Rome is full of disunity and division which, most likely happened slowly, over time.

Most believers don't wake up one day deciding to rebel against God. It happens after a little sin here and a little sin there — left unchecked — and exposure to sinfulness and worldly philosophies. In time, zeal for the Lord fades and sinning becomes a way of life. Then God becomes angry, because the truth of His righteousness is not being made known to others through the lives of these believers who are now living in a fleshly, carnal manner, displeasing the Lord.

Think about your own life. If you are not living righteously, as God commands, then you are suppressing truth, His truth. You are withholding the verity of God's righteousness to the world, and you will incur His wrath.

2. GOD REVEALS HIS WRATH BECAUSE MEN DO NOT GLORIFY GOD.

> **Rom. 1:19 because what may be known of God is manifest in them, for God has shown it to them.**
> **1:20 For since the creation of the world His invisible *attributes* are clearly seen, being understood by the things that are made, *even* His eternal power and Godhead, so that they are without excuse,**

All of mankind can intuitively see in this beautiful world and universe that there is a God, and they can see that He is extremely powerful. God's general revelation of Himself in creation — which He *has manifest in them* and *shown it to them* — gives man no excuse for not living righteously, and that is all the more true for believers who know the truth of God's Word.

> **Rom. 1:21 because, although they knew God, they did not glorify *Him* as God, nor were thankful, but became futile in their thoughts, and their foolish hearts were darkened.**
> **1:22 Professing to be wise, they became fools,**
> **1:23 and changed the glory of the incorruptible God into an image made like corruptible man—and**

birds and four-footed animals and creeping things.

1:21. The downward spiral into sinning as a way of life begins by becoming unthankful. Having a gratitude-attitude is so critical, for it demonstrates that all we have — physical, spiritual, intellectual, emotional, material — indeed, *everything!* — has been given to us by our gracious God. A thankful heart and mind recognize that truth and show a debt of gratitude.

When a believer becomes *unthankful*, the companion sin of *complaining* creeps in, and initial steps have been taken down the path of further sinfulness and not glorifying God. Then the thinking becomes *futile* (empty, vain, foolish) — and the heart grows *dark* — characterized by the darkness of sin rather than the light of righteousness.

1:22. Those who enter into a life of sinning may consider themselves as wise, but they actually become *fools*. The Greek word translated *became fools* is translated *lost flavor* in the Sermon on the Mount:

> **Matt. 5:13** You are the salt of the earth; but if the salt loses its *flavor*, how shall it be seasoned? It is then good for nothing but to be thrown out and trampled underfoot by men. (emphasis mine)

Sinning saints are unsalty and flavorless, and therefore, spiritually useless.

1:23. Somewhere along the line an exchange occurs — worshipping and glorifying God is traded for worshipping and glorifying other things. In the case of pagan unbelievers, it may be actual idols or statues that represent gods and goddesses. For believers, it could be one or more things that replace God as primary in their lives — a focus on retirement, travel, hobbies, personal pleasures, sports, cars, real estate, or numerous other things.

Incidentally, I have never heard a Christian admit to being idolatrous. Most are blind to their exchanging of God for something else. Like the Laodicean church, they think they are "rich, have become wealthy, and have need of nothing" — but, in reality, they are "wretched, miserable, poor, blind, and naked" (Rev. 3:17). If believers remain on that pathway and do not confess their unrighteous behavior, they remove themselves from the narrow way of discipleship, and sinning grows worse over time. They enter the downward spiral of defeat that ends in negative reward at the Judgment Seat of Christ.

The bottom line is that, because of man's sinfulness, God is not being glorified in the world. While this is generally true for all mankind, it is exponentially true when believers are not glorifying Him, as with some of these Christians in Rome. Consequently, — and tragically! — believers exchange glorifying God for self glory and the prospect of glorification at the Judgment Seat for shame. The word *glory* is used sixteen times in Romans, and the words *glorify* and *glorified* another five times, so the concept of *glory* is important to Paul's thesis. We ignore it at our own peril.

Paul also wrote about Christians who exchange glory for shame in one of his other epistles:

> **Phil. 3:18-19** For many walk, of whom I have told you often, and now tell you even weeping, *that they are* the enemies of the cross of Christ: whose end *is* destruction, whose god *is their* belly, and *whose* glory *is* in their shame—who set their mind on earthly things.

Before giving a third and final answer to the question — *Why does God reveal His Wrath?* — we must first answer another question...

HOW DOES GOD REVEAL HIS WRATH?

Three answers will be given to this question, and in every case, His wrath is revealed in the form of *temporal* judgment. There is no mention of Hell or the lake of fire. The revealing of God's wrath is how He judges *now*, and Paul's primary application is to believers.

1. GOD REVEALS HIS WRATH BY TURNING THOSE WHO CONTINUE IN SIN OVER TO UNCLEANNESS.

> **Rom. 1:24 Therefore God also gave them up to**

> uncleanness, in the lusts of their hearts, to dishonor their bodies among themselves,
> 1:25 who exchanged the truth of God for the lie, and worshiped and served the creature rather than the Creator, who is blessed forever. Amen.

1:24. *Uncleanness* is moral impurity. These believers have started down the path of defiling their bodies with sexual sins. Because that is what they have chosen for their lives, God gives them over to it. Imagine God taking His hand of grace and protection off one of His children and essentially saying to them: "My child, you have chosen not to live righteously, producing faith-filled works and, in so doing, you are no longer glorifying Me by your life. Consequently, because you have exchanged glory for shame, I give you over to your ways of uncleanness. I will no longer keep you from destroying yourself."

1:25. The downward spiral is now in full force. It only gets worse from this point forward. The exchange has led them to replace truth with error, the lies of the enemy. This is how Christians are deceived into thinking they are okay spiritually when, in reality, they are a mess. They are believing error, even with respect to their own lifestyle. What a terrible tragedy!

2. GOD REVEALS HIS WRATH BY TURNING THOSE WHO CONTINUE IN SIN OVER TO VILE PASSIONS.

> Rom. 1:26 For this reason God gave them up to vile passions. For even their women exchanged the natural use for what is against nature.
> 1:27 Likewise also the men, leaving the natural use of the woman, burned in their lust for one another, men with men committing what is shameful, and receiving in themselves the penalty of their error which was due.

1:26. The Greek word translated *vile* means "dishonorable and shameful." It is also translated that way in other places in the New

Testament. A Greek synonym for *vile* is also used in v. 27, translated *shameful*. How low can a sinning believer go?

Christians can commit any imaginable sin! Don't ever arrogantly suggest you would never stoop to a certain level. God warns: 1 Cor. 10:12, *Let him who thinks he stands take heed lest he fall.* These believers who have chosen the downward spiral of sin and have exchanged glory for shame are now committing the sin of homosexuality.

1:27. Homosexuality is sexual sin between those of the same gender — whether female with female or male with male. These sins are near the bottom of the downward spiral of sinning, and once again, God gives those who choose this lifestyle over to their vile passions.

Homosexuality is not natural. That's obvious to reasonable people whose thoughts haven't become futile or their hearts darkened. God made us male and female; thus, biologically, male pronouns are he/him, while female pronouns are she/her. Our culture is now being bombarded with the depravity of transgenderism, as many are now trying to transform their bodies into the opposite gender, and this wave of transgenderism is being aggressively pushed on young children. When man descends down the spiral, he turns everything upside down, perverting sexual relations and destroying the family.

Surprisingly, these sins now pervade the church and Christianity. How horrible for anyone — especially a child of God — to be given over to vile passions by God. Of course, that does *not* mean God pushes vile passions on people. God forbid! It simply means He lets them have their way. He removes His hand of grace, and that is how he demonstrates His wrath in this present age. The result is self-destruction. In the case of these vile passions, it results in various sorts of diseases and a complete rewiring of the brain to accept such things as normal. Not surprisingly, suicide rates are much higher for those engaged in the sins of homosexuality and transgenderism.

Incidentally, Christians should never show hatred or violence toward homosexuals or transgenders. Rather, we should show them Christ-like love. Of course, that does not mean condoning their sin, but we must genuinely love them as human beings made in the image of God, whom God loves. If they are unregenerate, they need salvation in the initial sense. If they are believers, they need to repent and return to fellowship with the Lord, who will abundantly pardon. We see His heart in the story of the prodigal son. He is the father, welcoming back home His repentant child. Third, God reveals His wrath...

3. GOD REVEALS HIS WRATH BY TURNING THOSE WHO CONTINUE IN SIN OVER TO A DEBASED MIND.

> **Rom. 1:28 And even as they did not like to retain God in *their* knowledge, God gave them over to a debased mind, to do those things which are not fitting;**

The word *debased* is also used in 2 Tim. 3:8:

> **2 Tim. 3:8** Now as Jannes and Jambres resisted Moses, so do these also resist the truth: men of corrupt minds, *disapproved* concerning the faith. (emphasis mine)

The word *debased* means "worthless and rejected as a castaway; disapproved." God says that He gives those who remain on the downward spiral of sin — including believers — over to themselves. In this case, He gives them over to a debased mind — a way of thinking that is worthless and rejected by Him. These believers are considered castaways by God so that when they meet Him at the Judgment Seat of Christ, they will face the punishment of the unfaithful servant in the parable of the talents:

> **Matt. 25:30** And cast the unprofitable servant into the outer darkness. There will be weeping and gnashing of teeth.

Outer darkness is not Hell, as so many think. It is the darkness outside Christ's bright, Messianic ruling realm, known as New Jerusalem. Those believers (called *servants* in Matt. 25:14-30) who are excluded from New Jerusalem will be consigned to the earthly realm of the kingdom. They will weep and gnash their teeth, an oriental idiom for conscious regret. These castaways are those believers who continue in the sins listed in vs. 29-31, which will be explained below.

We return now to give the third and final answer to our initial question, *Why does God reveal His wrath?*

3. GOD REVEALS HIS WRATH BECAUSE MEN CONTINUE IN HORRIBLE SINS.

> **Rom. 1:29 being filled with all unrighteousness, sexual immorality, wickedness, covetousness, maliciousness; full of envy, murder, strife, deceit, evil-mindedness; they are whisperers,**
> **1:30 backbiters, haters of God, violent, proud, boasters, inventors of evil things, disobedient to parents,**
> **1:31 undiscerning, untrustworthy, unloving, unforgiving, unmerciful;**

Here is a brief snapshot of each one of these sins:

- *sexual immorality* — having sexual relations with someone to whom you are not married. Multitudes of Christians live in this manner. Incidentally, the Greek word translated *immorality* is *porneia*, from which we get our English word *pornography* (which is included with this sin).
- *wickedness* — all sorts of depravity
- *covetousness* — greed, wanting what you don't have
- *maliciousness* — ill-will; desire to injure
- *envy* — jealousy
- *murder* — unlawful killing, including abortion, suicide
- *strife* — contention
- *deceit* — trickery or flattery
- *evil-mindedness* — meanness or mischievousness
- *whisperers* — gossiping
- *backbiters* — slander
- *haters of God* — impious and God-forsaking
- *violent* — insolent and injurious; despiteful

- *proud* — arrogant and condescending
- *boasters* — braggardly
- *inventors of evil things* — instigating bad/evil
- *disobedient to parents* — refusal to obey parental authority
- *undiscerning* — lacking understanding and discernment
- *untrustworthy* — dishonest; lacking integrity
- *unloving* — without natural affection
- *unforgiving* — implacable and bitter
- *unmerciful* — merciless

Undoubtedly, this is not an exhaustive a list of sins, but representative. Notice what Paul adds at the end:

Rom. 1:32 who, knowing the righteous judgment of God, that those who practice such things are deserving of death, not only do the same but also approve of those who practice them.

Some of the believers at Rome know (*epignosis*) that what they are doing is deserving of death at the hand of God in judgment; nevertheless, they continue in these things, and they find gratification that others are doing the same. Is this camaraderie in evil?

Three times in 1:18-32 Paul emphasizes that God reveals His wrath by giving over those who are continuing in sin to their own ways. As mentioned earlier, He removes His hand of grace and lets them wallow in sin, because that's what they continue to choose. Were it not for God's grace, any one of us could end up like those in Rom. 1.

Perhaps you are continuing in sin of some sort. You can be sure that you are spiraling downward, whether you realize it or not. If you have one or more of these sins in your life, confess them immediately as sin before God and repent, turning away from those sins completely, looking to Jesus for victory going forward. He will abundantly pardon and bestow His grace. Otherwise, you will continue to spiral downward, exchanging glory for shame, and that will translate into negative reward at the Judgment Seat of Christ.

There is much at stake! Start living righteously so that you can hear, "Well done, good and faithful servant!"

In closing, consider these Scriptural warnings:

> **Rev. 16:15** Behold, I am coming as a thief. Blessed *is* he who watches, and keeps his garments, lest he walk naked and they see his **shame**.

> **1 John 2:28** Little children, abide in Him, that when He appears, we may have confidence and not be **ashamed** before Him at His coming. (emphasis added)

CHAPTER 7
ETERNAL LIFE FOR DOING GOOD?
ROMANS 2:1-24

Is *eternal* (age-lasting) *life*[1] received by faith alone or by doing good works? The answer may surprise you, but it depends on the context. Notice what Paul says about *eternal life* in the following verses:

> **Rom. 2:6-7** [God] *"will render to each one according to his deeds:"* eternal life to those who by patient continuance in doing good seek for glory, honor, and immortality.

These verses unquestionably refer to eternal life given as a reward for doing good deeds. How do we reconcile this with our understanding that eternal life is received by faith alone?

The key is understanding which aspect of eternal life Paul is referring to — the *gift* or the *reward*. I will differentiate between the two as we go along in the chapter.

Those who hold to the traditional, Reformation-driven interpretation of Romans — namely, that Paul is addressing matters of soteriology (*initial* salvation) in the early chapters of this epistle — struggle to explain verses such as those above. They also struggle to explain v. 13:

Rom. 2:13 For not the hearers of the law *are* just in the sight of God, but the doers of the law will be justified.

HERMENEUTICAL KEYS

These interpretive conundrums all fade away when the right hermeneutical (interpretive) keys are applied when reading and studying Romans. Thus far, we have learned two keys for interpreting Romans correctly:

1. Understanding that *justification* is not positional and legal, but conditional and behavioral, as explained in detail in Chapters 2-4.

2. Understanding that Paul is writing to *believers* about matters of sanctification unto maturity. He is *not* writing about matters of *initial* salvation (regeneration) for unbelievers. Thus in 1:16, *gospel* refers to the good news of kingdom inheritance for those who qualify and *salvation* refers to the ongoing process of *soul-salvation*, culminating in reward at the Judgment Seat of Christ — as noted in Chapters 5-6.

Once these keys are understood, confusion fades away, as we shall see. When interpreting the latter half of Rom. 1 in light of the above keys, it becomes obvious that Paul is not warning unbelievers about the consequences of sinning, although the principle applies to unbelievers as well. Rather, Paul warns *children of God* to beware of living unrighteously, for one sin typically leads to another and another, and so on. Before long, the believer is trapped in a downward spiral of sinning which grows worse with each iteration. God's wrath is revealed against those who continue in these sins (see 1:18-32)..

Believers incur God's wrath for: 1. suppressing truth (v. 18), 2. not glorifying God (v. 21), and 3. committing horrible sins, which are an offense to God, worthy of death (vs. 22-32). God reveals His wrath by giving sinning believers over to: 1. uncleanness (v. 24), 2. vile passions (v. 26), and 3. a debased mind (v. 28).

Unfortunately, most Christians don't think the latter half of Rom. 1 applies to them, because they assume the list of sins and God's wrath upon these sinners describes the condition of unbelievers. Those who interpret in this manner have an incorrect understanding of justification, which has been passed down from the Reformation. Paul applies the text to believers specifically!

INCORRECT RESPONSES TO SINNING

It is important to keep the context of Rom. 1 in mind, for as we now enter into Rom. 2, Paul warns the church at Rome of four incorrect responses to sinning. Incidentally, these are responses that any believer of any era of the church age could have toward sinning.

1. HYPOCRISY

> Rom. 2:1 Therefore you are inexcusable, O man, whoever you are who judge, for in whatever you judge another you condemn yourself; for you who judge practice the same things.
> 2:2 But we know that the judgment of God is according to truth against those who practice such things.
> 2:3 And do you think this, O man, you who judge those practicing such things, and doing the same, that you will escape the judgment of God?

2:1-2. The Jewish believers don't think they are guilty of the sins listed in ch. 1, because they keep the Mosaic law, which the Gentiles do not have. Although some of the Gentile believers are most likely guilty of the vile passions in vs. 23-27 — for those things were more typical of the Roman culture — the Jews, nevertheless, are culpable of many of the sins listed in vs. 29-32. Paul lets them know they are hypocritical and will not be excused. Nineteenth century British pastor and theologian Robert Govett (1813-1901) comments:

> Knowledge of what is right, and condemnation of what is evil are not enough. Judgment at last will be according to works. The apostle now commences convicting the Jew of his sinfulness, and exposure to the wrath of God. He [the Jew] could quite agree with all that Paul said against 'those wicked idolaters, the Gentiles.' But the Holy Ghost

now shows him to be under the same penalty and wrath of God, because he was guilty of the same transgressions which had been specified in the former chapter.[2]

2:3. The Jews must be thinking their close relationship with Jehovah and their keeping of the most important aspects of the law (at least in their minds) exempts them from judgment. But Paul says, "There is no partiality with God" (v. 11). Jehovah is not merely loving, He is righteous.

What often accompanies hypocrisy is an "I'm-better-than-you" attitude. It's the same attitude the Pharisees had, shown in their condescending attitude toward others. Jesus referred to this:

> **Luke 18:9** He spoke this parable to some who trusted in themselves that they were righteous, and despised others:
> **10** Two men went up to the temple to pray, one a Pharisee and the other a tax collector.
> **11** The Pharisee stood and prayed thus with himself, "God, I thank You that I am not like other men—extortioners, unjust, adulterers, or even as this tax collector.
> **12** I fast twice a week; I give tithes of all that I possess."
> **13** And the tax collector, standing afar off, would not so much as raise *his* eyes to heaven, but beat his breast, saying, "God, be merciful to me a sinner!"
> **14** I tell you, this man went down to his house justified *rather* than the other; for everyone who exalts himself will be humbled, and he who humbles himself will be exalted.

Many modern fundamentalists have the same attitude as these first century Pharisees. They do not commit immorality or homosexuality, so they think they are okay spiritually and far more accepted by God than those who are committing the "big" sins. But they seem to overlook the fact that they are full of pride, bitterness, gossip, dishonesty, coveting, lust, hatred, and a host of other things, all of which are also listed in the latter half of Rom. 1. Do they think they will escape the wrath of God? Will they be able to hide their sins because they are not as severe as the sins of others? Christians must awaken to truth. There is no partiality with God! Better to fall on your face before Him in humility *now*, than be ashamed in His presence at the Judgment Seat of Christ. A second incorrect response to the sins listed in Romans 1 is:

2. IMPENITENCE

> **Rom. 2:4 Do you despise the riches of His goodness, forbearance, and longsuffering, not knowing that the goodness of God leads you to repentance?**
> **2:5 But in accordance with your hardness and your impenitent heart you are treasuring up for yourself wrath in the day of wrath and revelation of the righteous judgment of God,**

2:4. We serve a marvelous God, who is good and patient and who suffers long with us, despite our sinning. He could judge instantly, but He forbears, because His goodness leads us to repent — i.e., to turn away from our sinning and start living righteously. That's what God wants from His children. He allows many to continue in their ways an entire lifetime, giving perpetual opportunities to repent and return to Him. God said to the Israelites:

> **Ezek. 33:11** I have no pleasure in the death of the wicked; but that the wicked turn from his way and live.

This is also true in our age, for He is the same — yesterday, today, forever!

2:5a. Believers presume upon God's goodness when they continue in sin, thinking God will not judge them, because their sin is so less offensive than others who are committing the "big" sins. In reality presuming upon God's goodness is hardness of heart, callousness that results in impenitence, which is a refusal to repent. Notice what God says about those who are guilty of presuming in this manner:

2:5b. *You are treasuring [storing] up for yourself wrath in the day of wrath and revelation of the righteous judgment of God.* Judgment is being stored up for the future, and you will experience the full force of God's wrath at the Judgment Seat of Christ. You will be naked and ashamed, for you will *not* be glorified and your reward will be negative, for you will be cast into the darkness outside, the relative darkness outside His bright ruling realm. There, in the earthly realm of the kingdom, you will weep and gnash your teeth, that is, consciously regret your foolish lifestyle decisions during this life. So take God up on His offer of repentance *now,* and you will be truly joyful *later.* How will God judge His children at the Bema?

> Rom. 2:6 Who *"will render to each one according to his deeds":*
> 2:7 **Eternal life to those who by patient continuance in doing good seek for glory, honor, and immortality;**
> 2:8 **but to those who are self-seeking and do not obey the truth, but obey unrighteousness—indignation and wrath,**
> 2:9 **tribulation and anguish, on every soul of man who does evil, of the Jew first and also of the Greek;**
> 2:10 **but glory, honor, and peace to everyone who works what is good, to the Jew first and also to the Greek.**

THE PROSPECT OF A NEGATIVE VERDICT

2:6. The word *render* means to recompense, repay. The repayment will be according to one's *deeds,* which BDAG defines as "that which displays itself in activity of any kind — of the deeds of humans, exhibiting a consistent moral character."[3] This definition is important, for it emphasizes that *deeds* are a summation of one's behavior.

I once had a discussion with a theologian friend about the word *work* in 1 Cor. 3, which is translated from the same Greek word translated *deeds* in Rom. 2:6:

> 1 Cor. 3:13 each one's <u>work</u> will become clear; for the Day will declare it, because it will be revealed by fire; and the fire will test each one's <u>work</u>, of what sort it is.
>
> 14 If anyone's <u>work</u> which he has built on it endures, he will receive a reward.
>
> 15 If anyone's <u>work</u> is burned, he will suffer loss; but he himself will be saved, yet so as through fire. (emphasis added)

My friend insisted that our behavior will not be on trial at the Judgment Seat of Christ, because all believers have been positionally, legally justified (in his view, which is the traditional Reformation model). Thus, he claimed that our *work* must be that which we do for the Lord. (Is that not interpreting *theologically* rather then *biblically*?). If our work for Him is done out of pure motives, it will be rewarded; otherwise, it will not, he claimed.

At that time I did not know about BDAG's definition of *deeds*, but I pointed to the word *works* used in Gal. 5:16 — *the works of the flesh are evident*. It is the same Greek word. Here's the point: If Galatians uses *works* to refer to behavior, then 1 Cor. 3:13-15 and Rom. 2:6 refer to behavior as well, for they are translated from the same Greek word. Our *deeds* (aka *works*), are a summation of our behavior. So there is no wiggling out of the prospect of a negative verdict at the Judgment Seat. God will *render* [recompense] *to each according to his deeds* [behavior], and many Christians will *suffer loss* (1 Cor. 3:15).

Interestingly, as noted in Chapter 2 of this book, all mankind will be repaid according to their *works* — what they have done, how they have lived (see 2 Cor. 5:10 and Col. 3:23-25). That is true of all the judgments recorded in the Scriptures. But the emphasis in Romans is on believers at the Judgment Seat of Christ, as seen in v. 16:

REVEALING THE SECRETS OF MEN

> **Rom. 2:16** in the day when God will judge the secrets of men by Jesus Christ, according to my gospel.

That which is secret and hidden will be made manifest. This is clearly a reference to believers, because Paul adds, *according to my gospel. His gospel* is the good news of kingdom inheritance for those who persevere in righteousness and suffering for Jesus' sake. Robert Govett writes:

> Here is a word to believers: this is the sowing time. According to the quantity and quality of the seed sown will be the harvest. Christ calls then His disciples to fill up this day with good works. But it is not enough to begin well, to start off with great zeal, and then to cool and … nay, even to turn back! It must be 'patient continuance in well doing.' So says the Saviour. The seed on the good ground "are they, who in an honest and good heart having heard the word, keep it, and bring forth fruit with patience," Luke 8:15 … God's prize shall more than repay the difficulties and troubles of service.[4]

2:7. To those who do good God gives eternal life, but this is not referring to the *gift* of eternal life, which is received by faith alone, resulting in regeneration (Eph. 2:8-9; Titus 3:5). This is the *reward* of eternal life, which is bestowed on those who live righteously and patiently endure until the coming of Christ.

The Greek word translated *eternal* is *aionios* and means *age-lasting* or *age-during (eonion)* or *for the age*. It does *not* mean "forever" or "never-ending" and, therefore, should not have been translated *eternal*. Thus, *age-during life* will be enjoyed in the coming millennial age. If you are not familiar with this concept, I would encourage you to pause reading here and read Addendum 1 entitled, "Eternal Is Not Forever" before continuing.

It is humorous, in a sad sort of way, to see how traditionalists try to explain Rom. 2:7 according to their soteriological understanding of salvation and justification in the book of Romans. It's like putting a square peg in a round hole — it just doesn't work.

THE REWARDS OF ETERNAL LIFE

What rewards does God give to those who do good? Several are mentioned:

- *Glory* — glowing in some degree — as seen in Christ's transfiguration and also in 1 Cor. 15. Those who are not glorified will be naked and ashamed (Phil. 3:18-19).
- *Honor* – an elevated position of ruling with Jesus in His New Jerusalem.

Matt 10:32-33 Whoever confesses Me before men, him I will also confess before My Father who is in heaven. But whoever denies Me before men, him I will also deny before My Father who is in heaven.

Luke 9:26 Whoever is ashamed of Me and My words, of him the Son of Man will be ashamed when He comes in His *own* glory.

- *Immortality* — but the word is not correctly translated. Several commentators point out that this word should actually be *incorruption*, referring to an incorruptible body. In fact, the same Greek word is translated *incorruption* several times in 1 Cor. 15. I've often wondered if those who are consigned to the darkness outside will have bodies of incorruption — I doubt it. I would think they would have regular human bodies that can function on Earth, not incorruptible bodies that function in ethereal realms, but that is merely speculation on my part.
- *Peace* — calmness of soul that will characterize those who are with Christ in New Jerusalem. Those who weep and gnash their teeth will not have peace of soul, but rather turmoil within.

These are glorious rewards: life for the millennial age, glory, honor, incorruption, and peace.

2:8-9. In contradistinction, negative reward will be given to those who are self-seeking and disobedient. Paul sums this up: *indignation and wrath, tribulation and anguish, on every soul of man who does evil, of the Jew first and also of the Greek.*

While righteous believers will be rewarded with peace, unrighteous believers will be recompensed with tribulation and anguish.

I have a theory that those who do not hear "Well done!" at the

Judgment Seat of Christ will be consigned to Earth for a period of time during the Millennium, where they will be tasked with "fixing" their sin problem for a period of time (a hundred years or several hundred?) — whatever the Lord decides — until they come to the end of self and can truly be declared justified. Then God will receive them into New Jerusalem for the remainder of His kingdom era. I can't prove that; it's mere speculation, but it seems appropriate to the character of God. Arlen Chitwood read what I wrote here before publication and shared something with me that I did not know:

> A. Edwin Wilson held a similar view, with reasoning behind his thoughts. He felt that, as the Millennium progressed and the earth's population increased, additional rulers would be required. And, if so, these rulers would have to be taken from those rejected at the beginning of the Millennium.
>
> Wilson suggested a possible gradation among all of the called relative to being called out (those being rejected at the beginning), though he didn't carry matters beyond that, since we're dealing more with speculation than not. Then, you have called attention to the seeming only logical means as to how this could be carried out, if done, at a time, or times, beyond the beginning of the Millennium.[5]

This is fascinating and worthy of pondering further. A third incorrect response to the sins listed in 1:18-32 is:

3. DENIAL OF GUILT

Paul makes the emphatic point that God's judgment is impartial and applies to all believers, both Jewish and Gentile.

Rom. 2:11 For there is no partiality with God.

This is important for both Jews and Gentiles to hear, because the Gentile believers may tend to think they are exempted from judgment, because they do not have the law, like the Jews. The Jewish believers may tend to think they are exempted from judgment because they have the law and keep it, for the most part, unlike the Greco-Romans. How does Paul respond to this incorrect thinking?

> **Rom. 2:12 For as many as have sinned without law will also perish without law, and as many as have sinned in the law will be judged by the law**
> **2:13 (for not the hearers of the law *are* just in the sight of God, but the doers of the law will be justified;**
> **2:14 for when Gentiles, who do not have the law, by nature do the things in the law, these, although not having the law, are a law to themselves,**
> **2:15 who show the work of the law written in their hearts, their conscience also bearing witness, and between themselves *their* thoughts accusing or else excusing *them*)**
> **2:16 in the day when God will judge the secrets of men by Jesus Christ, according to my gospel.**

2:12. The word *perish* leads many traditionalists to think Paul is talking about Hell, but that is not the meaning of this Greek word. To *perish* is to become lost or destroyed or rendered useless. Paul is saying that those who are guilty of committing one or more of the sins in the latter half of Rom. 1, will experience the consequence of losing their soul at the Judgment Seat, which means they lose their reward (see Matt. 16:24-27). Their works will be tested by fire and nearly everything will burn up, because they are characterized by works of the flesh, not fruit of the Spirit.

2:14-15. That applies, whether they are Jews, having the Mosaic law, or Gentiles, *not* having the law, because all believers have the work of the law written in their hearts. Furthermore, even unbelievers know the essence of right and wrong, because all have a conscience.

THE FUNCTION OF THE CONSCIENCE

The purpose of conscience is described in v. 15 — to accuse (condemn a particular thought or action as inappropriate) or excuse (accept a particular thought or action as appropriate). Seeing that all men have a conscience, all are without excuse and will one day stand before God as judge, giving an account for how they behave, whether righteously or unrighteously.

That is especially true of believers, for we have the law written on our hearts. In this sense, it seems that New Testament Christians have entered into one of the glories of the New Covenant even in advance of God giving that covenant to Israel at the end of the Tribulation (see Jer. 31:31-34).

Thus, even Gentiles are culpable for their sinning, because although they don't have the Mosaic law, their conscience leads them to obey the law nonetheless. When they do so, they confirm that all men can live righteously.

2:16. Those who do not live righteously will be exposed by God when He reveals all things.

2:13. Incidentally, the Jews are not guiltless if they are sinning, because God doesn't justify (declare righteous) those who merely hear the law, only those who do it! The Jews constantly heard the law read in synagogue, but that was not good enough. How many countless thousands of Christians hear the Word of God preached in church every Sunday for decades throughout their lives? But that's not good enough! God doesn't want mere hearers of the law; He wants *doers* of the law — those who apply what they are hearing through obedience (see James 1:22). A fourth incorrect response to the sins listed in the latter half of Rom. 1 is found in vs. 17-24.

4. BOASTING

> Rom. 2:17 Indeed you are called a Jew, and rest on the law, and make your boast in God,
> 2:18 and know *His* will, and approve the things that are excellent, being instructed out of the law,

> 2:19 and are confident that you yourself are a guide to the blind, a light to those who are in darkness,
> 2:20 an instructor of the foolish, a teacher of babes, having the form of knowledge and truth in the law.
> 2:21 You, therefore, who teach another, do you not teach yourself? You who preach that a man should not steal, do you steal?
> 2:22 You who say, "Do not commit adultery," do you commit adultery? You who abhor idols, do you rob temples?
> 2:23 You who make your boast in the law, do you dishonor God through breaking the law?
> 2:24 For *"the name of God is blasphemed among the Gentiles because of you,"* as it is written.

2:17-18. The Jews boasted that they were God's chosen people. They had the sign of circumcision in their flesh to prove it. Notice four glorious benefits possessed by Israel:

1. The Mosaic law
2. The one true God
3. The Word of God
4. The Custodians of God's truth

2:19-20. The Jews viewed themselves as guides and lights and instructors and teachers. Their audience? — the Gentiles, who were blind and in darkness and foolish and babes. How arrogant! But Paul pushes back:

2:21-22. "You might think of yourselves as teachers of others, but do you teach yourself? You might preach 'Do not commit adultery!' quoting the seventh commandment to your Gentile brethren, but don't you commit adultery?" Paul probably has in mind the sin of lusting.

He goes on to say: "You preach 'thou shalt not steal,' but don't you steal?" Paul probably has in mind stealing in their business dealings by charging exorbitant prices. "You abhor idolatry, but aren't you guilty of robbing temples?" Perhaps Paul has in mind their robbing of God by withholding their tithes and offerings.

2:23-24. "You boast in the law, but don't you break the law too? Because of this, the name of your God is blasphemed among the Gentiles."

Boasting in the law while dishonoring God through disobedience is a terrible testimony! Apparently, the Gentiles were mocking Jehovah as being the God of lawbreakers — for His people break His laws.

PHARISEES AND MODERN FUNDAMENTALISTS

During the time of Christ the Pharisees were guilty of doing the same things. They were in outward conformity to the law, for the most part. But inwardly, their hearts were full of pride and breaking the spirit of God's laws.

Is modern Christianity any different? Many fundamentalist groups boast in a similar manner. They think they have the truth and others don't, and they think they are earnestly contending for the faith by fighting with other evangelical Christians who have different views than their own. They go so far as to brand their brethren as heretics on the internet and separate from them. They love to do all of this publicly, convincing themselves they are being true to God's Word — considering it a badge of honor. They often refer to themselves proudly as "fightin' fundamentalists." No, they would not consider themselves to be murderers, but they sure have vitriolic hatred in their hearts, and that is murder in God's eyes, according to Jesus. They are lawbreakers too, guilty of committing several of the sins named in Rom. 1.

Moreover, they are typically hyper-separational, setting their own rules for how people should dress and what kind of music they should listen to and what Bible versions they should read — and a host of other rules they call "standards," which are not addressed in the Bible, but which they have made as rules for themselves and often for their churches. Meanwhile, they look down at any believer or church that has "lesser standards" than their own. It is prideful and condescending, yet it happens all the time in fundamentalism!

They are modern Pharisees who disgrace the name of Christ in the culture, yet they see no need to repent, because they arrogantly think they are living righteously. May God have mercy on fundamentalist Christianity!

Do *you* have a condescending attitude toward others who are sinning, even though you are guilty of sinning also? Do you think others are unrighteous, but you are righteous? Beware of boasting and arrogance! What will be your reward?

> **Rom. 2:6-7** [God] *"will render to each one according to his deeds:" eternal life to those who by patient continuance in doing good seek for glory, honor, and immortality.*

Eternal life for doing good? Absolutely! Those who live righteously will be richly rewarded by God. Ah, but remember also...

> **Rom. 2:8-9** but to those who are self-seeking and do not obey the truth, but obey unrighteousness—indignation and wrath, tribulation and anguish, on every soul of man who does evil, of the Jew first and also of the Greek.

Which verdict applies to you?

CHAPTER 8
THE RIGHTEOUS REQUIREMENTS OF THE LAW
ROMANS 2:25-29

This text is the interpretive pinnacle of the book of Romans. What one does with these verses, in the context of the first two chapters of Romans, determines how the rest of the book will be interpreted. As pointed out repeatedly in the previous chapters, evangelical Christianity predominantly interprets the first four chapters of Romans as soteriological, meaning Paul is talking about matters of *initial* salvation. That interpretation is not Scriptural, but theological, driven by the theology of the Reformers.

SIX HERMENEUTICAL KEYS FOR RIGHTLY DIVIDING ROMANS

By way of brief review, the following six hermeneutical keys must be understood if one is to "rightly divide" the epistle to the Romans:

1. Paul directs this letter to the *believers* in the church at Rome — both Jews and Gentiles.

2. His ultimate purpose is to dispel the disunity and division within the church which has largely fallen out along ethnic lines — Jews vs. Gentiles (and in particular, Greeks, who were the sophisticated subset of Gentiles, as opposed to the barbarians).

3. Paul's *gospel* of *salvation* in 1:16 is the good news that believers can be sanctified, set apart unto holiness, and if they continue on this pathway throughout life, they can inherit rewards at the Judg-

ment Seat of Christ. In other places in the New Testament this is called "the saving of the soul" (e.g., Matt. 16:24-27; Phil. 2:12-13; Heb. 10:39; James 1:21; 1 Pet. 1:9 — notice works are involved in this aspect of ongoing salvation).

4. Paul's *gospel* reveals two things:

- 1:17, God's righteousness — to those believers who progress from initial faith (regeneration) to continuing faith (sanctification). In other words, God justifies (declares righteous) those believers who are living righteously, producing faith-filled works.
- 1:18-32, God's wrath — to those believers who live unrighteously. God gives them over to their ways, and they end up spiraling downward and self-destructing. Apparently, some of the believers at Rome were already on this path and were not justified in God's eyes, thus the immediate consequence of disunity and division and the ultimate consequence of disinheritance at the Judgment Seat of Christ.

5. Paul takes the Jewish believers to task in Rom. 2, because of their condescending attitude toward the Gentiles. The Jews, who were in outward conformity to the Mosaic legal requirements, thought they were accepted by God. Paul points out they were just as guilty as the Gentiles, because although they did not commit the so-called "big" sins of homosexuality and immorality and adultery, etc., they were guilty of many of the other sins listed in Rom. 1 – such as pride, hatred, strife, coveting, malice, greed, bitterness, and a host of other things.

6. Paul warns that God will judge all believers according to their *deeds* (*works*): Those who continue patiently in doing good will inherit the rewards of age-lasting (millennial) life, glory, honor, peace, and incorruption (2:7,10). In contrast, those who are self-seeking and do not obey the truth, but continue in unrighteousness, will be repaid with indignation and wrath, tribulation and anguish (2:8-9).

Paul emphasizes that God judges impartially; He does not show favoritism to Jews simply because they are His covenant people (2:11). Those who sin *without law* (Gentiles) will perish (lose their soul, i.e., reward), as well as those who sin *in the law* (Jews) (2:12). God justifies those Jewish believers who are truly obedient to God's moral law, not merely hearers of the law (2:13).

God also justifies those Gentile believers who are righteous, even though they don't have the law, seeing that God has given a conscience to all men. Believers have a special advantage, for they have the law written on their hearts.

THE OLD TESTAMENT ROOTS OF CIRCUMCISION

Rom. 2:25-29 is the critical pivot point for understanding Rom. 3-4. Paul continues his rebuke of the Jewish believers who think they are accepted by God — despite their sinning — because they are circumcised, which is the symbol of being Jewish and God's covenant people. Keep in mind the Old Testament history of this rite.

> **Gen. 17:9** God said to Abraham: "As for you, you shall keep My covenant, you and your descendants after you throughout their generations.
>
> **10-11** This *is* My covenant which you shall keep, between Me and you and your descendants after you: every male child among you shall be circumcised … and it shall be a sign of the covenant between Me and you.
>
> **13** He who is born in your house and he who is bought with your money must be circumcised, and My covenant shall be in your flesh for an everlasting covenant.
>
> **14** And the uncircumcised male child, who is not circumcised … that person shall be cut off from his people; he has broken My covenant."

Circumcision of the males was the indispensable requirement for being Jewish, for being God's covenant people. Those who refused to circumcise were excommunicated from Israel and from the covenant with Jehovah, and that was a very serious thing indeed. Commentator James Dunn (1939-2020) says:

THE RIGHTEOUS REQUIREMENTS OF THE LAW   109

This sense of circumcision's importance had been strengthened in the Hellenistic period [323 BC—32 BC] by way of reaction to Hellenism's distaste for the rite, and ever since the Maccabees, circumcision had been seen as an absolutely essential expression of Israel's national identity and religion.

Those listening to Paul's letter would thus recognize the connection of thought without difficulty: circumcision was fundamental to the typical Jew's self-understanding, the mark of his religious distinctiveness, the badge of national privilege, the seal of God's covenant favor to Israel his chosen people.[1]

In 2:25-29 Paul shares 4 earth-shattering truths for the Jewish believers:

1. IF YOU ARE A LAWBREAKER, THEN YOUR CIRCUMCISION IS NULLIFIED.

> **Rom. 2:25 For circumcision is indeed profitable if you keep the law; but if you are a breaker of the law, your circumcision has become uncircumcision.**

This is profound! Paul declares that those Jewish believers who live disobediently to the law (i.e., the *moral* aspects of the law) have essentially identified as non-Jews, non-circumcised. That's radical, because it means they are no longer accepted as God's covenant people! The Jews never imagined their breaking of the law would nullify God's covenant with them, as long as they were circumcised, but Paul arrests their attention with this new revelation.

Those Jews who continue in sinfulness — even the sins they consider "lesser" in offense — are no different than the uncircumcised Gentiles toward whom they have been critical and condescending. God does not consider them His covenant people. Paul is really stirring the pot here, but it gets more intense in the following verses. A second earth-shattering truth is found in v. 26. Most of this chapter's content will focus on this particular point.

2. IF AN UNCIRCUMCISED GENTILE KEEPS THE RIGHTEOUS REQUIREMENTS OF THE LAW, HE WILL BE CONSIDERED CIRCUMCISED IN GOD'S EYES.

> **Rom. 2:26** Therefore, if an uncircumcised man keeps the righteous requirements of the law, will not his uncircumcision be counted as circumcision?

If uncircumcised Gentiles live righteously — by obeying God's *moral* commands — they are counted as circumcised in God's eyes, that is, under the covenant and accepted by God. In light of what they knew from Gen. 17, this truth is shocking to the Jews! Dunn puts it plainly:

> The clear implication of Paul's teaching: that in order to become a full member of the covenant, a full participator in the blessings God had promised to the people of Israel, it was not necessary to be circumcised.[2]

Think of it! Any believer — Jew or Gentile — who lives righteously, in accordance with the law's righteous demands, is justified in God's eyes and stands to inherit the rewards of age-lasting (millennial) life, glory, honor, peace, and incorruption. That is glorious!

THE RIGHTEOUS REQUIREMENTS OF THE LAW VS. THE RITUAL ASPECTS

Take careful notice of the term, *the righteous requirements of the law*. This term is absolutely essential to comprehend, for it marks a turning point in Jewish understanding of the law. Paul teaches, not just here in Romans, but also in his other epistles, that the *ritual* aspects of the law are now defunct because of Christ. To the Colossians, Paul wrote:

> **Col. 2:11-14** In Him you were also circumcised with the circumcision made without hands, by putting off the body of the sins of the flesh, by the circumcision of Christ, buried with Him in baptism, in which you also were raised with *Him* through faith in the working of God, who raised Him from the dead. And you, being dead in your

THE RIGHTEOUS REQUIREMENTS OF THE LAW

trespasses and the uncircumcision of your flesh, He has made alive together with Him, having forgiven you all trespasses, having wiped out the handwriting of requirements [KJV: *ordinances*] that was against us, which was contrary to us. And He has taken it out of the way, having nailed it to the cross.

16-17 So let no one judge you in food or in drink, or regarding a festival or a new moon or sabbaths, which are a shadow of things to come, but the substance is of Christ.

In Colossians Paul nullifies rituals for Jewish believers, such as observing the feasts and sabbaths. In Galatians Paul nullifies rituals such as dietary laws when rebuking Peter for not eating with the Gentiles when the Jews from Jerusalem showed up. In Romans Paul nullifies rituals such as circumcision. The bottom line is that the keeping of ritualistic laws is *not* required for sanctification, for either Jewish or Gentile believers — those who are *in Christ* — (including *all* the rituals in the Mosaic law, things such as laws regarding ceremonial uncleanness, leprosy, etc.)

God wants His children to observe His moral laws, which are not merely for Jews, but for all mankind. Jesus announced to the Jews:

Luke 16:16 The law and the prophets *were* until John. Since that time the kingdom of God has been preached, and everyone is pressing into it.

In other words, the era of the Mosaic law officially ended when John the Baptist, the forerunner of Jesus arrived. From that point forward, the emphasis would be on the kingdom of heaven (New Jerusalem) and how to qualify for inheritance in it, which is *not* by keeping the ritualistic aspects of the Mosaic law, but by keeping the moral law of God. Jesus summarized the moral law of God (the ten commandments) in two simple commands:

Matt. 22:37-38 Jesus said … "You shall love the Lord your God with all your heart, with all your soul, and with all your mind. This is the first and great commandment.

39 And *the* second *is* like it: *You shall love your neighbor as yourself.*

> **40** On these two commandments hang all the Law and the Prophets."

Jesus later elevated the second command to a higher standard:

> **John 13:34** A new commandment I give to you, that you love one another; as I have loved you, that you also love one another.

Immediately following His teaching about the vine and branches, which is about believers remaining in fellowship with God, Jesus said:

> **John 15:8** By this My Father is glorified, that you bear much fruit; so you will be My disciples.
> **9** As the Father loved Me, I also have loved you; abide in My love.
> **10** If you keep My commandments, you will abide in My love, just as I have kept My Father's commandments and abide in His love.
> **11** These things I have spoken to you, that My joy may remain in you, and *that* your joy may be full.
> **12** This is My commandment, that you love one another as I have loved you.

Jesus doesn't mention anything about observing ritualistic aspects of the law, such as circumcision or dietary laws or feast days or sabbaths.

When the rich, young ruler came to Jesus asking how he could inherit eternal (i.e., age-lasting) life, how did Jesus answer him?

> **Mark 10:17** Now as He was going out on the road, one came running, knelt before Him, and asked Him, "Good Teacher, what shall I do that I may inherit eternal life?"
> **18-19** So Jesus said to him … "You know the commandments: *do not commit adultery, do not murder, do not steal, do not bear false witness, do not defraud, honor your father and your mother."*
> **20** And he answered and said to Him, "Teacher, all these things I have kept from my youth."
> **21** Then Jesus, looking at him, loved him, and said to him, "One

thing you lack: Go your way, sell whatever you have and give to the poor, and you will have treasure in heaven; and come, take up the cross, and follow Me."

22 But he was sad at this word, and went away sorrowful, for he had great possessions.

The rich man apparently struggled with coveting. That was his big sin, thus he would need to find victory over that sin in order to inherit a place of ruling in the kingdom of the heavens. Notice Jesus doesn't say anything about observing ritualistic aspects of the law, such as circumcision or dietary laws or feast days or sabbaths.

James puts it this way in his epistle to the Jews who had scattered in the diaspora:

Jas. 2:8-9 If you really fulfill *the* royal law according to the Scripture, *"You shall love your neighbor as yourself,"* you do well; but if you show partiality, you commit sin, and are convicted by the law as transgressors.

10 For whoever shall keep the whole law, and yet stumble in one *point*, he is guilty of all.

11 For He who said, *"Do not commit adultery,"* also said, *"Do not murder."* Now if you do not commit adultery, but you do murder, you have become a transgressor of the law.

12 So speak and so do as those who will be judged by the law of liberty.

James refers to it as the *royal law* and the *law of liberty* — and just like Christ's teaching, James says nothing about observing ritualistic aspects of the law, such as circumcision or dietary laws or feast days or sabbaths.

Paul summarizes the righteous requirements of the law later in Romans:

Rom. 13:8b He who loves another has fulfilled the law.

9 For the commandments, *"You shall not commit adultery," "You shall not murder," "You shall not steal," "You shall not bear false witness," "You shall not covet,"* and if *there is* any other commandment, are *all*

summed up in this saying, namely, *"You shall love your neighbor as yourself."*

10 Love does no harm to a neighbor; therefore love *is* the fulfillment of the law.

Just as in the teachings of Jesus and James, Paul says nothing about observing ritualistic aspects of the law, such as circumcision or dietary laws or feast days or sabbaths.

THE RIGHTEOUS REQUIREMENTS WRITTEN ON THE HEART

What are the righteous requirements of the law which must be observed by a child of God if he or she would be sanctified unto maturity and qualified to inherit rewards at the Judgment Seat of Christ? They are the moral commands of God, which transcend time and ethnicity — the opposites of the sins in Romans 1:18-32. The Mosaic law is *not* applicable to believers — those who are *in Christ* — but we are, nevertheless, obligated to keep God's moral law. Call it the royal law ... the law of liberty ... the law of Christ ... the law of love — they all refer to the same thing, which is summed up in Matt. 22:37-40.

Now that you are *in Christ*, the moral law of God is written in your heart (Rom. 2:15). It seems that God gives to believers *now* what He promises to Israel in the New Covenant, which will officially be given to the nation at the end of the Tribulation when they repent of national sins and embrace Jesus as Messiah.

> **Ezek. 36:26-27** I will give you a new heart and put a new spirit within you; I will take the heart of stone out of your flesh and give you a heart of flesh. I will put My Spirit within you and cause you to walk in My statutes, and you will keep My judgments and do *them*.

> **Jer. 31:33** But this *is* the covenant that I will make with the house of Israel after those days, says the LORD: I will put My law in their minds, and write it on their hearts; and I will be their God, and they shall be My people.

While these are promises for future Israel, the same essentially happens when anyone believes on Jesus for the gift of eternal life. We become regenerated; old things pass away, all things become new; we are henceforth designated as being *in Christ*, and the law is written on our hearts (Rom. 2:15), regardless of national ethnicity. Jews and Gentiles who are *in Christ* are *the one new man in Christ*.

> **Eph. 2:14-16** For He Himself is our peace, who has made both one, and has broken down the middle wall of separation, having abolished in His flesh the enmity, that is, the law of commandments contained in ordinances, so as to create in Himself one new man from the two, thus making peace, and that He might reconcile them both to God in one body through the cross, thereby putting to death the enmity.

In Christ, there are no Jews or Gentiles, but simply "Christians." This is what the disunified believers at Rome need to grasp.

DEAD TO THE RITUAL ASPECTS OF THE LAW

Key to resolving the disunity is for the Jewish believers to see they are now dead to the ritual aspects of the law through Christ.

> **Rom. 7:4** Therefore, my brethren, you also have become dead to the law through the body of Christ, that you may be married to another —to Him who was raised from the dead, that we should bear fruit to God.

Evident from the overall context of Romans is that Paul abrogates the Mosaic *rituals*, but not the *moral* law of God, which is based on the character of God and transcends time. To that end, notice what he says in 2:26:

> **Rom. 2:26 Therefore, if an uncircumcised man keeps the righteous requirements of the law, will not his uncircumcision be counted as circumcision?**

Remember that Paul is talking to Jewish believers, and he shocks them by claiming: When a believing Gentile keeps the righteous requirements of the law (i.e., the moral law of God), he is counted by God as righteous and, therefore, as if he were circumcised, having entered into a favored relationship with God.

We now come to the crux of the matter, the pinnacle of application. It is found in Rom. 8 – which will be discussed in a future chapter, but a sneak preview might be helpful.

> **Rom 8:4** that the righteous requirement of the law might be fulfilled in us who do not walk according to the flesh but according to the Spirit.

Are we obligated to fulfill *the righteous requirement of the law?* Absolutely! And how do we do so? Through the Holy Spirit, who enables us to walk according to the Spirit rather than according to the flesh. When that happens, we are living from faith to faith, being justified by faith-filled works of righteousness that please God — and we will be rewarded with age-lasting life and glory and honor and peace and incorruption at His Judgment Seat. Those who are *not* fulfilling the righteous requirements of the law are not justified and can expect to be repaid with wrath and tribulation and anguish. Paul now shares a third earth-shattering truth with the Jewish believers.

3. IRONICALLY, RIGHTEOUS GENTILES, EVEN THOUGH PHYSICALLY UNCIRCUMCISED, WILL JUDGE UNRIGHTEOUS JEWISH BELIEVERS, WHO INSIST ON CLINGING TO THEIR RITUALS AND CIRCUMCISION AND MERE OUTWARD OBSERVANCE OF THE LETTER OF THE LAW.

> **Rom. 2:27** And will not the physically uncircumcised, if he fulfills the law, judge you who, even with your written code [KJV: *the letter*] and circumcision, are a transgressor of the law?

James Dunn clarifies:

In contrast to "fulfilling the law" "the letter" must mean something like the literal meaning, an understanding of the law which stays at the level of the ritual act and outward deed.[3]

It is as if Paul is saying, "You can hold on to your rituals all you want, Jewish believers, and you can merely observe the *letter* of the law, not the *spirit* of the law, but if you do not fulfill the righteous requirements of the law — if you do not obey your new Master, Jesus Christ, *inwardly* — you will be judged by those who truly live righteously, and that includes Gentiles who never had the Jewish rituals." Dunn adds:

> By resting on the law, in the false confidence that what the law requires is a strict observance of the practice of circumcision and the maintenance of ... its attendant laws, the devout Jew is actually transgressing the law. He has missed the point of the law and of circumcision. What he counts as "doing the law" Paul counts as transgressing the law!
>
> In consequence it will not be a case of the faithful Jew passing judgment on the lawless Gentile ... [see 2:1–3], but rather a case of the law-fulfilling Gentile (by his faith and life) passing judgment on the law-transgressing Jew—this is what God's judgment of human secrets will reveal in the day of judgment (2:16).[4]

That brings Paul to a fourth and final earth-shattering truth that he shares with the Jewish believers:

4. PHYSICAL CIRCUMCISION IS MERE OUTWARD OBSERVANCE OF THE MOSAIC RITUALS; HEART CIRCUMCISION IS INWARD OBSERVANCE, LED BY THE SPIRIT, AND THEREFORE ACCEPTED BY GOD.

> **Rom. 2:28-29 For he is not a Jew who is one outwardly, nor is circumcision that which is outward in the flesh; but he is a Jew who is one inwardly; and circumcision is that of the heart, in the Spirit, not in the letter; whose praise is not from men but from God.**

Incidentally, this is what the law and the prophets called for:

Deut. 10:16 Therefore circumcise the foreskin of your heart, and be stiff-necked no longer.

Jer. 4:4 Circumcise yourselves to the LORD, and take away the foreskins of your hearts, you men of Judah and inhabitants of Jerusalem, lest My fury come forth like fire, and burn so that no one can quench *it*, because of the evil of your doings.

In fact, if Israel had been taken captive by enemies as God's judgment for their sinfulness, when they later turned back to the Lord, God promised something very special:

Deut. 30:4 If *any* of you are driven out to the farthest *parts* under heaven, from there the LORD your God will gather you, and from there He will bring you.
5 Then the LORD your God will bring you to the land which your fathers possessed, and you shall possess it. He will prosper you and multiply you more than your fathers.
6 And the LORD your God will circumcise your heart and the heart of your descendants, to love the LORD your God with all your heart and with all your soul, that you may live.

Even from the Old Testament law and prophets, it's obvious where God puts the emphasis. God always desired Israel's inward obedience, i.e., a circumcised heart. But His people merely obeyed outwardly, focused on their circumcised flesh, which is the context of Rom. 2.

Jesus dealt with the sin of mere outward obedience in the Sermon on the Mount. The Jews claimed they were not committing adultery, but they were lusting. They claimed they were not murdering, but they were hating others. They claimed they were not stealing, but they were charging high prices and high interest rates for lending.

MERE OUTWARD OBEDIENCE AND OBSERVANCE OF RITUALS (I.E., RULES)

In addition to mere outward observance of the moral law, the Jewish believers continued to keep the rituals — observing feast days and sabbaths, eating only kosher foods, and making sure all the males were circumcised. The Pharisees were guilty of this during the time of Christ, and their influence upon the Christians continued for decades after, even as far as Rome.

Sadly, the fundamentalist segment of the church of Jesus Christ, in large part — as mentioned in the previous chapter — is guilty of living in like manner. The emphasis is on outward obedience and keeping a list of ritualistic rules they have made for themselves that are not found in the Bible, then expecting everyone to abide by them. Those who do not, are looked down upon and considered unspiritual or, at the very least, less spiritual. What a tragedy! As a result, the church of Jesus Christ is full of disunity and division, just like the church at Rome.

Thus, rightly interpreting the book of Romans is critical for application to twenty-first century believers. Dunn says:

> Paul looks for a circumcision of the heart that completely replaces the physical rite and does not merely complement it, for a lawkeeping which can be completely independent of so much of the law, the ritual law, which Jews regarded as fundamental, with all the authority of Moses behind them.
>
> Not only is the requirement of circumcision to be redefined (properly defined) in a way which renders the outward rite unnecessary, but the very name "Jew" is to be redefined (properly defined) also, as one whose Jewishness (= praiseworthiness) is dependent not on what spectators can see and approve, but on what God alone can see and approve (the hidden secrets of the heart—2:16).[5]

God wants His children to live righteously, inwardly obeying Him, not committing any of the sins listed in the latter half of Rom. 1 — many of which are inward sins, secret sins that no one knows about except the one who is sinning. Those who live in this manner are circumcised in heart, which God can see and which He justifies.

They will be rewarded with age-lasting (millennial) life and glory and honor and peace and incorruption.

On the other hand, God condemns mere outward obedience, and observance of rituals. For the Jews, the rituals included such things as observing feast days and sabbaths and circumcision and dietary laws. For modern Christians rituals are lists concocted by pastors and churches, or lists put together in the minds of believers either consciously or subconsciously, the keeping of which they think makes them spiritual.

What is missing? Faith-filled works of righteousness that God justifies. That is what Paul is going to deal with next, in Rom. 3-4.

Are you fulfilling the righteous requirements of the law by surrendering to the Holy Spirit in faith?

CHAPTER 9
THE MYSTERY OF THE ORACLES
ROMANS 3:1-20

Driven by the goal of dispelling the disunity and division in the church that have been spurred on by ethnic prejudices and carnality, Paul spends the first two chapters in Romans rebuking both groups of believers for sinning:

- The Gentiles — for succumbing to the more obvious outward sins of the Greco-Roman culture (e.g., immorality and debased forms of licentious living).
- The Jews — a) for observing the *letter* of the law *outwardly*, while ignoring the *spirit* of the law *inwardly*, by committing sins of the heart (e.g., bitterness, hatred, lust, pride, strife, etc.), and b) for clinging to the ritual aspects of the law, thinking their physical circumcision guarantees covenant acceptance, even though God is focused on circumcision of the heart.

Now in Rom. 3 Paul presents three rhetorical arguments that he anticipates from the Jewish believers.

1. WHAT GOOD IS "JEWISHNESS?"

Rom. 3:1 What advantage then has the Jew, or what *is* the profit of circumcision?

The Jews want to know: "If circumcision is only profitable when we are keeping the law, then what's the benefit of being Jewish and becoming circumcised?" Surely in their minds is also the shocking comment of Paul that when uncircumcised Gentiles keep the righteous requirements of the law, God views them *as if they were circumcised.* So again, what's the advantage of Jewishness and circumcision?

If I were Paul, I would probably shout back at them, "You've missed the point!" They are arguing that Jewishness and circumcision are worthless if those things don't keep them in covenant favor with God. The point is that they should stop sinning, for their inward lawbreaking and mere observance of rituals while ignoring *the righteous requirements of the law* has essentially nullified God's covenant acceptance of them.

Paul is implying: "The covenant is *conditional* — contingent on your obedience — which God made clear to you at Mt. Sinai." Of course, they all know what God had said at Sinai:

> **Exod. 19:5-6a** Now therefore, if you will indeed obey My voice and keep My covenant, then you shall be a special treasure to Me above all people. And you shall be to Me a kingdom of priests and a holy nation.
>
> **8a** Then all the people answered together and said, "All that the LORD has spoken we will do."

It seems Paul's audience has forgotten that the covenant is *conditional*, dependent on their obedience. God expects His law to be fulfilled consistently, though not perfectly, which is why He gave them the sacrifices, so they could seek forgiveness [the Old Testament equivalent of 1 Jn. 1:9 for New Testament believers]

The law is not to be willfully and presumptively disobeyed! Thus, Paul is not discounting the covenant itself; he is admonishing their "covenant presumption" which is the Old Testament equivalent of

Christians continuing in sin on the presumption of God's grace in the New Testament (Rom. 6:1ff). Paul's response to their objection now makes sense. They're probably expecting Paul to say, "There is now no advantage to being Jewish, seeing that Christ has come." But that is *not* what Paul says. Notice the answer he gives to his question:

> **Rom. 3:1 What advantage then has the Jew, or what is the profit of circumcision?**
> **3:2 Much in every way! Chiefly because to them were committed the oracles of God.**

Are there advantages to being God's chosen people? Absolutely! — The main advantage is that God entrusted Israel with the *oracles* of God. According to the *Oxford Dictionary*, an oracle is "a priest or priestess acting as a medium through whom advice or prophecy was sought from the gods in classical antiquity, or a place at which such advice or prophecy was sought."[1]

The Jewish people were God's oracles to the nations, in the sense that they were God's priests, who had been given the revelation of God, the Holy Scriptures, for the whole world. That calling is profound! God gave to Israel the law and the prophets, and look how *we* have benefitted from the Scriptures, even in the twenty-first century. That is true for all cultures in every era of time since the law and prophets were given by God to the Jews. Commentator James Dunn says:

> For a gentile readership the word "oracle" would evoke the thought of inspired utterances preserved from the past, often mysterious and puzzling in character, awaiting some key to unlock their meaning. Paul may well imply then that the Jews had been entrusted with the stewardship of safeguarding and preserving these oracles of God until the coming of the key, that is, the gospel of Christ Jesus, which unlocked the mystery of what had always been God's purpose but which had remained hidden hitherto until this time of the End (cf 11:25–27; 16:25–26).[2]

One of the passages Dunn suggests reading is Romans 16:25-26:

Rom. 16:25-26 Now to Him who is able to establish you according to my gospel and the preaching of Jesus Christ, according to the revelation of the mystery kept secret since the world began but now made manifest, and by the prophetic Scriptures made known to all nations, according to the commandment of the everlasting God, for obedience to the faith—

PAUL'S GOSPEL

Why does Paul use the term "my gospel?" In what sense was it "his?" Arlen Chitwood believes, and so do I, that this is the gospel of kingdom inheritance given to Paul by Jesus, when Paul spent three years in Arabia. He was commissioned to share this gospel with the Gentiles, so that the Holy Spirit could use it to call out *sons to glory*, those who will reign with Jesus as His bride and co-rulers in the coming kingdom. It was this particular gospel that the prophets were curious about and which the angels desire to look into, for it results in the deposing of the angelic realm as rulers and the elevation of *sons to glory* as rulers in their place. That is the mystery of which Paul speaks. Peter adds:

1 Pet. 1:7-9 That the genuineness of your faith, *being* much more precious than gold that perishes, though it is tested by fire, may be found to praise, honor, and glory at the revelation of Jesus Christ, whom having not seen you love. Though now you do not see *Him*, yet believing, you rejoice with joy inexpressible and full of glory, receiving the end of your faith—the salvation of *your* souls.

This *gospel* is referring to the *salvation of the soul*, resulting in inheritance for persevering in the Christian life. Reading on, Peter says something very interesting:

1 Pet. 1:10-11 Of this salvation the prophets have inquired and searched carefully, who prophesied of the grace *that would come* to you, searching what, or what manner of time, the Spirit of Christ who was in them was indicating when He testified beforehand the sufferings of Christ and the glories that would follow

> **12** To them it was revealed that, not to themselves, but to us they were ministering the things which now have been reported to you through those who have preached the gospel to you by the Holy Spirit sent from heaven—things which angels desire to look into.

How does this relate to Romans 3:2? The *oracles* — in a *general* sense — are the law and prophets given to Israel, its custodians. But the oracles — in a *specific* sense — are the *mystery* of Jews and Gentiles as one *in Christ* — Christians of the church age — to whom is extended the gospel of kingdom inheritance. Those who believe this gospel and produce faith-filled works of righteous will experience the salvation of their souls at the Judgment Seat of Christ.

What about those Jews who do *not* embrace Paul's gospel? That raises another rhetorical argument that Paul anticipates from the Jewish believers:

2. IS GOD'S FAITHFULNESS NULLIFIED BY ISRAEL'S FAITHLESSNESS?

> **Rom. 3:3 For what if some did not believe? Will their unbelief make the faithfulness of God without effect?**

A predominant segment of the Jews, in fact, the nation overall, did not embrace Jesus as Messiah. Consequently, despite Paul sharing his gospel of kingdom inheritance with individual Jewish believers, Israel as a nation failed in its mission to steward the oracles. That is, Israel failed to embrace and proclaim the mystery of being *in Christ* and the glories of kingdom inheritance for those who qualify. Paul was carrying the torch, but national Israel was not! James Dunn says:

> They had failed God's trust: either because having preserved the oracles of God for so many generations they had now failed to recognize the real meaning of them as given by the gospel; or because they had never recognized the real meaning in the first place, and in discharging their responsibility to the Gentiles as they saw it (2:19–20), they were presenting and living by a misconception of their covenant and the law (2:21–29).[3]

Does national Israel's faithlessness nullify God's faithfulness? Furthermore, does the failure of individual Jewish believers to live righteously and proclaim the gospel of kingdom inheritance destroy God's plan? Has His covenant been in vain? Should God ditch Israel and start over? Paul gives an emphatic answer by quoting Ps. 51:4, David's psalm of penitence:

> **Rom. 3:4 Certainly not! Indeed, let God be true but every man a liar. As it is written:** *"That You may be justified in Your words, and may overcome when You are judged."*

God is always true! He is always faithful! It is man who fails God; not the other way around. Dunn confirms:

> God's faithfulness is not determined by Jewish unfaithfulness. As God remained faithful to his covenant with Israel in the past, despite Israel's unfaithfulness, so he will remain faithful to Israel in the present and future, despite Israel's continuing unfaithfulness in rejecting the gospel. Paul cannot allow that Israel's unfaithfulness has nullified God's choice of Israel ... for the simple reason that such an admission would undermine his own gospel; such is the continuity between God's purpose for Israel and the gospel of his Son.[4]

Paul anticipates a third rhetorical argument from the Jewish believers:

3. IF GOD REMAINS FAITHFUL IN SPITE OF ISRAEL'S FAITHLESSNESS, THEN WOULDN'T IT BE CONTRARY TO HIS NATURE TO JUDGE SIN?

> **Rom. 3:5 But if our unrighteousness demonstrates the righteousness of God, what shall we say? Is God unjust who inflicts wrath? (I speak as a man.)**

The argument suggests that when Israel is sinning and living in unbelief, God's righteousness shines all the more. In other words, if

His faithfulness and goodness are put on display, why would He condemn His people? Wouldn't that be tantamount to opposing His righteousness toward them?

Paul uses this argument to underscore Israel's presumption and irrationality in claiming they deserve God's favor because they are circumcised (in spite of sinning). But in resorting to this argument, the Israelites don't make any sense. They think that for God to maintain a righteous, faithful image means He will not judge them. Of course, that is complete nonsense, which Paul makes clear in v. 6:

> **Rom. 3:6 Certainly not! For then how will God judge the world?**

If Israel insists on using that outlandish argument, then the whole world can use it.

WILL BELIEVERS BE JUDGED FOR SINNING?

Incidentally, this is the argument essentially used by most evangelicals when they claim that God doesn't judge His children because they are *in Christ* and, therefore, have His positional righteousness (the Reformation doctrine of justification). I was taught this for years.

Ironically, Chapter 7 of my first book, *The End of the Pilgrimage*, entitled "Judged for Sinning?" — in which I give eight reasons why Jesus will judge believers for their sinfulness at the Judgment Seat of Christ — is one of the most attacked subjects in my kingdom inheritance writings. Many object, claiming, "God won't judge us for our *sins*; He will only judge us for our *works*." What? That's a nonsensical argument! Your *works* are your *deeds* — what you do, how you live your life. Your life is characterized, either by deeds of fleshliness and sinning or deeds of Spirit-led fruitfulness, to the glory of God (see Gal. 5:16-25). Your *works* (*deeds*) are either "good and faithful" or "wicked and slothful" (see Matt. 25:23,26).

Most Christians can't fathom the idea of being judged for a lifetime of sinning. They think all their sins are covered and, therefore, they have nothing to worry about when they meet Jesus. They don't believe there is such a thing as negative reward, and they certainly can't imagine anything negative happening at the Bema. They expect to be rewarded in some degree, even if their life has been characterized by what the Scriptures define as carnality. This way of thinking is completely contrary to Christ's warning about the need for one's soul to be saved at the Judgment Seat (see Matt. 16:24-27).

Thus, the argument used by these Israelites is essentially the same argument used by most Christians today, namely: "God can't judge us for sinning, because He is righteous, and we have His righteousness through Christ; His favor has been bestowed upon us. It would be unjust for God to judge His children and exclude us from the kingdom of heaven." Isn't that essentially what we have been taught throughout our lives? That thinking pervades modern evangelical Christianity. First century *Jewish* presumption has become twenty-first century *Christian* presumption.

If God doesn't judge His own children for sinning, then how can He judge the world for sinning? Peter claims that judgment begins at the house of God (1 Pet. 4:17). But He will also judge the world! Paul puts it this way in Corinthians:

> **2 Cor. 5:10** For we must all appear before the judgment seat of Christ, that each one may receive the things *done* in the body, according to what he has done, whether good or bad.

James Dunn says:

> The world we inhabit is a morally ordered world; man's sense of being morally responsible, whether in terms of gentile conscience or of Jewish law, simply confirms the revelatory postulate that there will be a final day of reckoning at which God will provide and "render to each according to his works" (2:6).[5]

Before moving on, Paul repackages this argument in vs. 7-8:

Rom. 3:7 For if the truth of God has increased through my lie to His glory, why am I also still judged as a sinner?

> **3:8 And *why* not *say*, "Let us do evil that good may come?"—as we are slanderously reported and as some affirm that we say. Their condemnation (judgment) is just.**

This problem just doesn't want to go away. The Jewish believers continue to think they can sin with immunity, because of God's faithfulness to His covenant people, and as already pointed out, many New Testament-era children of God think the same. In fact, some of the believers (probably the Gentiles) had charged Paul with teaching that the Jews could sin with immunity, because they were God's chosen ones. Paul makes clear that those rumors are slanderous; he has never taught this, and he is confident those who have spread these lies will be judged by God.

God continues to be faithful to each one of His children, despite our sinning and unbelief. But God's faithfulness does not mean He ignores sin. No, judgment day is coming for *all* — for Israel, for Jews and Gentiles who are *in Christ*, and even for the unregenerate world. So don't go on thinking you can sin with immunity, simply because God is true and righteous. Paul drops this line of thinking for now, but he will pick it up again in chapters 9-11. Nevertheless, his point has been made: God is faithful, but that doesn't give His children a license to sin — neither Jews nor Gentiles. Paul summarizes that nicely in v. 9:

> **Rom. 3:9 What then? Are we better *than they?* Not at all. For we have previously charged both Jews and Greeks that they are all under sin.**

Keep in mind that Paul is talking to believers. So his point in vs. 9-18 is *not* that the whole world is sinful. His audience already knows the world is sinful, and while the verses in the next section certainly *apply* to the whole world, that is not Paul's focus. He applies this unified thought in vs. 9-18 to Jewish and Gentile *believers* — as if to say — the gospel of kingdom inheritance is to Jewish believers first, but also to Gentile believers. When embraced, it results in salvation of the soul, and the reward of age-lasting life, glory, honor, peace, and incorruption (2:7, 10). In 3:10-18 Paul indicts both Jews and Gentiles:

> **Rom. 3:10 As it is written:** *"There is none righteous, no, not one;*
> *3:11 There is none who understands; there is none who seeks after God.*
> *3:12 They have all turned aside; they have together become unprofitable; there is none who does good, no, not one."*
> *3:13 "Their throat is an open tomb; with their tongues they have practiced deceit"; "the poison of asps is under their lips";*
> *3:14 "Whose mouth is full of cursing and bitterness."*
> *3:15 "Their feet are swift to shed blood;*
> *3:16 Destruction and misery are in their ways;*
> *3:17 And the way of peace they have not known."*
> *3:18 "There is no fear of God before their eyes."*

Paul starts this string of quotations from the book of Ecclesiastes, then gives several passages from the Psalms and then a final lengthy one from Isa. 59.

THERE IS NONE RIGHTEOUS — NOT EVEN THOSE UNDER THE LAW

James Dunn says:

> The message is clear ... no one within the law can claim to be righteous either because he is within the law or because (he thinks) he keeps the law. Paul's adaptation of the quotation reemphasizes the point: "There is none righteous, *not even one.*" The later, larger quotation from Isa 59:7–8 (vv 15–17) makes the same point: this is Israel being challenged from within its own scriptures for its own lawlessness and lack of righteousness.[6]

Paul's purpose is to indict the Jewish believers who continue to think they are favored by God and are largely exempt from His judgment because of their status as God's covenant people and their identification with the covenant via the mark of circumcision. Consequently, they continue in their condescension toward the Gentiles. So Paul demonstrates from their own Scriptures that they are just as culpable of sinfulness as the Gentiles.

He asks in v. 9, "Are *we* (Jews) better than *they* (Gentiles)?" The answer is a resounding "No!" In fact, all are under sin. Now there's something important to catch here. Dunn concludes that Paul is referring to the *power* of sin, and I would agree with that, since the Scriptures teach Christ has already paid the *penalty* of sin for all mankind. (That will be more fully explained in Rom. 5).

> The prepositional formula *"under* sin" (as in 7:14 and Gal 3:22) and the personification subsequently (most clearly 5:12, 21; 6:6, 12–23; 7:8–11) indicate that Paul understands "sin" as a force (or power) within the world, which functions in and upon man to negative effect ... The strength of the imagery of kingly rule or slave ownership (5:21; 6:12–23; 7:14) should not be discounted, since evidently this power can exercise a *force majeure* [i.e., major force] which results in death (5:21; 6:16, 21, 23; 7:9, 11).[7]

Dunn also refers to a commentator named Kaye, who concludes that *"hamartia* [the Greek word for *sin*] consistently in Romans means "sinful act, or the guilt consequent upon such acts." So that adds weight to the view that Paul is referring, *not* to the *penalty* of sin (singular), but to the *power* of sins (plural) upon all men. Once again, it is important to remember that Paul is speaking to *believers*, so his point to the Jewish believers in the church at Rome is that *all* are under the *power* of sinning, both Jewish and Gentile believers. In Rom. 6-8 he tells believers how to be freed from sin's power by appropriating the indwelling Spirit of God. We will get to that in a future chapter.

The resounding point Paul wants these Jewish believers to understand is in v. 19:

Rom. 3:19 Now we know that whatever the law says, it says to those who are under the law, that every

mouth may be stopped, and all the world may
become guilty before God.

The Jews are the ones under the law, so Paul says to the Jewish believers, "You are just as culpable and guilty of sinning as the Gentile believers." Your own law indicts you! And then Paul delivers the final blow in v. 20:

Rom. 3:20 Therefore by the deeds of the law no flesh will be justified in His sight, for by the law *is* the knowledge of sin.

Dunn refers to this as the "theological underpinning of the whole argument."[8] Paul says something very similar in Galatians:

DEEDS (WORKS) OF THE LAW DO NOT JUSTIFY

Gal. 2:16 Knowing that a man is not justified by the works of the law ... for by the works of the law no flesh shall be justified.

In the context of Galatians, Paul is rebuking Peter for not eating with the Gentiles.

In the context of Romans 1-3, what are *"deeds of the law?"* Is it synonymous with fulfilling the *righteous requirements of the law*, that is, keeping the moral law of God? —the law of Christ? —the law of liberty? —the royal law? —the law of love? No! *Deeds (works) of the law* are one and the same as keeping the *ritual* aspects of the law. Paul's showcase illustration here in Romans is circumcision. In Galatians it is dietary laws, and in Colossians it is observance of feasts and sabbaths.

So Paul is emphasizing that no one can be declared righteous merely by keeping the ritual deeds of the Mosaic law. Incidentally, Paul is not talking about matters of initial salvation, or regeneration. He is talking to believers about matters of sanctification — living righteously, set apart unto God. James Dunn says:

"by works of the law" ... This is the first appearance of a key phrase whose importance for understanding Paul's thought in this letter can hardly be overemphasized, but which has in fact frequently been misunderstood by successive generations of commentators. How did Paul intend his Roman readership to understand it? ... Given ... Paul's polemic against Jewish over-confidence based on having the law, the answer is not difficult. "Works of the law" must refer to the attitude attacked in chap. 2; it must denote the "works" referred to there, particularly circumcision ... "works of the law" are *not* the same as *doing* the law (2:13–14), or *fulfilling* the law (2:27); "works of the law" are *not* the same as "the work of the law written in the heart" (2:15), "the circumcision of heart by the Spirit" (2:29). "Works of the law" are rather something more superficial, at the level of "the letter" (2:27, 29), an outward mark indicative of ethnic solidarity (2:28), something more limited than "the patient perseverance in good work" (2:7). In the context of the argument in 2:1–3:8 then, "works of the law" can be defined somewhat crudely as doing what is necessary to be (become, or remain) within the covenant.[9]

By warning the Jewish believers that mere *works* (*deeds*) of the law will not result in God declaring them righteous, Paul has essentially taken a giant pin and deflated the balloon of Jewish ego. The Jewish believers at Rome can no longer think they are better than the Greco-Roman believers merely because they are God's chosen people who are circumcised. Keeping the Jewish rituals cannot make a person righteous!

INABILITY OF RULES TO SANCTIFY

Though I have said this several times in the previous chapters, it bears repeating. The practical application for twenty-first century believers is this: Keeping a list of rules will not sanctify you. God wants inward obedience from a circumcised heart. He wants you to fulfill the righteous requirements of the law *by faith* (which will be made clear in Rom. 4). *That* is what Paul's gospel is all about — the *mystery* of the oracles.

In closing, keep in mind that Paul later says, "whatever is not from faith is sin" (14:23). He also says, "love is the fulfillment of the law" (13:10). Christians who merely keep a list — expecting a daily ritual of devotions to sanctify or holding to certain separational "standards" that presumably make them spiritual — are some of the most condescending, unloving people I know. Furthermore, they tend to take on the role of the Holy Spirit in the lives of others, which gets messy very quickly.

If we love others as Jesus loves us, we will truly be fulfilling *the righteous requirements of the law*. The Christian life *begins* with grace — "For by *grace* you have been saved, through faith" (Eph. 2:8-9) — and it *continues* by grace — "Being justified freely by His *grace*" (3:24). Faith is the *means* by which we access God's grace — "We have access by faith into this grace in which we stand" (5:2). The Holy Spirit is the *catalyst* — "That the righteous requirement of the law might be fulfilled in us who do not walk according to the flesh but according to the Spirit" (8:4).

THE PURPOSE OF THE OLD TESTAMENT RITUALS

Many years ago I sought to understand why God would command Israel through the Mosaic law to keep so many rituals — all those restrictive ordinances governing their diet; laws specifying what would make them unclean and how they could become clean again; regulations for handling leprosy; requirements for observing certain holy days and for making restitution; strange edicts (in my way of thinking) about not mixing fabrics and not cooking a young goat in the milk of its mother — on and on these laws continue – 613 laws in total! Of course, circumcision, which was the capstone of all the laws, marked their identification with Jehovah and His law.

What was God's purpose in all this? Was He trying to overload His people with rules and regulations? Not at all! When I preached through the Pentateuch, many years ago, I came to realize that the intent of each of the rituals was to point Israel's attention to one of the ten commandments, God's moral laws. In other words, each ritual served a bigger purpose, and the purpose was twofold: 1) to serve as an outward, daily reminder of their need to live holy and righteous, by obeying God's *moral* laws, and 2) to alert them to their constant failure to live righteously and thus, their need to offer sacrifices to seek forgiveness for violating God's laws.

THE DANGER OF LETTING RITUALS SUPERSEDE GOD'S MORAL LAWS

Thus, the rituals were designed with a lofty purpose in mind: to keep Israel focused on obeying God's *moral* laws. The problem was that through the centuries — and especially during the era of the Pharisees — the *rituals* supplanted the *moral* laws. Israel focused on the rituals at the expense of the deeper moral meaning behind them.

Paul says at the end of v. 20 that the purpose of the Jewish rituals is to bring knowledge of sin. Ironically, the Jews boasted in their keeping of the rituals, but the rituals were designed to deflate the Jews, to cause them to see their inability to keep the law and thus their need for God's grace!

Sadly, the Jews leaned on the rituals as a crutch of sorts, thinking that by the *deeds* (*works*) of the law they were in favor with God, though they were disobeying God inwardly, committing the "heart sins" listed in Romans 1:18-32. That is the serious spiritual problem Paul is dealing with in Romans as he confronts the Jewish believers. Ritual observance is part of their psyche, because of the influence of the Pharisees.

Twenty-first century Christians — particularly those who claim to be *fundamentalists* — must come to realize that ritual observance in modernized forms is also part of their psyche, for that is what they have been taught all their lives. By God's grace we must cast off our ritualism and the thinking that it makes us spiritual, and learn to walk in the Spirit, thereby fulfilling the righteous requirements of the law!

CHAPTER 10
SOUL-SALVATION BY GRACE THROUGH FAITH
ROMANS 3:21-4:8

At this juncture, it would be wise to drop back for a moment and briefly review the flow of the narrative in Romans.

1:1-17 Paul writes to *believers*, both Jews and Gentiles. The *gospel* (vs. 16-17) is the good news that those believers who are producing faith-filled works of righteousness are considered justified by God and will be rewarded with kingdom inheritance. *Salvation* in Romans is not *initial* salvation (regeneration) that results when one initially believes on Jesus; it is *ongoing* salvation (sanctification) for those who *continue to believe,* resulting in the saving of the soul. The apostle's ultimate goal is to resolve the disunity and division in the church, caused by carnality and ethnic prejudices, with the goal being, as Paul wrote in Eph. 4:13: *Till we all come to the unity of the faith and of the knowledge of the Son of God, to a perfect man, to the measure of the stature of the fullness of Christ.*

1:18-32 Paul rebukes both Jewish and Gentile believers for sinning and warns of God's wrath upon those who continue in sinfulness. The Gentile believers are predominantly guilty of committing outward sins, such as immorality and other forms of licentious living that characterize the Greco-Roman culture. The Jewish believers, on the other hand, are guilty of observing the *letter* of the law *outwardly,* while ignoring the *spirit* of the law *inwardly,* by committing sins of the heart (e.g., bitterness, hatred, lust, pride, strife, etc.)

2:1-29 Paul admonishes the Jewish believers for clinging to the ritual aspects of the law, thinking their physical circumcision guarantees covenant acceptance, even though God is focused on circumcision of the heart. He shocks the Jews by claiming God accepts even uncircumcised Gentiles who are living righteously.

3:1-20 Paul teaches that the Jewish believers are just as sinful as the Gentile believers, and he emphasizes that mere *deeds of the law* do not sanctify or mean that one is living righteously. The first section of Romans (1:1-3:20) ends with this conclusion:

> **Rom. 3:20** Therefore by the deeds of the law no flesh will be justified in His sight, for by the law *is* the knowledge of sin.

DEEDS OF THE LAW VS. THE WEIGHTIER MATTERS

Deeds of the law is a term Paul uses to refer to observing the ritual aspects of the law (things like circumcision, dietary laws, observing feast days and sabbaths) — and expecting those things to make one sanctified and righteous — which they do not! He uses this term in contradistinction to another — *the righteous requirements of the law* — that is, fulfilling the moral law of God, which is truly righteous living.

Once again, I remind that this has nothing to do with initial salvation; Paul is writing to believers about the saving of the soul, which is about living righteously and inheriting rewards at the Judgment Seat of Christ. His point is that observing the Mosaic rituals cannot save the soul. They merely highlight Israel's sinfulness and need to keep *the righteous requirements of the law*, which Jesus referred to as the *weightier matters of the law* — the moral law of God, summed up in the two great commandments — love the Lord your God with all your heart, and soul, and mind, and love your neighbor as yourself.

We made application of the truths taught in Romans to the Christian life and the mentality of many Christians that "keeping a list" and/or "holding to standards" makes them spiritual. God forbids this mentality, and wants His children to obey the law of Christ, the law of love. On this important foundation, we can now understand the next key section of the epistle.

> **Rom. 3:21 But now the righteousness of God apart from the law is revealed, being witnessed by the Law and the Prophets,**
> **3:22 even the righteousness of God, through faith in Jesus Christ, to all and on all who believe. For there is no difference;**

3:21. *The righteousness of God*, interpreted in light of 1:16-17, is God's salvation (deliverance) of His *faithful* children — those who are living righteously by fulfilling *the righteous requirements of the law*. If they remain on the pathway of discipleship, they will be rewarded and will become His bride and co-rulers in the Messianic kingdom, serving together with Him in New Jerusalem. Thus, the *salvation* mentioned in Rom. 1:16 and throughout the entire epistle, is not initial salvation, the salvation of your spirit when you got saved (regenerated). It is ongoing soul-salvation, which Jesus talked about in Matt. 16:24-27, James mentions in 1:21 of his epistle, and Peter discusses in 1 Peter 1:10-16.

This is what Paul calls "the gospel of Christ" in Rom. 1:16 and "my gospel" in 16:25-26, which was hidden in Old Testament times, but is now made manifest:

> **Rom. 16:25-26** Now to Him who is able to establish you according to my gospel and the preaching of Jesus Christ, according to the revelation of the mystery kept secret since the world began but now made manifest, and by the prophetic Scriptures made known to all nations, according to the commandment of the everlasting God, for obedience to the faith—

The law and the prophets predicted the mystery of the gospel that Paul had been commissioned to share, and which he had faithfully revealed to "all nations" — not merely to Jews, but to the Gentile world.

OBEDIENCE TO THE FAITH

Notice the last phrase of 16:26, *for obedience to the faith*. This cannot be the gospel of initial salvation for sinners (unbelievers), for it is by works. It is the gospel of ongoing salvation (sanctification unto righteousness) for saints. Again, it is the good news that those Jews and Gentiles who believe this gospel and produce faith-filled works of righteousness will experience the salvation of their souls at the Judgment Seat of Christ. In what sense is this salvation *apart from the law*? Commentator James Dunn says:

> "apart from the law" means apart from the law understood as a badge of Jewishness, understood as the chief identifying characteristic of covenant membership by those "within the law." It is precisely this link between law and God's righteousness which Paul ... seeks to sever; it is precisely this presumption, that works of the law ensure the Jew's final vindication by God because they maintain his status and identity as a member of God's people, that Paul seeks to destroy by his abrupt "apart from the law."[1]

3:22. Rather, Paul says, it is "through faith in Jesus Christ, to all and on all who believe." Dunn adds:

> Expressed as an antithesis to "works of the law" (3:20), it is clearly intended to denote *the basis of a relationship which is not dependent on specific ritual acts, but is direct and immediate, a relying on the risen Christ rather than a resting on the law.*[2]

CONTINUING TO BELIEVE GOD

The verb *believe* in v. 22 is an active present participle and should read: "on all who are believing." *Young's Literal* (YLT) translates this verse: "and the righteousness of God [is] through the faith of Jesus Christ to all, and upon all those believing."[3] Dunn confirms this understanding:

As with 1:16 the present tense of the verb ("to all who believe") may well imply that Paul was thinking of this attitude of reliance on Christ not simply as the beginning of the relationship with God (experience of God's righteousness) but also as the continuing (indeed lifelong) basis of that relationship.[4]

In other words, those believers who keep believing God to carry out faith-filled works of righteousness are the ones who are declared righteous by God. Isn't that the point of Heb. 11? Those believers from olden times trusted God, by faith, to fulfill *the righteous requirements of the law*. Even those in Heb. 11 who were from the era of the Mosaic law were heroes of the faith, not because they kept the rituals of the law, but because they believed God to live and act righteously. There is no mention anywhere in Heb. 11 of people of faith keeping the Mosaic rituals.

Here's the point, child of God: You cannot live righteously merely by having daily devotions and going to church. You cannot live righteously merely by having separational "standards." You can only live righteously by trusting the Holy Spirit who lives within to enable you to obey God! That is the point of climax in Rom. 3:22.

At the end of the verse Paul says *there is no difference*. In other words, this isn't only for Jews; it is for *all* believers, regardless of their ethnic heritage, as long as they meet God's conditions. Undoubtedly, Paul emphasizes the inclusivity of the offer, because the Jews to whom he is writing have a condescending attitude toward the Gentiles, thinking they are better spiritually.

Romans 3:23 now makes sense.

Rom. 3:23 for all have sinned and fall short of the glory of God,

While this principle applies to all mankind, Paul is not applying it to unbelievers in the context of Rom. 3, even though virtually everyone uses it in their evangelistic presentations, especially when using the Romans Road method of witnessing. Paul is applying this principle to *believers*, all of whom *have sinned* and "are missing out on the glory intended for them—the tenses denoting a continuing consequence of past sins."[5]

But there's good news, and it's Paul gospel — the gospel that was a mystery in Old Testament times but is now revealed.

SOUL-SALVATION IS ALSO BY GRACE THROUGH FAITH

> **Rom. 3:24 being justified freely by His grace through the redemption that is in Christ Jesus,**

Being justified is God declaring that you are living righteously, qualifying for the salvation of your soul at His Bema Seat.

Notice that justification is a gift of God's grace. This caused the Reformers to think Paul was speaking of initial salvation, which is certainly by grace, through faith (Eph. 2:8-9). But that's not Paul's point here. He is saying that soul-salvation is also by God's grace, through faith. The believer must continue to access God's grace, by faith (5:2), in order to live righteously and, therefore, victoriously. Dunn makes this clear:

> It is this humbling recognition—that he has to depend *entirely* from start to finish on God's gracious power, that he can receive acquittal only as a gift—which lies at the heart of faith for Paul ... The indispensable starting point for any good that man does is his acceptance of God's embrace and his continual reliance on God's enabling to accomplish that good.[6]

Paul makes the same emphatic point in Galatians 3:

> **Gal. 3:2** This only I want to learn from you: Did you receive the Spirit by the works of the law, or by the hearing of faith?
>
> **3** Are you so foolish? Having begun in the Spirit, are you now being made perfect by the flesh?
>
> **5-6** Therefore He who supplies the Spirit to you ... *does He do it* by the works of the law, or by the hearing of faith? — just as Abraham *"believed God, and it was accounted to him for righteousness."*

Paul is talking about being *sanctified* by grace through faith, and he quotes the same passage from Gen. 15:6 about Abraham as quoted in Romans 4:3. As we shall see, God's pronouncement in Genesis is *not* speaking of Abraham's *initial* belief in Jehovah (which, incidentally, is nowhere mentioned in the Scriptures), but his *ongoing* exercising of faith, that is, believing God for righteous living. Thus, *soul-salvation by grace through faith* is also found in the Old Testament.

Like initial salvation of one's spirit, so the ongoing salvation of one's soul is ...

> **Rom. 3:24b-25a through the redemption that is in Christ Jesus, whom God set forth *as* a propitiation by His blood, through faith, to demonstrate His righteousness,**

THE CROSS WORKS BOTH DIRECTIONS

Christ's redemptive work on Calvary is both retroactive and proactive. Dunn says:

> On the one hand it certainly denotes a historical action of Christ, the act of ransoming, the provision of a ransom payment ... But on the other hand, in Paul's mind there may well have been also the implication that this redemption is an offer still available "in Christ Jesus." If so, the two aspects would be held together in Paul's mind by his ... conviction that the believer is united with Christ not only in the here and now, but also with Christ in his dying and rising again.[7]

I personally think this past and present application of Christ's blood redemption is also seen in Eph. 1:7:

> **Eph. 1:7** In Him we have redemption through His blood, the forgiveness of sins, according to the riches of His grace.

All of our *past* sins were forgiven when He saved us initially, but all of our *present* sins are forgiven only when we confess them on the basis of 1 Jn. 1:9.

Incidentally, back in Rom. 3:25 — *whom God set forth as a propitiation by His blood* — YLT translates the word *propitiation* as *mercy seat*, for the Greek word used here was what the Septuagint translators used to convey the idea of *mercy seat* in the Old Testament. Of course, the mercy seat was where the high priest of Israel applied the blood of the lamb on the annual Day of Atonement, when atoning for the sins of the nation. Christians need to keep in mind that the Old Testament sacrifices, including those on the Day of Atonement, were for a redeemed people to confess their ongoing sins to God.

CONTINUED CLEANSING ON THE BASIS OF 1 JOHN 1:9

This is pictured for New Testament believers in the "cleansing" of 1 Jn. 1:9. God forgives and *cleanses* us from *all* unrighteousness. Only the Passover signified the *initial* application of blood, as pictured in *initial* salvation. 1 Jn. 1:7 gives a beautiful picture of what happens in the heavenlies when children of God keep their sins confessed.

> **1 John 1:7** But if we walk in the light as He is in the light, we have fellowship with one another, and the blood of Jesus Christ His Son cleanses us from all sin.

The point is that being considered justified (righteous) at the Bema Seat of Christ for living righteously is made possible because of Christ's redemptive work on Calvary. So, in that sense, His justification of believers who live righteously is also given as an act of His grace.

The thrust of Romans 2-3 is that the Jewish believers were putting their confidence in their rituals, including circumcision, depending on *that* to sanctify them and justify them before God, rather than Christ's redemption and resurrection.

What about faith-filled *Old Testament* saints? Paul includes them in v. 25b

Rom. 3:25b because in His forbearance God had

> **passed over the sins that were previously committed,**

Commentator James Dunn clarifies:

> Former sins were passed over, either because Jesus' death demonstrates the sacrificial system to be effective (at least so far as inadvertent sins were concerned), or because Jesus' death as the death of sinful man is effective for the persons of faith who came before him as well as for those who come after.[8]

Thus, people like Noah and Job—and multitudes of others who lived righteously—were also justified by faith in ancient times, long before Christ had come. Having talked about the past, Paul returns to the present in v. 26.

> **Rom. 3:26 to demonstrate at the present time His righteousness, that He might be just and the justifier of the one who has faith in Jesus.**

Dunn demonstrates that this is for believers:

> Christ's death deals with the believer's sins and destroys the power of sin for the one "in Christ" … restoring to communion with God the one who identifies himself with the dead and risen Christ in trustful commitment.[9]

"TRUSTFUL COMMITMENT"

The key is "trustful commitment" — those who *are believing*, according v. 22 — and that is what the next section emphasizes as well.

> **Rom. 3:27 Where *is* boasting then? It is excluded. By what law? Of works? No, but by the law of faith.**

Paul says to these first century Jewish believers: "Don't brag about the fact that you are Jewish and have the mark of circumcision and keep the sabbaths and feast days and hold to a kosher diet. Those things do not make you righteous!"

By way of application, Paul says to twenty-first century Christians: "You cannot boast about *keeping your list* or holding to your *separational standards*. Living righteously and pleasing God does not come by these things, but by depending on Jesus to enable you to live righteously, so stop thinking you are more spiritual than others because you hold to certain rituals." God is looking for those who will keep on believing Him.

> **Rom. 3:28 Therefore we conclude that a man is justified by faith apart from the deeds of the law.**

Could Paul say it any more clearly? Believers are considered righteous by God only to the extent that they are living by faith, producing faith-filled works of righteousness, not by merely carrying out religious rituals of some sort. Those who continue to think this is talking about initial salvation have ignored the context! This is practical theology for you and me and for Christians everywhere!

To his Jewish audience, Paul asks:

> **Rom. 3:29-30 Or *is He* the God of the Jews only? *Is He* not also the God of the Gentiles? Yes, of the Gentiles also, since *there is* one God who will justify the circumcised by faith and the uncircumcised through faith.**

Notice that phrase, *there is one God*. This is the same phrase used in James 2:19. The Jews were monotheistic, believing in Jehovah, the one true God. They certainly did not believe in myriad gods and goddesses, who governed over their own regional constituents. That being the case, if God is One, wouldn't He treat all people the same, especially seeing He is impartial (2:11)? He treats Jewish believers who are circumcised the same as Gentile believers who are uncircumcised. All believers who live righteously, *by faith*, are considered "circumcised in heart" (2:26).

DEPENDING ON THE RISEN CHRIST

> **Rom. 3:31 Do we then make void the law through faith? Certainly not! On the contrary, we establish the law.**

Does living by faith negate the Mosaic law? Absolutely not! The moral law of God transcends time and ethnicity. God expects all of His children — both Jewish and Gentile believers — to fulfill *the righteous requirements of the law* by depending on the risen Christ. Faith-living results in righteousness of life, obeying the weightier matters of the law, which pleases God. Only the Jewish *rituals* have been nullified, for they do not make one righteous. They merely accentuate man's sinfulness. But now that Christ has come, we depend on His righteous provision within to enable us to obey God.

Paul now moves into Romans 4 and gives two Old Testament illustrations. Before examining vs. 1-8, a point of emphasis needs to be made. Romans is written to both Jewish and Gentile believers who are living sinfully. Paul dealt with the *Gentile* sinning in ch. 1. Their situation is not nearly as complicated as the Jewish one, for the Gentiles never had the Mosaic law. So they need to simply stop their sinning and, of course, now they have Christ to enable them. But Paul's focus in chapters 2-3 has predominantly been the *Jewish* believers, who are trapped in a web of Mosaic rituals, thinking that *deeds of the law* make them righteous.

Paul is now going to use as illustrations two Old Testament Jewish believers, revered by all the Jews: Abraham and King David. Both of these men were accepted by God — but why? Was it because they kept the Jewish rituals? No, it was because they simply believed God to fulfill *the righteous requirements of the law.*

> **Rom. 4:1 What then shall we say that Abraham our father has found according to the flesh?**

4:2 For if Abraham was justified by works, he has *something* to boast about, but not before God.

4:3 For what does the Scripture say? *"Abraham believed God, and it was accounted to him for righteousness."*

THE ILLUSTRATION OF ABRAHAM

4:3. Paul quotes Gen. 15:6. The evangelical Christian world largely interprets this as Abraham's *initial* salvation, because they interpret Rom. 3-4 as referring to *initial* salvation. But as we have demonstrated repeatedly, that is not a valid interpretation, because Paul is not talking to *unbelievers* about matters of *initial* salvation. He is talking to *believers* about matters of *ongoing* salvation, sanctification and living righteously. That is overwhelmingly clear from the context. It's difficult for some Christians to accept that, because they have been so indoctrinated with theology that has been passed down from the Reformation.

Politicians know that if you repeat something long enough — even if it's blatantly untrue — the general public will eventually accept it as true. That tactic is as old as the devil himself. He has had five hundred years to indoctrinate Christians with Reformation interpretations of Romans rather than what the book of Romans actually teaches. Consequently, tradition dies hard. Thus, it is extremely difficult teaching most Christians the correct interpretation of Romans, because they refuse to believe other than what they have been taught. I am thankful for those Christians who have seeking hearts and minds. I believe the Lord continues to bless them spiritually by unveiling truth from His Word.

Arlen Chitwood sums up v. 3 quite well:

> This event is looked upon by some individuals as the point in Abraham's life where he was saved. But that *CANNOT possibly be correct.* The context of the statement in Gen. 15:6 has to do with that which God had previously revealed about Abraham and his progeny realizing an inheritance in another land (cf. Gen. 13:14-17; 15:2-21), which is the contextual setting of the statement in Romans as well

(4:1-22). And it was *in THIS realm that Abraham exercised faith, believed God.*

Abraham had believed God relative to this same issue prior to the events of Genesis chapter fifteen, while still in Ur (cf. Gen. 12:1-3; Heb. 11:8). And his belief concerning this issue, once in the land, is simply a continuing belief in God's fulfillment of that which He had previously promised ... Eternal salvation is NOT in view anywhere in this passage.[10]

Here's the bottom line: By Gen. 15, Abraham is a man who has believed God for many years and has followed the Lord from Ur (a chic, pagan city of his day) to Canaan land. In the early verses of Gen. 15, Abraham asks God if Eliezer, his servant, will become his heir. God tells Abraham "no," then assures him that his heir will come from his own body and his descendants will become as the stars of heaven:

> **Gen. 15:5** Then He brought him outside and said, "Look now toward heaven, and count the stars if you are able to number them." And He said to him, "So shall your descendants be."
> **6** And he believed in the LORD, and He accounted it to him for righteousness.

Verse 6 is quoted by Paul in Rom. 4:3 and Gal. 3:6. In both cases, Paul is talking about matters of ongoing sanctification by faith, not initial salvation (regeneration) by faith. Before moving on to King David, Paul adds something very interesting in v. 4:

BEWARE THE "GOD OWES ME" ENTITLEMENT MENTALITY REGARDING REWARDS

> **Rom. 4:4 Now to him who works, the wages are (KJV: *reward is*) not counted as grace but as debt.**

The Christian life is all about *doing* — as 2:7 says, "doing good" — as 2:13 says, "doers of the law" — i.e., *the righteous requirements of the law.* To live righteously and do good one must behave in a certain manner and that involves works of sorts. But Paul has been speaking to Jews throughout the context of ch. 2-3 about the futility of doing mere works of the law (keeping the rituals) — that is the context. So in v. 4 Paul essentially says to those Jewish believers who are focused on doing the Mosaic rituals, "You have the mentality that God *owes* you for doing deeds of the law."

Think about this for a moment. Paul has already made the point that doing *works of the law* does not justify; those deeds don't make you righteous. They merely bring knowledge of sin and guilt (3:19-20). Thus, Paul implies: "Expecting God to repay you for doing mere *deeds of the law* is foolish, because you are lawbreakers when it comes to the weightier matters of the law; your reward will be negative. God rewards those who fulfill *the righteous requirements of the law by faith* — while trusting Him to graciously reward as He sees fit."

Isn't that the point made by Jesus in the parable of the workers in Matt. 20:1-16? That parable begins:

Matt. 20:1 For the kingdom of heaven is like a landowner who went out early in the morning to hire laborers for his vineyard.

The *kingdom of heaven* is New Jerusalem, the realm of reward in the coming Messianic kingdom. That's what Jesus was teaching about in this parable. He tells of a landowner needing to hire laborers to harvest the crop in his vineyard. The first round of workers hired very early in the morning want to negotiate a fair wage for their labor. They represent the Jews who cling to mere *deeds of the law* and have an entitlement mentality — "God owes us for keeping the Mosaic rituals!" More workers are hired later in the day — some at the third hour, some at the sixth, some at the ninth,, and some at the eleventh. *They* see no need to negotiate; they simply trust the landowner to pay them fairly. They represent Jews who keep *the righteous requirements of the law by faith* and trust God to reward as He sees fit.

At the end of the workday, the landowner pays all the workers a full day's wage, even those who did not work a full day. When those hired first get their agreed-upon wage, which is the same as given to everyone else, they complain: "But we worked all day! Those hired later only worked part of the day. We should get more money!" The landowner tells them they have been paid according to their agreement; they have no business telling him what he can and cannot pay the others. How do we understand this?

> **Rom. 4:4 Now to him who works, the wages are (KJV: *reward is*) not counted as grace but as debt.**

In light of Christ's parable and the context of Rom. 2-3, the application is now clear. Those believers who have an entitlement mentality will not receive eternal rewards; they will get only what they bargained for: bragging rights for doing deeds of the law. Their debt has been repaid here on Earth. On the other hand, look at v. 5:

> **Rom. 4:5 But to him who does not work but believes on Him who justifies the ungodly, his faith is accounted for righteousness,**

These believers are not merely focused on keeping the Mosaic rituals with an entitlement mentality. They are focused on believing God to fulfill *the righteous requirements of the law*. Consequently, God justifies them; they will be rewarded when they meet Him in judgment. This also applied in ancient times — consider Abraham and King David who lived in this manner and with this attitude. Paul now illustrates by using David's repentance.

THE ILLUSTRATION OF KING DAVID

> **Rom. 4:6 just as David also describes the blessedness of the man to whom God imputes righteousness apart from works:**
> **4:7-8 *"Blessed are those whose lawless deeds are forgiven, and whose sins are covered; blessed is the man to whom the LORD shall not impute sin."***

This is a quote from Ps. 32. David wrote this psalm of penitence after his sin of adultery with Bathsheba, and after he had sought forgiveness, cleansing and restoration from God. David's purpose is to share with others how graciously God deals with those who confess their sins and the glorious blessedness of forgiveness. Of course, this has nothing to do with initial salvation. This is about sanctification and cleansing, going forward living righteously, even after sinning and confessing those sins.

The word *impute* means "to take inventory and conclude." This does not mean we are credited with Christ's righteousness when we are saved. It simply means that when a believer confesses sins and moves on, living righteously, God no longer reckons His child to be sinful, but righteous. King David did not have to work his way back into fellowship with God, nor do you when you confess your sins. God instantly pardons and cleanses and considers you as one of His righteous ones.

Do you have an entitlement mentality, expecting God to reward you for keeping your list and holding to your standards? Or do you have a spirit of righteousness through faith? — obeying God by trusting Him for help? To close this chapter, notice again the following verses:

Rom. 3:23-24 For all have sinned and fall short of the glory of God, being justified freely by His grace through the redemption that is in Christ Jesus.

These verses — like the rest of Romans — are also written to believers. Don't fall short of God's glory by continued sinning. Confess your sins, as the psalmist did, and go on living righteously by the grace of God, through faith in our Lord Jesus Christ.

CHAPTER 11
HIS RESURRECTION FOR OUR RIGHTEOUS LIVING
ROMANS 4:9-25

I have learned through many years of pastoring that repetition is essential to comprehension for most people, particularly when introducing Bible truths that are unfamiliar. Even those who catch what is being taught the first time around (a small percentage) tend to appreciate repetition also, for it helps to reinforce the teaching in their minds as well. That being said, please forgive me for repeating some concepts yet again.

We must remember that Paul is not teaching about initial salvation. He is writing to believers about the saving of the soul, which is about living righteously and inheriting rewards at the Judgment Seat of Christ. His point is that observing the Mosaic rituals cannot save the soul. The application for modern-day believers is that "keeping a list" and/or "holding to standards" does not make one spiritual. God forbids this mentality, and wants His children to obey the law of Christ, the law of love. To that end, He has given to His children Jesus Himself, living within, as our enabler.

JUSTIFIED BY CONTINUED FAITH IN JESUS

Rom. 3:22 specifies that we can live righteously as believers when we continue to believe Jesus in our daily lives, depending on Him to enable us to live righteously, in a manner that pleases God. Rom.

3:24 specifies that we are justified (declared righteous by God) freely, as an act of His grace, when we appropriate this truth. It's not a matter of keeping a list to make us spiritual, but rather depending upon Him for daily victory over sins. Paul sums it up in:

> **Rom. 3:28** Therefore we conclude that a man is justified by faith apart from the deeds of the law.

Believers are living righteously when they are depending on Jesus as opposed to keeping the Mosaic rituals or, by way of application in our modern culture, keeping a list of religious rules. In the first eight verses of ch. 4, Paul refers to two Old Testament heroes whom all the Jews revered, to illustrate his point.

FATHER ABRAHAM AND KING DAVID

Abraham lived righteously, but not by keeping the law, for he lived before the Mosaic law was given. He lived righteously by believing God and acting accordingly. Paul quotes Gen. 15:6:

> **Rom. 4:3** For what does the Scripture say? *"Abraham believed God, and it was accounted to him for righteousness."*

This cannot be referring to Abraham's *initial* "salvation," for we don't know when Abraham first believed God. All we know is that he left the city of Ur much earlier in his life, when God told him to go to Canaan land. His life was characterized by faith-filled works. In Gen. 15:6 he believes God's announcement that Eliezer will not be his descendant, but one who would come from his own body. On this basis, God's pronounces in Gen. 15:6 that Abraham believed God, as he had done all through the years, so that God considered him a righteous man.

King David is used as an illustration in 4:7-8. After David sinned with Bathsheba, he eventually recognized his sin, confessed it, and made it right with God. Of course, our great God who is faithful and just, forgave David and considered him righteous once again. Paul's point in 4:6 is that God considered David as living righteously, once his sins were confessed and forgiven. This was of faith, not of works of the law; that is, David did not have to earn God's forgiveness and cleansing by practicing the rituals of the law.

Granted, David offered sacrifices in the tabernacle under the Old Testament sacrificial system, so works were involved in a righteous lifestyle. However, his forgiveness was not contingent on *works of the law*. God simply forgave when David, by faith, offered sacrifices and sought God's forgiveness. The same is true of you, when you confess your sins (which is a work on your part). You don't have to read your Bible and pray for thirty days or keep a list of religious rules before you will be forgiven. You simply believe on the basis of 1 John 1:9 that God has forgiven you, and when you do, God reckons you righteous!

WHICH VERB IS BEST? — *ACCOUNTED, IMPUTES, RECKONED,* OR *CREDITED?*

Notice the words *accounted* in v. 3 and *imputes* in v. 6:

> **Rom. 4:3** *"Abraham believed God, and it was <u>accounted</u> to him for righteousness."*

> **4:6** just as David also describes the blessedness of the man to whom God <u>imputes</u> righteousness apart from works: (underlining added)

In both cases — *accounted* and *imputes* — the Greek word *logizomai* is used, which means "to reckon, count, compute, calculate, count over; hence, to take into account, to make account of."[1] Strong's Concordance adds: "to take an inventory.[2]" This Greek word *logizomai* is used eleven times in Rom. 4, and a total of nineteen times in the book of Romans overall, so it's a very important word.

In Romans 4, the NASB uses the verb *credited* in every case, which is not the best translation. The ESV uses the verb *counted* in every one of these verses, which is better. But YLT wins the prize for getting it right, for in every verse it uses the verb *reckoned*, which is the best translation, in my opinion.

NOT IMPUTED WITH CHRIST'S RIGHTEOUSNESS

Imputed is not a good translation of this Greek word *logizomai*, and here's why. Ever since the Reformation, Protestants, including Baptists, have been led to believe that when we are saved, Christ's righteousness is *imputed* (i.e., credited) to our account. However, the Reformation doctrine of positional justification is unscriptural, as discussed in previous chapters in this book. It is not taught in Galatians or Hebrews or Romans, not even in the Old Testament. Justification is God's reckoning that a person is righteous if they are *living* righteously, by faith.

The verb *impute* implies that we have been credited with His righteousness, and that it happened automatically, at initial salvation, regardless of how we are living. That is incorrect! Even the dictionaries have been tainted by Reformation doctrines. One of the definitions given for the word impute is, "In *Theology [to]* ascribe (righteousness, guilt, etc.) to someone by virtue of a similar quality in another: *Christ's righteousness has been imputed to us.*"[3] Interestingly, not only have dictionaries been corrupted by Reformation doctrines, so have many Greek lexicons.

I believe YLT has chosen the best word to translate the Greek word *logizomai* into English: *reckoned*. In other words, God does the accounting, He takes inventory and reckons. He can see that this person over here is living righteously, while that person over there is not. *Logizomai* does not mean that His righteousness is credited to our account. Thankfully, He has given us the provision of Christ in us, but that is no guarantee that we will appropriate His provision and actually *live* righteously.

ALL WHO QUALIFY ARE ACCOUNTED AS RIGHTEOUS

In vs. 9-10 Paul returns to his continuing argument, which is a series of questions:

> **Rom. 4:9 Does this blessedness then come upon the circumcised only, or upon the uncircumcised**

> also? For we say that faith was accounted to Abraham for righteousness.
> 4:10 How then was it accounted? While he was circumcised, or uncircumcised? Not while circumcised, but while uncircumcised.

4:9a. Paul asks rhetorically if the blessedness of God declaring a person righteous is only for Jews under the covenant — those who are circumcised — or if it applies to others also. The answer is obvious — it applies to all!

4:9b-10. After all, Abraham was not yet circumcised when God said this about him. Those instructions were not given to him until Gen. 17 which, chronologically, follows *after* ch. 15

God declares as righteous those who are believing Him and thereby living righteously, *apart from* "works of the law."

CIRCUMCISION IS IRRELEVANT

> Rom. 4:11 And he received the sign of circumcision, a seal of the righteousness of the faith which he had while still uncircumcised, that he might be the father of all those who believe, though they are uncircumcised, that righteousness might be imputed to them also,
> 4:12 and the father of circumcision to those who not only are of the circumcision, but who also walk in the steps of the faith which our father Abraham had while still uncircumcised.

4:11. To make sure his audience is crystal clear on the matter, Paul reemphasizes that Abraham was reckoned as righteous *before* he was ever circumcised. Commentator James Dunn says:

> Abraham's circumcision was dependent on his *previously* having been accepted by God and on his already having been reckoned righteous —not the other way round.[4]

HIS RESURRECTION FOR OUR RIGHTEOUS LIVING

The key to being reckoned as righteous is not doing mere religious rituals, it is living by faith, depending on God to live uprightly. Dunn says:

> The point has thus been established that Abraham's righteousness was dependent solely on a believing which clearly preceded circumcision and which therefore is clearly distinct from works of the law.[5]

4:12. Consequently, he is the spiritual father of all who live by faith, both Jews and Gentiles. Dunn adds:

> Because faith is the crucial factor, all those who believe as he did are his children, whether circumcised or uncircumcised. He is the father of the circumcised, but they enter into their full sonship only when they exercise faith as Abraham did, in a way which shows it to be independent of circumcision. And uncircumcised Gentiles who believe can properly call Abraham "our father" too."[6]

FULL SONSHIP – FIRSTBORN INHERITORS

Notice that Dunn uses the term *full sonship* — which is the idea of becoming a mature, firstborn son — as summed up by the Greek word *huios* in this context.

Interestingly, in the book of Galatians, Paul takes up the same subject, contrasting those believers who merely do works of the law vs. those believers who live by faith, and here is what he concludes:

> **Gal. 3:5-6** Therefore He who supplies the Spirit to you and works miracles among you, *does He do it* by the works of the law, or by the hearing of faith?—just as Abraham *"believed God, and it was accounted to him for righteousness."*
>
> 7 Therefore know that *only* those who are of faith are sons of Abraham.

The word *sons* here is the Greek word *huios*. These believers are *sons* of Abraham, not in a legal sense, but in the sense that they are living by faith. Thus, only those believers who are living by faith —

in contrast to those who are living by mere works of the law (rituals, or a list of some sort) — are firstborn inheritors, who will be rewarded at the Judgment Seat of Christ. This is, unequivocally, the message shared over and over again in Paul's epistles, and for that matter, throughout the entire New Testament.

We must cast off the Reformation doctrine handed down through the centuries, which teaches that all who are in Christ have positional justification — a legal standing of righteousness before God, regardless of how they are living. That unscriptural teaching has led generations of Christians to believe the Judgment Seat of Christ will be a glorified awards ceremony, having no serious negative consequences. Consequently, Satan has, through this errant doctrine, led multitudes of believers down the wide path that leads to destruction. Instead of becoming sons to glory and being given clothing of glorification and crowns of righteousness, signifying rulership, they will be cast into the darkness outside of the ruling realm of His kingdom, naked and ashamed. What a tragedy!

DESCENDANTS AS THE STARS OF HEAVEN

Paul introduces a new word in v. 13:

> **Rom. 4:13 For the promise that he would be the heir of the world *was* not to Abraham or to his seed through the law, but through the righteousness of faith.**

The new word is *promise*, which Paul uses four times in this chapter. What is this promise? The answer is found in the context of Gen. 15:6, which Paul quotes in Rom. 4:3.

> **Gen. 15:5** Then He brought him outside and said, "Look now toward heaven, and count the stars if you are able to number them." And He said to him, "So shall your descendants be."

According to Dunn, the Jews understood this to mean that Abraham's descendants would inherit the earth.[7] While we know that the nation of Israel will inherit a place of ruling on Earth in the Millennium, the actual promise made in Gen. 15:5 is that Abraham's descendants will be like the stars of heaven. Some believe these stars are church-age believers who are found righteous and faithful and consequently rewarded with the privilege of serving as Christ's bride and co-rulers in the age to come. They will reign over the Earth, from heavenly New Jerusalem. God told Daniel:

> **Dan. 12:3** Those who are wise shall shine like the brightness of the firmament, and those who turn many to righteousness like the stars forever and ever.

Thus, God promises Abraham that his descendants will be like the stars of heaven, that is, inheritors in the kingdom of the heavens. That is likely what is meant by the phrase: "the promise that he would be heir of the world," if we interpret it in the context of Gen. 15. These "stars" will rule over the earth in the Messianic age, as Abraham's descendants.

THE PROMISE FULFILLED THROUGH THE RIGHTEOUSNESS OF FAITH

Abraham believed that God would fulfill this promise, and God declared Abraham righteous, for he acted in faith rather than unbelief. This promise would not be fulfilled through works of the law, for the law had not yet been given. In fact, in Gal. 3:17 Paul says the (Mosaic) law came 430 years after this. Even the rite of circumcision had not been given yet to Abraham. Rather, this promise would be fulfilled through the *righteousness of faith*. In other words, Abraham's descendants will inherit the Earth and rule over it—that is, those who live righteously, by faith, just like Abraham. How would this come about? Arlen Chitwood describes:

> God is presently in the process of accomplishing a work which will result in "many sons" being brought "unto glory" (Heb. 2:10; *cf.* Rom. 8:18, 19). These "sons" are mainly individuals being removed from the nations presently holding the sceptre, with a view to these sons one day holding the sceptre. The immersion in the Spirit of those believing

on the Lord Jesus Christ places them "in Christ," a part of *the one new man*. And because they are positionally "in Christ" (Who is Abraham's Seed), this allows God to recognize them as "Abraham's seed, and heirs according to the promise (*cf.* Rom. 4:13; Gal. 3:26-29)."[8]

POTENTIAL HEIRSHIP, NOT AUTOMATIC

Because of our relationship as being *in Christ*, believers are *potential* heirs; not *automatic* heirs. As Paul already pointed out in 4:13, heirship will be given to those spiritual descendants of Abraham who live righteously, by faith, as he lived. What about those believers who think keeping a list of rules or rituals will result in being accepted by God? Paul deals with that problem in vs. 14-15:

> **Rom. 4:14-15 For if those who are of the law *are* heirs, faith is made void and the promise made of no effect, because the law brings about wrath; for where there is no law *there is* no transgression.**

Those who have legalistic behavior nullify the promise, for they are not living by faith. They will not be inheritors in the age to come. Indeed, they bring God's wrath upon themselves, for that is the function of the law: to condemn. Paul continues:

> **Rom. 4:16-17a Therefore *it is* of faith that *it might be* according to grace, so that the promise might be sure to all the seed, not only to those who are of the law, but also to those who are of the faith of Abraham, who is the father of us all (as it is written, *'I have made you a father of many nations'*).**

Dunn sums up nicely:

God's intention, as attested by Gen 15:6, was that the promise of grace through faith might embrace all who are willing to accept that same grace, whether Jews or not, just as Abraham did.[9]

That's the only way God's promise of Abraham becoming a father of many nations could be fulfilled (Gen. 17:5). We come to an odd parenthesis of sorts in vs. 17b-18:

> **Rom. 4:17b-18 in the presence of Him whom he believed—God, who gives life to the dead and calls those things which do not exist as though they did; who, contrary to hope, in hope believed, so that he became the father of many nations, according to what was spoken,** *"So shall your descendants be."*

ABRAHAM BELIEVED THE IMPOSSIBLE

From a human standpoint, Abraham's situation was impossible. He and Sarah were old and had no children, their bodies were "good as dead" (Heb. 11:12). Yet God had promised that his heirs would come from his own body. Amidst this perplexing dilemma, Paul says that Abraham believed in the Creator God, "who gives life to the dead (i.e., He resurrects)" and calls into existence things that do not exist (which is what He did in Gen. 1:1, *ex nihilo*). If anyone can bring life from "good-as-dead" bodies, Creator God can. Abraham trusted in this incredible God to solve his impossible situation, and contrary to hope, Abraham believed and became hopeful, and God brought His promise to pass in this man's life. He indeed, became the father of many nations. Paul continues:

> **Rom. 4:19 And not being weak in faith, he did not consider his own body, already dead (since he was about a hundred years old), and the deadness of Sarah's womb.**
> **4:20-21 He did not waver at the promise of God through unbelief, but was strengthened in faith, giving glory to God, and being fully convinced that what He had promised He was also able to perform.**

4:22 And therefore *"it was accounted to him for righteousness."*

Remember the words the angel Gabriel said to Mary when announcing the virgin birth:

Luke 1:37 "With God nothing will be impossible."

That applies here as well! Abraham believed God can do anything! Revel in the truth of vs. 20-21. Abraham did not waver in unbelief. He continued in faith, convinced that if God promised, He would carry it out.

As a result, God reckoned Abraham as righteous, because he believed God as he lived out his life. Paul makes abundantly clear that God declared Abraham righteous, not because he submitted to circumcision or carried out certain rituals. Rather, God declared Abraham righteous because he simply trusted God throughout his life. He hoped in God's faithfulness even amidst his hopeless predicament.

GOD WANTS SIMPLE FAITH

Folks often say to me, "I don't know if I have done enough to be rewarded at the Judgment Seat." Be encouraged! From Abraham's life we learn that it's not necessarily about *how much* we do; it's about trusting Him day by day, living righteously, pleasing Him by our life. It's not necessarily about how many jobs we take on in our local church, though God certainly wants us to have a servant's heart. Sometimes believers get so focused on what they *do* to the point that *doing things* becomes a ritual of sorts. It certainly makes them *feel* better.

Again, the emphasis in this entire passage is on Abraham's heart of faith, trusting God's promises, believing what He has said. This is so practical for the Christian life. Dunn says:

> God's extending righteousness to his human creation is not a once-for-all event, whether in the past or in the future. It is God's accep-

tance of persons, whether as an initial acceptance, or as a repeated sustaining (God's saving acts), or as his final acquittal. What makes a person thus acceptable to God is nothing he or she is or does, but simply the kind of faith which Abraham exercised, as described in Gen 15:6.[10]

> **Rom. 4:23-24 Now it was not written for his sake alone that it was imputed to him, but also for us. It shall be imputed to us who believe in Him who raised up Jesus our Lord from the dead,**

We should learn from Abraham's faith. God tells us that He deliberately included the account of Abraham's faith — and God's reckoning of him as righteous — for our benefit. God will also reckon us to be righteous if we believe Him as did Abraham.

The climax is found in v. 25, which is a profound statement about Jesus:

RAISED FOR OUR RIGHTEOUS LIVING

> **Rom. 4:25 who was delivered up because of our offenses, and was raised because of our justification.**

Jesus *died* so we can have forgiveness of sins, a subject that Paul will develop further in Rom. 5. But Jesus *arose* from the grave so we can live righteously, having power over the gravitational pull of sins in our lives. Bob Wilkin said:

> An alternate translation for Rom 4:25 might be *raised for our righteous living* (i.e., raised that we might live righteously in our experience).[11]

By rising again, Jesus became the victor over sin — which means we can have victory over sin too!

Do you have victory in your Christian life? Jesus was raised so you could live righteously. What a marvelous truth — His resurrection for our righteous living!

CHAPTER 12
REJOICING IN HOPE OF GLORY
ROMANS 5:1-11

Have you been singing the blues in your Christian life? Are pressures bearing down upon you? Have you grown discouraged? Then the text for this chapter is just what you need! For it is like a ray of sunshine.

Paul now pivots from Abraham, who lived as an example of faith-living, to the glorious benefits we have when we are living a justified life, in like manner as father Abraham. He gives five benefits, which will be shared below, but first, notice the statement of summary and conclusion in 5:1:

> **Rom. 5:1 Therefore, having been justified by faith, we have peace with God through our Lord Jesus Christ,**

Notice the phrase, "having been justified by faith." This could include the justification that occurred at our initial salvation, when we first believed on Jesus for eternal life. For at the point of regeneration we were declared righteous — not in a positional, legal sense, but in the sense that all of our past sins were forgiven. Those who continue to live righteously, depending on Jesus by faith for victory over sins, are justified in an ongoing sense. However, those believers who turn to a life of repeated sinning are not justified and need to confess their sins, as did King David after he had sinned with Bathsheba, thereby returning to fellowship with God and experiencing the blessedness of forgiveness. Paul referred to that incident in 4:6-8. Once David confessed his sins and became restored to fellowship, God once again reckoned him as righteous, justified.

ONGOING FAITH IN THE RESURRECTED CHRIST

Of course, the immediate context of 5:1 and the statement "having been justified by faith" is Abraham and his ongoing faith in God's promises. Consequently, God considered him *justified*. Thus, in v. 1 Paul is not referring to *all* believers. He is referring to those believers who are living righteously. That is what the context dictates. Dunn says:

> This is clearly Paul's recapitulation of the exegetical conclusion, reached in 4:22, and its extension to all who believe, in 4:23–24.[1]

> **Rom. 4:22** And therefore *"it was accounted to him* [Abraham] *for righteousness."*
> **23-24** Now it was not written for his sake alone that it was imputed [reckoned] to him, but also for us. It shall be imputed [reckoned] to us who believe in Him who raised up Jesus our Lord from the dead,

The word *believe* is an active present participle, which simply means it involves continuing action, thus it should read: "to us who *are believing* in Him who raised up Jesus." Paul has been talking about Abraham's ongoing life of faith and God's declaration of him as a righteous man because he continued to believe God. These are clearly matters of sanctification or, we could say, soul-salvation. Paul says quite clearly that Abraham's life of faith is held up as an example for us as New Testament believers. That is the context when Paul concludes in Rom 5:1, "Therefore, having been justified by faith ..." Dunn continues:

What Paul asserts of himself and his readers ("having been justified") is what Gen 15:6 asserted of Abraham. The point, which he reiterates from chap. 4, is that God justifies *by faith*—God holds a person in good standing, reckons him an acceptable partner in covenant relationship, simply on the grounds of that person's trust, his humble acceptance of God's unconditional promise to act for him.

Since the covenant with Abraham is still so much in the background, the Roman congregations would be unlikely to make the mistake of reading the aorist tense ("having been justified") as though it excluded other tenses. That is to say, they would be unlikely to regard their justification, their acceptance by God, simply as an act finished and past. Paul's use is a good deal more flexible.

And though his emphasis here is on what initially makes a person acceptable to God, the implication of the scriptural background and covenant connotations is that God's acceptance is no single once-for-all (far less merely passive) act; rather, it is God's reaching out to embrace and sustain up to and including the final verdict of acquittal. We might even paraphrase, therefore, "Since we too have now been drawn into God's promise and its fulfillment through our acceptance of that promise...."[2]

THE BENEFITS OF LIVING RIGHTEOUSLY, BY FAITH

Paul now enters into a discussion of the glorious benefits that we, as believers, have when we are living righteously, by faith, as Abraham. He gives five benefits:

1. LIVING AT PEACE WITH GOD

This is made possible through our Lord Jesus Christ, who has reconciled us to God, according to v. 10. Vincent says that *peace* here in v. 1 is "Not *contentment, satisfaction, quiet* ... but the state of *reconciliation* as opposed to enmity (v. 10)."[3]

Interestingly, John Niemela points out that there is a textual dispute here.[4] The Majority Greek text is fairly evenly divided as to two interpretive options:

a. Indicative – "we have peace." Hodges says:

The nature of this peace is of course *judicial*, since justification is the act of God as our Judge.[5]

b. Subjunctive – "let us have peace." Niemela says:

Those who see this [the subjunctive] as the correct reading believe that the experience of peace with God, rather than the positional reality, is in view.[6]

Commentators are on both sides. For example, Zane Hodges prefers the indicative, while Marvin Vincent and A.T. Robertson prefer the subjunctive. In fact, Robertson says the Greek "can only mean: *Let us enjoy peace with God* or *Let us retain peace with God.*"[7] Since I do not hold to *positional* justification, I also do not hold to *positional* peace and, therefore, hold to the *subjunctive* option.

PEACE IS CONDITIONAL, NOT POSITIONAL

Keep in mind that when we were initially saved, we became reconciled with God and thus, going forward, we are no longer His enemies, as we shall see in a moment in v. 10. But when we choose a lifestyle of sinning, we are not maintaining peaceful relations with God, but rather hostility, which incurs His wrath — all the more reason why we must live righteously by faith! How important that we retain peace with God and thereby remain reconciled to Him.

When a husband and wife are having marital problems, they might need to go to a counselor, so they can learn how to reconcile with each other and restore their marriage. During that process they remain husband and wife, but they need to reconcile. In like manner, when believers, who are God's children, continue in sinning, they remain His children, but they desperately need to reconcile with God and restore fellowship with Him, thereby returning to righteousness, so they can once again have peace with God. Righteousness is a condition for peace.

Isa. 32:17 The work of righteousness will be peace, and the effect of righteousness, quietness and assurance forever.

Jas. 3:18 Now the fruit of righteousness is sown in peace by those who make peace.

Rom. 14:17 For the kingdom of God is not eating and drinking, but righteousness and peace and joy in the Holy Spirit.

Isa. 48:22 and **57:21** "There is no peace," says the Lord, for the wicked."

Furthermore, in describing sinners, Rom. 3:17 says, "the way of peace they have not known." Those believers who are walking in the Spirit are living in peace, for the fruit of the Spirit is love, joy ... peace. In other words, peace comes when people are living righteously, which can only be appropriated through Jesus Christ. Paul emphasizes this in his epistle to the Colossians:

Col. 1:19-20 For it pleased *the Father that* in Him [Jesus Christ] all the fullness should dwell, and by Him to reconcile all things to Himself, by Him, whether things on earth or things in heaven, having made peace through the blood of His cross.
21-23 And you, who once were alienated and enemies in your mind by wicked works, yet now He has reconciled in the body of His flesh through death, to present you holy, and blameless, and above reproach in His sight—if indeed you continue in the faith, grounded and steadfast, and are not moved away from the hope of the gospel which you heard.

We have the glorious prospect of enjoying peace with the God of the universe through His Son Jesus Christ, which is a marvelous benefit! But it is incumbent upon us to retain that peace. A second benefit of being justified by faith is:

2. ACCESSING GOD'S GRACE

Rom. 5:2a through whom also we have access by faith into this grace in which we stand.

The standard textbook definition for grace is "unmerited favor," but we can do better than that. James Dunn says:

> Paul's thought is of the infinite resource of God's favor (including the royal power to translate that favor into practical effect) which lies behind the curtain of this visible world; it is that which Christ has secured for those who seek to approach God through him, trusting themselves to him.[8]

In a practical sense, God's grace is His *divine enablement*. We cannot function apart from God's grace, His divine enablement, but grace comes with a warning:

Jas. 4:6b God resists the proud, but gives grace to the humble.

Those living in sinfulness are not humble, nor are those who think they can handle their own problems. But God has unlimited grace available, that He bestows on His children who are humbly believing Him for it. Notice that Rom. 5:2 says we access His grace by faith. So if you want God's help in your daily life, claim His promises for grace: "My grace is sufficient" (2 Cor. 12:9). He also promises to give *more grace* when we need it (James 4:6a). In fact, He freely welcomes us to ask:

Heb. 4:16 Let us therefore come boldly to the throne of grace, that we may obtain mercy and find grace to help in time of need.

A third benefit of being justified by faith is:

3. REJOICING IN HOPE OF GLORIFICATION

Rom. 5:2b and rejoice in hope of the glory of God.

The Greek word translated *hope* does not have the same meaning as our English word. We think of hope as a feeling that something *might* happen, but in the Bible sense of the word, hope is confident expectation. Thus, to *rejoice in hope of the glory of God* is confident expectation that you will be glorified when you meet Jesus in judgment, as long as you have met His conditions. Those who are justified not only possess that hope (confidence), they also *rejoice* in it. The word *rejoice* could also be translated *boast*; but this is not selfish boasting; it is selfless glorying in God's will.

It is not boasting in the rituals of the law (as the Jews were doing) or rejoicing in keeping our lists and standards (as many modern Christians do). It is the idea of exulting in the truth that God promises to glorify those of His children who are living righteously, by faith, those whom He considers to be justified. It is appropriate to boast in this glorious privilege, because it is the ultimate fulfillment of God's purpose for this age.

In other words, this is His plan, His will. He has established the entire system of rewards because He is gracious and loving and wants His creation to be restored and to share in His glory. Those who live righteously, by faith, will hear "Well done!" at the Bema Seat of Christ. They will be out-resurrected (Phil. 3:11) to serve as Christ's bride and co-rulers in New Jerusalem for the entire millennial age. For God to graciously offer this system of reward is beyond comprehension. In fact, Paul said:

> **1 Cor. 2:9** Eye has not seen, nor ear heard, nor have entered into the heart of man the things which God has prepared for those who love Him.

To think that we, as believers, can confidently expect to be rewarded, if we live righteously, by faith! This should bring great joy of heart and boasting in the Lord. Are you on this pathway of inheritance? A fourth benefit of being justified by faith is:

4. GLORYING IN TRIBULATIONS

> **Rom. 5:3-4** We also glory in tribulations, knowing that tribulation produces perseverance; and perseverance, character; and character, hope.

5:3. How are tribulations a benefit, and why should we glory in them? If we respond rightly to trials, they will lead us to a glorious end. Ironically, the word *glory* in v. 3 is from the same Greek word translated *rejoice* in v. 2 — it also means *to boast*. Why would anyone want to boast in tribulations, which are trials? James put it this way:

> **Jas. 1:2-3** My brethren, count it all joy when you fall into various trials, knowing that the testing of your faith produces patience.
> **4** But let patience have *its* perfect work, that you may be perfect and complete, lacking nothing.

We should boast (in a positive sense) in our trials, knowing that God is using them to produce perseverance in our lives, which God rewards. The theme of the book of Hebrews is *persevering unto reward*, which is not "grit-your-teeth, keep-on-hangin'-on" theology. Perseverance is not merely trying harder, it is continuing to live righteously, by faith, even when the going gets tough, by depending on God's grace, His divine enablement. Jesus said:

> **Matt. 11:28** Come to Me, all *you* who labor and are heavy laden, and I will give you rest.
> **29** Take My yoke upon you and learn from Me, for I am gentle and lowly in heart, and you will find rest for your souls.
> **30** For My yoke *is* easy and My burden is light.

PERSEVERANCE PRODUCES "APPROVEDNESS"

5:4. When you learn to persevere, despite the trials and burdens of life, maintaining a sweet spirit of submission before the Lord, your perseverance will produce *character*. This word is not the best translation because it's too vague in English. According to Hodges, the Greek word translated *character* could be translated "approvedness."[9] Although that's a bit awkward in English, it accurately sums up the idea of the word. This same basic Greek word is used in 2 Tim. and James:

2 Tim. 2:15 Be diligent to present yourself *approved* to God. (emphasis added)

Jas. 1:12 Blessed *is* the man who endures temptation; for when he has been *approved*, he will receive the crown of life which the Lord has promised to those who love Him. (emphasis added)

Tribulations produce perseverance and perseverance produces "approvedness." All believers should strive to be approved by Jesus in their daily living, so they can ultimately be approved at His Judgment Seat. That is the highest of acclamation, and will result in great reward. Paul also talked about this in Philippians.

Phil. 3:14 I press toward the goal for the prize of the upward call of God in Christ Jesus.

Peter also talked about this, referring to it as *abundant entrance into the kingdom* — see 2 Peter 1:5-11.

"APPROVEDNESS" PRODUCES HOPE

Notice the end of Rom. 5:4 — *character* or "approvedness" produces *hope*, that is, confident expectation of reward. Dunn says:

> The whole process produces hope because it indicates that the process of salvation is under way: when suffering is experienced not as a contradiction to faith or occasion to renounce God, but as a strengthening of patience and maturing of character, it stimulates hope in the grace that is having such effect. The whole process produces hope because for Paul it is ... the process whereby God recreates humanity in his own image—what he refers to elsewhere as the wasting away of the visible man which is the necessary complement to the renewal of the hidden man (2 Cor 4:16).[10]

By "process of salvation" Dunn means soul-salvation, resulting in the revealing of the sons of glory (Rom. 8:19), for which creation eagerly awaits. This prospect should bring great hope to righteous believers.

> **Rom. 5:5a Now hope does not disappoint [i.e., make ashamed].**

Many believers will be ashamed at the Judgment Seat, for they will be naked, i.e., they will not be given clothing of glorification, which is encasement in light. Adam and Eve were apparently glorified before the fall, but when they sinned, they lost that encasement of light and became naked and ashamed.

Traditional Christianity teaches that all Christians will be glorified, but that is not correct. Only those who have persevered in righteousness and have been approved by God will be glorified in some degree. If you are on the narrow path that leads to life, then rejoice (boast) in your tribulations, for you possess *hope* of glorification. You will not be ashamed. The tribulations are doing God's work in your life, bringing you to the point where you will be able to stand before Jesus "mature and complete, lacking nothing," as James 1:4 indicates. A fifth benefit of being justified by faith is:

5. EXPERIENCING GOD'S LOVE IN THE SOUL

> **Rom. 5:5 Now hope does not disappoint, because the love of God has been poured out in our hearts by the Holy Spirit who was given to us.**

I have read many revival histories over the years, and one intriguing concept that occasionally comes up in times of revival is being overwhelmed with God's love — so much so that the person was afraid it would kill them. Is this too much of a good thing? I don't know, but it sounds thrilling. Paul prayed in Eph. 3 that the believers ...

> **Eph. 3:17** being rooted and grounded in love, may be able to comprehend with all the saints what *is* the width and length and depth and height—to know the love of Christ which passes knowledge; that you may be filled with all the fullness of God.

God's love is multi-dimensional and beyond comprehension, yet Paul prays that the saints will be able to comprehend its "mind-blowing" proportions. Those who are being justified by faith regularly experience this love of God being poured out in their soul. The result is a keen awareness of God's love, along with an intensified love for others, just as He has. Thus, we have His provision to love others as He loves us — what a marvelous truth!

FAITH AND HOPE AND LOVE

Interestingly, the trio of faith, hope and love are all mentioned in Rom. 5:1-5. In 1 Cor. 13 Paul said faith, hope, and love are the three virtues that abide or remain. It's as if the essence of spiritual life is summed up in merely three simple words. Ironically, though the words are simple, the truths they represent are complex and profound, and therefore grasped by few believers. Perhaps that is because only a small minority are being justified by faith.

Incidentally, Paul's use of the faith-hope-love triplet in 1 Cor. 13:13 is not a lone reference. The three words are used together in several places in the New Testament, in addition to Rom. 5:1-5 (see Gal. 5:5-6; Col. 1:3-5; 1 Thess. 1:2-3; 5:8; Heb. 10:22-24). So this is a very important concept, repeated throughout the New Testament. Repetition in the Scriptures means that God does not want us to miss truth that is far-reaching and consequential.

In fact, the entire book of Romans is essentially an exposition of faith, hope, and love. *Faith living* is the Christ-life of victory, which Paul deals with extensively in Rom. 6-8. *Hope living* is kingdom preparedness, which Paul speaks about here in ch. 5, but again in chs. 8, 15. *Love living* is the ultimate demonstration of Christ's character and attributes through our lives, which Paul emphasizes in chs. 13-15. I believe *love living* is also recognizing His plan to save all mankind, which is seen later in ch. 5 and also in chs. 9-11, 14. It's all here in Romans, summarized in 5:1-5.

By way of review, those who are living righteously, by faith, are experiencing five glorious benefits:

1. Living at peace with God

2. Accessing God's grace
3. Rejoicing in hope of glorification
4. Glorying in tribulations
5. Experiencing God's love in their soul

In the next few verses of Rom. 5, Paul pauses for a moment to explain how all of this is made possible.

> **Rom. 5:6 For when we were still without strength, in due time Christ died for the ungodly.**
> **5:7 For scarcely for a righteous man will one die; yet perhaps for a good man someone would even dare to die.**
> **5:8 But God demonstrates His own love toward us, in that while we were still sinners, Christ died for us.**

CHRIST DIED FOR SINNERS, BUT WHICH SINNERS DOES PAUL HAVE IN MIND?

Christ didn't die for the righteous; He died for sinners, and He did so out of great love. Why would Paul stop to say this to believers, who comprise his audience? In fact, Paul even includes himself — "we being without strength" (weak) (v. 6) — "we being sinners" (v. 8). Keep in mind that Paul's focus in ch. 2-4 has been the *Jewish* believers, who think they are being sanctified and approved before God by keeping the Mosaic rituals. Paul has hammered away at this incorrect thinking in the previous three chapters of his epistle, demonstrating some key points:

1. Even believers sin but must confess those sins and choose to go on living righteously.
2. Mere works of the law do not produce righteousness (soul-salvation).
3. Righteousness is obtained by continued faith in Jesus.

He already made these points in Rom. 3, which I have annotated below:

Rom. 3:21-22a But now the righteousness of God apart from the law is revealed ... even the righteousness of God, through faith in Jesus Christ, to all and on all who believe [literally, *are believing* – this is a present, active participle].

23-26 For all have sinned and fall short of the glory of God [even believers!], being justified freely by His grace through the redemption that is in Christ Jesus, whom God set forth as a propitiation by His blood, through faith, to demonstrate His righteousness ... that He might be just and the justifier of the one who has faith in Jesus [*ongoing faith* in Jesus is implied].

This is consistent with what the apostle John says:

1 John 1:6 If we say that we have fellowship with Him, and walk in darkness, we lie and do not practice the truth.

7 But if we walk in the light as He is in the light, we have fellowship with one another, and the blood of Jesus Christ His Son cleanses us from all sin.

THE ONGOING EFFICACY OF CHRIST'S BLOOD ATONEMENT

Christ's blood atonement is not merely efficacious for *initially* saving us from our sins (as pictured by the Passover); it is efficacious for *continuing* to save us from our sins when we confess them and live righteously (as pictured by the Old Testament sacrificial system). That is Paul's point in 3:10, 23 and here again in 5:8.

> **Rom. 5:8 But God demonstrates His own love toward us, in that while we were still sinners, Christ died for us.**

Even as believers, we need His continued forgiveness and cleansing because we are *still sinners*. Now v. 9 makes sense:

> **Rom. 5:9 Much more then, having now been justified by His blood, we shall be saved from wrath through Him.**

SAVED FROM WRATH

Having been initially justified (declared righteous) by His blood, we can continue being justified (declared righteous) by His blood. Indeed, if we continue on that path, we will be *saved from wrath*. Dunn says:

> Paul obviously seeks to strike a balance between the once-for-allness of what has already happened ("we have been justified/reconciled") and the not yet of a salvation in process but as yet incomplete (including "the redemption of the body"—8:23).[11]

Of course, *salvation* in these chapters of Romans, as established by Paul in 1:16, is soul-salvation, progressing in sanctification. *Wrath* (*saved from wrath*, v. 9) does not refer to Hell, as so many have incorrectly taught. *Wrath* is God's judgment, which in this present life is God giving us over to our own ways, which is a dreadful prospect. In the future, it is negative reward at the Judgment Seat of Christ, which is even more dreadful. In this context, vs. 10-11 now make sense:

> **Rom. 5:10 For if when we were enemies we were reconciled to God through the death of His Son, much more, having been reconciled, we shall be saved by His life.**
> **5:11 And not only *that*, but we also rejoice in God through our Lord Jesus Christ, through whom we have now received the reconciliation.**

REMAINING RECONCILED AND JUSTIFIED

Reconciliation is restoration to favor with God through Jesus Christ, so that we are no longer his enemy. We were initially *justified* (declared righteous) and *reconciled to* (restored to favor with) God when we were initially saved — and that means we have the prospect of living peaceably with God. But, having been justified and reconciled, we are *saved* (i.e., we maintain *ongoing* salvation — sanctification or soul-salvation) *by his life.*

In other words, Jesus died and shed His blood to justify us and reconcile us to God by forgiving all our past sins. Jesus rose, victorious over sin and death, to continue justifying us when we live righteously by continued faith in Jesus — "He was raised because of our justification" (4:25). Just as *justification* has two stages (*initial*, for the past, and *ongoing*, for the present), so also *reconciliation* is twofold. That is why Paul says, *"Having been justified by faith, let us retain peace with God through our Lord Jesus Christ"* (v. 1). As if to say: *remain reconciled with God.* When we do, we can say with Paul:

5:11. *We ... rejoice in God through our Lord Jesus Christ, through whom we have now received the reconciliation.*

OUR MINISTRY OF RECONCILIATION

Consequently, we have a responsibility:

> **2 Cor. 5:18-19** Now all things *are* of God, who has reconciled us to Himself through Jesus Christ, and has given us the ministry of reconciliation, that is, that God was in Christ reconciling the world to Himself, not imputing [reckoning] their trespasses to them, and has committed to us the word of reconciliation.

What is the ministry of reconciliation to which we are called? It is defined earlier in the text.

> **2 Cor. 5:14-15** For the love of Christ compels us, because we judge thus: that if One died for all, then all died; and He died for all, that those who live should live no longer for themselves, but for Him who died for them and rose again.

Did you notice the double aspects of reconciliation that we are to share with people?

1. God has reconciled the world to Himself through the death of Jesus Christ, so that He does not reckon you as being under the penalty of sin (2 Cor. 5:18-19). This is what I call *salvation in the first*

degree and applies to all mankind, whether they realize it or not. (see the *Four Degrees of Salvation* in Addendum 2).

2. God wants you to reconcile with Him through His Son Jesus (*third degree salvation*, for those who believe Him for eternal, age-lasting life). Then He wants you to stop living for yourself and live righteously (*fourth degree salvation*, for those who continue believing Him for sanctification unto reward). *Second degree salvation* is for those who never believe Jesus for age-lasting life (either because they don't know about this marvelous gift or don't understand it), yet they believe God and live righteously. The benefits of this degree of salvation are significantly less. See Addendum 2 for a full explanation. Zane Hodges says:

> The reconciliation in view here [in Rom. 5:11] ... is effected by Christ's death, but must also be received by men ... This double aspect of reconciliation is also presented by Paul in 2 Cor 5:18-21. There God is seen as "reconciling the world to Himself" at the cross and subsequently sending forth messengers "pleading" with men to "be reconciled to God." True reconciliation with God required God's initiative in the death of Christ, and it requires our response to Him by faith.[12]

THE GOAL OF RECONCILIATION

What's the goal of urging men to reconcile with God? Is it to lead them to pray a prayer so they can go to Heaven when they die? No! It's to encourage them to believe Christ's promise of eternal (age-lasting) life, then continue believing on the resurrected Christ, who dwells within, as the provision to *live righteously*.

> **2 Cor. 5:15** that those who live should live no longer for themselves, but for Him who died for them and rose again.

This is repeated by Paul in 2 Cor. 5:

> **2 Cor. 5:20** Now then, we are ambassadors for Christ, as though God

were pleading through us: we implore *you* on Christ's behalf, be reconciled to God.

21 For He made Him who knew no sin *to be* sin for us, that we might become the righteousness of God in Him.

The verb *might become* is in the subjunctive mood (in Greek), which is the mood of potential. In other words, this does not automatically happen when someone is initially saved. Rather, it is the *goal* of the Christian life, made possible by Christ's death, but conditioned on living righteously. Yet, so often, the emphasis in so-called "soulwinning" is about leading a person to pray a prayer to invite Jesus to save them, as if that were the end in itself, and then the ambassador has done his/her duty.

No! That's only the beginning! The Great Commission of Jesus (Matt. 28:19-20) is focused on teaching people to reconcile with God and then stay reconciled by living righteously, by depending on Jesus. Dunn says:

> God's purpose to draw humankind back into proper relationship with him is something accomplished not in a once-for-all instant, either in the death of Jesus or in the event of conversion, but in an ongoing process in which the power of Christ's risen life ... plays a controlling role.[13]

No wonder Paul says:

Rom. 5:11. *We ... rejoice in God through our Lord Jesus Christ, through whom we have now received the reconciliation.*

Are you rejoicing in hope of glory? You are, if you are living righteously and remaining reconciled to God. If you are not living righteously, then bow before Jesus and reconcile with Him today!

CHAPTER 13
GRACE WINS!
ROMANS 5:12-21

The latter half of Romans 5 presents two kings — the *King of Sin* and the *King of Grace*. It is appropriate to call them *kings*, because sin and grace are both said to *reign* in v. 21. When speaking of *sin*, it is also appropriate to refer to its sidekick *death* as reigning also, and the sidekick of *grace* is *life*, which also reigns with grace.

Rom. 5:12-21 is one of the most important sections of the book of Romans. Indeed, in my opinion it is one of the most important sections in the New Testament. These verses serve as a resounding conclusion to the first five chapters of Romans, as Paul prepares to make practical application to the Christian life in chs. 6-8.

ANOTHER OLD TESTAMENT ILLUSTRATION — ADAM

In v. 14 Paul introduces another Old Testament character who has not yet been mentioned — Adam. Why does he do this? Keep in mind that in the first five chapters of Romans Paul has primarily targeted the Jewish believers and their reliance on the Mosaic law, thus the patriarch Moses is clearly implied. To broaden the circle to include Gentile believers, Paul steps back further in time, first bringing in Abraham as an illustration of living by faith.

Remember that God promised to Abraham that he would become "heir of the world" (Rom. 4:13), a "father of many nations"

(Gen. 17:5), because he believed God and lived by faith. Thus, Paul includes all believers — for Abraham is not only the *genetic* father of the Jews, he is also the *spiritual* father of those who believe in Jesus Christ (the church). Furthermore, he is the father of those believers — Jewish or Gentile — who *continue* believing in Jesus for daily victory — the sons to glory! Abraham's heritage will ultimately extend to the entire world. Gen. 17:5 says *all nations* and Gen. 12:3 says *all families*. So Paul steps back from Moses to Abraham, and then goes back all the way to Adam, the progenitor of the human race. For Adam is the father of *all* mankind.

SALVATION FOR ALL MANKIND

Thus, God's saving plan in sending Jesus is not merely for the Jews or Israel, nor is it merely for those who believe Him for eternal (age-lasting) life (i.e., church-age believers). It is for *all mankind*! What a glorious truth that traditional theology does not recognize.

The book of Revelation pictures future universal worship of Jesus around His throne that includes this song:

> **Rev. 5:9** "You are worthy ... for You were slain, and have redeemed us to God by Your blood out of every tribe and tongue and people and nation."

> **5:13** And every creature which is in heaven and on the earth and under the earth and such as are in the sea, and all that are in them, I heard saying: "Blessing and honor and glory and power *be* to Him who sits on the throne, and to the Lamb, forever and ever!"

But that is the *end* of the story. We must see the whole panorama, beginning with a brief summary of Rom. 5:12-21:

Through Adam, *sin* entered into the world, resulting in man spiraling downward to death. Through Christ *grace* entered into the world, resulting in resurrection and life for all, leading to reigning (v. 17) in His kingdom, for those who appropriate the life. Thus, Paul writes of two kings, so to speak — *sin*, with its prince of *death* (represented by the first Adam) — and *grace*, with its princes of *right-*

eousness and *life* (represented by Jesus, the last Adam). As Paul is going to explain, *grace* wins! Glory!

But again, that is the *end* of the story. We must start at the beginning, which is quite dismal:

ONE MAN INTRODUCED SIN INTO THE WORLD

Rom. 5:12 Therefore, just as through one man sin entered the world, and death through sin, and thus death spread to all men, because all sinned—

Jan Bonda (1918-1997) was a Dutch Reformed pastor in the Netherlands who changed much of his Reformation theology after studying Romans. He wrote an excellent book: *The One Purpose of God*, in which he comments:

> Following Augustine, tradition speaks of original sin or hereditary sin. It says: Because Adam sinned, humankind sinned even before birth, and as a result all must die! This line of thinking is at odds with what Paul wrote earlier. All evidence suggests that in speaking about God's "reckoning" of sins, Paul refers to sins committed by the individual himself and does not speak in terms of hereditary sin as a guilt of the first human, which is "reckoned" as the sin of all his posterity.[1]

In a footnote, Bonda adds:

> The Vulgate renders Romans 5:12 as "in quo omnes peccaverunt" ("in whom all sinned"). Augustine understood these words as a reference to hereditary sin: "in Adam all have sinned" (*Enchiridion*, 26). He taught that because of original sin unbaptized children will be eternally lost; nevertheless they will suffer the lightest degree of punishment (*Enchiridion*, 93).[2]

He continues on in the main text:

All human beings are ... slaves to sin (Rom. 6:6, 17). They do not commit sin because they are forced to do so; they are the ones who sin and they themselves bear responsibility for what they do. That is the element of truth in the doctrine of hereditary sin. But tradition has burdened this doctrine with other implications. It suggests that, because of this link with our ancestors, hereditary sin is a matter of inescapable fate! And its final consequence will be that the vast majority of humankind will end in perdition. That is the opposite of what Paul is arguing![3]

Zane Hodges adds:

The entrance of sin and death into mankind's experience has become universal. *And so* the result of its entrance through one man is that **death came to all men because all have sinned.** This statement is plain and direct. Yet in one of the strangest turns in the exegesis of Romans, this straightforward statement has been made to teach that all mankind sinned in Adam as its seminal head. But no such idea is found here or anywhere else in the Bible.

Paul's meaning is quite uncomplicated. Death became a universal experience precisely *because all* human beings *have sinned.* In other words, "the wages of sin is death" (see 6:23).

Paul is not concerned here with the "mechanics" of the transmission of a sinful nature from generation to generation. It is enough to know that what Adam and Eve did in the garden has produced descendants who, without exception, have committed sin.[4]

Verse 12 says sin *entered* — as if Adam opened the door and Sin (personified) crept in, pervading all of humanity, bringing death in its wake. If the text were to end there, then the fate of mankind would be dismal indeed, for the King of Sin and Death would win. However, that is not the right ending, for Paul makes quite clear that the King of Grace and Life wins!

Skipping the huge parenthesis (vs. 13-17) for the time being, we can see the continuity of the text from v. 12 to vs. 18-19:

Rom. 5:12 Therefore, just as through one man sin

> entered the world, and death through sin, and thus death spread to all men, because all sinned—
> 5:18 Therefore as by the offence of one *judgment came* upon all men to condemnation; even so by the righteousness of one *the free gift came* upon all men unto justification of life.
> 5:19 For as by one man's disobedience many were made sinners, so by the obedience of one shall many be made righteous.

SIN (SINGULAR) VS. SINS (PLURAL)

Mankind has two problems: sin (singular) and sins (plural). Understanding the distinction is critical. Sin (singular) is the natural inclination to commit sins (plural), which put us at enmity with God. James Dunn says:

> "Sin" is ... the force which functions as the antecedent to particular acts of sin, that power which man experiences influencing his desires and choices to act against his best interests as a creature of God (the analysis already provided in 1:18–32).[5]

As both Bonda and Hodges pointed out earlier, sin and death became mankind's universal problem because of Adam introducing it into the world, but it is not passed along in some sort of genetic (seminal) sense, as is commonly taught, based on assumptions. Rather, Rom. 5:12 is clear: "death spread to all men, *because all sinned*."

Death is the penalty for sin (singular), and the implication is that, apart from some radical solution on God's part, death would be never-ending separation from God. But thanks be to God, Jesus has delivered mankind from sin and death by His redemption.

> **2 Tim. 1:10** Jesus Christ ... has abolished death and brought life and immortality to light.

Heb. 2:14-15 Inasmuch then as the children [i.e., mankind] have partaken of flesh and blood, He Himself likewise shared in the same, that through death He might destroy him who had the power of death, that is, the devil, and release those who through fear of death were all their lifetime subject to bondage.

John the Baptist emphasized that Jesus is the Lamb of God who takes away the sin (singular) *of the world!* The Lamb of God imagery implies that He paid the penalty for sin (singular) by His blood atonement — as typified by the Old Testament lambs. Consequently, no one will experience never-ending separation from God. That is why Jesus is called *the Savior of the world* (John 4:42) and *the Savior of all men* (1 Tim. 4:10). He has already saved every person from sin, which is man's universal problem via Adam, whether the individual realizes it or not.

Incidentally, this is why we know that babies and young children that die will not be condemned. The penalty for sin has already been paid for all mankind. Jesus is the Savior of all men, and that includes babies and young children too. We see this truth taught here in our text also:

Rom. 5:18 Therefore, as through one man's offense judgment came to *all* men, resulting in condemnation, even so through one Man's righteous act the free gift came to *all* men, resulting in justification of life.

19 For as by one man's disobedience *many* were made sinners, so also by one Man's obedience *many* will be made righteous. (italics added)

The word *made* in Rom. 5:19 means "designated" or "constituted." The use of *all* in v. 18 and *many* in v. 19 refer to all humanity. This is also seen in v. 15:

Rom. 5:15 For if by the one man's offense *many* died, much more the grace of God and the gift by the grace of the one Man, Jesus Christ, abounded to *many*. (italics added)

CHRIST'S DEATH RECONCILED THE WORLD TO GOD

James Dunn says:

> The "many" would be recognized as an acceptable variation for the "all men" of v 12, since it is humankind in the mass which Paul clearly has in view in both cases ... Paul was viewing the epoch of Adam as a whole, from beginning to end; for though the rule of the present age has not yet finished, in that all have not yet died, nevertheless the fact remains that death is the inescapable bottom line for all without exception, as certain for those belonging to this age now or in the future as it was for those already dead ...
>
> For the second time in the verse, Paul uses ... "the many," to once again underline the epochal significance of Christ's gracious act: it has affected an epochful of humanity, humankind in that age in the mass; and it has determined the character of that epoch from beginning to end as the age of overflowed grace.[6]

This marvelous truth is also found in Corinthians:

> **1 Cor. 15:22** For as in Adam *all* die, even so in Christ *all* shall be made alive.

> **2 Cor. 5:19** God was in Christ reconciling *the world* to Himself, not imputing their trespasses to them. (emphasis added)

God has already reconciled the entire world to Himself through Christ. Even though *all* mankind has a sin problem that results in sinning ("because all have sinned") and ultimately death (in the sense of never-ending separation from God), Jesus paid mankind's sin penalty. Consequently, *all* humans have been redeemed by Jesus and reconciled to God and can live righteously. This is wonderfully good news!

THE LAMB SLAIN BEFORE THE FOUNDATION OF THE WORLD

The death of Jesus is both *retroactive* and *proactive*. He is the Lamb slain before the foundation of the world. His death continues to redeem every generation of mankind — prior to His historical death and even long after it. Consequently, *all* mankind has been saved — *in this sense*. This is salvation in the "first degree," which makes possible salvation in greater degrees (see Addendum 2). Additional salvation is necessary, because mankind still has a problem — choosing to commit sins (plural), for which he will be judged.

Unbelievers will give an account at the Great White Throne *after* the Millennium. Believers (those who are *in Christ*) will give an account at the Judgment Seat of Christ *before* the Millennium. That is why Paul proclaimed:

> **Acts 17:30-31** God ... commands all men everywhere to repent, because He has appointed a day on which He will judge the world in righteousness by the Man whom He has ordained. He has given assurance of this to all by raising Him from the dead.

Thankfully, the death of Jesus offers greater degrees of salvation which, if received, can result in righteous living and preparedness for meeting Him in judgment — see Addendum 2 for more details.

Having understood the big picture of Rom. 5:12-21, we can now go on to the parenthesis in vs. 13-17, looking at the important details:

> **Rom. 5:13 (For until the law sin was in the world, but sin is not imputed when there is no law.**
> **5:14 Nevertheless death reigned from Adam to Moses, even over those who had not sinned according to the likeness of the transgression of Adam, who is a type of Him who was to come.**

ADAM A TYPE OF THE ONE TO COME

5:13. Hodges translates the word *imputed* in v. 13 as *itemized*, commenting:

> Paul's idea seems to be that in the period before the law a specific list of sins could not be drawn up which had universal application to all men … Though badly defaced, the law is nevertheless written on each conscience in a way that permits God to judge individuals as individuals … But the absence of law means that man's failures cannot be codified into a specific list of infractions.[7]

5.14. Despite the imprecision of counting before the law was given, man, nevertheless, sinned and was under the sentence of death as in any generation, even those who did not transgress as in like manner as Adam (willful disobedience to a direct command). Why does Paul bother to make this point? I personally think there are three reasons:

1) To demonstrate that humanity from Adam all the way to the end of time, have shared or will share in this inescapable human problem: sin resulting in death;

2) To announce that Jesus provided the way of escape from sin's reign of death for all mankind (both retroactively and proactively) through Jesus Christ; and

3) To show Israel that because they were given the law, they are all the more culpable.

The end of v. 14 says that Adam is a type of Him who was to come. How can Adam be a type of Jesus, seeing that Adam sinned, but Jesus did not? Adam represents the entire human race in his sin and death, just as Christ represents the entire human race in His grace and life. Furthermore, as Dunn puts it:

> Adam is the exemplar or pattern of Christ in that both are epochal figures: both by one decisive act determine the character of the subsequent epoch for those belonging to that epoch … As Adam by his transgression determined the character of the present age, so Christ has determined the character of the age to come.[8]

That leads to v. 15:

> **Rom. 5:15 But the free gift *is* not like the offense. For if by the one man's offense many died, much more the grace of God and the gift by the grace of the one Man, Jesus Christ, abounded to many.**

CHRIST'S GIFT OF LIFE FOR THE *MANY*

Man did not *do* anything for Christ's redemption. Christ simply offered Himself as a gift to mankind. In v. 15, it seems *the free gift* is not referring specifically to the gift of eternal life. Rather, it is referring to *the gift of Jesus* as a sacrifice to redeem mankind in a more general sense. Adam sinned and thereby gave the "gift" of *death* to mankind, while Jesus died and gave the gift of His *life* to mankind — entirely as an act of grace on His part.

Notice again the dual usage of the word *many*, which has to mean *all*. Adam's offense resulted in the death of *all mankind* — referred to as *many*. To be parallel, Christ's gift abounding to *many*, must mean *to all mankind*.

> **Rom. 5:16 And the gift *is* not like *that which came* through the one who sinned. For the judgment *which came* from one *offense resulted* in condemnation, but the free gift *which came* from many offenses *resulted* in justification.**

Paul repackages what he has already said, adding a few new details. Adam's sin resulted in *condemnation*. This is not the best translation. *Condemnation* — according to Moulton and Milligan, as quoted in Hodges — means: "the punishment following a judicial sentence" or "penal servitude." This prompted Hodges to write:

> *The judgment* passed on Adam led to a *penalty*, i.e., *servitude to sin*. Adam was now spiritually dead, and physically dying, and in this condition he fell under *bondage to sin*.[9]

In contrast, Christ's free gift results in "restoration of the criminal, the fresh chance given to him."[10]

The word *justification* in v. 16 doesn't merely mean *righteousness*; it means *righteous acts*. It is the same Greek word translated *righteous act* in v. 18 — referring to Christ's righteous act of dying on Calvary, and it is the same Greek word translated *righteous acts* in:

> **Rev. 19:8** And to her it was granted to be arrayed in fine linen, clean and bright, for the fine linen is the *righteous acts* of the saints. (emphasis added)

DEGREES OF SALVATION

Thus, Jesus *reverses* mankind's slavery to sin, resulting in first degree salvation for all, so that man can produce righteous acts by believing God (second degree salvation) and avoid the lake of fire. When a person believes on Jesus for eternal (age-lasting) life, all of their past sins are forgiven (third degree salvation). Thus, they are justified at that point in time. Those who continue, by faith, to live righteously, remain justified, for they are carrying out righteous acts through Jesus Christ who enables (fourth degree salvation). This results in reward, as seen in v. 17:

> **Rom. 5:17 For if by the one man's offense death reigned through the one, much more those who receive abundance of grace and of the gift of righteousness will reign in life through the One, Jesus Christ.**

GRACE'S REIGN OF LIFE

In contrast to sin's reign of death, Paul here showcases grace's reign of life. The word *receive* in v. 17 is an active present participle, thus a continuing tense. It literally translates, "those who *are receiving* abundance of grace and the gift of righteousness [by faith, 3:22] will reign." Hodges says,

The future tense in this verse is precisely analogous to the future in 5:9.[11]

Rom. 5:9 Much more then, having now been justified by His blood, we shall be saved from wrath through Him.

Those who are living righteously, by faith — and are therefore, considered justified by God — will be saved from wrath, both *now* in this life and at the Bema Seat of Christ. That is essentially the same as saying those who are receiving God's abundant grace to live righteously by faith will reign in life — *now*, through victory over sinning — and *in the age to come*, through co-rulership with Christ. God's grace is abundant! He keeps giving more grace, whenever we need it and ask Him for it, so that we can live victoriously.

One more important detail needs to be added to the exposition of v. 18:

> **Rom. 5:18 Therefore, as through one man's offense *judgment* came to all men, resulting in condemnation, even so through one Man's righteous act *the free gift came* to all men, resulting in justification of life.**

The word *condemnation* in v. 18 is the same as in v. 16 and means "servitude to sin." The word *justification* (Greek *dikaiosis*) in v. 18 is a slightly different noun than used in v. 16 (Greek *dikaioma*). In v. 16 it means "righteous acts," but in 5:18 and 4:25 the word means "righteous living," according to Bob Wilkin. Thus, he says it should be translated in 5:18b, *through one righteous action grace came for all men to produce righteous living sourced in [God's] life.*[12]

As mentioned in a previous chapter. The Christian life is not about praying to ask Jesus to be your Savior so you can go to Heaven when you die. It is believing on Jesus for eternal (age-lasting) life, then appropriating God's abundant grace to live righteously. The purpose of the Christian life is summed up in:

2 Cor. 5:15 He died for all, that those who live should live no longer for themselves, but for Him who died for them and rose again.

21b that we might become the righteousness of God in Him.

RIGHTEOUS BEHAVIOR THE PURPOSE OF THE CHRISTIAN LIFE

Just as Adam's sin results in judgment (servitude to sin) for all men, for all have sinned, so Christ's righteous act (crucifixion) results in the free gift to all men unto righteous living which is sourced in Christ's resurrected life.

All mankind will ultimately be saved and living righteously by the end of all the ages. For multitudes, it will come after they have spent time in the lake of fire, which is remedial. But in the end, *all* will be saved — *every* knee will bow and *every* tongue will confess that Jesus Christ is Lord to the glory of God the Father, and that includes things in heaven, things on earth, and things under the earth (Phil 2:10-11). *Every* means *every* and *all* means *all*!

> **Rom. 5:20-21** Moreover the law entered that the offense might abound. But where sin abounded, grace abounded much more, so that as sin reigned in death, even so grace might reign through righteousness to eternal life through Jesus Christ our Lord.

Perhaps for the benefit of the Jewish believers, Paul adds: "The law entered that the offense might abound." This must have been shocking news for the Jews to hear! Dunn says, "Far from being an answer to sin, as his fellow Jews naturally assumed, it increased sin!"[13] Hodges adds:

> Sin undergoes "enlargement" through the coming of the law. The law is the divine magnifying glass under which man's sinfulness can in no way be minimized. But in sharp contrast to this grim reality, in which sin has been powerfully magnified by the law, stands God's magnificent grace.[14]

Where sin abounded, grace *superabounded*. Grace always trumps sin, and we should be most thankful for that!

THE KING OF SIN VS. THE KING OF GRACE

In the final analysis we find two kings in Rom. 5 — the King of Sin, who reigns in death, and the King of Grace, who reigns through righteousness to life for the age. Hodges concludes:

> God's grace reigns when the believer reigns "in life" through Jesus Christ. That is to say, when the believer gains victory over sin, grace is reigning in his life experience.[15]

Verse 18 describes the *provision* for righteous living, which is sourced in God's life, producing soul-salvation. Verse 21 describes the *reward* for righteous living, which leads to eternal (age-lasting) life, in the sense of rulership (v. 17). That is why crowns are promised in the Scriptures for the faithful:

> **2 Tim. 4:7-8** I have fought the good fight, I have finished the race, I have kept the faith. Finally, there is laid up for me the crown of righteousness, which the Lord, the righteous Judge, will give to me on that Day, and not to me only but also to all who have loved His appearing.

> **Rev. 2:10b** Be faithful until death, and I will give you the crown of life.

Will you be rewarded for being faithful and living righteously?

CHAPTER 14
BURIED IN DEATH, RISEN IN LIFE
ROMANS 6:1-14

Chapters 6-8 of Romans put into practice the important theology of the earlier chapters. Notice that Paul starts with an important question:

> **Rom. 6:1** What shall we say then? Shall we continue [literally, *persist*] in sin that grace may abound?

GRACE ABOUNDS, BUT DON'T KEEP SINNING!

Paul anticipates questions arising from the believers at Rome, so he proactively squelches them before they can ever be asked. Keep in mind how the apostle ended the previous chapter:

> **Rom. 5:20b-21** Where sin abounded, grace abounded much more, so that as sin reigned in death, even so grace might reign through righteousness to eternal life through Jesus Christ our Lord.

Grace abounds much more than sin. That is a glorious thought! Despite man's overwhelming sins, grace always triumphs — literally *superabounds* — when man accepts it from God. Thus, Paul starts out ch. 6 by cutting off at the pass the incorrect line of thinking that because God's grace always abounds and wins the victory over sin,

God's children can keep on sinning and experience God's abounding grace.

Some might tend to think, "Well, I can just keep on sinning then, since God's grace is going to cover it." That's a terrible conclusion! The objective in the Christian life is to stop sinning, so that we might live in holiness, pleasing God. For as seen in the previous two chapters, the purpose of the Christian life is summed up beautifully in two verses:

> **2 Cor. 5:15** He died for all, that those who live should live no longer for themselves, but for Him who died for them and rose again.
>
> **21** For He made Him who knew no sin *to be* sin for us, that we might become the righteousness of God in Him.

The goal of the Christian life is living righteously, victorious over sin, living as Jesus lived! That should drive our daily decisions and thoughts and emotions (aspects of the soul).

HOLINESS, THE PATHWAY TO SOUL-SALVATION

Starting in ch. 6, Paul begins a detailed discussion of soul-salvation, which is essentially the process of sanctification. Incidentally, *sanctification* comes from the Greek word *hagiasmos*, which is from *hagios*, meaning *holy*. The Greek word *hagiasmos* is used twice in Rom. 6:

> **Rom. 6:19b** Just as you presented your members *as* slaves of uncleanness, and of lawlessness ... so now present your members *as* slaves *of* righteousness for holiness.
>
> **22** But now having been set free from sin, and having become slaves of God, you have your fruit to holiness, and the end, everlasting life (i.e., life for the age). (parenthesis added)

Those who are living in holiness, finding victory over sin as a general rule of life, are on the pathway of soul-salvation. If they continue on that narrow way throughout life, they will be rewarded when they meet Jesus in judgment. Some Christians respond to this by thinking, "Okay, then I'll live a holy life!" Not so fast! A word of warning: You cannot produce holy living by yourself. Multitudes of Christians *try*, but it merely becomes an effort of one's own strength and flesh.

Paul has already dealt with the first century Jewish error of attempting to keep the Mosaic rituals for holiness. "It won't work," Paul essentially says, "You need Jesus, and you must depend on Him by faith." Of course, the twenty-first century version of the first century Jewish error is the mindset of many evangelical Christians, that "if I keep a list of rules or standards, I will be spiritual." Again, you need Jesus, and you must depend on Him by faith. The songwriter wrote: "The arm of flesh will fail you, ye dare not trust your own."[1]

THE CHRIST-LIFE OF VICTORY

To live a holy life that will result in hearing "Well done!" at the Bema Seat, we need Jesus, His life being lived through ours. This is often called the "Christ-life." Some refer to it as the *abundant life*, the *deeper life*, the *exchanged life*, or the *Spirit-filled life*. This happens when believers appropriate the provision of Jesus within to live victoriously over sin. Paul is going to tell believers how to do that here in ch. 6.

Notice Paul's answer to their hypothetical question, "Shall we continue [literally, *persist*] in sin that grace may abound?" —

Rom. 6:2a Certainly not! [KJV: *God forbid!*]

The word *God* is not in the Greek text, prompting some English translations to use other exclamatory phrases:

- (NKJV) Certainly not!
- (NASB) May it never be!
- (HCSB) Absolutely not!
- (ESV) By no means!

Any one of these captures the idea. Paul is horrified by the thought.

Rom. 6:2b How shall we who died to sin live any longer in it?

Here Paul introduces a new concept that he is going to flesh out in the next several verses. His use of the pronoun "we" refers to all those who have believed Jesus for eternal life (life for the age), children of God. "We" (Christians) should not persist in sinning, thinking that God's grace will abound and cover our sins, because we died to sin. The KJV says "are dead to sin," but Wm. Newell points out that is "wrong, for the tense of the Greek verb is the aorist, which denotes not a state but a past act or fact."[2] The NKJV is correct in saying "we who died to sin." The Bible Knowledge Commentary adds,

> Death to sin is separation from sin's power, not the extinction of sin." It is being *"set free from sin* (vv. 18, 22).[3]

How should we live in light of this truth? Paul said, "I die daily" (1 Cor. 15:31), and Jesus said:

> **John 12:24** Most assuredly, I say to you, unless a grain of wheat falls into the ground and dies, it remains alone; but if it dies, it produces much grain.

Neither Jesus nor Paul are talking about dying *to sin*. That already happened when we were regenerated. We are never commanded to die *to sin*. We are merely told to reckon the fact that we died to sin (when we were initially saved). Both Jesus and Paul are talking about dying *to self* — that is, choosing to humble ourselves and subject ourselves to the will of Christ every day of our lives.

Paul then tells believers — those who are already children of God — three things we need to *know* and three things we need to *do* if we want to live victorious Christian lives.

1. WE NEED TO KNOW THAT WE HAVE BEEN IMMERSED IN CHRIST'S DEATH, BURIAL, AND RESURRECTION.

> **Rom. 6:3** Do you not know that as many of us as were baptized into Christ Jesus were baptized into His death?

IS THIS WATER BAPTISM?

Commentators are split as to the nature of this baptism. Some (e.g., Newell) assume it is referring to *water* baptism as identifying the new believer in Christ, picturing His death and resurrection. But the problem with this understanding is that, based on the wording of v. 3, it then sounds as if water baptism is part of salvation (which is not the case). I agree with James Dunn and Alva McClain and Zane Hodges and numerous others that this text does *not* refer to water baptism. More likely, it is a metaphor for what happens at the point of regeneration in a *spiritual* sense.

The word *baptism* means "immersion." But it also can mean "placed into."[4] At the point of initial salvation, believers are baptized [i.e., placed into] the body of Christ by the Holy Spirit, becoming united with Him.

> **1 Cor. 12:13** For by one Spirit we were all baptized into one body—whether Jews or Greeks, whether slaves or free—and have all been made to drink into one Spirit.

> **Gal. 3:27** For as many of you as were baptized into Christ have put on Christ.

> **Col. 3:3** For you died, and your life is hidden with Christ in God.

To be sure, water baptism is a vivid *picture* of this spiritual transaction, but it does not contribute in any way to our salvation. Paul adds more detail in v. 4:

> **Rom. 6:4** Therefore we were buried with Him

> through baptism into death, that just as Christ was raised from the dead by the glory of the Father, even so we also should walk in newness of life.
> 6:5 For if [since] we have been united together in the likeness of His death, certainly we also shall be *in the likeness* of *His* resurrection,

At the point of being baptized into Christ, we were spiritually immersed in His death, buried with Him, and raised with Him, the result being that we now walk in newness of life. The *Bible Knowledge Commentary* says:

> The Greek word [translated] "newness" ... speaks of life that has a new or fresh quality. The resurrection of Jesus was not just a resuscitation; it was a new form of life. In the same way the spiritual lives of believers in Jesus have a new, fresh quality. Also, a believer's identification with Jesus Christ in His resurrection, besides being the start of new spiritual life now, is also the guarantee of physical resurrection.
>
> This work of God at salvation in identifying a believer with Christ's death, burial, and resurrection—thus separating him from sin's power and giving him a new quality of life—is the basis of the Holy Spirit's continuing work in sanctification.[5]

There is a second thing we must *know* if we want to live victoriously:

2. WE NEED TO KNOW THE GLORIOUS BENEFITS OF BEING CRUCIFIED WITH CHRIST.

> Rom. 6:6 Knowing this, that our old man was crucified with *Him,* that the body of sin might be done away with, that we should no longer be slaves of sin.
> 6:7 For he who has died has been freed from sin.

Three benefits are mentioned:

a. The *old man* was put to death. The term "old man" is a metaphor for the former, unregenerated spirit, which was crucified at the point of regeneration. God gave a new, regenerated spirit.

> **2 Cor. 5:17** Therefore, if anyone *is* in Christ, *he is* a new creation; old things have passed away; behold, all things have become new.

> **Col. 3:9b-10** You have put off the old man with his deeds, and have put on the new *man* who is renewed in knowledge according to the image of Him who created him.

It is biblically accurate to say the old nature no longer exists, for it was crucified, put to death. Granted, believers continue to sin, but that is not because of the old nature, for it is gone. A second benefit of having died with Christ in His crucifixion is:

b. The body of sin *might be* "done away with" (literally, "rendered powerless"). The Bible Knowledge Commentary says:

> The phrase 'the body of sin' does not mean that a human body is sinful in itself. It means that one's physical body is controlled or ruled by sin.[6]

Alva McClain (1888-1968) writes:

> "The body of sin" ... is the body we have, in which sin finds an instrument: the tongue, the hands, the mind. Sin does not find its source in the body. Sin finds its source in the will, but uses the body as an instrument.[7]

Zane Hodges adds:

> By the term *body of sin* Paul evidently means the aggregate total of all the sins committed through our physical bodies.[8]

6:6. *That the body of sin might be done away with.* The verb *might be* is in the Greek subjunctive mood, which is the mood of potential. In other words, this *could* happen, but it's not guaranteed — just as in 2 Cor. 5:21, *that we might become the righteousness of God in Him* — which is also in the subjunctive mood. It is possible, if certain conditions are met.

The power of sin in the believer's life can be "done away with" (NKJV); "destroyed" (KJV); "brought to nothing" (ESV); "abolished" (HCSB); "made useless" (YLT).

The best translation is: *rendered powerless*. Alva McClain says:

> The Greek word here gives the idea of sin being annulled, or rendered inoperative.[9]

In other words, your body does not have to remain under sin's power, for sin can be rendered powerless in your life. The tiger of sin can become toothless and declawed. A third benefit of having died with Christ in His crucifixion is:

c. Believers no longer have to be enslaved to sin. When you were saved, you died with Christ and rose with Him in a spiritual sense. Your former, unregenerated spirit was crucified, and you were given a new regenerated spirit, so that you can now walk in newness of life. You are no longer under sin's dominion — sin is no longer your master. As a result, sin has been rendered powerless in your life, and you have been freed from sin.

6:7. The Greek word translated *freed* is most often translated *justified* in the book of Romans. It's the idea that when you were regenerated, God forgave all your past sins and declared you righteous. You were acquitted, not in a positional sense, as the Reformers taught, but *at that point in time*. In that sense, you were freed from sin, and sin was rendered powerless because of your death, burial and resurrection with Christ. To the extent you live righteously by appropriating the grace of God, by faith, you will remain righteous.

Going forward, sin's dominance in your life can be rendered powerless or inoperative, but you have to make that decision. Thankfully, you have the *provision* to live righteously, and His name is Jesus.

When my dad died, he died to the IRS and taxes and bills from vendors. I had to pay them on behalf of my mom. My dad is resting easy in his grave, not in the least bit worried about bills or taxes or the IRS, or vendors of any type. He is never going to pay them anything again. He died to all of that. So with you, child of God. When you got saved, you died to sin *in Christ*. Sin is powerless to rule over you. It can't touch you, unless you allow it to come after you, and that would be foolish.

Christians need to know this!

1. We need to *know* that we have been immersed in Christ's death, burial, and resurrection (vs. 3-5).

2. We need to *know* the glorious benefits of being *crucified* with Christ (vs. 6-7).

Finally...

3. WE NEED TO KNOW THE GLORIOUS BENEFITS OF BEING RESURRECTED WITH CHRIST.

> **Rom. 6:8** Now if [since] we died with Christ, we believe that we shall also live with Him,
> **6:9** knowing that Christ, having been raised from the dead, dies no more. Death no longer has dominion over Him.
> **6:10** For *the death* that He died, He died to sin once for all; but *the life* that He lives, He lives to God.

Three benefits are mentioned:

a. We are *alive* with Jesus. This does not merely mean that we will be resurrected one day in the future. It means we are alive *right now* — because *He lives!* Vincent says this life is:

> "participation of the believer's sanctified life with the life of Christ rather than participation in future glory, which is not the point emphasized."[10]

We have new life in Christ now!

> **2 Tim. 1:9-10** [God] has saved us and called *us* with a holy calling, not according to our works, but according to His own purpose and

grace which was given to us in Christ Jesus ... *who* has abolished death and brought life and immortality to light through the gospel.

A second benefit of having risen with Christ is:
b. We are no longer under death's dominion. Those who do not believe on Jesus for eternal life have never been crucified with Him, nor have they been buried with Him, nor have they been resurrected with Him. That being the case, they can never rule with Him, but will remain in the grave during the Millennium. But because we have risen with Him, we will be resurrected before the Millennium. Furthermore, we can live righteously through Jesus and thereby qualify to rule with Him in His kingdom. Jesus said to Martha at the gravesite of Lazarus:

> **John 11:25-26** (YLT) Jesus said to her, 'I am the rising again, and the life; he who is believing in me, even if he may die, shall live; and every one who is living and believing in me shall not die — to the age;

A third benefit of having risen with Christ is:
c. We can live unto God. We have the provision to live the Christ-life of victory, for the resurrected Jesus lives within. He died to sin *once* (i.e., *once for all*), but He lives unto God. So can you!

> **Gal. 2:20** I have been crucified with Christ; it is no longer I who live, but Christ lives in me; and the *life* which I now live in the flesh I live by faith in the Son of God, who loved me and gave Himself for me.

If you choose to remain in the prison cell of sin, it is because you have failed to take the key of *faith* and open up the cell.

Many will remember the television program, *The Andy Griffith Show*, set in a small, rural town in 1950s America. Andy was the sheriff, Barney was the deputy, and Otis was the town drunk. Every Saturday night Otis would get drunk on illegal moonshine. Rather than getting arrested and fined by Andy or Barney, he would check himself into the local jail, often putting himself in the cell. The next morning, after sleeping it off, he would let himself go of his own accord, knowing that the key was hanging on the wall right outside the cell, well within reach. In a much greater spiritual sense, when you sin, you admit yourself to sin's prison, it's "lock-up." But it's of your own doing. You can walk out free whenever you want, by using the key of faith, depending on Jesus for victory. Why, then, do so many insist on remaining in sin's prison?

By way of review, notice what God wants all of His children to know:

1. We have been immersed in Christ's death, burial, and resurrection (vs. 3-5).

2. We enjoy the glorious benefits of having been crucified with Christ (vs. 6-7):

- Our old man has been put to death and replaced with a new man.
- Our body of sin *might be* rendered powerless.
- We no longer have to be enslaved to sin.

3. We enjoy the glorious benefits of having been resurrected with Christ (vs. 8-10):

- We can live with Jesus.
- We are no longer under death's dominion.
- We can live unto God.

However, merely *knowing* something doesn't mean it is benefitting us. Every child of God must choose to *believe* the truth and put it into action in everyday living, by God's grace.

Paul goes on to challenge believers to *do* three things with these truths, if they would live victoriously.

1. RECKON IT TO BE SO.

> **Rom. 6:11 Likewise you also, reckon yourselves to be dead indeed to sin, but alive to God in Christ Jesus our Lord.**

To *reckon* is "to do the accounting or take inventory; calculate." God wants you to *reckon* that you are dead to sin and alive to God. Think about it and consider it to be so! Don't ever doubt, for the accounting is true. Consider it to be so, and never let yourself be convinced otherwise! You are indeed dead to sin, if you are a child of God, and that brings with it all the glorious benefits already discussed. Alva McClain says:

> Whenever a young man who may be a member of an Orthodox Jewish family becomes a Christian, the father says, "This son is to me dead." He turns him out of his house. He never speaks to him again. If friends come in and ask about his son, he says, "My son is dead." He is not actually dead, but the father considers that boy as dead.[11]

In like manner, you are dead to sin, even though sin is very much alive. There is a second thing God wants you to *do* so you can live victoriously:

2. DON'T ALLOW SIN TO BE YOUR MASTER.

> **Rom. 6:12 Therefore do not let sin reign in your mortal body, that you should obey it in its lusts.**

Sin is very happy to get back up on the throne of your life, and sin would love to depose your new Master, Jesus Christ. But sin does not have the power or authority to do that, unless you allow it. So don't allow sin to rule in your life, because if you do, then you will start submitting to sin as your master. Remember what James said about the downward spiral of sin:

> **Jas. 1:15** Then, when desire has conceived, it gives birth to sin; and sin, when it is full-grown, brings forth death.

I marvel how the Scriptures personify Sin and Death. Perhaps they are actual, sentient beings. John Milton viewed them that way in his *Paradise Lost*.

The point is that when sin is once again allowed to become your master, then death follows in its wake.

Of course, as a child of God, you are guaranteed to be resurrected before the Millennium. But God wants you to live the Christ-life now, so that God is glorified and you can receive the inheritance of co-rulership with Jesus when you meet Him in judgment. Those who submit to sin as their master will self-destruct and wither spiritually. Eventually, we will study Rom. 8, where Paul warns:

> **Rom. 8:6-7** For to be carnally minded *is* death, but to be spiritually minded *is* life and peace. Because the carnal mind *is* enmity against God; for it is not subject to the law of God, nor indeed can be.

Those who submit to sin as their master become carnal (fleshly). God gives them over to their ways (Rom. 1:18ff), and they could very possibly die prematurely because of their own foolish choices that lead down the path of death. So don't allow sin to be your master. There is a third thing God wants you to *do* so you can live victoriously:

3. USE YOUR BODY PARTS AS TOOLS FOR RIGHTEOUSNESS.

> **Rom. 6:13** And do not present [KJV: *yield*] your members *as* instruments of unrighteousness to sin, but present [KJV: *yield*] yourselves to God as being alive from the dead, and your members *as* instruments of righteousness to God.

The verb translated *present* or *yield* is the same Greek word used in Rom. 12:1 "*present* your bodies a living sacrifice, holy, acceptable to God." The first time the word *present* is used in 6:13 it is in the *present tense*, implying continued action — "don't keep yielding your body parts to sin and unrighteousness." The second time the word *present* is used in 6:13 it is in the *aorist tense*, implying a once-for-all yielding. So here's the idea: "don't continue yielding your body parts to sin; come to a decisive turning point in your life in which you choose to yield your parts to God going forward."

SPIRITUAL CRISIS MOMENTS

I believe this implies — and I know this to be true from my own experience — that God sometimes uses spiritual crisis moments in our lives to bring us to the end of self, so we yield ourselves to God, which generally remains the default going forward. Sanctification is generally a steady process, if one remains yielded to the Lord, but it will occasionally be punctuated by crises. These "I surrender all" moments can be very helpful to get us on track spiritually. It doesn't mean you will always live righteously from that point on, but it means your new way of life will be characterized by righteousness rather than sinfulness.

Your hands and feet and mouth and brain and eyes and ears — and even your private parts — can be used to commit sins that lead to spiritual deadness, or they can be used to do righteous deeds for God that lead to life and vibrancy. In fact, the Greek word translated *instruments* is sometimes translated *weapons* in the New Testament. Thus, your body — through its various parts — can be used as weapons, metaphorically, for either good or evil. Vincent speaks of sin and righteousness as "rulers of opposing sovereignties, and enlisting men in their armies."[12] So make choices to present yourself to righteousness rather than to sin. Live for Jesus!

> **Rom. 6:14 For sin shall not have dominion over you, for you are not under law but under grace.**

What a glorious promise! Sin cannot rule over you! James Dunn says:

> The reason it is possible for believers to avoid a habitual surrender to sin at one point or other in their lives is that sin shall no longer have the dominant say in their lives, because they are not under the law but under grace ... *Grace is the only power which can break the mastery of sin.* It is only as believers live their lives "under grace," in dependence on God's gracious power to sustain and restore, that the power of sin can be defeated, that the enticing voice of self-satisfaction ... can be ignored.[13]

THE POWERLESSNESS OF SIN TO REIGN, OF ITSELF

The bottom line is that sin is powerless to reign in your life. But you can allow sin to usurp the authority of Christ in your life. Indeed, that happens whenever you choose to ignore the key of faith and commit sins, thereby putting sin back on the throne. However, the throne of your life rightfully belongs to Jesus now, for He has redeemed you and regenerated you, by His grace. Your obligation is to live for Him, not for the old master of sin.

To the Jewish believers at Rome, Paul adds, "For you are not under the law but under grace." The Mosaic rituals have been abolished. Attempting to keep them will not make you spiritual. The same applies to twenty-first century Christians with their rituals, rules, lists, and standards. Commentator William Harrison says:

> The phrases "sin will not have dominion over you, for you are not under the law but under grace," could be put in reverse and read as "sin will have dominion over you if you are under the law and not grace" ... If a believer neglects the grace of God which empowers us to live for Him [and] falls into legalism ... this brings failure. Trying to live the Christian life through your own strength [also] brings failure.[14]

Only Jesus can make you alive and spiritual. You died *with Him*, you were buried *with Him*, you were raised to newness of life *with Him*. Reckon it to be so!

CHAPTER 15
WHO'S YOUR MASTER?
ROMANS 6:15-23

In a spiritual sense, you are enslaved to only one of two possible masters — there are no alternatives. Incidentally, you are the one who decides which master you are going to serve. It is not forced upon you by God or anyone else.

Rom. 6:1-14 teaches that when you were initially saved (regenerated), you died with Christ, you were buried with Him, and you rose with Him — in a spiritual sense, of course. As a result, you were immersed (or *placed*) into Christ by the Holy Spirit, so that you have been united with Him, and you are now part of His body. This is what it means to be *in Christ*. Consequently, you are now dead to sin and alive unto God through Jesus Christ. You possess newness of life, and God wants you to walk in it.

Specifically, God wants you to do three things:

1. **Reckon it to be so.** Consider it, do the accounting, and resolve in your mind that this is so!
2. **Don't allow sin to be your master.** You have been freed from sin, so don't go on living in the jail house of sin.
3. **Use your body parts as tools for righteousness.** Your hands and feet and mouth and brain and eyes and ears can be used to commit sins that lead to spiritual deadness, or

they can be used to do righteous deeds for God. He wants you to use your body for His glory.

Paul is now going to develop those themes further in Rom. 6:15-23.

> **Rom. 6:15** What then? Shall we sin because we are not under law but under grace? Certainly not!

This is similar to the question asked earlier:

> **Rom. 6:1-2a** What shall we say then? Shall we continue in sin that grace may abound? Certainly not!

Once again, Paul emphatically insists that believers should not continue in sinning now that grace has abounded over sin and the law. Grace is not a license to sin! Paul uses idiomatic language to make his point: *Certainly not!* Why would someone who has died to sin continue to make sin their master? As if to imply: How foolish! In v. 16 Paul gives a good summary of his point.

> **Rom. 6:16** Do you not know that to whom you present yourselves slaves to obey, you are that one's slaves whom you obey, whether of sin *leading* to death, or of obedience *leading* to righteousness?

WHICH ONE IS YOUR MASTER?

Here the two masters are exposed — *sin* leading to *death* or *obedience* leading to *righteousness*.

Obedience must be driven by *faith* in our new Master, Jesus Christ (per Rom. 4-5). Thus, it is faith-filled obedience to God, leading to righteousness. Which one is your master? *Sin* or *Obedience*?

Jesus said something similar, using a different metaphor

Matt. 7:13 Enter by the narrow gate; for wide *is* the gate and broad *is* the way that leads to destruction, and there are many who go in by it.

14 Because narrow *is* the gate and difficult *is* the way which leads to life, and there are few who find it.

The two ways are not two places — Heaven and Hell — but rather, two possible ways of living chosen by believers: sinfulness or sanctification (set apart to holiness). You are the one who chooses which master you are going to serve.

Notice the word *present* in v. 16. You *present* yourself as the *slave* of either sin or obedience. The word *present* can also be translated *yield* — the same word used in 6:13 and 12:1.

Christ has saved you and given you newness of life. The old master is gone; the new master Jesus Christ is now your rightful authority. But you must choose whether or not you are going to submit to Him. He will never force you. Children of God are just as free to choose *sin* as *obedience*, even though choosing *sin* is nonsensical, because the consequence is dreadful.

Paul adds a personal parenthesis of sorts in vs. 17-18:

Rom. 6:17 But God be thanked that *though* you were slaves of sin, yet you obeyed from the heart that form of doctrine to which you were delivered.
6:18 And having been set free from sin, you became slaves of righteousness.

6:17. Many commentators think the "form of doctrine to which you were delivered" refers to the doctrine of salvation by grace through faith — that is, the truths regarding initial salvation — but that doesn't fit the context. Zane Hodges translates the last half of v. 17:

> *You have obeyed from the heart that form of teaching in which you were instructed* ... My rendering is also reflected in the Jerusalem Bible which reads: *You submitted without reservation to the creed you were taught.*[1] (italics added)

Hodges later adds:

> Paul is grateful to God for the Christian experience of the Roman believers. In their unconverted days they had been slaves of sin, but after their conversion they had obeyed from the heart (i.e., sincerely) the form of teaching in which they had been instructed. That is to say, they had responded obediently to the Christian teaching they had received.[2]

In the context of the book of Romans, Paul is *not* talking about unbelievers getting saved. He is talking about believers pursuing discipleship *after* their salvation. These believers at Rome are having some carnality issues, largely because of ethnic prejudices, which had resulted in division and disunity, but they were a far cry from their behavior before becoming regenerated. For that, Paul is truly grateful to the Lord. But he wants them to keep on growing and choosing obedience as their master, by faith. That's the only way they are going to experience the salvation of their souls and the only way they are going to resolve their in-house problems as the church at Rome.

"SLAVES" OF RIGHTEOUSNESS

6:18. Paul refers to the outcome of this decision as "slavery" — you are either sin's slave or the slave of obedience. Why does Paul use this unusual terminology? The answer is given in v. 19:

> **Rom. 6:19a I speak in human *terms* because of the weakness of your flesh.**

Robert Govett claims:

> This is a sort of apology for the calling the service of God a slavery (v. 18).[3]

It seems that by "human terms" Paul means he is using a metaphor that they will all understand, especially in the Roman world. Man, by his weak nature, is prone to be *enslaved* — to be subject to or subservient to someone other than self. Wm. Newell says:

> Man hates this fact. He boasts his independence, whether it be in the realm of intellect—"free thought!" in the matter of private wealth—"independent!" or in the manner of government—"free!" But it is all really a delusion ... What we most earnestly assert is that not only Paul here, but our Lord Himself, and Scripture generally, sets forth that *only those that know the truth and walk therein, are free.*
>
> The Jews (in John 8:33ff) horribly rebel against our Lord's saying: "If ye abide in My word, then are ye truly My disciples: and ye shall know the truth, and the truth shall make you free! ... Every one that committeth sin is the bondservant [slave] of sin ... If the Son shall make you free, ye shall be free indeed." There is no freedom out of Christ. "Whose service is perfect freedom" is the beautiful expression of obedience to God.[4]

One of the spiritual laws of the universe is that people are either enslaved to sin leading to death or obedience leading to righteousness. Seeing that believers have died to sin in Christ, why would any child of God choose to keep living in sin? Thus, Paul reiterates:

> **Rom. 6:19b For just as you presented your members *as* slaves of uncleanness, and of lawlessness [wickedness] *leading* to *more* lawlessness [wickedness], so now present your members *as* slaves *of* righteousness for holiness.**

Notice the last phrase, "slaves of righteousness for holiness." Zane Hodges, in his translation, adds the word "producing" before holiness. He comments:

> The phrase *producing holiness* translates *eis hagiasmon*. BDAG reminds us that outside of Biblical literature the word *hagiasmos* frequently signals "personal dedication to the interests of the deity." In the NT it has come to mean especially "the state of being made holy." In this

context, however, an element of the basic meaning seems implicit in the context of being slaves to righteousness. The Greco-Roman world was familiar with the concept of someone who was permanently attached to a pagan temple as a servant of the god who was worshipped there.[5]

Here's the point — A slave of righteousness is a believer who is totally dedicated to serving the Lord Jesus Christ. Ironically, real freedom can only come through obedience to Jesus Christ, for it leads to righteousness and life, which will be seen in v. 23.

> **Rom. 6:20 For when you were slaves of sin, you were free in regard to righteousness.**
> **6:21 What fruit did you have then in the things of which you are now ashamed? For the end of those things *is* death.**

Those who are enslaved by the power of sin find that righteousness is powerless in their lives. What a tragedy when sin continues in the life of a Christian, for it is shameful and results in death, as these Roman believers knew from their former ways of living. There is no spiritual fruit in a life of enslavement to sin, only spiritual death.

WHAT IS DEATH?

William Harrison writes:

> Death here does not refer to Hell. The word "death" means "separation" or "to be inactive" ... When we sin we lose fellowship with God and are separated from such fellowship ... When we live in death, we do not bear fruit or works for God and instead are "inactive," like a corpse that doesn't do anything except rot and make things stink for others.
>
> Shall we go ahead and sin since we are under grace? No, it has consequences and we'll lose out on experiencing the abundant life that God has for us. Instead we'll waste our lives as we waste away

and become like dead people, who produce nothing of value with our lives ... and bring sadness to those around us.[6]

Hodges says:

> For Paul, death is not the mere cessation of physical existence but is also an experience that is qualitatively distinct from true life. As Paul puts it in Eph 4:18, the unregenerate are "alienated from the life of God, because of the ignorance that is in them." But as he will show clearly in the following two chapters, such "alienation" from God's life is experienced also by the Christian when he submits to the desires of his spiritually-dead physical body.[7]

Interestingly, a theologian friend of mine, John Sweigart, in an unpublished journal article, demonstrates from the suzerain-vassal treaties of ancient times, that one of the definitions of *death* is "loss of dominion." Sweigart says:

> In addition to being used as a separation metaphor, [DEATH] also can mean "loss of dominion." This can be seen in the life of Adam and Eve who not only were separated from God by being driven out of the garden but also lost their kingship and priesthood over creation in the same judgment.
>
> This meaning fits admirably well in Paul's whole discussion in Romans 6-8 ... So, the result is that "life" means "dominion" and "death" means loss of dominion. In Romans 6:23 it may mean "the wages of sin lead to loss of dominion. This loss of dominion applies to both this life and the life to come.[8]

This is important to understand, especially in light of the final two verses of ch. 6.

Rom. 6:22 But now having been set free from sin, and having become slaves of God, you have your fruit to holiness, and the end, everlasting life.

NOT THE GIFT OF ETERNAL LIFE, BUT THE REWARD

Everlasting life (*eonian life*, or *life for the age*) — as seen in this verse — is not considered a present possession, but rather the conclusion for a life that has borne fruit unto holiness. So this cannot be referring to initial salvation, or the *gift* of eternal life, because holy living is the *prerequisite* for this *eonian* life. Therefore, Paul must be referring to the *reward* of eternal (*eonian*) life for living obediently.

In their former lifestyle the Roman believers were enslaved to sin and bore no spiritual fruit. But now they are God's slaves (i.e., His servants) and bearing fruit in holiness. Their "end" — their verdict at the Judgment Seat — is "everlasting life" (*life for the age*). If Sweigart is correct, that means they will be rewarded with *dominion* — co-rulership with Jesus.

The word *end* is translated from the Greek word *telos*, which means "conclusion," or "outcome." In this case, the outcome is *reward* for the faithful child of God. However, those who hold to Calvinism do not view this as reward, but rather, "the final verdict" for a "true" child of God. Because they hold to *perseverance* doctrine, Calvinists never know if they will have salvation at the end of life — because their behavior tomorrow and thereafter may be atrocious, indicating they were never actually a child of God. They must await the verdict of "final salvation" from Jesus at the Judgment Seat to know whether they are allowed to enter Heaven. What a terrible way to live! Calvinist doctrine causes perpetual doubt regarding one's salvation (i.e., regeneration). Reformed Pastor John Piper says:

> Works ... are the necessary fruit of justifying faith, which confirm our faith and our union with Christ at the last judgment.[9]

So, in essence, a Calvinist Christian really doesn't know if he is actually saved and "on his way to Heaven" or not until he hears Jesus announce that he has "final salvation." Doesn't this negate their credo of *sola fide*, which is Latin for "by faith alone"? A salvation that has to be confirmed *by* works is a salvation *of* works! That is *not* what Paul is talking about!

The *end* that Paul mentions, regards matters of Christian living, thus *eternal (age-lasting) life*, in this context, is the goal of coming to know Jesus in a deeper, fuller way, experiencing His abundant life, and living in holiness — with the outcome being reward, dominion in the age to come.

In other words, those who live righteously *now*, are enjoying the benefits of appropriating their eternal life *now*. They are walking in newness of life, and they will be rewarded when they meet Jesus with the privilege of ruling with Him in His kingdom.

The last verse of ch. 6 must be interpreted *in this same context*.

> **Rom. 6:23 For the wages of sin *is* death, but the gift of God *is* eternal life in Christ Jesus our Lord.**

WHY DOES PAUL REFER TO THE GIFT OF ETERNAL LIFE?

The wages (or payment) for a believer who continues throughout life enslaved to sin is *death*. Keep in mind that Paul is speaking to believers, thus his use of the word *death* — as already noted by Hodges — includes alienation from God's life here and *now* and even *then*, for their verdict will be "wicked and lazy servant" (Matt. 25:26) at the Bema. Consequently, they will be consigned to the darkness outside New Jerusalem, which means they will be relegated to the earthly realm of the kingdom, where they will consciously regret their foolish life choices by weeping and gnashing their teeth.

In contrast to the wages of sin — death in its many forms — the gift of God is eternal life. Why would Paul use the word *gift* in this context? Because the gift keeps on giving! Bible teacher Dale Taliaferro explains:

> This is about the walk, not about coming to Christ. If I present myself as a slave, it is death. But if I present myself to God, depending on him, the gift of God is eternal life. When I trust, I have the gift of life. If I trust again, I have the gift of life. This is not a once-for-all issue. It is a walk. This is not about how to be "saved" (as the old paradigm knows it), but how to walk. God promises me a wholly different life. We must die before living.[10]

The word *gift* comes from the Greek word *charisma*, which is a bestowal of God's grace. Seeing that Paul is writing to believers about walking in newness of life, we can conclude he is not talking about initial salvation, thus we must interpret Rom. 6:23 to mean:

The payment for a believer's life of sinning is death — loss of dominion in the next age. But those who live righteously by faith, appropriating God's bestowals of grace (His gifts!), will be rewarded with dominion in the next age.

Rom. 6:15-23 is summed up in Gal. 6:7-8:

Gal. 6:7 Do not be deceived, God is not mocked; for whatever a man sows, that he will also reap.
8 For he who sows to his flesh will of the flesh reap corruption, but he who sows to the Spirit will of the Spirit reap everlasting life.

Everlasting life in Gal. 6 and also in Rom. 6 is not referring to our present possession that assures our presence in the millennial kingdom. It is the verdict of "Well done!" for those believers who live enslaved to obedience unto righteousness rather than enslaved to sin unto death. They will be chosen to wear crowns and co-rule as His bride.

Who's your master? — Sin leading to death or obedience leading to righteousness and life?

CHAPTER 16
THE DEADENING EFFECTS OF LEGALISM
ROMANS 7

In Romans 8, Paul describes how to have victory over sinning in the Christian life. In ch. 7 he describes how *not* to have victory — and, of course, that is by depending on the law. A large segment of his audience are Jewish believers who continue to cling to the rituals of the Mosaic law, expecting the keeping of those rituals to sanctify and make them spiritual and pleasing to God. Of course, that is incorrect. In ch. 8 Paul explains that the way to have victory over sinning is by depending on the Holy Spirit, the Spirit of Christ who lives within.

The church of Jesus Christ is predominantly Gentile. Granted, some Jews have embraced Jesus as Messiah and have believed Him for eternal (age-lasting) life. Regardless, the principles in Rom. 7 apply to Gentiles all the same, because all believers have the problem of indwelling sin, which will be discussed in this chapter. The tendency of believers is to deal with indwelling sin through reliance on self and some system of their own devising. However, Paul's point is that systems of man's devising fail miserably.

> Rom. 7:1 Or do you not know, brethren (for I speak to those who know the law), that the law has dominion over a man as long as he lives?

LEGALISM IS BINDING

Paul directs his attention "to those who know the law." In the first century culture, that would have been the Jews. Zane Hodges believes they would have been a minority in the church at Rome — and for that matter, in most of the churches Paul had established — but they were an *influential* minority, for they knew the Old Testament Scriptures.[1] Not to mention, the Messiah was Jewish. What is the equivalent in the twenty-first century church? It is those believers who think they must hold to certain rules or standards or lists to be sanctified and spiritual in God's eyes.

Multitudes of individual believers and many churches have fallen prey to this mentality — especially, large segments of fundamentalism. So we must be careful not to "tune out" when reading that Paul is speaking to "those who know the law." That includes those believers who have a legalistic approach to spirituality, and it is quite possible for any believer to fall prey to legalism's clutches, for it usually happens unwittingly.

RELEASED FROM THE LAW — THE ILLUSTRATION OF A SPOUSE THAT DIES

Paul says, "Don't you know that the law has dominion (rule) over a man as long as he lives?" He is making the point that the Mosaic law can only have authority in a person's life as long as they are alive. Once they have died, the law cannot rule over them. The apostle illustrates with an example from the Mosaic law itself — the commands about divorce and remarriage. However, it is important to understand that Paul's purpose here is not to speak to the doctrine of divorce and remarriage, per se, merely to use it as an illustration of the extent of the law's authority over a Jewish person. Notice what he says:

> Rom. 7:2 For the woman who has a husband is bound by the law to *her* husband as long as he lives. But if the husband dies, she is released from the law of *her* husband.

> **7:3 So then if, while *her* husband lives, she marries another man, she will be called an adulteress; but if her husband dies, she is free from that law, so that she is no adulteress, though she has married another man.**

The Mosaic law specified that a married woman was bound to her husband in marriage as long as he was alive. The law allowed divorce under certain extenuating circumstances, but that is not Paul's point here. He is speaking generally, emphasizing that the law required marriage for life. If the wife married someone else while the husband was alive, she was considered an adulteress. But once her husband had died, the wife was free to marry another, for she was free from the "law" of her husband. Again, this is not intended as a treatise on divorce and remarriage, but rather as an illustration. So what's his point?

"MARRIED" TO JESUS – YOUR NEW "SPOUSE"

> **Rom. 7:4 Therefore, my brethren, you also have become dead to the law through the body of Christ, that you may be married to another—to Him who was raised from the dead, that we should bear fruit to God.**

In a spiritual sense, those Jews who had become believers in Jesus Christ were dead to the law. Remember back to what Paul had taught in Rom. 6. Those who are regenerated have died with Christ and risen with Him. From that point forward, believers are free from any legal system that binds.

> **Gal. 3:13** Christ has redeemed us from the curse of the law, having become a curse for us.

Because you died to the law, the law no longer has dominion over you. Your new "spouse," so to speak, is Christ. Incidentally, this passage is *not* teaching that you are now Christ's bride. The determination as to which believers comprise the bride of Christ will be at the Judgment Seat of Christ. They are His faithful servants who will be glorified to co-rule with Him as bride and co-regent in the Millennium. Paul is simply applying the illustration of vs. 2-3 to the Christian life: You died to the law; you are now married to Christ.

What is the purpose of this new union, according to v. 4? "That we should bear fruit to God." We are now to live in holiness and righteousness and, thankfully, that is made possible by Jesus.

> **Rom. 7:5 For when we were in the flesh, the sinful passions which were aroused by the law** [Hodges: *the yearnings for sin that the law produced*] **were at work in our members to bear fruit to death.**
> **7:6 But now we have been delivered from the law, having died to what we were held** [back] **by, so that we should serve in the newness of the Spirit and not *in* the oldness of the letter.**

FORMER FRUIT UNTO DEATH

7:5. Prior to believing on Jesus for eternal life, the Jews did not have the Holy Spirit dwelling within. Consequently, their fruit was unto death (spiritual deadness). That is because the law was a dominating presence and actually prompted inward yearnings to sin. Zane Hodges explains how this happens:

> In the light of Paul's subsequent statement about the law arousing lust (v 7), it is likely that he has in mind the way negative commands so easily awaken yearnings for forbidden sin ... These yearnings were ones that the law actually produced, as in fact it did in the case of the command not to covet (v 7).[2]

Perhaps this can be illustrated by a sign placed on a newly painted park bench that reads, "Do not touch! Wet paint." What does everyone want to do? They want to touch it, in spite of the order *not* to touch it. Paul says the law had that effect. The sinful urges within our bodies — fueled by the fires of the law — resulted in our bodies bearing fruit to death (spiritual deadness). Hodges adds:

> As Paul will make clear a little later, this is not a reflection on the law itself. On the contrary, it is the result of the law's counterproductive influence on the flesh.[3]

Bob Wilkin comments:

> Paul was describing the view of the law held by the Pharisees of his day. Their legalistic devotion to the law, rather than to the One who gave the law, was a terrible error. When Jews came to faith in Christ for everlasting life and gave up trying to be justified by means of the law, often they would continue to look to the law as the means of sanctification.[4]

NOW FREE TO LIVE IN NEWNESS OF LIFE

7:6. Without the aid of the Holy Spirit, our inward yearnings are dominated by fleshly responses. Since we have died to the law and, therefore, have been delivered from the law's dominance in our lives, we can live in newness of life through the Holy Spirit, rather than oldness of the letter (i.e., the law). Law-living (legalism) leads to spiritual deadness, for the law holds back and hinders. On the other hand, Spirit-filled living leads to spiritual life and vibrancy, leading us onward and upward.

> **2 Cor. 3:6b** The letter kills, but the Spirit gives life.

That being the case, why would any Christian, who has died to the law through union with Christ, return to the law's dominance in their lives? Is that not an outright rejection of the Holy Spirit? Is it not setting oneself up for defeat and failure? Tragically, legalism holds back multitudes of Christians from victorious Christian living.

In the next couple of verses, Paul makes an important clarification:

> Rom. 7:7 What shall we say then? *Is the law sin?* Certainly not! On the contrary, I would not have known sin except through the law. For I would not have known covetousness [i.e., lust] unless the law had said, *"You shall not covet."*
> 7:8 But sin, taking opportunity by the commandment, produced in me all *manner of evil* desire. For apart from the law sin *was* dead.

THE LAW PUTS A SPOTLIGHT ON SIN

7.7. After warning in v. 5 of the law's tendency to produce yearning to sin, Paul asks, "Is the law itself sinful?" For the third time within two chapters, he answers emphatically, "Certainly not!" Rather, its purpose is to shine a spotlight on sin.

Paul gives an example: He would have never known that coveting (i.e., lusting) is sin, without the law, which commands, "You shall not covet." Zane Hodges says:

> How sin did this has already been suggested (in v 5) in Paul's mention of "the yearnings for sin" that the law awakens. But the responsibility for that lies with sin itself. All that the law actually did was to make Paul aware of the evil dispositions his own heart was capable of harboring. In this way, sin took advantage ... by stimulating and drawing forth from Paul the sinful desires inherent in his sinful nature.[5]

7:8. Apart from the law, sin is dead; that is, sin is not a moral dilemma unless God announces that something is a moral dilemma through the law. When God says, "Thou shalt not," He is defining what is sinful. Incidentally, the "sinful nature" to which Hodges refers is defined by Paul in v. 17 as "sin that dwells in me." Thus, I prefer to call it "indwelling sin." We all have indwelling sin — it is resident in the *soul* aspect of our being — and that is why our souls need saving, which is a lifelong process called *sanctification* in which we become more and more conformed to Jesus Christ.

PAUL'S PERSONAL STRUGGLE WITH SIN

In v. 9 Paul becomes transparent about a time when he stumbled into sinning in his own life.

> **Rom. 7:9** I was alive once without the law, but when the commandment came, sin revived and I died.

Paul uses the first-person pronoun "I" in this chapter numerous times to refer to his own personal struggles with sin and the law. This has prompted many theologians to claim Paul is talking about his life prior to regeneration. That view especially appeals to Calvinists, because of their adherence to *perseverance* doctrine, which I explained in previous chapters. Those who hold to Calvinism cannot imagine that Paul could struggle in this manner as a believer. Nevertheless, Paul is talking to believers about matters of sanctification! It would make no sense for him to give an example from his life before the time he was regenerated.

His statement in v. 9 also would not make sense if referring to his life as a Pharisee. The Pharisees, of course, were wrapped up in legalism and, therefore, deadness. Paul says, "I was alive once without the law." He is speaking of his life after believing on Jesus, when he was dead to the Mosaic rituals and alive unto Christ. But something happened to steal away his victory over sinning. He confesses, "the commandment came, sin revived, and I died." In other words, in a moment of weakness, Paul resorted to legalism ("the commandment came"), and he stumbled into sinning ("sin revived"), as the Mosaic law shined a spotlight on his sin. The sin produced spiritual deadness in his soul ("I died"), and he remained in that condition for some time, as long as he continued in legalism. Didn't this also happen to Peter at Antioch (see Gal. 2:11ff)?

> **Rom. 7:10 And the commandment, which *was* to bring life, I found to *bring* death.**
> **7:11 For sin, taking occasion by the commandment, deceived me, and by it killed *me*.**

Paul describes how the principle of v. 5 impacted his own life. The law produced in him a yearning to sin. Could that be lust as mentioned in v. 7? By yielding to sin, Paul discovered that his Christian life became spiritually dead. In fact, the sin, which took advantage of him via the commandment of God, "killed him" — fellowship with God was instantly severed. That raises a question:

> **Rom. 7:12 Therefore the law *is* holy, and the commandment holy and just and good.**
> **7:13 Has then what is good become death to me? Certainly not! But sin, that it might appear sin, was producing death in me through what is good, so that sin through the commandment might become exceedingly sinful.**

THE LAW IS NOT THE PROBLEM

The apostle wants to make something very clear. He insists that the law is holy and just and good. The law is not to blame for his sinning! Far from it! Sin is the problem — it used the law to arouse desires, so that Paul yielded, and sin produced deadness. The law of God merely did its job of putting a spotlight on sin, making it appear sinful, in fact, "*exceedingly* sinful," because when someone sins in spite of the law to the contrary, it is bald-faced defiance of God's will and, therefore, extremely sinful.

> **Rom. 7:14 For we know that the law is spiritual, but I am carnal, sold under sin.**

In contrast to the law, which is spiritual, believers who yield to sin are carnal, fleshly, sold out as slaves of sin. By choosing to sin, they place themselves back under sin's dominion. They present their members as instruments of unrighteousness to sin rather than presenting them to God. That had happened to Paul at some point earlier in his Christian life. He exposes his past errors in Rom. 7 so we can learn from his mistakes.

> **Rom. 7:15 For what I am doing, I do not understand. For what I will to do, that I do not practice; but what I hate, that I do.**

PAUL'S FRUSTRATION AND INNER TURMOIL

Do you sense Paul's frustration? Do you feel his pain? In the first sentence of this verse, he admits to spinning his wheels and not accomplishing anything of spiritual value. In the latter half of the verse, he describes sin's grip — when a child of God is unable to do what they know is right and can only continue in what they know is wrong, otherwise known as *habitual sinning*. This behavior confirms the law's function of doing good — keeping a spotlight on sin.

> **Rom. 7:16 If, then, I do what I will [wish] not to do, I agree with the law that *it is* good.**

But then Paul says something unusual.

> **Rom. 7:17 But now, *it is* no longer I who do it, but sin that dwells in me.**

What does he mean by this? Is Paul passing the blame? Not at all! He is simply being specific. When Paul says "it is not I who keep sinning," ("doing what I wish *not* to do"), he is referring to his *inner man*, i.e., the realm of the *spirit*. That will be confirmed in a moment, in vs. 22, 25.

His spirit had been regenerated. He had died with Christ, and risen with Him, and he is now in union with Christ — and that is true of all believers, those who are *in Christ*. The old man died, and the new man lives, which is a reference to your regenerated spirit (Rom. 8:16; 2 Cor. 5:17). Consequently, you have a new master, Jesus Christ. The old master, sin, is powerless to rule over you. But you can continue to submit to the old master.

INDWELLING SIN RESISTS THE SAVING OF THE SOUL

How can that happen, if your old man is gone? Because while your *spirit* has been saved (regenerated), your *soul* has *not* been regenerated. Rather, your *soul* is in the process of being saved, but that happens over time, as you submit to your new Master. In that realm of your being, there will be a constant struggle, and the struggle is because of "sin that dwells" in you, i.e., *indwelling sin.*

So while your old nature has been eradicated, replaced by the new — and that happened in the realm of your *spirit* when you were initially saved — your *soul* is in the process of change, aka *sanctification*. Indwelling sin resists the saving of your *soul* — "it is no longer I who do it, but sin that dwells in me" (v. 17).

Paul is *not* passing the blame. Rather, he is *pinning* the blame on the rightful realm of his being — not his *spirit*, or *body*, but his *soul* — specifically, *sin* that continues to dwell within his soul, *indwelling sin.*

When you got saved, though your spirit changed instantaneously, your soul and body did not change. You were still the same weight and height and subject to the laws of gravity and, for that matter, aging. You also woke up the next morning after being regenerated the same person in your thinking and feelings and volition (mind, emotions, will). Those old thought patterns and raging emotions that characterized you *before* salvation were still there. But since you were given a new Master, you were then able to start cooperating with Him to bring change to your soul. Hopefully, that has happened in your life as you have become more and more changed into His image, over the course of time, step-by-step, by making choices to walk in the Spirit rather than in the flesh. God is merciful and gracious to His children throughout the process, for He knows that it takes time.

> Rom. 7:18 For I know that in me (that is, in my flesh) nothing good dwells; for to will is present with me, but *how* to perform what is good I do not find.
> 7:19 For the good that I will *to do*, I do not do; but the evil I will not *to do*, that I practice.

THE FLESHLY SOUL OF A BELIEVER

By using the term *flesh* Paul is not referring to the body. Gnostics believe the body is evil, and that goes back to Manichaeism (third century AD). If the body were the problem, then we should flagellate our flesh, as some do, or become ascetics, at the very least, denying the body privileges. But that is not biblical. The problem is not the body, per se, it is the soul. A fleshly soul is self-seeking, having sinful desires, worldly pursuits, and enjoying material pleasures. Fleshly behaviors are often carried out in the body, but they are rooted in the soul, so the body, per se, is not evil. The *flesh* within the soul is evil (see v. 18) – i.e., *sin that dwells in me* or *indwelling sin*. Thus, the soul needs to be saved from sinning and indulging in fleshly appetites.

It is in the realm of the soul that we think impure *thoughts* and entertain sinful ideas. It is in the realm of the soul that our *feelings* want something and succumb to the urge. It is in the realm of the soul that we make *willful choices* to disobey God. Paul says "to will is present with me" (v. 18). In other words, in his spirit, his innermost being, Paul desires to do right and wishes to carry that out, but he doesn't know how to carry out those wishes in his sinful soul. In fact, he frankly admits (paraphrase): "I can't seem to do the good that I want to do, and the evil that I want to avoid, is what I end up doing." What a perplexing problem! — a *spirit* that wants to do right; a *soul* that doesn't want to cooperate because of indwelling sin but, instead, teams up with the *body* to do evil deeds.

> **Rom. 7:20 Now if I do what I will not *to do*, it is no longer I who do it, but sin that dwells in me.**
> **7:21 I find then a law, that evil is present with me, the one who wills to do good.**

As Christians we discover a new law (principle) that governs our lives by default. Although we have died to sin, and sin is no longer our master, we find that sin aggressively works to usurp the authority of our new Master. Our regenerated spirit wants to live righteously, but indwelling sin (fleshliness) in the soul continually fights against doing right. Is that your experience? It certainly was Paul's, at least at one point in his Christian life.

> **Rom. 7:22 For I delight in the law of God according to the inward man.**
> **7:23 But I see another law in my members, warring against the law of my mind, and bringing me into captivity to the law of sin which is in my members.**

THE "LAWS" TO WHICH PAUL REFERS

Paul has already given one law (principle):

1. **The law of indwelling sin** (v. 21) — "evil is present with me" — which is the propensity in the soul to sin. Then he adds three more laws!

2. **The law of God** (v. 22) — the moral aspect of the Mosaic law — the ten commandments, summed up by Jesus in two commands in the New Testament: Love God and love your neighbor — aka, *the law of Christ* (cf. Gal. 6:2). This is the desire in one's regenerated spirit (the "inward man") to live righteously.

3. **The law of sin in the members** (v. 23) — i.e., the body, which carries out the evil that has been festering in the soul, and often results in addictions. For example, lust in the soul often manifests in fornication or adultery in the body. Cravings in the soul to take in a substance that will make one feel good or alter the mind and/or consciousness, often leads to alcohol or drug addiction, which involves the body.

4. **The law of the mind or thoughts** (v. 23). Seeing that the law in the members (i.e., the body) wars against the law of the mind, the context implies that Paul views the law of the mind as good. It wants to do right and maybe thinks about the downsides of addiction or sexual fornication, but is often overwhelmed by bodily cravings, so that the law of sin in the members wins out.

With two of these laws working against us in the soul and body, how can we ever live righteously, finding victory over sin? Paul expresses this same frustration in v. 24:

> **Rom. 7:24 O wretched man that I am! Who will deliver me from this body of death?**

THE GLORIOUS ANSWER AMIDST DESPERATION

Do you sense his desperation? Do you feel his pain? Victory over sin seems like a no-win situation. Is this not the same thing you experience as a child of God? If the chapter were to end here, we would be in a miserable condition with no way out. But thankfully, there is relief from this dilemma in v. 25:

> **Rom. 7:25 I thank God—through Jesus Christ our Lord! So then, with the mind I myself serve the law of God, but with the flesh the law of sin.**

Jesus is the answer! He cuts through the overwhelming presence of sin in the soul that plays out in the body. Paul concludes by saying the mind wants to serve the law of God (rooted in the spirit) but the flesh (the soul in league with the body) wants to serve the law of sin. That is a dilemma, but Paul says the way to navigate this common problem in Christianity is through Jesus Christ.

In the next chapter he will explain how to have victory over sinning through Jesus Christ. But in Rom. 7, he has made very clear how *not* to have victory over sinning. For first century Jews, it is through continued dependence on the Mosaic rituals for pleasing God. Practicing circumcision and keeping the dietary laws and sabbaths and feast days and the 613 other Mosaic laws will not please God, for it will not make one spiritual. By way of application for twenty-first century believers, spiritual deadness and defeat are ensured for those who think they must hold to certain rules or standards or lists to be sanctified and acceptable to God.

Legalism in all of its forms is deadening, for "the letter kills, but the Spirit gives life." Jesus is the answer!

Paul is going to break through the gloom of ch. 7 in the next chapter, which is about living in the power of the Holy Spirit, who alone brings life. If you are living in legalism, forsake that sinful approach to God and seek His forgiveness. Learn the principle that "the law of the Spirit of life in Christ Jesus has made me free from the law of sin and death" (Rom. 8:2). By all means, beware the deadening effects of legalism!

CHAPTER 17
HOW TO HAVE VICTORY OVER SINNING
ROMANS 8:1-11

Rom. 7 is a miserable treatise on spiritual defeat and the deadening effects of legalism, which we covered in the previous chapter. I would describe it like a thunderstorm, concluding with a "thunderclap" crescendo:

> **Rom. 7:24** O wretched man that I am! Who will deliver me from this body of death?

FROM DESPERATION AND DEFEAT IN CH. 7 ...

What desperation and defeat! Unfortunately, that is the way multitudes of Christians live, accepting it as normal, because so many have succumbed to defeat and legalism in some form. First century Pharisaism is merely one form of legalism — clinging to the Mosaic rituals, even after Christ has come, expecting that by keeping the 613 Old Testament commandments, a believer is sanctified and made spiritual. But Paul condemns that way of thinking. Nevertheless, Pharisaism is alive and well, even in the twenty-first century, through the keeping of certain rules or standards or lists for a sanctified life. Again, it doesn't work. Legalism is deadening, regardless of the form it takes.

TO JOYFULNESS AND VICTORY IN CH. 8!

If Paul's emphasis in ch. 7 is how *not* to have victory over sinning, then his emphasis in ch. 8 is how to have victory in the Christian life — and that is the normal Christian life. Anything less is abnormal. Watchman Nee asks in his classic book, *The Normal Christian Life:*

> What is the normal Christian life? ... It is something very different from the life of the average Christian.[1]

He sums up the normal Christian life in the biblical words of the apostle Paul in Gal. 2:20, "I live no longer, but Christ lives His life in me"[2] (which is Rom. 6-8 summed up in a sentence).

In this chapter we move out of the storm clouds of defeat in Rom. 7 and into the sunshine of victory in Rom. 8, and what a glorious chapter of Scripture this truly is!

In 7:24 Paul asks, "Who will deliver me from this body of death?" The Greek word *hruomai*, translated *deliver*, according to Zane Hodges:

> is a functional equivalent for the idea in the Greek word-group *sozo/soteria*, "to save," "salvation."[3]

Thus, Paul's heart-cry is, "Who will *save* me from this wretchedness in my soul!" Seeing that God had already saved his spirit when he was regenerated, Paul is obviously speaking of soul-salvation, which is the ongoing process of sanctification for those who cooperate with God (Phil. 2:12-13). Jesus referred to it as entering the narrow gate and the difficult path that leads to life (Matt. 7:13-14; see also Matt. 16:24-27, cf. James 1:21).

JESUS IS THE ANSWER

What answer does Paul give to his question of desperation, "Who will save me?"

Rom. 7:25a I thank God—through Jesus Christ our Lord!

Jesus is the answer to your ongoing problem of indwelling sin! He can save you from spiritual deadness by enabling you for spiritual victory over sinning. Paul will unfold that glorious truth in Rom. 8. Notice the first verse:

> Rom. 8:1a *There is* therefore now no condemnation to those who are in Christ Jesus,
> 8:1b who do not walk according to the flesh, but according to the Spirit.

WHAT IS THE MEANING OF "NO CONDEMNATION"?

The word *condemnation* can be confusing, for it conjures up a picture of Hell for most Bible readers. Unfortunately, that is how tradition has trained us, which is incorrect. Adding to the confusion, the Alexandrian Greek manuscripts omit the latter half of v. 1 entirely. Zane Hodges explains:

> Regrettably the words *who do not walk in relation to the flesh but in relation to the Spirit* (found in KJV, NKJV) are omitted by most modern translations (e.g., NIV, NASB, JB). This omission by modern translators is due to their reliance on a few older Greek manuscripts that differ from the Majority Text.[4]

Bob Wilkin adds:

> The vast majority of Greek manuscripts (undivided Majority Text and even codex Alexandrinus, a key Critical Text manuscript) support the longer reading. So does the context.[5]

Keep in mind that Paul is speaking to believers, so this *condemnation* cannot be referring to Hell! What is this condemnation? Zane Hodges clarifies:

> Contrary to the widely held opinion that in 8:1 Paul is discussing the truth of justification as the removal of all condemnation, Paul's statement has a quite different meaning.[6]

Bob Wilkin adds:

> Hodges is certainly understating the case to say that the result is "a quite different meaning." This meaning is the exact opposite of the traditional understanding.[7]

NO PENAL SERVITUDE

When discussing *condemnation* as used in Rom. 5:16, 18 (see Chapter 13), we quoted Moulton and Milligan's definition for the word: "the punishment following a judicial sentence" or "penal servitude."[8] In light of this definition, Hodges translates Rom. 8:1 as follows:

> Therefore there is now no servitude to sin for those who are in Christ Jesus, who do not walk in relation to the flesh but in relation to the Spirit.[9]

This translation fits the context of Rom. 7 perfectly, where Paul has been talking about his past experience of servitude to sin — *as a believer*. He cannot seem to find victory and cries out for deliverance — for the saving of his soul from continued sinning. Thus, John Niemela writes regarding Rom. 8:1:

> Some may imagine that omitting the phrase, "who do not walk in relation to the flesh but in relation to the Spirit" ... would negate Hodges's exposition of v 1. It does not ... Pretend that the critical text's omission of walking by the Spirit were right. Would the verse then suggest that all believers would automatically escape penal servitude? No, both prior and following context teach that the escape is not automatic. It requires walking by the Spirit.
>
> Romans 7:13-25 described Paul as a believer making a futile effort to escape penal servitude by the flesh. Romans 8:1ff sets forth walking by the Spirit as the only way for believers to escape penal servitude.[10]

THE CHRIST-LIFE OF VICTORY

> **Rom. 8:2 For the law of the Spirit of life in Christ Jesus has made me free from the law of sin and death.**

Paul shares another law (or principle) — the law of the Spirit of life in Christ — or simply, the Christ-life. As noted in 6:3-4, we died with Christ and rose with Him at the point of our regeneration. Furthermore, we were baptized (i.e., placed) into Christ's body by the Holy Spirit (see 1 Cor. 12:13). We were placed into Jesus, and He placed His Spirit in us. Going forward, the law of sin and death is powerless to rule over us, for we now have the provision to yield our members to righteousness rather than to sinning, and thereby live the Christ-life of victory. The Holy Spirit is the divine catalyst. Victorious living is not automatic, of course, but those who choose to walk in the Spirit will experience victory through Christ.

An outstanding book on this subject is *Victory in Christ* by Charles Trumbull.[11] This book influenced me greatly early in my ministry. I would encourage you to read it. Trumbull points out that one of our biggest mistakes is not taking God at His Word. We must *believe* what God says in Rom. 6-8.

WALKING IN THE SPIRIT

Thus, the simple answer to the dilemma of Rom. 7 is to walk in the Spirit rather than the flesh. Incidentally, *to walk* is to take reiterated steps — just one step at a time. I once had a young Christian couple come to me and say, "Living the Christian life is so overwhelming! It's like climbing a massive mountain!" I responded to them, "No, you have the wrong metaphor; God's Word describes it as one step at a time, keeping your eyes focused only on the next step." That really helped them, and that is essentially what Paul says here — *take step after step in the Spirit rather than in the flesh*. If you do that, you will no longer be serving sin but Christ Jesus. There is freedom from sinning for those who walk in the Spirit.

Rom. 8:2 is a marvelous statement of truth. The only way we will ever experience victory is if we take this truth *by faith*. God says, "the law of the Spirit of life in Christ Jesus" — the same Spirit who dwells within us as believers — "has made me free from the law of sin and death!" Take it by faith, begin to walk in the Spirit, and experience the deliverance from sin that Paul so desperately sought at the end of Rom. 7. What, then, is "the law of the Spirit of life in Christ Jesus?" Paul develops that in the following verses:

> **Rom. 8:3 For what the law could not do in that it was weak through the flesh, God *did* by sending His own Son in the likeness of sinful flesh, on account of sin: He condemned sin in the flesh,**

What a glorious thought! We *can* obey God; we *can* live righteously; we *can* fulfill the law's righteous requirements — by walking in the Spirit!

THE LAW'S WEAKNESS REMEDIED BY CHRIST

Paul makes the point that the law never helped anyone walk in victory; only God can do that. He did it when He sent His Son Jesus to conquer sin by taking it upon Himself on the cross of Calvary. He died and rose, in part, so that God's children might have the ability through the Spirit to fulfill the righteous requirements of the law.

The verb *condemned* in v. 3 has a slightly different meaning than the noun *condemnation* in 8:1 and in 5:16, 18. To *condemn* is "to pronounce a sentence on." The idea is that God sentenced sin through Jesus Christ *in His flesh*. Ironically, the flesh was the very thing Paul struggled with, according to Rom. 7.

What Paul could not do in *his* flesh (for in *his* flesh "nothing good dwells," 7:18), Christ did in *His* flesh, for Jesus was without sin. This seems to be a dual reference, not only to the incarnation of Christ and His physical death, but also to Christ's soul, which was pure and untainted by sin, unlike man's. Hodges says:

Thus the death of Christ is also a sentence of doom upon sin in the flesh, destroying its present power and presaging its final removal from the experience of the one who is "righteous by faith" (1:17).[12]

> **Rom. 8:4 that the righteous requirement [Hodges: *action*] of the law might be fulfilled in us who do not walk according to the flesh but according to the Spirit.**

FULFILLING THE RIGHTEOUS REQUIREMENT OF THE LAW

The term *righteous requirement* is the same Greek word translated *righteous action* in 5:18. Hodges points out:

> As Paul has already asserted, the Christian is "not under the law but under grace" (6:14). Thus Paul does not mean here that a Christian can operate under the law and carry out its "requirements," but rather that the righteous action which the law stipulated, but failed to produce (see 7:15-25), can be achieved under grace. Understood this way, the singular of *dikaiōma* ... occurs because Paul's statement is a statement of principle. What Paul is affirming is that the thing that couldn't be done by living under the law can in fact be achieved by walking in relation to the Spirit.[13]

This is the very thing Paul could not do in his flesh! He could not fulfill the righteous actions of the law. Instead, his flesh kept driving him to continue sinning. But now, through the Spirit of Christ, he realizes that he — and *we*, by extension — have the *provision* to obey and live righteously, no longer in defeat and deadness. We can live in victory and vibrancy of life, pleasing God

Look again at v. 4. The term *might be fulfilled* is in the subjunctive mood, which is the Greek mood of potential. It's not guaranteed to happen; it will happen only if the condition is met. The condition is: walking in the Spirit rather than the flesh.

How does one walk in the Spirit? It requires *surrender* of your will to the Spirit's will in everyday living (Eph. 5:18; 12:1) and *faith*, believing that God will enable you through the Spirit to live righteously (Gal. 2:20). One additional requirement for walking in the Spirit is found in v. 5:

> **Rom. 8:5 For those who live according to the flesh set their minds on the things of the flesh, but those *who live* according to the Spirit, the things of the Spirit.**

THE MIND ORIENTED TOWARD THE SPIRIT

Notice how important it is to have your mind predisposed to walking in the Spirit. Hodges uses the word *oriented*.[14] Your spiritual orientation must be aligned with walking in the Spirit rather than the flesh.

> **Col 3:2** Set your mind on things above, not on things on the earth.

The word *mind* here is the same Greek word used for *mind* in Rom. 8:5. The point is that a believer who is focused on worldly or fleshly things is never going to find victory, because their mind is not predisposed or oriented to spiritual things. In the next few verses, Paul distinguishes between the two ways of thinking about spiritual matters.

> **Rom. 8:6 For to be carnally minded *is* death, but to be spiritually minded *is* life and peace.
> 8:7 Because the carnal mind *is* enmity against God; for it is not subject to the law of God, nor indeed can be.**

THE CARNAL MIND VS. THE SPIRITUAL MIND

Notice the distinction between the carnal and the spiritual mind. The NASB refers to this as *the mind set on the flesh* vs. *the mind set on the Spirit*. As explained in the previous chapter, the *flesh* does not necessarily refer to the *body*. Our problem is not the *body*, per se, it is the *soul*, specifically *indwelling sin*. A fleshly soul is self-seeking, having sinful desires, worldly pursuits, and enjoying material pleasures. Fleshly behaviors often are carried out in the body, but they are rooted in the soul, so it's not the body, per se, that is evil. It is the *flesh*, or *indwelling sin*, which Paul refers to as "carnality" in these verses.

A carnal or fleshly mindset produces spiritual deadness. but a spiritual mindset produces life and peace. Here's why: Those believers who have a carnal mindset are at enmity with God. Fellowship with Him has been severed; the relationship is strained. There is a need for confession and forgiveness and reconciliation with God. A believer is not subject to God's moral law and can't be, as long as their mindset is carnal.

This explains why so many believers are defeated rather than victorious. It also explains how believers can live in a perpetual state of disobedience to God. Their spiritual orientation is not given over to God. As long as a child of God remains focused on worldly pleasures, they are doomed to fail. I dread to think of the consequences at the Judgment Seat of Christ for a life lived in this manner! In the next two verses, Paul shares the difference between believers and unbelievers, to demonstrate the marvelous *provision* we have *in Christ*.

> **Rom. 8:8 So then, those who are in the flesh cannot please God.**
> **8:9 But you are not in the flesh but in the Spirit, if indeed the Spirit of God dwells in you. Now if anyone does not have the Spirit of Christ, he is not His.**

Paul is speaking of our position as being "in the Spirit" because we have believed on Jesus for eternal (age-lasting) life, as opposed to being "in the flesh" (like unbelievers, who are perpetually in the flesh). Unbelievers don't have the Spirit of Christ thus, cannot please God. Bob Wilkin comments:

> When Paul speaks of being *in the flesh*, he is speaking of being in that state in one's position. He is not speaking of walking in that state in

one's experience ... Believers are *in the Spirit*, but may walk *according to the Spirit* or *according to the flesh*. Unbelievers are *in the flesh* and only walk *according to the flesh*.[15]

Why does Paul mention this? The answer is found in v. 10:

Rom. 8:10 And if Christ *is* in you, the body *is* dead because of sin, but the Spirit *is* life because of righteousness.

OUR PROVISION IN CHRIST

Paul wants the believers at Rome to realize the marvelous *provision* they have because they are *in Christ*, a provision that is spiritually priceless. Yes, the body remains spiritually dead because of sin. But we have the glorious benefit of the Spirit of life dwelling within our spiritually "dead" bodies. He breathes spiritual life into us when we choose to walk in the Spirit, thereby producing righteousness. Paul brings this to a climax in v. 11:

Rom. 8:11 But if the Spirit of Him who raised Jesus from the dead dwells in you, He who raised Christ from the dead will also give life to your mortal bodies through His Spirit who dwells in you.

Zane Hodges says:

Although Christians live in physically mortal bodies that are already spiritually dead because of sin (v 10), the Spirit can impart to these mortal bodies an experience of life. In its context here, this statement must not be taken as referring to our future resurrection. Instead, it refers to the life and peace produced by the mindset of the Spirit (v 6b). Thus the Spirit can overcome the death that characterizes the fallen state of our present mortal bodies (v 10) and can make them vehicles for expressing the divine life within us.[16]

What a marvelous concept! The same God who raised Jesus from the dead, will breathe life into our mortal bodies when we are appropriating our provision, drawing upon the Spirit's enabling power. The result will be a righteous lifestyle, a reflection of Christ's image to others around us, and a soul that is being saved, on the pathway to becoming a son to glory. Are you on that pathway?

CHAPTER 18
THE REVEALING OF GOD'S GLORIFIED SONS
ROMANS 8:12-19

If the Lord Jesus were to say to me, "For the rest of your life, I want you to preach and teach only *one* chapter from the Scriptures to the church of Jesus Christ; choose your chapter wisely"— I would indubitably and without hesitation choose Rom. 8.

THE MOST GLORIOUS CHAPTER IN ALL OF SCRIPTURE

Rom. 8 is a thrilling chapter of victory! It tells how children of God can become victorious over sinning in their Christian lives. It tells how they can progress from being mere *children* of God to *sons* of God — *sons to glory,* as Heb. 2:10 refers to them. It tells of the future revealing of the sons of God as a new order of rulers who will ascend to positions of rulership formerly held by angelic beings. It tells how this revealing will accompany the restoration of Earth to its former glory. It tells how this is the culmination of God's plan for mankind, and how all creation is eagerly awaiting this, even now, which is evident in man's inner longings for a utopian world and his headlong pursuit of communism, which is a Satanic counterfeit. In the end of the chapter, it tells of the marvelous love of God in leading and training these sons of God, preparing them for glorification. In spite of all the persecution and suffering they will face on the pathway to glorification, He will comfort them with His love, so that nothing will be able to separate them from God's love. I think Rom. 8 could possibly be the most glorious chapter in all of Scripture.

This is the purpose for your salvation! It's not so you can go to Heaven when you die. It's so you can draw upon your spiritual provision — Jesus Christ living within — to live victoriously and thereby experience the saving of your soul so you can qualify to co-rule with Him in His kingdom. That is the ultimate purpose for eternal life (life for the age). But you must qualify for this degree of salvation; it is not automatic. Sadly, *very few* churches teach these truths and, consequently, *very few* believers know about them. Even fewer are preparing to qualify. Shockingly, some churches actually preach *against* these truths. May we faithfully preach these profound truths from the rooftops to believers everywhere! In fact, these themes should dominate the preaching and teaching ministry of churches everywhere, and should characterize our Christian living and witness. Before God's sons can be revealed, they must be prepared, and that is ongoing in the present age.

> **Rom. 8:12 Therefore, brethren, we are debtors—not to the flesh, to live according to the flesh.**
> **8:13 For if you live according to the flesh you will die; but if by the Spirit you put to death the deeds of the body, you will live.**

INDEBTED TO LIVE IN THE SPIRIT

8:12. Paul starts v. 12 with the word *therefore*, which is a word of summary and conclusion. Whenever this word is used in the Scriptures, we should stop and determine what it is *there for*. As seen in the previous chapter, vs. 1-11 are about the importance of believers choosing to cooperate with God and walk in the Spirit rather than in the flesh. Paul puts a great deal of emphasis on the importance of having our minds *set* on the things of the Spirit rather than the flesh. He goes so far as to say this is our *obligation*.

Now that Christ has delivered us from sin's power, we are

indebted, not to live according to the flesh, but according to the Spirit. Griffith Thomas writes:

> We are debtors to live "after the Spirit," and this necessarily means a mortification of everything fleshly and sinful. It is only as we fulfil these obligations that we can realise our true life of sonship and look forward with absolute assurance to the coming glory.[1]

CARNALITY KILLS

8:13. Those believers who remain indebted to the flesh, even though they have been delivered from sin's power, are carnal and do not have that assurance. Incidentally, the word *carnal* comes from the Latin root word *carn*, which means *flesh*. From this root word we get other words such as *carnivorous*, which means flesh-eating; *carnage*, which is the destruction of flesh, whether animals or people; *chili con carne*, which is chili with flesh or meat; and even *carnival*, which in its original meaning is the idea of a fleshly, indulgent sort of revelry that dates back to ancient times. God says to believers in v. 6:

> **Rom. 8:6a** To be carnally minded *is* death.

In fact, in 7:9 Paul admitted that he "died" when he gave in to sin. Obviously, he is speaking spiritually, not physically. His fellowship with God was instantly severed. Rom. 7:11, *For sin, taking occasion by the commandment, deceived me, and by it killed me.* In the context, Paul is referring to legalism, which caused him to stumble and sin. But whether sinning in legalism or in license, sin deadens. It zaps our spiritual vitality. Thus, to summarize 8:12-13 (my paraphrase):

> Don't succumb to the flesh, for fleshliness produces deadness! On the other hand, if you put to death the deeds of the body (your fleshly choices to sin) by depending on the Holy Spirit, you will live — you will have vibrancy of spiritual life.

The *death* and *life* mentioned in this text are not merely referring to here and now — that is, in this present age — for how we live our lives *now*, determines how we will live out our lives in the next age, the millennial age. The choices you are making today will either come back to haunt you in the next age or they will come back to bless you. We begin to see this principle unfold in v. 14:

> **Rom. 8:14 For as many as are led by the Spirit of God, these are sons of God.**

GOD'S CHILDREN VS. HIS SONS

Those who choose to walk in the Spirit as their mode of life are considered God's *sons*. Some may wonder, "Aren't *all* believers God's sons?" Technically, no! Unfortunately, because of some mistranslations in the KJV — which I believe were theologically motivated — multitudes of Christians have been led to believe we are all *sons* of God. For instance, notice how the King James translates theses verses:

> **John 1:12 (KJV)** But as many as received him, to them gave he power to become the sons of God, *even* to them that believe on his name:

> **Phil. 2:15 (KJV)** That ye may be blameless and harmless, the sons of God, without rebuke, in the midst of a crooked and perverse nation, among whom ye shine as lights in the world;

> **1 John 3:1a (KJV)** Behold, what manner of love the Father hath bestowed upon us, that we should be called the sons of God.

The word *sons* in these verses is not correct, because in all of the verses mentioned, the Greek word translated *sons* is *teknon*. But *teknon* doesn't mean *son*; it means *child* (actually, *children* in the plural) and should have been translated as such. Children are posterity, regardless of age, male and female. Believers are repeatedly called "children of God" in the New Testament, because we are God's posterity, regardless of our age. When we were initially saved, He re-created us spiritually (2 Cor. 5:17), thus we are His children. It is, therefore, correct to refer to God as our Father. The word *teknon* is used in v. 16.

Rom. 8:16 The Spirit Himself bears witness with our spirit that we are children of God,

Zane Hodges says:

This verse is often misunderstood as a reference to some kind of inner (mystical) witness *to* (as opposed to *with*) our human spirit that gives us a subjective assurance that we are born again. Paul knows nothing of this kind of "inner witness."[2]

John Niemela adds:

The popular view [of this verse] is that the Holy Spirit witnesses *to* our human spirit, rather than *along with* our spirit ... The form of the word ... argues for seeing both the Holy Spirit and our human spirit jointly giving testimony that we are regenerate, because both know that we believed Christ's promise of everlasting life.[3]

If you doubt that you are God's child and that the Holy Spirit lives within you, even though you have believed on Jesus for eternal life, it is very likely because you were *taught* to doubt by some preacher who holds to incorrect theology — and that has done a great deal of damage in Christianity!

Bob Wilkin contributes a note in Hodges's Commentary:

Taking Rom 8:16 as a verse about assurance of everlasting life not only misunderstands the passage entirely, but actually strips believers of assurance since they cease looking to Christ's promise only (e.g., John 5:24). Instead, they now look introspectively for some sort of mysterious feeling. Such a practice is self-defeating since our feelings cannot be objectified or trusted.[4]

If you believed on Jesus, then take God at His Word that you possess eternal life, whether or not you have "warm fuzzies" in your soul. Look again at v. 16:

Rom. 8:16 The Spirit Himself bears witness with our spirit that we are children of God,

The word *children* is the Greek word *teknon*, which is the word used for all believers — they are children of God. However, a different Greek word — *huios* translates as *son*. Though most Christians are probably unaware of this, only some children of God are considered *huios*, or *sons*. Nineteenth century commentator, Robert Govett, said: "We become '*children* of God' by His grace. We become '*sons* of God' by obedience."[5] Arlen Chitwood says:

> All Christians are referred to as "children" (Gk., *teknon*), but Scripture does not use "sons" (Gk., *huios*) in the same all-encompassing manner. Though all Christians are "sons" because of *creation*, the New Testament usage of the Greek word *huios*, referring to Christians through this means, appears only within contexts where *regality is seen and where Christians are seen actively progressing toward the goal set before them*. In this respect, the word is used relative to Christians in complete keeping with that which "sonship" portends — with *rulership*.[6]

There are only three texts of Scripture in which the word *sons* is applied to Christians — Rom. 8, Gal. 3-4, Heb. 12 — and in all three of these instances, the concept of *adoption* is also being discussed. (Note: Adoption is also discussed in Eph. 1, but not concurrent with the word *sons*).

THE BIBLICAL MEANING OF ADOPTION

The word *adoption* in Greek is *huiothesia*. The way the word *adoption* is used in our culture is entirely different than the way it is used in the Scriptures. Of course, we refer to adoption as legally taking someone else's child and raising that child as our own. In Greco-Roman culture, adoption was the idea of declaring an adult as one's legal child and heir, and given all the rights and privileges of the father, even if that one was not the natural firstborn child.

An example of this is seen in the classic 1959 film *Ben Hur*. The protagonist, Judah Ben Hur, who is a young, wealthy, Jewish man, is wrongly accused by the Romans and sentenced to slavery in the galley of a Roman warship. In the course of battle, the ship sinks and Judah saves the ship's captain from drowning. The captain, Quintus Arrius, is also a Roman Senator. Out of gratitude he adopts Judah Ben Hur as his legal heir and gives him the family signet ring, which carries all the power and authority of that family.

Add to that the picture of Jewish adoption in the Scriptures. Sons would typically receive an equal inheritance of the father's wealth. But one son was particularly chosen to take on the father's name and business affairs, and would continue as spiritual leader of the family. He would receive a double portion so as to enable him to carry out his responsibilities. Typically, that would be the firstborn, but sometimes the firstborn was disinherited and another would be chosen. By way of example, Jacob had twelve sons, who each received an equal portion of his estate upon his death. Reuben, who was the firstborn, was disinherited from that position for sinning and offending his father. Instead, Joseph — who was much younger — was chosen as firstborn for being faithful, and his two sons (Ephraim and Manasseh) were both honored as inheritors.

In the New Testament we think of the prodigal son, who essentially disinherited himself by his behavior, until he repented and returned back home. The father held a feast and put on him the best robe and the father's signet ring. I believe this signifies the returned son was being promoted to firstborn son. The elder son had an attitude of arrogance and non-repentance, so he was essentially disinherited. He represents the Pharisees in the text, while the restored prodigal represents repentant Israelites.

Notice what happens to those believers who are led by the Spirit of God:

> **Rom. 8:14 For as many as are led by the Spirit of God, these are sons [Greek *huios*] of God.**
> **8:15 For you did not receive the spirit of bondage**

> again to fear, but you received the Spirit of adoption [Greek *huiothesia*] by whom we cry out, "Abba, Father."

REWARDED WITH ADOPTION

8:14. Those believers who consistently walk in the Spirit rather than the flesh will be rewarded with adoption — the position of firstborn inheritor — when they meet Jesus at the Judgment Seat of Christ. They will receive a double inheritance, as will be seen in a moment.

8:15. Incidentally, Paul encourages the believers to aspire to this status of adoption by walking in the Spirit, for they have not received a spirit that will lead them back into enslavement to sin via legalism. Rather, they have received the Holy Spirit of God, who leads believers to adoption. He is seeking out *sons to glory* — those who can refer to God as "Abba, Father," which is a term of endearment reserved for those who are in close fellowship with Him. Of course, we understand the prerequisite that is found everywhere in the context. The believer must cooperate with the Holy Spirit and live righteously rather than catering to the flesh. Zane Hodges writes:

> In Paul's much earlier epistle to the Galatians, he clearly distinguished between a "minor child" (*nepios*) and a "son" (*huios*). The former is a child "not yet of legal age" ... who is under the governance of a tutor (the law), while the latter is the "adult son" who is no longer under this tutor (see Gal 4:1-7). If the Galatians passage is compared carefully with Rom 8:14-17, their similarities will be quite obvious.
>
> Both passages contain the words for "son" (Gal 4: 4, 6; Rom 8:14 [also vv 19, 29, 32]) and "heir" (Gal 4:1, 7; Rom 8:14, 17). Both refer to the Spirit's cry, "Abba, Father" (Gal 4:6; Rom 8:15), and both use the word "adoption" (*huiothesia*: Gal 4:5; Rom 8:15) in the technical sense of "adoption of children" ...
>
> In the light of Paul's teaching in Gal 4:1-7, it is natural here to take the expression *the sons of God* ... as a reference to the life-experience of the adult son who is not under the law. In contrast to

the earlier struggle (described in Rom 7:7-25) in which the regenerate inner man strived vainly to fulfill God's law, now the one *led by the Spirit* lives the life of an adult son who is no longer under the law.[7]

THE SPIRIT OF ADOPTION – NEITHER LICENTIOUS NOR LEGALISTIC

To summarize, Hodges is saying that only those believers who learn to walk according to the Spirit of adoption (liberty and freedom) rather than according to some system of legalism (bondage and fear) will be adopted as sons to receive the double portion of inheritance, for they are being led by (i.e., walking in) the Spirit. They are neither licentious nor legalistic.

In the context of both Romans and Galatians, Paul is condemning legalism, thus legalists will not inherit a place of rulership in the kingdom, for they remain juvenile and have not matured as adults. Think of the high percentage of Christians who live licentiously, on the one hand, and those who live legalistically, on the other. Presumably, they will not be inheritors in the kingdom of Christ.

ADOPTION IS NOT AUTOMATIC AT INITIAL SALVATION

Unfortunately, traditionalists believe this adoption is automatic, at the point of salvation, for all believers. Some readers may be familiar with the "Patch-the-Pirate" children's song, "I'm Adopted." Here are the lyrics:

> I am adopted; I'm a child of the King.
>   God is my Father, and he owns ev'rything.
>   He walks beside me; He's my very best friend.
>   Praise God, I'll never be lonely again.
>
> My Father chose me, and He loves me, I know.
>   He will be with me wherever I go.
>   I'll never worry; I have joined royalty.
>   I am a member of the King's family. Chorus

Chorus:
>   I'm adopted, hallelujah! I've got a new song.
>   I'm adopted, hallelujah! I fin'ly belong.
>   I've got a brand new family overflowing with love.
>   I'm a child of my Father above.[8]

Those lyrics represent commonly-held theology in evangelical Christianity, including fundamentalist Christianity. But that is erroneous theology that came out of the Reformation. You were not automatically adopted when initially saved (regenerated). You will be adopted at the Judgment Seat of Christ, *if* Jesus deems that you lived righteously, walking in the Spirit consistently. Otherwise, you will not be adopted, and you will not receive the standing of a mature, firstborn son. You will not receive the double inheritance. You will merely receive the basic inheritance that all children of God receive — and what is that?

> **Rom. 8:16-17 The Spirit Himself bears witness with our spirit that we are children [Greek, *teknon*] of God, and if children, then heirs—heirs of God and joint heirs with Christ, if indeed we suffer with *Him,* that we may also be glorified together.**

WHO ARE GOD'S HEIRS?

All children of God are His basic heirs. They will be resurrected before the Millennium and will dwell in His kingdom, but not necessarily in the realm of the kingdom of heaven, New Jerusalem. Only the "good and faithful" children who hear "Well done!" will be adopted and given the double inheritance of co-heirship with Christ. They will also be co-glorified with Him. They will co-rule with Him in New Jerusalem, which will hover over the earth, as the heavenly realm of the kingdom, where Christ will dwell with His bride.

Those children of God who hear the verdict "wicked and lazy servant" will be consigned to the darkness outside New Jerusalem. In other words, they will dwell on the earth, consciously regretting that they did not walk in the Spirit and thereby qualify for double inheritance. Zane Hodges says:

> In the Christian family there are both children (*heirs of God*) and also a Firstborn Son [v. 29, *that He might be the firstborn among many brethren*] ... This second heirship—co-heirship with Christ—is predicated on "co-suffering" that leads to "co-glorification." ... The word *if* ... indicates the conditional nature of this statement. It is false grammar to say that the "if" clause treats this as a definite fact. The construction means no more than the expression "on the assumption that" and leaves fully open the opposite possibility.[9]

WHO ARE CHRIST'S JOINT-HEIRS?

I used to think, because it was what I was taught, that *all* believers are heirs of God and joint-heirs with Christ. In fact, in my mind, I was essentially taught to put a period at the end of the phrase, "joint-heirs with Christ." In my circle of Christianity, we never seemed to read the last part of v. 17 or, at the very least, we never emphasized it. But it is critical to understanding the entire verse.

What is the prerequisite to adoption and co-rulership with Christ? Verse 14 makes clear that it is being led by (i.e., walking in) the Spirit. Verse 17 adds the condition, *if* we suffer with Him (i.e., with Jesus). G.H. Lang says:

> The sharing of Christ's sufferings now is our training and qualifying for sharing His glory hereafter; as well as the glory being the compensation graciously promised for the sufferings ... Those who refuse the distinction between simple heirship to God and joint heirship with the Messiah, make the former as well as the latter to become conditional upon suffering with Christ; and thus would the loss of those who avoid suffering become vastly greater, their salvation itself being imperilled.[10]

THE PREREQUISITE OF SUFFERING

Sadly, some Christians never suffer with Jesus. Paul implies why that is the case.

> **2 Tim. 3:12** Yes, and all who desire to live godly in Christ Jesus will suffer persecution.

If you haven't suffered for Him, then it is likely you haven't been living godly in Christ Jesus. Jesus said:

> **John 15:20** If they persecuted Me, they will also persecute you.

The apostles speak of rejoicing in suffering for Jesus *now*, which will result in being exceeding joyful *then*, in His presence:

> **1 Pet. 4:12-13** Beloved, do not think it strange concerning the fiery trial which is to try you, as though some strange thing happened to you; but rejoice to the extent that you partake of Christ's sufferings, that when His glory is revealed, you may also be glad with exceeding joy.
> **14** If you are reproached for the name of Christ, blessed *are you*, for the Spirit of glory and of God rests upon you. On their part He is blasphemed, but on your part He is glorified.

> **Phil. 3:10-11** that I may know Him and the power of His resurrection, and the fellowship of His sufferings, being conformed to His death, if, by any means, I may attain to the [out]-resurrection from the dead. (parenthesis mine)

There are conditions for being adopted as a firstborn son, and the conditions are persevering in righteous living through the enabling power of the Holy Spirit, and enduring the sufferings of Christ for His glory.

> **2 Tim. 2:12** If we endure [KJV: *suffer*, because it is enduring in suffer-

ing], we shall also reign with *Him*. If we deny *Him*, He also will deny us. (parenthesis mine)

THE REWARD OF SUFFERING

This has nothing to do with salvation; it is in the context of sanctification unto reward. Paul shares a comforting thought in Rom. 8:18:

> **Rom. 8:18 For I consider that the sufferings of this present time are not worthy *to be compared* with the glory which shall be revealed in us.**

Anything we might have to endure for Jesus' sake during our lifetime of seventy or eighty years is nothing compared to the glory He will reveal in us during the next thousand years.

> **2 Cor. 4:17** For our light affliction, which is but for a moment, is working for us a far more exceeding *and* eternal weight of glory,

Though our present sufferings are real, they are "light" compared with the *reward* for suffering — a superlative degree of glory in the next age! What a marvelous thought! He will reveal His glory in us, that is, in those believers who are led of the Spirit and therefore are deemed adopted as sons. *When* is this revealing and *what* is it? Lang writes:

> Romans 8:19-25. The passage speaks of "the revealing," the unveiling, "of the sons of God" as being their "adoption." This word does not refer to the new birth into the family of God, but to the final possible outcome of that birth. The Roman noble could choose any one of his male children to be heir to his titles and estates. This youth he led before the Senate and declared in due form that this was his son and heir.
>
> Thereupon the robe of a youth was removed and he was given that of manhood. Similarly, it is not yet made manifest to the universe which of the family of God will reign with Christ; but when the present body of humiliation gives place to a body like unto the

glorified body of Christ it will be made clear: "When Christ [Who is already] our life shall be manifested, then shall we also be manifested with Him in glory" (Colossians 3:4).[11]

So many assume Col. 3:4, which Lang has just quoted, is automatic for all believers, but it is not. In the context of Col. 3, the passage is quite clear that this reward is conditional, for those who qualify. Paul talks there about putting off sins and putting on the graces of our Lord Jesus Christ. He concludes the chapter with these words:

> **Col. 3:23-24** And whatever you do, do it heartily, as to the Lord and not to men, knowing that from the Lord you will receive the reward of the inheritance; for you serve the Lord Christ.
>
> **25** But he who does wrong will be repaid for what he has done, and there is no partiality.

THE REVEALING OF THE SONS TO GLORY

How marvelous to think the adopted sons of God will be revealed in full glory! Glory, of course, is encasement in light in full splendor — think of Christ's transfiguration and the Old Testament *shekinah* glory. God is literally going to share some of His glory with His adopted sons, for all to see.

Those who live godly in Christ Jesus will suffer in some manner. People will revile you and say all kinds of evil against you falsely for Jesus' sake. They will despise you and treat you disdainfully, as if you don't know what you're talking about. They will brand you a heretic. Surprisingly, a high percentage of the persecution will come from other Christians who disagree with you. The apostle Paul said:

> **1 Cor. 4:10** We *are* fools for Christ's sake, but you *are* wise in Christ! We *are* weak, but you *are* strong! You *are* distinguished, but we *are* dishonored!
>
> **11** To the present hour we both hunger and thirst, and we are poorly clothed, and beaten, and homeless.
>
> **12-13** And we labor, working with our own hands. Being reviled,

we bless; being persecuted, we endure; being defamed, we entreat. We have been made as the filth of the world, the offscouring of all things until now.

Most of this treatment Paul received at the hands of the Jews, his own countrymen, who were believers in an Old Testament sense. They could not tolerate his teaching about Jesus and kingdom inheritance. Do you ever get treated like that? If not, then perhaps you are not living godly in Christ Jesus.

If you are enduring suffering of some type, be assured. Those who think of you disdainfully will one day see you revealed in full glory as an adopted son of God. When you are revealed as a son to glory, they will be amazed that the one they had despised and rejected is being honored by Jesus and held in high esteem as one of the rulers of the new age, in full glory. Whereas in the present age they view you as a mere caterpillar, a worm, one day in the future they will see you in full glory as a magnificent butterfly — one having power and authority as delegated by Jesus Himself. That is why Paul can say:

Rom. 8:18 For I consider that the sufferings of this present time are not worthy *to be compared* with the glory which shall be revealed in us.

The revealing of God's glorified sons is coming, child of God, so don't lose heart! Stay the course and persevere, by the grace of God. Keep walking in the Spirit!

CHAPTER 19
BIRTH OF A NEW AGE
ROMANS 8:19-25

When I was a kid in the late 1960s and early '70s, I remember hearing on occasion a song entitled, *The Age of Aquarius*. It was sung by a group called *The Fifth Dimension*, whose name is apropos to the song. That pop song was quite popular during my childhood, because those were the heyday years of the hippie and new age movements. The title of the song especially piqued my curiosity because my birthday is in February, and falls under the so-called sign of Aquarius. As a Christian I have always steered clear of horoscopes and astrology, because I realize those subjects promote the evil side of the supernatural realm, which I understand is quite dangerous.

LONGING FOR UTOPIA

The song's lyrics long for a new age, when "peace will guide the planets, and love will steer the stars" — a time of "harmony and understanding, sympathy and trust abounding; no more falsehoods or derisions; golden living dreams of visions; mystic crystal revelation; and the mind's true liberation."[1] It's all so new age of course. But doesn't this represent the longing of man throughout all of time for a new age of peace and harmony?

Some may remember the 1971 Coca-Cola advertisement,

which was one of the most popular of all time. One hundred young people from all over the world are standing on a hill, singing "I'd like to teach the world to sing in perfect harmony."[2] Again, it was a hippie, new-age song — which Coke gladly exploited — but it expressed a longing for world peace and harmony and love.

I have a book in my library entitled, *Utopian Thought in the Western World*, in which the authors — over the course of more than 800 pages — review the history of utopian ideals, from Thomas More to Francis Bacon to Karl Marx, and dozens of others throughout history. [3]Naturally, Jesus Christ is mentioned numerous times, as one who had utopian ideals, but how ironic is that? We know He is the *only one* who can truly bring world peace and harmony and love, and He will do so when He returns the second time and launches His millennial kingdom. Then all the world will truly sing, "Joy to the world, the Lord has come!"

The heart of man longs for a golden age, a utopia of peace, harmony and love on earth. Is that not what Paul refers to in 8:19?

> **Rom. 8:19 For the earnest expectation of the creation eagerly waits for the revealing of the sons of God.**

Notice the phrases, *earnest expectation* and *eagerly waits*. The deep longing in man's soul is for God's glorified sons to be revealed, though man doesn't realize that this is the only true way to have world peace. Instead, man blindly pursues Satanic counterfeits that destroy peace (e.g., communism).

Why is the revealing of God's glorified sons critical to the birth of the new age?

1. BECAUSE IT RESULTS IN REGIME CHANGE

Arlen Chitwood says:

> According to Rom. 8:19-23, the entire creation (as it pertains to the earth, both the material creation and redeemed man) presently

groans and travails, awaiting "the manifestation of the sons of God" (a new order of sons — *taken from among redeemed man, NOT angels*).[4]

GOD'S FIRSTBORN SONS AT PRESENT

What is this "new order of sons," of which Chitwood speaks? God presently has two firstborn sons, that is, those who are given a double inheritance. First and foremost, the Bible speaks of Jesus as being firstborn.

Col. 1:15 He is the image of the invisible God, the **firstborn** over all creation.

Col. 1:18 And He is the head of the body, the church, who is the beginning, the **firstborn** from the dead, that in all things He may have the preeminence.

Heb. 1:6 But when He again brings the **firstborn** into the world, He says: *"Let all the angels of God worship Him."*

Rev. 1:5 Jesus Christ, the faithful witness, the **firstborn** from the dead, and the ruler over the kings of the earth.

Second, Israel is God's firstborn son.

Exod. 4:22 Then you shall say to Pharaoh, "Thus says the LORD: 'Israel *is* My son, My firstborn.

Despite Israel's sinning and God's consequent divorcing of Israel as His "wife," God has never withdrawn the status of firstborn. He has a future plan for Israel, based on His covenants. Israel will repent, Jesus will return, and the nation will become restored as Jehovah's "wife" (see Jer. 3 and Hosea).

GOD'S FUTURE FIRSTBORN — THE SONS TO GLORY

God's third firstborn son is the faithful subset of the church — those who hear "good and faithful" at the Judgment Seat of Christ. They live according to the Spirit rather than the flesh, and they willingly suffer for Jesus. They will become adopted as the firstborn sons to glory to co-rule with Jesus in the heavenlies. The writer to the Hebrews refers to them:

> **Heb. 12:22-23** But you have come to Mount Zion and to the city of the living God, the heavenly Jerusalem, to an innumerable company of angels, to the general assembly and church of the firstborn *who are* registered in heaven, to God the Judge of all, to the spirits of just men made perfect."

In the context of Heb. 11, the great faith chapter, and God's preparation of His sons to glory in the early verses of ch. 12, these are the qualified ones who will co-rule with Jesus in New Jerusalem. Rom 8:29 refers to Jesus as being "the **firstborn** among many brethren." Jesus, the firstborn over all, will launch His kingdom, having two realms:

1. The *earthly* realm, with firstborn son Israel as premier ruler over the nations.
2. The heavenly realm, with the adopted firstborn sons of the church age as rulers with Christ in the heavenlies (New Jerusalem).

THE NEW ORDER TO REPLACE THE SATANIC ORDER

But there is something about the revealing of these sons to glory that will be quite astounding. It is the reason why all of creation has earnest expectation and eagerly awaits — that is, has a deep longing — for God's glorified sons to be revealed, which signals the new age of peace and love. The present age poses a major obstacle to the coming of the new age, namely, the *rulers* of this age, which Paul speaks about in Ephesians.

> **Eph. 6:12** For we do not wrestle against flesh and blood, but against principalities, against powers, against the rulers of the darkness of this age, against spiritual *hosts* of wickedness in the heavenly *places*.

Satan is the prince of the power of the air. He controls the kingdoms of this world and has delegated his authority to the demonic realm to rule with him in the heavenlies. In fact, when Satan tempted Jesus in the wilderness and offered Him all the kingdoms of this world, Jesus never challenged Satan's authority over Earth. But Satan's rule over the heavenlies, along with his echelons, will one day be removed and replaced with the sons to glory. Notice something interesting Paul said in 1 Cor. 2:

> **1 Cor. 2:6** We speak wisdom among those who are mature, yet not the wisdom of this age, nor of the rulers of this age, who are coming to nothing.
>
> **7-8** But we speak the wisdom of God in a mystery, the hidden *wisdom* which God ordained before the ages for our glory, which none of the rulers of this age knew; for had they known, they would not have crucified the Lord of glory.
>
> **9** But as it is written: *"Eye has not seen, nor ear heard, nor have entered into the heart of man the things which God has prepared for those who love Him."*

Had Satan and his echelon known of God's plan to replace them with Jesus and His army of glorified sons that Jesus redeemed and is now preparing as His future co-rulers, they (Satan and his echelon) would *never* have crucified the Lord of glory.

RIGHTEOUSNESS AND PEACE

The reason why the revealing of the sons of glory is what all creation *earnestly expects* and *eagerly awaits* is that it will signal the removal of sin and wickedness, to be replaced by obedience and righteousness, and that will result in peace. In order for peace and harmony to prevail on Earth, there must first be righteousness.

Isa. 32:17 The work of righteousness will be peace, and the effect of righteousness, quietness and assurance forever. (see also James 3:18)

As long as Satan is ruler over Earth, there can never be peace or harmony or love. Only when Satan is ultimately defeated and cast into the lake of fire with his echelon and Jesus ascends to the throne with His echelon will there be peace on earth, goodwill to men. Christ's co-regents will be a new order of rulers comprised of adopted, firstborn, glorified, redeemed humans who will replace the former order of supernatural beings. This transference of power is found in the book of Revelation. Arlen Chitwood notes:

> Revelation chapters one through three present *the complete Church* in heaven following the present dispensation. Events of the judgment seat are depicted; and when that depicted is one day realized, *the overcomers*, those found worthy to rule the nations with Christ, will be made known.
>
> The scene which follows in chapter four is ... *a relinquishment of crowns by angelic rulers* (vv. 10, 11), with a view to *a new order of rulers* — Christians having previously been shown qualified through decisions and determinations rendered at the judgment seat (chs. 1-3) — taking these crowns and ruling the earth in the stead of the present order of rulers, in the stead of angels (Rom. 8:18, 19).[5]

G.H. Lang writes:

> There exists a government of the universe conducted by great angels and their subordinates. Many of these have fallen from their original allegiance to God and prostitute their offices and powers to corrupt His realms. It is therefore inevitable that a re-arrangement shall come in that heavenly government. This will be effected by Christ and His glorified followers being invested with the whole of that heavenly authority. For it is written that "not unto angels hath God subjected the inhabited earth to come" (Hebrews 2:5).[6]

Why is the revealing of God's glorified sons critical to the new age?

2. BECAUSE IT BRINGS SUBSTANTIAL DIMINISHING OF THE CURSE

> **Rom. 8:20-21 For the creation was subjected to futility, not willingly, but because of Him who subjected *it* in hope; because the creation itself also will be delivered from the bondage of corruption into the glorious liberty of the children of God.**

The sin of Adam resulted in the curse of Genesis 3. Consequently, creation has been corrupted and plunged into a state of deterioration — its potential greatly diminished. That is why Paul refers to it as "subjected to futility" (i.e., purposelessness or frustration — the idea of being kept from fulfilling its ultimate purpose). This was thrust upon the earth, not of its own will. Actually, God did this, with a hopeful future in mind. In fact, this *hope* is likely a veiled reference to the *proto-evangelium*, "the first gospel," in Gen. 3:15, in which God promised to one day crush the serpent's head.

God subjecting the creation "in hope" could also explain why mankind longs for utopia — he holds out hope for something better and grander than what we presently experience. Nevertheless, man presently toils and labors by the sweat of his brow to make the earth productive, and women bear children in pain and suffering. Furthermore, Christ's serpent-enemy is always working to oppose Him (and us).

TRANSFORMATION OF EARTH DURING THE TRIBULATION

Some prophecy teachers and creation scientists believe God's judgments during the Tribulation will bring about the redemption of the present heavens and earth, producing the following glorious results:

1. Greenhouse effect of water vapor canopy in the upper atmosphere which shields out harmful radiation from the sun
2. Interactive hydrologic system with no storms
3. Healthy atmospheric conditions — no pollution, higher concentration of oxygen (aids in healing and overall vitality)
4. Much longer lifespans

5. Earth more habitable — pre-flood topography, shallower oceans, more land mass, no deserts or polar caps

6. A world of peace and prosperity, where war and crime and overt sin will not be tolerated

7. Population explosion

8. Highly advanced civilization

As a result of these changes, Earth will revert back in large measure to the way it was before the Flood of Noah's day.

A MAGNIFICENT MILLENNIAL EARTH

Isa. 35:1-2 The wilderness and the wasteland shall be glad for them, and the desert shall rejoice and blossom as the rose; it shall blossom abundantly and rejoice, even with joy and singing.

Isa. 35:6b For waters shall burst forth in the wilderness, and streams in the desert.

Isa. 40:4 Every valley shall be exalted and every mountain and hill brought low; the crooked places shall be made straight and the rough places smooth;

Isa. 11:6 The wolf also shall dwell with the lamb, the leopard shall lie down with the young goat, the calf and the young lion and the fatling together; and a little child shall lead them.

7 The cow and the bear shall graze; their young ones shall lie down together; and the lion shall eat straw like the ox.

8 The nursing child shall play by the cobra's hole, and the weaned child shall put his hand in the viper's den.

9 They shall not hurt nor destroy in all My holy mountain, for the earth shall be full of the knowledge of the LORD as the waters cover the sea.

CHANGES FORTHCOMING FOR MANKIND

What a glorious Earth is forthcoming in the new age! Mankind will also be favorably impacted:

Isa. 2:4b They shall beat their swords into plowshares, and their spears into pruning hooks; nation shall not lift up sword against nation, neither shall they learn war anymore.

Isa. 35:5-6a Then the eyes of the blind shall be opened, and the ears of the deaf shall be unstopped. Then the lame shall leap like a deer, and the tongue of the dumb sing.

Isa. 11:10 And in that day there shall be a Root of Jesse, who shall stand as a banner to the people; for the Gentiles shall seek Him, and His resting place shall be glorious.

Isa. 65:20a No more shall an infant from there *live but a few* days, nor an old man who has not fulfilled his days; for the child shall die one hundred years old.
   21 They shall build houses and inhabit *them;* they shall plant vineyards and eat their fruit.
   22 They shall not build and another inhabit; they shall not plant and another eat; for as the days of a tree, *so shall be* the days of My people, and My elect shall long enjoy the work of their hands.
   23 They shall not labor in vain, nor bring forth children for trouble; for they *shall be* the descendants of the blessed of the LORD, and their offspring with them.

Arlen Chitwood says:

God, in complete accord with the pattern established in Gen. 1:1-2:3, is presently working six more days to restore man. And once man has been restored (once God's work in man's redemption has been completed), the material creation will be "delivered from the bondage of corruption" (Rom. 8:21). The curse will be lifted, and this will be followed by God resting a seventh day, resting from His redemptive work (as in the established pattern [Gen. 2:1-3]).[7]

Why is the revealing of God's glorified sons critical to the new age?

3. BECAUSE IT MARKS THE GLORIOUS LIBERTY OF CHRIST'S REIGN.

Let's flip around the order of the verses and see v. 22 before v. 21:

> Rom. 8:22 For we know that the whole creation groans and labors with birth pangs together until now.
> 8:21 because the creation itself also will be delivered from the bondage of corruption into the glorious liberty of the children of God.

LABOR PAINS LEADING TO BIRTH

8:22. Notice the language of childbirth — *groans, labors, birth pangs, delivered*. Women who have had children can relate to this terminology. God uses the specific language of childbirth to refer to the birth of the new age. All creation presently *groans and labors with birth pangs*. In fact, creation has done that since the curse, including plants and animals and mankind. All are under the weight of sin and its consequences, not only mankind, but also Earth itself. This has been ongoing for millennia, but it's all leading somewhere.

Oftentimes, women suffer throughout the pregnancy, not just at the end. There is morning sickness, and then discomfort, not being able to sleep properly, indigestion, etc. I feel sorry for women having to share their limited internal space with a child, who stretches and kicks and punches as it does gymnastics in the womb. It's quite uncomfortable and even painful. Then as the due date draws nigh, the pains increase. Oftentimes, there are "false" labor pains. But ask any pregnant woman — they are *not* false! Then comes the actual labor, which is quite intense.

8:21. In Paul's metaphor birth pangs likely refer to the tribulation period, the final seven years on Earth, during which God will bring tremendous pain to the earth, as he transforms this globe into its pre-flood state. Chitwood claims:

> This is what Revelation chapters five through nineteen are about. They are about *effecting a redemption of the creation* subjected by man's

fall to "the bondage of corruption" (Rom. 8:20, 21), bringing to pass "the times of restitution ['restoration'] of all things" (Acts 3:21).[8]

Of course, man will experience great pain and suffering during the tribulation, as God seeks to bring His nation and even Gentiles to the point of repentance. After all the pain and suffering — not only for millennia of time, but also for the final seven years of intensity — the "child" comes forth. When the "child" is finally birthed, the pain ends and the joy begins. In fact, notice the contrasting terms in v. 21: "Delivered *from* the bondage of corruption" — that is, all creation delivered from the pain and suffering of this old, corrupted world. "Delivered *to* the glorious liberty of the children of God" — that is, the ones who are adopted as "sons," and that is the joyous part. What, then, is the child in this metaphor? I personally think it is two-fold:

THE FIRST "CHILD" IN THE METAPHOR

1. The child is the repentant nation of Israel restored to fellowship with Jehovah and ready to take up her place as priest among the nations.

> **Isa. 66:7 (NASB)** Before she travailed, she brought forth; before her pain came, she gave birth to a boy.
>
> **8** Who has heard such a thing? Who has seen such things? Can a land be born in one day? Can a nation be brought forth all at once? As soon as Zion travailed, she also brought forth her sons.
>
> **9** "Shall I bring to the point of birth and not give delivery?" says the LORD. "Or shall I who gives delivery shut *the womb?*" says your God.
>
> **10** Be joyful with Jerusalem and rejoice for her, all you who love her; be exceedingly glad with her, all you who mourn over her,

God is describing something rather remarkable here. After Israel goes through the intense suffering and labor pains of the tribulation, she will give re-birth to herself as a spiritual nation, and it will happen instantly. God promises not to delay Israel's restitution as a nation. She will literally come forth in a day! Ironically, this is dramatically different from Israel's formation as a nation in 1948, which took years and much effort before it ever came to fruition.

NATIONAL ISRAEL'S REPENTANCE

Once national Israel repents near the end of the tribulation, Jesus will return, and there will no longer be a need for continued labor. The nation will be re-born, and according to v. 8, so will the earth, i.e., the promised land. The New Covenant will be implemented, and all the world will rejoice with Israel.

Then notice that immediately after Israel is birthed, she in turn gives birth to her children — Who are these "children?" Chitwood says:

> The reference to "sons" [NASB] being brought forth is also seen in the travailing and deliverance in Romans chapter eight. The time when the creation will *be delivered from the present groaning and travailing together in pain* is the time of "the manifestation of the sons of God" [v. 19].
>
> This chapter in Romans deals more specifically with the adoption of Christians as firstborn sons and their being manifested as such. Israel though has already been adopted and is presently God's firstborn son [*cf.* Ex. 4:22, 23], though an unbelieving son. And Israel must be brought forth as well [actually first and foremost].
>
> The creation will be delivered from its present groaning and travailing in pain only when the complete contingent of the Sons of God [Christ, Israel, and the Church following the adoption] have been manifested for all to see.)[9]

THE SECOND "CHILD" IN THE METAPHOR

What is the second child that is brought forth in the birthing metaphor?

2. The adopted sons of God (Rom. 8:14-19), the sons to glory (Heb. 2:10), also known as, the bride of Christ (Rev. 19:7-8); the church of the firstborn (Heb. 12:23); the overcomers (Rev. 2-3). The

coming forth of the adopted sons of God signals the birth of the new age of Jesus, the establishment of His millennial kingdom, after He deposes Satan and his echelons.

> **Rev. 11:15b** (*Weymouth's Translation*, 1903) The sovereignty of the world now belongs to our Lord and His Christ; and He will be King until the Ages of the Ages.

Of course, Jesus will ascend to the throne, along with His bride — the adopted, glorified sons of God. One additional adjective that could be added to the list of *adopted* and *glorified* is *redeemed* — look at v. 23:

> **Rom. 8:23 Not only *that*, but we also who have the firstfruits of the Spirit, even we ourselves groan within ourselves, eagerly waiting for the adoption, the redemption of our body.**

Even God's children, who have the "first-fruits" of the Holy Spirit (even in advance of the launching of the New Covenant with Israel), groan with the rest of creation — but in our case, we (i.e., those who understand this concept) long to be adopted as firstborn sons, thereby receiving the "full harvest." Sadly, most Christians assume this is automatic.

THE REDEMPTION OF THE BODY

In Rom. 8:23, redemption of the body is equated with the *adoption*, which is not conferred upon believers at the point of regeneration. Rather, it is given by Jesus as a reward to those who live righteously and suffer with Him. He will bestow this glorious reward, along with crowns, at His Judgment Seat, and it is equated with redemption of the body. I used to equate the redemption of the body with resurrection, but Chitwood clarifies otherwise from the Scriptures:

> *The redemption of the body*, as seen in Rom. 8:23 [not to be confused with the resurrection of the body], has to do with the future adop-

tion into a firstborn status and is part and parcel with the salvation of the soul.[10]

In one of his other books, Chitwood adds:

"The redemption of the body" has to do with *placing man back in the position which he occupied prior to the fall and, in this position, allowing man to realize the reason for his creation, which is regal.* This is the way matters are set forth in both Rom. 8:15-23 and Phil. 3:20, 21.

The word "change" in Phil. 3:21 (referring to changing our body of humiliation) is a translation of the Greek word *metaschematizo*, which refers to *an outward change.* An outward change though would necessitate *a previous inward change,* described by the Greek word *metamorphoo* (Rom. 12:1, 2 [translated, "transformed"]). Christians who allow the Spirit to perform a present inward change in their lives will one day realize the corresponding outward change, finding themselves *enswathed in Glory,* with their bodies "fashioned like unto" *Christ's body of Glory* (Phil. 3:21).

Thus, the adoption, the change in our body of humiliation, the redemption of the body, occurs at a time following the resurrection and rapture. This will be *the capstone of all which preceded, placing man back in the position which Adam occupied before the fall, though with regal garments.* And, accordingly, it will precede and anticipate Christ's millennial reign.[11]

HOPING FOR THE ADOPTION

This section of the epistle closes with vs. 24-25:

> **Rom. 8:24 For we were saved in this hope, but hope that is seen is not hope; for why does one still hope for what he sees?**
> **8:25 But if we hope for what we do not see, we eagerly wait for *it* with perseverance.**

As children of God, we *hope* — i.e., *confidently expect* — that we will be adopted and glorified if we have lived righteously and suffered with Jesus. Use of the word *hope*, of course, implies that we haven't already received the adoption, otherwise, there would be no need to hope for it. But we look for it, we long for it, *with perseverance* (i.e., endurance). In other words, never stop hoping for the adoption. Live as if it could happen any moment.

When you stand before Jesus to hear His verdict on your life, will you be clothed in garments of light or left naked and ashamed? The apostle John had these same themes on his mind when he wrote:

> **1 John 2:28** And now, little children, abide in Him, that when He appears, we may have confidence and not be ashamed before Him at His coming.

CHAPTER 20
PROMISES FOR FIRSTBORN SONS
ROMANS 8:26-39

I used to view all the references to *salvation* in the New Testament as having singular meaning — referring to regeneration, or "salvation from Hell, so we can go to Heaven when we die." I also assumed *justification* is essentially equivalent to salvation in the singular sense. That is what I was always taught. Thus, I formerly thought that Rom. 8:29-30 describes the process of salvation from God's perspective. However, that traditional teaching — which came out of the Reformation — is quite problematic in texts like this and in other places where salvation or eternal life include *works* (see Luke 10:25; John 6:27; Rom. 2:7; 6:22; Gal. 6:7-8; 1 Tim. 6:12, to name only a few).

THE DUALISTIC MEANINGS OF SALVATION AND ETERNAL LIFE

Then I came to realize that salvation has two possible meanings in the Scriptures, depending on context:

    a) Initial salvation by faith alone, in which one's spirit becomes regenerated, and

    b) Ongoing salvation of the soul (aka, sanctification) by cooperating with God to live obediently and do works pleasing to the Lord, which ultimately result in inheritance and reward at the Judgment Seat. Apart from this dualistic understanding of salvation and eternal life, Scripture will be misinterpreted and misapplied, and theological gymnastics will be necessary for explaining passages.

Thank the Lord, I now understand the Bible more clearly, and I don't have to put my theological "square pegs into round holes" to explain Scripture. Consequently, I now understand that Rom. 8:29-30 does *not* describe the process of salvation from God's perspective. These verses describe the process of sanctification unto reward from God's perspective — and not as automatic, but conditional.

When that is understood — and that fits the context of the preceding verses as well as the overall book of Romans — then Rom. 8:26-39 makes much more sense. God apparently included this section of Scripture on the heels of the previous section (8:12-25) to bring comfort and encouragement to those who are on the pathway to becoming firstborn sons to glory. He wants us to remain faithful amidst persecution, so we can move on to maturity and glorification, by His grace. To that end, God makes five promises in this text to encourage us to persevere in hope, a theme which is presented in v. 25:

> **Rom. 8:25** But if we hope for what we do not see, we eagerly wait for *it* with perseverance.

PROMISE #1: THE HOLY SPIRIT PRAYS FOR FIRSTBORN SONS

> **Rom. 8:26** Likewise the Spirit also helps in our weaknesses. For we do not know what we should pray for as we ought, but the Spirit Himself makes intercession for us with groanings which cannot be uttered.
> **8:27** Now He who searches the hearts knows what the mind of the Spirit *is*, because He makes intercession for the saints according to *the will of* God.

God's will, in this context, is that His children not get deterred by the sufferings of this present time, but continue on to becoming sons to glory by living righteously. To that end, encouragement is given in v. 18:

Rom. 8:18 For I consider that the sufferings of this present time are not worthy *to be compared* with the glory which shall be revealed in us.

How blessed we are as believers in Jesus Christ, not merely to possess eternal (age-lasting) life, but also to have the Holy Spirit as our divine Helper. Zane Hodges comments:

> Although it is true that our sufferings cannot be compared with the coming glory (8:18), still we are weak and groan even in the midst of Christian victory (v 23). Thus we urgently need divine **help in our weaknesses**. And this is precisely what we receive through the indwelling Spirit, who *likewise also* (in addition to producing His first fruits within us [v 23]) gives us this help.
>
> In fact, *our weaknesses* are manifest precisely in our times of prayer when, under the pressures of suffering, we try to make intelligent requests from God. But we have no real ability to assess any stressful situation we are in and to know precisely what it is really necessary for us **to pray for** at such times. Into this gap, Paul assures us, comes the intercessory work of **the Spirit** who dwells within us.[1]

GROANINGS WHICH CANNOT BE UTTERED

How grateful we should be that the Spirit of God prays for us to be victorious in times of suffering, so that we will remain steadfast unto glorification! Jesus also prays for us (see v. 34)! Nevertheless, a phrase of v. 27 troubled me for many years — the *groanings which cannot be uttered*. Does that mean the Spirit of God speaks to God in some inarticulate language that we don't understand? If so, that would be an odd thing for God to tell us. Hodges gives a much better explanation:

> Consequently, in the midst of our own **inarticulate groanings, the Spirit Himself makes intercession** for us. Although some commentators have thought that the *groanings*... referred to here are those of *the Spirit*, this seems quite improbable. The preceding context speaks clearly of our own groanings (... v 23) and the reference is surely to

that. When our own inability to know how to pray in the necessary way results in inarticulate ... expressions of anguish and concern, the Spirit intervenes. He prays the requests we ourselves do not know to pray.[2]

Does it not make more sense that the Holy Spirit takes our groanings (which is contextual, v. 23) and makes them prayer requests to God when we don't know how to pray amidst our particular situation? Why would God say that the Holy Spirit speaks to Him in an unintelligible groaning which we cannot understand or articulate? That makes no sense. Hodges's explanation, on the other hand, makes perfect sense.

Notice at the end of v. 27, the Spirit makes *intercession* for us. He prays for us amidst our pilgrimage throughout life, *according to God's will*. God's will is that we become mature, firstborn sons to glory. Jesus is praying specifically for that (v. 34) and so is the Holy Spirit (v. 27)! No wonder Paul says in v. 31, "If God is for us, who can be against us?" God makes a second promise to encourage us to persevere in hope:

PROMISE #2: ALL THINGS WORK TOGETHER FOR GOOD FOR FIRSTBORN SONS

> Rom. 8:28 And we know that all things work together for good to those who love God, to those who are the called according to *His* purpose.

This promise is commonly quoted and assumed to apply to all Christians with no conditions attached. The further assumption is made that all Christians surely love God, at least in some degree, or else they are not Christians. But that is driven by Calvinist *perseverance* doctrine. The truth is that *not* all Christians love God, and that is obvious in that they do not obey Him. Jesus said, "If you love Me, keep My commandments." He was speaking to His disciples who were believers.

Incidentally, Christians who love the Lord will, nonetheless, occasionally stumble and sin. But what distinguishes those believers is that they immediately confess their sins and maintain fellowship with the Lord. They obviously love God. On the other hand, those Christians who continue living in sinfulness and do not maintain regular fellowship with the Lord do not truly love the Lord — although they remain children of God. They may *claim* to love God, but their lifestyle betrays their real heart condition.

Those who love God, who are on the pathway of becoming one of God's glorified sons, can be assured that every circumstance of life, every trial, every burden, every persecution, is working in their favor. We tend to think of certain things in life as *bad*; e.g., circumstances that are not favorable to us, things we do not enjoy, things that cause pain and suffering. But God essentially says, "Everything that happens in your life is for your good, on the pathway to becoming a son to glory. If you continue to love me — and demonstrate it by your obedience — you can be sure that nothing can harm you irreparably or destroy you. All the circumstances of your life are in My hands, and they are all working for your good."

I have often used the illustration of baking a cake. No one would ever want to eat a cup of flour or sugar or oil or a spoonful of cinnamon — that would be awful! But blending them all together, they make a wonderful-tasting cake. By way of application, you may not want to endure the so-called *bad* things in life that cause pain and suffering, but brought together in your life with everything else, they are producing a mature, complete Christian, lacking nothing. With this promise in mind, remain joyful, trusting Jesus and loving Him. The third promise God makes to encourage us to persevere in hope is:

PROMISE #3: FIRSTBORN SONS ARE BEING CALLED AND JUSTIFIED, AND WILL BE GLORIFIED

> Rom. 8:29 For whom He foreknew, He also predestined *to be* conformed to the image of His Son, that He might be the firstborn among many brethren.
> 8:30 Moreover whom He predestined, these He also called; whom He called, these He also justified; and whom He justified, these He also glorified.

Does foreknowledge require unconditional foreordination? In other words, does God's knowledge of something happening *before it happens* mean that He has already predetermined its outcome? No! God certainly has the *power* to make things happen His way, if He wants, but He has given man freedom to make choices. He knows what every individual will choose in advance of their choosing, but He doesn't predetermine their choices or the outcome.

Rom. 8:29 says God *foreknows* those who will make choices to become conformed to the image of Christ (i.e., become sanctified). Knowing this, He also *predestines*, which is not the best word chosen by the translators. G.H. Lang says:

> For this unjustified word they went back to Catholic Versions, the Rheims and the Vulgate, which have *predestinavit*, whereas the earlier English Versions of Wycliffe and Tyndale had the softer and more accurate word "preordain" ... These later translators had reason for forsaking the Latin, and its restoration by the Authorized Version has had the disastrous effect of fixing in the mind of the English reader the fatalistic notion so foreign to Scripture.
>
> A thing may be foreordained without it being irreversible, for it may be ordained on conditions, which not being fulfilled the ordination lapses. And this is the case here.
>
> This conditional element has been given little, if any, weight in Calvinistic treatment of this theme and is often strongly repudiated. Yet it is quite evidently present, and it rules out completely every attempt to attach a fatalistic sense to these passages. God's foreordination was conditioned by something that He foreknew, and by its very terms is conditioned by the response of man.[3]

FOREKNOWLEDGE LEADS TO FOREORDINATION

So the best word choice is *foreordains* (conditionally) or Young's preferred word, *fore-appoints*. In other words, knowing those who will make choices to become sanctified, He *predetermines* their path. By the end of life, they will be sanctified and conformed to the image of Christ *if* they remain on that path. God will enable to this end, because He knows they have chosen this.

Some may argue that means God is making the choices for the individual. However, it doesn't mean that at all. The child of God will still endure temptations and trials and persecutions — any of which could derail him/her from going on to glorification — and that is obvious from the verses that follow. But God knows those of His children who will continue to choose rightly — not perfectly, but consistently — and He predetermines their path.

Why does God bother to predetermine or foreordain that those whom He foreknows will go all the way through to glory? So that Jesus might be the firstborn among *many* brethren. By foreordaining, He can begin to develop a relationship with them even now by chastening (child-training) the firstborn sons to glory (Heb. 12) so they will be prepared to rule with Him.

CALLED TO CONFORMITY TO CHRIST

Incidentally, this foreordination is not to initial salvation; it is to soul-salvation, conformity to the image of Christ. That requires not only obedience (walking in the Spirit, v. 14), but also suffering with Him (v. 17). Co-suffering leads to co-glorification.

Those whom God foreordains to be conformed to the image of Christ, He then *calls*. This ties v. 30 with v. 28, which says that *all things work together for good to those who ... are the called according to His purpose.* His purpose is that they be conformed to the image of Christ (v. 29) so they can be adopted as firstborn brethren (vs. 14-17), to become Christ's bride and co-rulers. This is what creation eagerly awaits.

> **Rom. 8:19 For the earnest expectation of the creation eagerly waits for the revealing of the sons of God.**

Zane Hodges says:

> In Pauline doctrine, to be "called" is not merely to be "invited" ... Rather, as BDAG states, "from the meanings 'summon' and 'invite'

there develops the extended sense *choose for receipt of a special benefit or experience, call.*"4

In other words, God *calls* in the sense that He chooses those whom He foreknows are on the pathway to becoming His glorified sons.

JUSTIFIED AND GLORIFIED

Next, He *justifies* them, but again, this has nothing to do with salvation. In the early chapters of this book I demonstrated that justification is not positional or legal, as the Reformers taught. To be justified is to be declared righteous at any given point in time, based on one's behavior, and ultimately at the Judgment Seat.

Bob Wilkin says:

> This justification is "vindication at the Bema of the believers who respond properly to the call."5

Those whom God justifies He *glorifies*. Only those who live righteously, by faith, will be given a garment of encasement in light; all others will be ashamed. Many commentators believe this is the "clothing" that Adam and Eve lost in the Fall that caused them to be naked and ashamed.

By way of summary, those whom God foreknows will become sons to glory, He foreordains their path, so they will become conformed to the image of Christ; then He calls, justifies, and glorifies them! Thus, vs. 29-30 describe the process of sanctification unto reward from God's perspective — and it is not automatic, but conditional. Since it's from *God's* perspective, then that means none of us can know if we have been foreordained by God as a son to glory. Even if we are confident that we are *presently* on the pathway to glory, we don't know if we will *remain* on that path. But knowing that God calls, justifies and glorifies those whom He foreknows will remain on the pathway to glory, God's promises should keep you persevering in hope. If you are presently on the pathway, by God's grace, remain on the path.

God makes a fourth promise to encourage us to persevere in hope:

PROMISE #4: FIRSTBORN SONS CAN SUCCEED, FOR GOD IS ON THEIR SIDE

> Rom. 8:31 What then shall we say to these things? If God *is* for us, who *can be* against us?
> 8:32 He who did not spare His own Son, but delivered Him up for us all, how shall He not with Him also freely give us all things?
> 8:33 Who shall bring a charge against God's elect? *It is* God who justifies.
> 8:34 Who *is* he who condemns? *It is* Christ who died, and furthermore is also risen, who is even at the right hand of God, who also makes intercession for us.

8:31. Think about it: If God is on your side, can anyone oppose you successfully? Of course not! So persevere, knowing He is "in your corner," so to speak. We will face great opposition, even from Christians who do not agree with the message of kingdom inheritance. They may try to "cancel" you (even Christians practice "cancel culture"), cloaked in spiritual-sounding garments, labeling their decision, "biblical separation." Yet more often than not, so-called "biblical separation" is unbiblical, driven by opinions, viewpoints, and personal preferences rather than biblical truth. We are obligated to separate from other believers in limited instances, but fundamentalism often defaults to hyper-separation, which is displeasing to Jesus, who prayed for unity amongst the brethren (read John 17).

Regardless of any opposition you may face — spiritual or psychological or physical — you can know that God is on your side, if you are walking in the Spirit. If you continue to have a right spirit amidst seasons of persecution and suffering, Jesus will reward you richly, for He promises:

> **Matt. 5:10** Blessed *are* those who are persecuted for righteousness' sake, for theirs is the kingdom of heaven.

11 Blessed are you when they revile and persecute you, and say all kinds of evil against you falsely for My sake.

12 Rejoice and be exceedingly glad, for great *is* your reward in heaven, for so they persecuted the prophets who were before you.

If you are taking a stand for righteousness and proclaiming truth, God is on your side! I pity those who try to cross the servants of God, for they will give an account one day and will watch as the faithful that they persecuted are revealed as adopted, glorified sons. That thought carries me through on difficult days.

EVERYTHING WE NEED TO SUCCEED

8:32. Seeing that God gave up His own Son to die for us, won't He give us everything we need to succeed, including strength to carry on? Hodges translates v. 32b, "How shall He not also graciously give us, together with Him, all things?"

The phrase *together with Him* implies something far greater than merely help *now*, as needed, although that is wonderful. It also suggests that one day He will give firstborn sons glorification in His presence!

8:33. *Who dares to bring a charge against God's elect?* The word *elect* is not a salvation term, but a sanctification term. G. Campbell Morgan says:

Election in Scripture is to the Church, and never to salvation.[6]

G.H. Lang adds:

The passages as to election and preordination do not apply to the question of salvation, but rather to the prospect of persons already saved.[7]

Shawn Lazar wrote an excellent book entitled, *Chosen to Serve: Why Divine Election is to Service, Not to Eternal Life.* The title speaks for itself.

8:34. *Who is he who condemns?* Is it your legalistic, fundamentalist brother? That's not his place, it's Jesus Christ's, who is *actually* qualified, who died and rose again and is seated at the right hand of God. Why does man think he can take on God's roles and responsibilities? Rest in knowing Jesus is praying for you! He knows when you're going through tough times, and He wants you to succeed. There's no one I would rather have on my team than Jesus. God makes a fifth promise to encourage us to persevere in hope:

PROMISE #5: FIRSTBORN SONS RECEIVE AN ABUNDANCE OF HIS LOVE

> Rom. 8:35 Who shall separate us from the love of Christ? *Shall* tribulation, or distress, or persecution, or famine, or nakedness, or peril, or sword?
> 8:36 As it is written: *"For Your sake we are killed all day long; we are accounted as sheep for the slaughter."*
> 8:37 Yet in all these things we are more than conquerors through Him who loved us.

8:35. Remember the context: God is speaking about firstborn sons, those who walk in the Spirit and suffer with Jesus. Does God love in degrees? In other words, does He love some more than others? The answer is yes, absolutely! We have somehow accepted the teaching that God loves everyone equally. To be sure, God loves all mankind, even sinners (*For God so loved the WORLD, that He gave ...*), but the Bible is clear that He loves in much greater degree those who fear Him and live righteously! We can demonstrate this from the Scriptures.

GOD'S FAITHFUL LOVE IS GREATER TO THOSE WHO FEAR HIM

> Ps. 103:11 (HCSB) For as high as the heavens are above the earth, so great is His faithful love toward those who fear Him.

The term *faithful love* is translated from the Hebrew word *chesed*, which means God's lovingkindness, His steadfast love. Unfortunately, the KJV and NKJV translate it *mercy*, which is only one aspect of this word *chesed*. *Faithful love* is about the best we can do in English without getting too wordy. Notice His *faithful love* is *great* toward those who fear Him, which implies it is not as great toward those who do not fear Him.

> **Ps. 103:17** (ESV) But the steadfast love of the LORD is from everlasting to everlasting on those who fear him ... to those who keep his covenant and remember to do his commandments.

God loves the whole world, but He shows far greater love toward those who fear Him and keep His commandments. Those who are obedient and live righteously get a much bigger dose of God's love, and that makes sense. If you have two adult children — one who honors you, heeds your counsel, shows love toward you, and desires to spend time with you — and another child who spurns you and rejects your counsel, not showing love toward you and doesn't care to spend time with you — while you love them both as your children, you are going to have far greater love for the faithful child who wants to spend time with you and honor you and heed your counsel.

In the context of Romans 8, God shows greater love toward those of His children who are becoming conformed to the image of His dear Son. Because He foreknows that they will keep obeying Him and loving Him, He showers the fullness of His love upon them. His overflowing love continues reassuring that all things work together for good in their lives — even so-called bad things — and nothing can separate them from His love — not tribulation or distress or persecution or famine or nakedness or peril or sword.

8:36. Paul then adds a quote from Ps. 44 about believers being hunted down and persecuted: *For Your sake we are killed all day long; we are accounted as sheep for the slaughter* (v. 36). That is why God's love is so important. His loving arms overwhelm us, not merely with protection and strength, but also with the assurance that He truly loves us, tremendously, regardless of what happens in our lives.

MORE THAN CONQUERORS

8:37. Despite fierce opposition, we are *more than conquerors through Him who loves us*. How can a child of God be *more than* a conqueror? You're either a conqueror or you're not, right? Firstborn sons are *more than conquerors* in that we not only defeat the enemy through Christ, we have His overflowing love (and the implication is: *they don't*). Keep in mind: His much greater degree of love is not for all children of God, but reserved for those who have chosen to honor Him, obey Him, and love Him, i.e., firstborn sons.

Christians in general love to claim the promises of Rom. 8, but those who are not living righteously should realize that these promises are not for God's carnal children. They are for those who are walking in the Spirit, becoming conformed to the image of Christ. If you are not an obedient child of God, then you don't love God, because Jesus said, "If you love me, keep my commandments" (Jn. 14:15; see also Jn. 15:10). If you don't love God, then all things are not working together for your good, and you are not called according to His purpose. You are not being justified and will not be glorified, and you cannot claim that nothing will separate you from God's love.

THE SURETY OF INHERITANCE

Rom. 8:31-39 is *not* about "eternal security," as it is commonly taught and applied. It is about the surety of inheritance for those who are living righteously. Bob Wilkin says:

> The believer who is walking according to the Spirit is one who is experiencing God's love even when he is undergoing persecution for his faith.[8]

> **Rom. 8:38-39 For I am persuaded that neither death nor life, nor angels nor principalities nor powers, nor things present nor things to come, nor height nor depth, nor any other created**

thing, shall be able to separate us from the love of God which is in Christ Jesus our Lord.

Notice in this list Paul includes matters of life and death, the supernatural realm, matters in the present and even matters in the future, all of creation, and even things at the highest levels and lowest levels. *Nothing — nothing at all!* — can separate firstborn sons from God's love! That should drive us to endure *anything* for God's glory. If we do, our future reward will be glorious, beyond description!

If you are on the pathway to becoming a firstborn son to glory, stay on that path, by claiming God's five promises to enable you to persevere in hope amidst suffering:

1. The Holy Spirit prays for firstborn sons.
2. All things work together for good for firstborn sons.
3. Firstborn sons are being called and justified, and will be glorified.
4. Firstborn sons can succeed, for God is on their side.
5. Firstborn sons receive an abundance of His love.

Are you claiming these promises of God?

CHAPTER 21
HAS ISRAEL BEEN REPLACED?
ROMANS 9:1-3

Are you aware that Martin Luther who launched the Protestant Reformation in the year 1517 was antisemitic?

THE HORRIFYING ANTISEMITISM OF MARTIN LUTHER

In the year 1543 Martin Luther penned a sixty-five thousand word book entitled, *On the Jews and Their Lies*. I never in all my years of Christian school, Bible college or seminary training heard about this, until I visited the Holocaust Museum in Washington, D.C. about twenty years ago. There, on display for all the world to see, are excerpts from Luther's book, in which he asks, "What shall we Christians do with this rejected and condemned people, the Jews?"[1] He gives the following seven answers:

1. I advise to set fire to their synagogues or schools ... This is to be done in honor of our Lord and of Christendom, so that God might see that we are Christians ...

2. I advise that their houses also be razed and destroyed.

3. I advise that all their prayer books and Talmudic writings, in which such idolatry, lies, cursing, and blasphemy are taught, be taken from them.

4. I advise that their rabbis be forbidden to teach henceforth on pain of loss of life and limb ...

5. I advise that safe-conduct on the highways be abolished completely for the Jews. For they have no business in the countryside ...

6. I advise that usury be prohibited to them, and that all cash and treasure of silver and gold be taken from them ...

7. I recommend putting a flail, an ax, a hoe, a spade, a distaff, or a spindle into the hands of young, strong Jews and Jewesses and letting them earn their bread in the sweat of their brow ... But if we are afraid that they might harm us or our wives, children, servants, cattle, etc., ... then let us emulate the common sense of other nations such as France, Spain, Bohemia, etc., ... then eject them forever from the country.[2]

This strong statement of antisemitism was written by the man who is hailed as a hero by Christians for starting the Reformation. Incidentally, if you thought that was awful — and it truly is — be aware that in the treatise, Martin Luther describes Jews as a "base, whoring people, that is, no people of God, and their boast of lineage, circumcision, and law must be accounted as filth."[3] He also said many other horrible things about the Jewish people that I do not want to repeat. His writings are readily available.

THE EFFECTS OF ANTISEMITISM ON THE HOLOCAUST

Granted, modern day Protestants, including Lutherans and others of a Reformed tradition condemn Luther's book and antisemitic ideas, but that didn't happen until the 1950s — *after* Hitler's Holocaust! By then the damage was done. Per Marc Ellis, late Director of the Center for Jewish Studies at Baylor University:

> With the rise of the Nazi Party in Weimar Germany, [Luther's] book became widely popular among Nazi supporters. During World War II, copies of the book were commonly seen at Nazi rallies, and the prevailing scholarly consensus is that it may have had a significant impact on justifying the Holocaust.[4]

THE EFFECTS OF ANTISEMITISM ON CHRISTIANITY

How can we have respect for a man's theology when we know he thought so disdainfully of the Jewish people? It is no wonder that Luther referred to the biblical book of James as an "epistle of straw." This Reformer did not understand the doctrine of justification, yet the vast majority of Protestantism — including multitudes of Baptists — continue to teach his version of Augustinian justification! Indeed, as I said in Chapter 1, I believe Satan hijacked the Reformation and has used it to confuse, fracture, and divide Christianity for the past five hundred years!

In fact, I am convinced that Martin Luther's theology dealt the death blow to kingdom inheritance doctrine taught by Jesus and the apostles. Jesus predicted this would happen in His parable of the leaven in the loaf:

> **Matt. 13:33** Another parable He spoke to them: "The kingdom of heaven is like leaven, which a woman took and hid in three measures of meal till it was all leavened."

The great medical doctor, pastor, and Bible teacher, Walter L. Wilson (1881-1969), wrote:

> In every place where leaven is mentioned, it is a type of evil teachings, evil doctrines and evil practices. It is always to be put away and cast out as an unclean thing. The Gospel is never called leaven. Nothing good is ever compared to leaven. Nothing good is ever said about leaven. In every place it is mentioned, leaven is defiling and is to be put away. (See Exodus 12:15; Leviticus 2:11; I Corinthians 5:6).
>
> Matthew 13:33 — The leaven in this case is a type of evil doctrines, taught by the apostate church. The woman is the apostate church, the meal is the Word of God, the leaven is wrong and evil teachings concerning the Word of God.[5]

THE EFFECTS OF ANTISEMITISM ON UNIVERSAL RECONCILIATION

Tragically, kingdom inheritance doctrine has been leavened (corrupted) in virtually all segments of Christianity, in large part due to Roman Catholicism as the first wave and Luther's Protestant Reformation doctrines as the second wave. But that's not all Luther left to us. His antisemitism snatched away from the church what I believe is the biblical doctrine of universal reconciliation, which is the teaching that God will ultimately save all mankind through Jesus Christ by the end of the ages, using the lake of fire as a remedial tool of purging, so that in the end:

> **Phil. 2:10-11** At the name of Jesus every knee should bow, of those in heaven, and of those on earth, and of those under the earth, and that every tongue should confess that Jesus Christ is Lord, to the glory of God the Father.

Jan Bonda, quoted earlier, lived from 1918-1997. He was a Dutch Reformed pastor in the Netherlands and would have been a young adult in his twenties during WW2. After studying the Scriptures intensely, he had to forsake much of his Reformed theological heritage and his views on Israel. Notice his keen insights:

> In all likelihood, no chapter of Scripture has been so much misunderstood by the church throughout the ages as Romans 9. In this chapter the church has read that God rejected Israel forever. It has also been interpreted as the cornerstone of the traditional doctrine of predestination. "I have loved Jacob, but I have hated Esau (v. 13, RSV), and "He has mercy on whomever he chooses, and he hardens the heart of whomever he chooses" (v. 8, RSV). The idea that God does not want to save all people began with the conviction that God does not want to save Israel.
>
> What has this doctrine of Israel's rejection brought about? The great catastrophe of our century tells us: The murder of almost six million Jews from 1940 to 1945 in post-Christian Europe would not have been possible without the preparatory work of this ecclesiastical tradition. Here the exegesis of Romans 9-11 played a major role.

The genocide was not committed by Christians, but by pagans who had rejected faith in Jesus. However, this would not have happened in Europe if through the centuries the church had taught the people to see Israel as the apple of God's eye; if the church had learned to focus her expectations on the great salvation that God would give to the world through Israel.[6]

To learn more about universal reconciliation, see my book, *The Savior of All Men: God's Plan to Reconcile All Through Jesus Christ*.

THE EFFECTS OF ANTISEMITISM ON ESCHATOLOGY – THE ERROR OF REPLACEMENT THEOLOGY

Despite these indicting statements by Bonda, *replacement theology* continues alive and well within Reformed Protestant Christianity, including multitudes of Reformed Baptist churches. *Replacement theology* teaches that because of Israel's disobedience, God has forsaken Israel and turned His attention to the church, which is now spiritual Israel. The promises in the Old Testament for Israel are being fulfilled by the church in a spiritual sense, as Israel's replacement.

Thus, replacement theology typically results in an a-millennial view of the end times, which dramatically reshapes the Scriptural view of eschatology, which is the doctrine of future events. Incidentally, replacement theology dates back long before Luther and the Reformation. Augustine (AD 354-430) wrote a booklet called, "A Tract Against the Jews," in which he promoted replacement theology. He expanded on this in his tome, *The City of God*.[7] In fact, the Roman Catholic Church was also impacted by Augustine's replacement theology, and that is why Roman Catholic churches — in like manner as Old Testament Israel — have priests, modeled after the Levitical system, and masses, which are essentially sacrifices.

Instead of quashing replacement theology during the Reformation, Luther's antisemitism fueled-the-fires all the more, popularizing it for modern Christianity. Consequently, this erroneous doctrine continues unabated into the twenty-first century.

THE RETURN OF NATIONAL ISRAEL AND THE SALVATION OF ALL MANKIND

In stark contrast to Augustine's and Luther's antisemitism and replacement theology, the apostle Paul demonstrates a deep love for the Jewish people and predicts a prominent future for national Israel. This is the clear teaching of Rom. 9-11. Furthermore, Israel's future salvation will be critical to the salvation of all mankind through Jesus Christ. Bonda says:

> The idea that God does not want to save all people began with the conviction that God does not want to save Israel.[8]

No wonder so few today believe in the salvation of all men! It seems that Protestant Christianity has been greatly shaped by the Reformation and its theology far more than most realize, even amongst those who claim not to hold to Reformation doctrines, such as dispensationalists.

Let's now see the loving heart of the Savior in Paul's position regarding Israel. As we begin to read in ch. 9, we must remember there are no chapter divisions in the original, so when Paul requests that he be accursed on behalf of Israel, he says that in the context of what he has just written at the end of ch. 8:

> **Rom. 8:38-39** For I am persuaded that neither death nor life, nor angels nor principalities nor powers, nor things present nor things to come, nor height nor depth, nor any other created thing, shall be able to separate us from the love of God which is in Christ Jesus our Lord.

PAUL INTERCEDES FOR ISRAEL, LIKE MOSES

Paul knows that even if he becomes accursed, God will love him regardless. He confidently steps in on Israel's behalf as an intercessor, just like Abraham did for Sodom, and Moses did for Israel in Old Testament times. Notice the first three verses of Rom. 9:

> **Rom. 9:1-2 I tell the truth in Christ, I am not lying,**

> my conscience also bearing me witness in the Holy Spirit, that I have great sorrow and continual grief in my heart.
> 9:3 For I could wish that I myself were accursed from Christ for my brethren, my countrymen according to the flesh.

Why does Paul wish himself accursed on behalf of Israel? And what does it mean to be *accursed*? To understand this, we need to jump ahead to 10:1 to see what Paul is desiring for Israel:

> **Rom. 10:1** Brethren, my heart's desire and prayer to God for Israel is that they may be saved.

By connecting this statement with his statements in the early part of Rom. 9, we discover that Paul's driving passion for Israel is that the nation would become "saved" — even to the point that Paul is willing to be accursed if it will result in Israel's "salvation." What is this *salvation*?

THE RE-OFFER OF KINGDOM INHERITANCE

The word *saved* in 10:1 must be defined in the same manner the word is used throughout the epistle of Romans, and considering the context of the book itself.

Many commentators believe Paul wrote Romans in AD mid-to-late 50s, when he was at Corinth (Zane Hodges says AD 56-57), within the "parenthetical era" of sorts, extending from the resurrection of Christ (around AD 32) to the end of the book of Acts (around AD 62) — a period of about thirty years. During this time frame the apostles re-offered kingdom inheritance to the entire generation of Israelites who were alive at the time of Christ's ministry. The re-offer is the focus of the book of Acts.

What is kingdom inheritance? By way of brief summary, Israel was deemed to be God's firstborn son (see Exod. 4:22) from the very beginning of the nation's existence and, as such, stands to inherit a place of rulership on Earth, over all the nations in Christ's forthcoming millennial kingdom. That had been promised in the Old Testament prophets.

However, during His three-year ministry on Earth, Jesus offered Israel something additional, something much grander. If the nation were to repent in the spirit of 2 Chron. 7:14 and return to fellowship with Jehovah, they would inherit a place of rulership, not merely on Earth, but in the heavenly New Jerusalem, which will be the millennial headquarters. It is not the third Heaven, per se, the place of God's dwelling. It is the city of reward that comes down from Heaven and hovers over Earth (see Rev. 21-22). New Jerusalem is described in the book of Revelation as having streets of gold and gates of pearl.

ISRAEL'S REJECTION OF THE OFFER

Jesus offered to national Israel a place of rulership in this heavenly realm of His kingdom, if the nation would return to fellowship with Jehovah by repenting of sins. Acceptance would result in the nation's "salvation." But the nation rejected Christ's offer and, instead, crucified Him. After the resurrection, God allowed the apostles to re-offer Christ's initial offer of kingdom inheritance through the end of the book of Acts, which ended just a few years before the destruction of Jerusalem by the Romans in AD 70. Because Israel rejected this offer of "salvation" — i.e., soul-salvation unto reward — Jesus is now making the same offer to Christians of the church age (see Matt. 21:43). However, the prerequisites for receiving this offer are living righteously, in dependence on Christ, and suffering with Him as a result of confessing Him before others.

At this point in the book of Romans, near the end of the thirty-year re-offer period, Paul is speaking to Jewish Christians about those Jews who have not yet believed Jesus is the Messiah. Nevertheless, at this particular point in Jewish history, this generation of Jews is regenerate, for they have believed God and have a zeal for Him. They are Old Testament believers — notice 10:2:

> **Rom. 10:2** For I bear them witness that they have a zeal for God, but not according to knowledge.

That same statement — *zeal for God without knowledge* — described Paul before He realized Jesus was indeed the Messiah. He was zealous for God, he was an Old Testament believer, but he did not understand about Jesus. Paul was ignorant of that aspect of the Scriptures — until he met Jesus on the road to Damascus.

PAUL WILLING TO BE ACCURSED IF ISRAEL WOULD BE "SAVED"

Thus, when Paul says that his heart's desire and prayer for Israel is that they might be "saved," he is not saying that he passionately desires for his fellow Israelites to be saved from Hell so they can go to Heaven (as is commonly interpreted in the Reformation tradition). Rather, Paul yearns for his fellow countrymen, who are already believers, to recognize Jesus as the Messiah and move forward with the salvation of their souls, that is, becoming sanctified and conformed to the image of Christ, by living righteously, in daily dependence on Jesus through faith, rather than depending on the Mosaic rituals. If they repent and live in this manner, they will become kingdom inheritors. Paul knows the thirty-year period of re-offering kingdom inheritance to that generation of Israelites is coming to a close, thus he cries out in 9:2-3:

> **Rom. 9:2-3** I have great sorrow and continual grief in my heart. For I could wish that I myself were accursed from Christ for my brethren, my countrymen according to the flesh.

The great sorrow and grief in Paul's heart sounds similar to the sentiment in the heart of Jesus near the time of His crucifixion:

> **Luke 19:41-42** Now as He drew near, He saw the city and wept over it, saying, "If you had known, even you, especially in this your day, the things *that make* for your peace! But now they are hidden from your eyes.
> **43-44** For days will come upon you when your enemies will build an embankment around you, surround you and close you in on every side, and level you, and your children within you, to the ground; and

they will not leave in you one stone upon another, because you did not know the time of your visitation."

Paul offers himself to become accursed if it will result in Israel's salvation.

WHAT IS THE MEANING OF "ACCURSED"?

Is Paul saying, "Lord, send me to Hell so that my countrymen might not have to go there?" No, as already determined, the salvation in this text is not initial salvation, or regeneration of one's spirit. Israel was already a regenerated nation, at this particular time in history, on the basis of the blood of the Passover lamb. This text — like the preponderance of the New Testament — is about soul-salvation, that is, sanctification unto reward.

The Greek word *anathema* means "excommunicated." Paul wishes to be excluded from kingdom inheritance if it will result in Israel's inheritance. But there's more to it than that. This Greek word *anathema* is used in the Septuagint to translate the Hebrew word *cherem* in the Old Testament, which means "to devote someone or something to destruction as an offering unto God." It was "under a ban," so to speak, for it belonged to God.

ACHAN TOOK OF THE "ACCURSED THING"

When the Israelites entered into Canaan land and the walls of Jericho were miraculously leveled, God specified that all of the wicked Canaanites in that city were to be killed, except for Rahab and her family who had turned to Jehovah. All others were to be killed, and all the material goods of value were to be brought into the tabernacle. It was all *cherem*, devoted to God as an offering of the first fruits of victory.

> **Josh. 6:17** Now the city shall be doomed by the LORD to destruction, it and all who *are* in it. Only Rahab the harlot shall live, she and all who *are* with her in the house, because she hid the messengers that we sent.

18 And you, by all means abstain from the accursed things, lest you become accursed when you take of the accursed things, and make the camp of Israel a curse, and trouble it.

19 But all the silver and gold, and vessels of bronze and iron, *are* consecrated to the LORD; they shall come into the treasury of the LORD.

Achan sinned by stealing what had been devoted to God — and that was a dreadful mistake, costing his life and defeat for Israel at the next battle of Ai. Paul uses this very word *cherem* (i.e., the Greek equivalent *anathema*), asking God to devote him as an offering to destruction — in this case, *disinheritance* — so that national Israel might receive kingdom inheritance. Arlen Chitwood writes:

> Israel's repentance was of such import that Paul, knowing and understanding the gravity of that involved, *was willing to go to the extent of relinquishing HIS OWN POSITION in Christ's coming kingdom IF the nation's repentance COULD be effected through such actions on his part.*[9]

THE SELFLESS INTERCESSION OF MOSES

How unselfish of the apostle! Just like the selfless intercession of Moses in the book of Exodus. You know the story. While Moses is up on the mountain with God, the people think he must have died, for he has been absent many days. So they have Aaron fashion a golden calf out of their gold jewelry which is melted down. They had undoubtedly learned about a golden calf for worship in Eygpt, for the Egyptians worshipped the apis bull as a god. Now Israel is doing the same, calling this calf "Jehovah," which God had forbidden in the ten commandments. Notice how the story develops, starting in Exod. 32:

> **Exod. 32:7** And the LORD said to Moses, "Go, get down! For your people whom you brought out of the land of Egypt have corrupted *themselves*.
>
> **8** They have turned aside quickly out of the way which I

commanded them. They have made themselves a molded calf, and worshiped it and sacrificed to it, and said, 'This *is* your god, O Israel, that brought you out of the land of Egypt!' "

9 And the LORD said to Moses, "I have seen this people, and indeed it *is* a stiff-necked people!

10 Now therefore, let Me alone, that My wrath may burn hot against them and I may consume them. And I will make of you a great nation."

Why didn't Moses take God up on His offer? Would it have been wrong for Moses to do so, seeing that God offered it? Instead, Moses intercedes with God for Israel:

> **Exod. 32:11** Then Moses pleaded with the LORD his God, and said: "LORD, why does Your wrath burn hot against Your people whom You have brought out of the land of Egypt with great power and with a mighty hand?
>
> 12 Why should the Egyptians speak, and say, 'He brought them out to harm them, to kill them in the mountains, and to consume them from the face of the earth'? Turn from Your fierce wrath, and relent from this harm to Your people.
>
> 13 Remember Abraham, Isaac, and Israel, Your servants, to whom You swore by Your own self, and said to them, 'I will multiply your descendants as the stars of heaven; and all this land that I have spoken of I give to your descendants, and they shall inherit *it* forever.' "
>
> 14 So the LORD relented from the harm which He said He would do to His people.

Moses is concerned about two things:

1. He is concerned that God will appear too harsh and judgmental to the Egyptians, so he pleads with God, "Turn from Your fierce wrath."

2. He is concerned that God's promises to Abraham, Isaac, and Jacob will not be fulfilled.

WHAT IF MOSES HAD NOT INTERVENED?

Granted, God said He would make a great nation of Moses, but Moses knows that means the salvation of all nations (promised to Abraham in Gen. 12:3) would never be accomplished, for the Abrahamic promises would be made null and void by the death of the nation.

Interestingly, Moses rejects God's offer. He doesn't want to become a great nation. He wants *Israel* to continue on, so she can be the tool through which God saves all the families of the earth. To that end, Moses asks God to spare the entire nation — including the sinful idolaters — not merely the righteous.

If Moses had not intervened on behalf of Israel, would God have spared Israel regardless? No!—Otherwise, this passage has absolutely no meaning. Thus, by stating these two objections — and thereby rejecting God's offer for himself — Moses does exactly what God wants him to do. He appeals to God's character and the specific promises to Abraham, that through him all of humanity will be saved. Based on Moses' intercession, God agrees to spare the people. Later, Moses returns to the Lord to make atonement for the sins of the people.

> **Exod. 32:31** Then Moses returned to the LORD and said, "Oh, these people have committed a great sin, and have made for themselves a god of gold!
> 32 Yet now, if You will forgive their sin—but if not, I pray, blot me out of Your book which You have written."

Moses essentially gives God a choice: Either forgive Israel's sin or blot me out of your book. As if to say, "I don't want inheritance if Israel can't have it."

THE BOOK OF LIFE

Many commentators believe the book mentioned here is the Book of Life. Because this same book is opened at the Great White Throne, many of those same commentators assume it is a record of those who are saved, i.e., regenerated. Thus, those not in the book are unsaved (unregenerate). However, I believe this assumption is incorrect. The Israelites were already a regenerated people as a result of the blood being applied in the first Passover. A comprehensive study of the Book of Life throughout the entire Bible reveals it is not a record of those who are regenerate; it is a record of those who have lived righteously and therefore stand to be rewarded.

Moses knows he is qualified to be in this book, so he asks God to forgive Israel, but if He will not, then Moses wants to be removed from this book. In other words, Moses offers to be disinherited from reward, so that Israel might be forgiven and spared God's judgment. Incidentally, if God had killed Israel for this sin, they would not have gone to Hell. Rather, like Sodom, they would have experienced instant death and, for Israel, it would have been in a disinherited state. Moses wants to take Israel's disinheritance upon himself as the substitute for the people. God honors Moses' request by sparing Israel, but does not take away Moses' inheritance.

> **Ps. 106:23** Therefore He said that He would destroy them, had not Moses His chosen one stood before Him in the breach, to turn away His wrath, lest He destroy *them*.

AS WITH MOSES, SO WITH PAUL — ISRAEL MUST CONTINUE!

This is exactly what Paul offers on behalf of Israel in Rom. 9. What is the significance of this? Both Moses and Paul were concerned that God's promises be fulfilled by Israel — that all of humanity would be saved. Yet the Reformation taught that disobedient Israel was replaced by another — the church of Jesus Christ, having different objectives. Incidentally, as pointed out earlier, this changes the entire scope of eschatology. This is *not* what God wants. He wants intercessors who will stand for Israel, even at their own peril, so Israel can fulfill its mission of saving the nations. Jan Bonda says:

> Thus we notice that God's purpose for Israel is not achieved automatically. It is realized only when Moses stands in the breach before God. God wants salvation for Israel, and through Israel he wants to

reach all nations with his redemption. He wants to achieve this through human beings (mortals!) who share in the same aim, and who want that so eagerly that they are willing to put their own salvation at risk! We completely miss the point Scripture is trying to make if we argue that God would have done this anyway, since it had been predetermined what he would do!

No, God himself puts everything at risk. If Moses had not intervened, Israel would not have received the forgiveness required for the fulfillment of the promise to the fathers. This Moses, who refuses to quit until God has assured him that he will forgive Israel and will dwell in their midst, appears as no other to be God's tool by which the divine intentions with Israel — and with all of humanity — can be realized.

Again we ask from the perspective of our tradition. Is it God's will that his children passively accept the perdition of the many? This story about Moses makes abundantly clear that this spirit of acquiescence is the complete opposite of what Scriptures teaches us about the will of God. Whoever is called by him is called not to accept passively the doom people have brought upon themselves. And those who do acquiesce cannot be the tools through which God realizes his purposes.[10]

THREE OPTIONS

What Bonda says about Moses is also true of the apostle Paul in Rom. 9, so that leaves us with three alternatives or options:

Option 1: We can acquiesce to man's will rather than God's and accept replacement theology, as Reformed Protestant Christianity has done.

Option 2: We can reject replacement theology but continue to embrace its logical conclusion — eternal conscious torment — the doctrine that the overwhelming majority of humanity will be tormented forever in the lake of fire, eternally separated from God, with no way of escape. Sadly, this is held by virtually all of Christianity, but as I said, it is the logical conclusion of replacement theology, it is not biblical doctrine. To repeat Bonda's profound statement:

The idea that God does not want to save all people began with the conviction that God does not want to save Israel.[11]

Option 3: We can choose to believe God wants all of Israel to be saved so they can lead all the nations to God through Jesus Christ, in fulfillment of the promise to Abraham.

GOD'S ANSWER TO PAUL

After offering himself to be accursed on behalf of Israel, Paul is given God's answer, and he writes about it in ch. 11:

> **Rom. 11:26-27** And so all Israel will be saved, as it is written [in Isa. 59:20]: *"The Deliverer will come out of Zion, and He will turn away ungodliness from Jacob; for this is My covenant with them, when I take away their sins."*

Then Paul gives God's purpose for saving Israel:

> **Rom. 11:32** For God has committed them all to disobedience, that He might have mercy on all.

Israel will finally become God's instrument for showering His mercy upon all mankind, unto salvation — and that prompts Paul to write:

> **Rom. 11:33** Oh, the depth of the riches both of the wisdom and knowledge of God! How unsearchable *are* His judgments and His ways past finding out!
> 36 For of Him and through Him and to Him *are* all things, to whom *be* glory forever. Amen.

Is not God most glorified in the salvation of all men? And is this not the ultimate of love?

THE GREATEST OF THESE IS LOVE

Paul sums up the Christian life in 3 words at the end of 1 Cor. 13

> **1 Cor. 13:13** Now abide faith, hope, love, these three; but the greatest of these *is* love.

In the next verse, he says: Pursue love. (14:1). I believe that FAITH living is the Christ life that leads to holiness and victory (Rom. 6, 7, and 8:1-11). HOPE living is kingdom preparedness that leads to reward (Rom. 8:12-39). LOVE living is universal reconciliation, the salvation of all mankind (Rom. 9-11, 14-15).

Love is what Abraham and Moses and Paul each had. How can Christianity be truly loving to mankind if it views Israel as replaced by the church? That's not God's will! Israel is His means of reaching the whole world with salvation! (Read Isa. 43). How can Christianity be loving if it expects the masses of humanity to burn forever and ever in the lake of fire? Is that God having mercy on all (Rom. 11:26)?

I prefer to believe that God will save all of humanity by the end of the ages. In small part, He will use the church to accomplish that goal, but in much greater part He will use Israel. May we, like Moses and Paul, yearn for Israel's salvation, for Israel's salvation is the key to the salvation of all. When you have this heart of love for Israel and mankind, then you have truly discovered the heart of God. That is why love is the greatest of these!

CHAPTER 22
ISRAEL'S FUTURE RESTORATION AND GLOBAL IMPACT
ROMANS 9:4-13

From the opening verses of Rom. 9, readers can clearly see Paul's loving heart for Israel — "my countrymen according to the flesh." i.e., his flesh-and-blood family and national heritage. The apostle longs for Israel's salvation — the nation's repentance, leading to millennial inheritance — which is consistent with the context of the book of Romans. To that end, the apostle is willing to be disinherited if it means Israel will be restored to fellowship. Incidentally, this is the same thing Moses had asked on behalf of Israel in the Old Testament.

Paul is obviously deeply concerned about Israel's rejection of Jesus as the Christ, the Messiah — the very Messiah for which they had been longing. He wants to be sure Israel doesn't perpetually remain on the sidelines, but that God fulfills His promises to the nation. God fully intends to bring Israel back to the forefront in time. Thus, the Holy Spirit inspires Paul to write this treatise, which spans from Rom. 9-11, regarding Israel's rejection and God's purpose to restore His chosen nation before this age ends and the millennial age begins. By the end of Rom. 11, the apostle is rejoicing — and we should be too!

WHAT SETS ISRAEL APART FROM OTHER NATIONS?

Paul lists eight things in vs. 4-5:

> **Rom 9:4** who are Israelites, to whom *pertain* the adoption, the glory, the covenants, the giving of the law, the service *of God,* and the promises; **9:5** of whom *are* the fathers and from whom, according to the flesh, Christ *came,* who is over all, *the* eternally blessed God. Amen.

1. ADOPTION

As already discussed in Chapter 18 of this book (Rom. 8), God has a plan of adoption for faithful saints of the church age, but Rom. 9 focuses exclusively on God's plan of adoption for national Israel.

Adoption, in a biblical sense, is the legal recognition of a mature son as firstborn, whether firstborn in a biological sense, or not. The *firstborn* is the child that the father considers worthy of receiving a double inheritance, which comes with the responsibility of carrying on the father's business affairs and functioning as the high priest of the family after the father's death.

Israel was first created by God as a nation through Jacob, then later designated as firstborn amongst the nations (see Exod. 4:22). God says something very interesting about Israel and the Jewish people in Isa. 43:

> **Isa. 43:1** But now, thus says the LORD, who created you, O Jacob, and He who formed you, O Israel: "Fear not, for I have redeemed you; I have called *you* by your name; you *are* Mine."

This is an endearing statement by God to His people, but there's something in the original Hebrew that needs to be pointed out. The word *created* is translated from the Hebrew *bara,* which means "to call into existence that which had no existence."[1]

God uses the same word *created* in Isa. 43:7:

Isa. 43:7 Everyone who is called by My name, whom I have created for My glory; I have formed him, yes, I have made him.

In the context, this refers to the Jewish people. God says He *created* Jacob — literally, He called Jacob into existence and all the individual Jews thereafter — *everyone who is called by My name* (*Israel*, meaning "prince with God"). That's quite a statement, for it doesn't use the normal language of procreation from one generation to another. Somehow, the Jewish people are not *merely* the products of reproduction, as the rest of mankind; they are God's unique people, called into existence by Him. We don't fully understand what that means, but it certainly implies something very special. Arlen Chitwood writes:

> *Because of creation,* Jacob is seen as *a son of God*; and, *through procreation,* all of his descendants are seen in Scripture individually as sons of God, with the nation as a whole seen collectively or corporately as *God's son.* And, following the adoption, the nation would be viewed as *God's firstborn son* (Ex. 4:22, 23). **[Exod. 4:22** Then you shall say to Pharaoh, "Thus says the LORD: 'Israel *is* My son, My firstborn.'"]
>
> This entire thought of *creation and sonship, followed by adoption,* is what separates and sets apart both the Jewish people individually and the nation of Israel as a whole from all the Gentiles (individually, or nationally). Scripture makes a sharp distinction between *Israel* on the one hand and *the Gentile nations* on the other. The Jewish people comprise a separate and distinct nation which is not to be "reckoned among the nations" — the Gentile nations (*cf.* Num. 23:9; Deut. 7:6; Amos 3:1, 2).[2]

What sets Israel apart from other nations?

2. GLORY

This is referring to the Shekinah glory, the blazing glow that hovered on Mt. Sinai like a consuming fire. Later, it became a pillar of cloud by day and pillar of fire by night that accompanied Israel on her journey through the wilderness. God was signifying to His people that He was personally in their midst. After the tabernacle was constructed, the glory of God filled the place.

> **Exod. 40:34-35** Then the cloud covered the tabernacle of meeting, and the glory of the LORD filled the tabernacle. And Moses was not able to enter the tabernacle of meeting, because the cloud rested above it, and the glory of the LORD filled the tabernacle.

The glory was unique to Israel. What sets Israel apart from other nations?

3. COVENANTS

God made several covenant promises in the Old Testament, for example:

- **Abrahamic** — God promised to make of Abraham a great nation, to bless all families of the earth through Him, and to give Canaan land to Abraham and his descendants.
- **Mosaic** — God promised to make Israel a kingdom of priests to propagate His blessing and glory to all the nations, *if* the nation would remain obedient to Him.
- **Davidic** — God promised to give David a descendant on the throne of Israel forever (*unto the age*, YLT).
- **New** — God promised a new era of forgiveness, with His word written on the heart.

All of the covenants are for Israel, including the *New* Covenant. Arlen Chitwood writes:

> Covenants are made with Israel (Rom 9:4). No covenant has been made or ever will be made with the Church … The Old Covenant (Mosaic, inseparably associated with the Abrahamic) was made with Israel; and the New Covenant, one day replacing the Old, will be made with Israel. BOTH *have to do with the theocracy*, as do ALL covenants made or to be made with Israel (Davidic, Palestinian, New).[3]

What sets Israel apart from other nations?

4. MOSAIC LAW

The Mosaic law was given on Mt. Sinai, and it was accompanied by angels, as stated in Acts 7:53, Gal. 3:19, and Heb. 2:2. Mt. Sinai was quite a spectacle at the time, with thunder and lightning and smoke and the sound of a trumpet blast and a great quaking. Needless to say, something important happened there, namely, God spoke to His people and gave the law that would guide them for fifteen hundred years.

5. SACRIFICIAL SYSTEM

The term *service of God*, which Paul uses in v. 4, refers to the Levitical system of blood sacrifices and offerings on the altar, initially at the tabernacle and later at the temple. Imagine the countless thousands of sacrifices made each year.

6. PROMISES

God made numerous promises to Israel, mainly through the prophets, which were promises of Messiah's coming and His glorious kingdom.

7. FATHERS (PATRIARCHS)

God set apart great and godly men, and then trained them and chastened them as needed to bring them to maturity — men like Abraham, Isaac, Jacob, Joseph, Moses, David, and plenty of others.

8. MESSIAH

Messiah was born of a Jewish virgin woman, descendant of King David, and He is over all, *God blessed throughout the ages*, is the way it reads literally in v. 5. This is a testimony to the divinity of Christ. What could be more marvelous than this!

Thus, Israel is distinct from all other nations, in that Israel has been given the adoption, the glory, the covenants, the law, the temple service, the promises, the fathers, and the Messiah Himself! No other nation can boast in these things. Arlen Chitwood claims:

> No Gentile nation can qualify to lay claim to anything in this list, for there is *no special creation* among any of the Gentile nations, allowing *sonship* and *a subsequent adoption* to exist. The only way that any Gentile nation can have any type [of] association with the things listed in this verse is seen in Gen. 9:25-27 …
>
> Of the three sons of Noah, *Shem* was the only one revealed to have a God (v. 26). And if either of the other two sons (Ham or Japheth), alienated from God in this respect, were to receive spiritual blessings, they would have had to "dwell in the tents of Shem" (v. 27). That is to say, they would have had to come to the one in possession of a God and spiritual blessings. They would have had to come to and ally themselves with Shem.
>
> And that is exactly the position in which *Israel and the Gentile nations* have found themselves throughout millenniums of time, find themselves today, and will always find themselves. Of all the nations on earth, *Israel, the nation descending from Shem through Abraham, Isaac, and Jacob, is the only nation having a God*; and the God Whom Israel possesses has decreed that *all spiritual blessings are to flow through the nation which He has singled out as His firstborn son.*
>
> Thus, for *the Gentiles* to be blessed — today, or at any time yet future — they would/will have to … come to the one in possession of a God and in possession of spiritual blessings … *Israel*.[4]

Given all of these wonderful benefits, shouldn't Israel have embraced Messiah at His first coming? Unfortunately, that did not happen due to misunderstanding who Jesus was. Paul, therefore, quashes what might have been in the minds of some in his day:

Rom. 9:6a But it is not that the word of God has taken no effect.

God's Word has not failed! The promises are just as sure as ever and will be fulfilled. Israel's present rejection of Jesus as Messiah in no way derails what God has promised for Israel in the future.

Paul then begins a lengthy section to explain that everything that has happened with Israel is in accordance with God's purposes — which leads to a second question:

WHO ARE ISRAELITES?

> **Rom. 9:6b For they *are* not all Israel who *are* of Israel,**

Paul restates what he had said earlier:

> **Rom. 2:28-29** For he is not a Jew who *is one* outwardly, nor *is* circumcision that which *is* outward in the flesh; but *he is* a Jew who *is one* inwardly; and circumcision *is that* of the heart, in the Spirit, not in the letter; whose praise *is* not from men but from God.

In other words, it's not merely about nationality. Zane Hodges says:

> For Paul, it is one thing to be an Israelite in the natural sense of that word, and another thing to be an Israelite spiritually.[5]

Jan Bonda writes:

> Not all who are descendants of Jacob truly belong to Israel, and not all who are born of Abraham are truly Abraham's children. *These words have been interpreted as follows:* God never indicated that his promise would be for all Israel; his promise to Abraham applies only to that part of Israel which he chooses from among all the Israelites.
>
> Therefore, what we now see happening to Israel is in full agreement with Scripture … So, why does the greatest part of Israel not share in God's salvation? God does not count them as true Israelites; true Israelites are only those who belong to that part of Israel that has been elected. They are those who accepted Messiah when he came, and possibly a few more in later times.

So this is a letdown! Paul and the other Jews had hoped that Jesus would save all Israel, but in retrospect it appears that God never intended to do so. Their expectations about God's promise to Israel were too high, and they will have to adapt them to reality, for the hope that all Israel would be saved is not grounded in Scripture … *This is the explanation that has become generally accepted in the church.* (italics mine).[6]

This bogus interpretation, which came out of the Reformation, has led to replacement theology and antisemitism (which was addressed in Chapter 21).

HOW DO WE KNOW THAT ISRAEL HAS NOT BEEN REPLACED?

1. Paul has just given eight benefits that set Israel apart from the other nations, and he uses the present tense. Thus, Israel is distinct from all other nations, in that Israel has been given the adoption, the glory, the covenants, the law, the temple service, the promises, the patriarchs, and the Messiah Himself! Paul assumes these things to be true even at the time of his writing, not merely true in Israel's past. For that matter, they are still true today!

2. Just a few chapters before this, Paul emphatically defends Israel's primacy even after the nation's rejection of Jesus as Messiah, asking:

> **Rom. 3:1** What advantage then has the Jew, or what *is* the profit of circumcision?
>
> 2 Much in every way! Chiefly because to them were committed the oracles of God.
>
> 3 For what if some did not believe? Will their unbelief make the faithfulness of God without effect?
>
> 4 Certainly not! Indeed, let God be true but every man a liar.

Israel's unbelief does not cancel out God's promises! Indeed, God will fulfill His Word regarding national Israel.

3. Jumping ahead to ch. 11, we find Paul's conclusion. He says that Israel's unbelief is only for a period of time:

Rom. 11:25b Blindness in part has happened to Israel until the fullness of the Gentiles has come in.

He insists that Israel will be saved and forgiven by God.

Rom. 11:26-27 All Israel will be saved ... *when I take away their sins.*

Paul reemphasizes that God's calling of His people cannot be derailed.

Rom. 11:29 For the gifts and the calling of God *are* irrevocable.

Then Paul shares the reason for Israel's present unbelief.

Rom. 11:32 For God has committed them all (both Jews and Gentiles) to disobedience, that He might have mercy on all.

THE PURPOSE FOR ISRAEL'S TEMPORARY UNBELIEF

Israel's temporary rejection of Messiah is so that God may have mercy on the Gentiles, but one day He will have mercy on His people once again, and they will be saved. So we can see that one of the arguments of replacement theology — that only *part* of Israel will be saved — is completely false and merely an unbiblical teaching of the Reformers.

Sometimes it's important to see the conclusion of the argument before seeing the argument itself. Paul begins to develop his argument in ch. 9:

> **Rom. 9:7** nor *are they* all children because they are the seed of Abraham; but, *"In Isaac your seed shall be called."* (God's promise to Abraham in Gen. 21:12)
> **9:8** That is, those who *are* the children of the flesh, these *are* not the children of God; but the children of the promise are counted as the seed.

> **9:9** For this *is* the word of promise: *"At this time I will come and Sarah shall have a son."*

Paul says that not even all of Abraham's children are Israelites, children of promise. The promise only applies to Isaac's lineage. So that would obviously rule out Ishmael, who is the child of the flesh referred to in v. 8. Abraham's consorting with Hagar wasn't a spiritual act; it was a fleshly one. He took matters into his own hands and tried to "help" God fulfill the promise. Nevertheless, the promised seed, the children of God, ultimately came through Sarah, not Hagar. Hodges says:

> It is not the children of the flesh who are children of God. To be truly children of Abraham, Paul implies, is to be the *children of God* ... By way of analogy, therefore, believing Israelites are *children of God* by faith in Christ, in contrast to unbelieving Israelites, who are not. Indeed, as mere physical descendants of Abraham, they are actually children of the flesh.[7]

The capstone of this line of thinking is found in Gal. 3:

> **Gal. 3:7** Therefore know that *only* those who are of faith are sons of Abraham.
> **8** And the Scripture, foreseeing that God would justify the Gentiles by faith, preached the gospel to Abraham beforehand, *saying, "In you all the nations shall be blessed."* (quoting Gen. 12:3)
> **9** So then those who *are* of faith are blessed with believing Abraham.

In keeping with the Old Testament narrative, Paul takes this one step further, and that leads to a third question:

HOW DID GOD CALL ISRAEL?

> **Rom. 9:10** And not only *this*, but when Rebecca also had conceived by one man, *even* by our father Isaac

9:11 (for *the children* not yet being born, nor having done any good or evil, that the purpose of God according to election might stand, not of works but of Him who calls),
9:12 it was said to her, *"The older shall serve the younger."*
9:13 As it is written, *"Jacob I have loved, but Esau I have hated."*

9:10-11. Not only did God choose Isaac over Ishmael, He also chose Jacob over Esau. God's choice had nothing to do with behavior, for He made His choice before Jacob and Esau were born. Paul makes that very clear in v. 11 — the purpose of God was *not of works but of Him who calls*. It was God's unilateral and arbitrary decision, not based on anything inherent in one twin or the other.

9:12. Furthermore, God chose the younger over the elder, as He also did with Isaac over Ishmael. Why God chooses in this manner, we do not know, but it's none of our business — God can do as He sees fit. We should only rejoice:

> **Rom. 11:33** Oh, the depth of the riches both of the wisdom and knowledge of God! How unsearchable *are* His judgments and His ways past finding out!
> 34 *"For who has known the mind of the LORD? Or who has become His counselor?"*

The promised seed came through Abraham, Isaac, and Jacob. Even though Esau has the same two parents as Jacob, Esau is not the father of any Israelites, i.e., children of God or children of promise. He became subservient to Jacob, who was God's choice as firstborn inheritor. Jacob, through his twelve sons, is the father of all Jews, naturally-speaking. The promises of God flow through him and his descendants. Hodges writes:

> Paul is simply reemphasizing that God sovereignly chose the vehicle through which His purpose for Israel was to be realized. Natural,

physical descent is not the basis for God's sovereign choice. Ishmael and Esau were both the "seed" of Abraham, but neither was the divinely chosen seed from which the nation itself would come.[8]

DOES GOD REALLY HATE ESAU?

9:13. Notice again the quote in v. 13: *"Jacob I have loved, but Esau I have hated."* This is a quote from Mal. 1. Throughout the centuries, Calvinists have used this verse as one of their hallmark passages to defend the doctrine of *unconditional election*, which is the "U" of Calvinism's T-U-L-I-P acrostic. Jan Bonda says:

> These words became one of the cornerstones of the doctrine of predestination … Out of the many God chooses a certain number of people he wants to save, while he does not want to save the rest.[9]

However, that is a misuse of the text, for in the context, God's focus is not on *individuals*, but on *nations*! Furthermore, this is *not* about matters of Heaven and Hell, as so many assume. God is talking about choosing a nation to fulfill His will on Earth. God does *not* elect some to salvation and others to damnation!

The passage says that God *loved* Jacob but *hated* Esau. *Hate* is a strong word. However, it needs to be understood in the broader context of the Scriptures. According to Rene Lopez:

> The term *hated* is an idiom understood as loving less (Gen. 29:30-31; Matt. 6:24; Luke 14:26; John 12:25). The concepts of *love* and *hate* are not to be viewed as feelings but a decision of God to bestow inheritance blessing on Jacob's descendants rather than Esau's.[10]

WHAT IS ISRAEL'S CALLING?

Paul now enters into a discussion of the lineage of Abraham — Isaac — Jacob. In a lengthy, but profound, explanation, Jan Bonda writes:

> All who have been born as descendants of Jacob are intended by God to become true Israelites in the fullest sense of the word. Of this

Jacob is the shining example. From his birth the promise was for Jacob. But he did not automatically become what God wanted him to be! Jacob is pictured for us as the man who wanted the blessing at the expense of his brother Esau. And that is not what God has in mind for Israel.

Israel has not been called to have the blessing for itself, but to be a blessing from God for all nations. For Jacob this means: to be first of all a blessing to his brother Esau. That he becomes in the night of his wrestling with God. In that night Jacob must fight for the blessing: "I will not let you go, unless you bless me!" There God gives him the name Israel, and there he receives the blessing: "And there he blessed him" ... (Gen. 32:22-32).

Now the past evil has been taken care of and the way is open for an encounter with his brother. In that night God makes him a different person. He has become Israel: a blessing for his brother Esau. We read about this in the story of his encounter with his brother that follows. He accompanies the gift, which he had sent to Esau, with the words: "Take, I pray thee, my blessing, that is brought to thee" ... (Gen. 33:11).

We have been conditioned to see Esau as the brother whom God had written off. But in fact the story teaches us that he is the brother who receives the blessing when Jacob has truly become *Israel*. And so, the people of Esau — Edom — is not written off; it is "written in!" After Jacob and Esau together buried their father — the problem between them had been solved for good! ...

The story teaches us what it means to be *Israel*. Jacob was born to be Israel, to be a blessing to his brother Esau, a blessing to all nations. But he does not become that until his struggle with God ... All Israel must become God's people. For to them "belongs the adoption" (Rom. 9:4) ... This implies that this continues to be God's intention for the Jewish people. It will yet be.[11]

How glorious to think that Israel's calling is to be a blessing to the nations! God pictures this in Jacob's meeting with Esau — and the preparation needed for that meeting — as recorded in Gen. 32-33. Indeed, all families of the earth will ultimately be blessed through Israel. That leads to an important fifth question:

WHAT KEEPS ISRAEL FROM FULFILLING ITS CALLING?

There are two obstacles to Israel's salvation, keeping the nation from fulfilling its adoption as God's firstborn son amongst the nations. Paul deals with both of these obstacles here in the epistle of Romans:

1. ISRAEL'S TRUST IN LINEAGE

Think of the attitude of the Pharisees: "We have Abraham as our father" (Matt. 3:9). But as Paul has just pointed out, lineage from Abraham is not what counts, for both Ishmael and Esau were Abraham's lineage, but the promise did not come through them. Even if the Pharisees were to amend their condescending attitude to: "We have Jacob as our father," we must ask: "Which Jacob?" — Jacob who snatched the blessing at Esau's expense? Or Jacob who wrestled with God, received the blessing, and willingly bestowed it on his brother? Not to mention, Paul has made quite clear that merely being an Israelite by *nationality* is not the same as being an Israelite *spiritually*, in God's eyes.

> **Gal. 3:7** Know that *only* those who are of faith are sons of Abraham.

Thus, part of Israel's problem is trusting in lineage, which has blinded the nation from seeing its need. But there is a second obstacle:

2. ISRAEL'S TRUST IN THE LAW

By depending on the Mosaic law's rituals to make them spiritual, the Jews are being self-righteous. Paul has spent several chapters on this problem, repeatedly emphasizing that what Israel needs is the righteous provision of Jesus living within through His Holy Spirit, for those who are led by the Spirit are the *sons* of God, the *huios*, the firstborn inheritors. However, because Israel has rejected Messiah, they do not have this provision to live righteously and, therefore, can only live in a fleshly manner.

HISTORY REPEATS ITSELF

Ironically, these are the same two problems within twenty-first century Christianity. As the old adage claims, "What goes around, comes around."

Trust in Lineage. Multitudes of Christians have been taught — through the perpetuation of Reformation doctrines — to trust their lineage, that is, to trust their relationship as God's children (and the errant doctrine of *positional* justification) to ensure a good report card at the Judgment Seat of Christ, regardless of behavior.

The attitude is: "We're Christians! We have all the blessings of salvation mentioned in the New Testament." But they fail to realize that many of those blessings are *not automatic,* bestowed at the point of regeneration. Rather, they are *conditional,* to be given at the Judgment Seat as the reward for persevering in righteous living and suffering on behalf of Christ.

Trust in Law. Multitudes of Christians also have the problem of trusting in the law, so to speak — not the Mosaic law, per se, but a law of their own devising — whether a list or set of rules or standards imposed by their church or denomination, expecting that keeping those things will make them spiritual.

Thus, the church's twenty-first century spiritual problems are really just repackaged versions of Israel's first century spiritual problems. If either of these problems characterizes you — and they often go together as a package — then confess it and forsake it immediately. Only then will you be able to go forward in victory. In closing this text, Hodges adds:

> The true force of Rom 9:7-13 is that there is clear Scriptural precedent for God's present dealings with His chosen nation. Israel has never received God's gracious mercy on the basis of mere physical descent from the patriarchs, nor has God's mercy been based on their works. This Scriptural precedent is fundamental to Paul's conviction that God's word has not failed (9:6).[12]

One day, when Israel finally realizes who Jesus is, they will have a complete reversal of attitude about their trust in their lineage and their trust in the law. When that happens, the nation will weep in repentance and truly become God's emissary and royal priesthood to the nations. What a day that will be!

CHAPTER 23
VESSELS OF MERCY PREPARED FOR GLORY
ROMANS 9:14-33

God chose Isaac over Ishmael and Jacob over Esau, to be the line through which the nation Israel would descend. That prompts the apostle to ask a question that could be on the minds of some of his readers:

> Rom. 9:14 What shall we say then? *Is there* unrighteousness with God? Certainly not!

Do God's decisions to select one over the other, nationally-speaking, imply that he is unjust or unfair? Paul's emphatic answer is: Certainly not!

> Rom. 9:15 For He says to Moses, *"I will have mercy on whomever I will have mercy, and I will have compassion on whomever I will have compassion."*

This is a quote from Exod. 33:19, and it is important to see the context of that verse in order to understand how Paul uses it in Rom. 9:

> Exod. 33:18-19 He [Moses] said, "Please, show me Your glory." Then He [God] said, "I will make all My goodness pass before you, and I

will proclaim the name of the LORD before you. I will be gracious to whom I will be gracious, and I will have compassion on whom I will have compassion."

When Moses asks to see God's glory, Jehovah describes Himself as gracious (merciful) and compassionate. It is God's prerogative to show mercy on certain ones, and not others, and that's what He does with Moses and the Israelites.

> **Rom. 9:16** So then *it is* not of him who wills, nor of him who runs, but of God who shows mercy.

JUSTICE FOR ALL, MERCY FOR SOME

Justice is different than mercy. *Everyone* is entitled to God's justice, for we are all sinful, but *no one* is entitled to His mercy. Imagine standing before a judge in a courtroom and demanding that the judge give you mercy for you are entitled to it. The judge would laugh in your face, making it very clear that the only thing you are entitled to is justice. The judge is under no obligation to show you mercy. Zane Hodges writes:

> The point Paul is making through the Exodus text is that when it comes to mercy and grace, God asserts His own prerogative to exercise this attribute toward the person, or persons, He Himself selects. But to state this fact is to make the case. No man can lay a legitimate claim on God for His mercy. It is man's need, inadequacy, or failure that calls forth mercy in the first place. To make it a human entitlement is to destroy its gracious character and turn it into a divine obligation.
>
> Thus if God acts in mercy/grace toward Isaac or towards Jacob, there is no unrighteousness in doing so. Neither Ishmael nor Esau was deprived of anything he had a right to claim. The bottom line in this matter of mercy is that mercy does not occur simply because someone wishes it or because someone runs, i.e., strives, for it. Rather it comes from the God who sovereignly bestows mercy on whom He will. Man's "will" and "desire" do not produce mercy, nor

do his most strenuous efforts, like those of a "runner" in a race. God, not man, determines who receives His mercy.[1]

Paul then shares the example of Pharaoh:

> **Rom. 9:17 For the Scripture says to the Pharaoh, *'For this very purpose I have raised you up, that I may show My power in you, and that My name may be declared in all the earth."* [quote from Exod. 9:16]
> **9:18 Therefore He has mercy on whom He wills, and whom He wills He hardens.**

GOD'S POWER AND GLORY MADE KNOWN TO THE NATIONS

Incidentally, this has nothing to do with matters of Heaven and Hell, as some like to suggest. Rather, it was God's choice not to show mercy to a pagan king who was the avowed enemy of Israel, but rather to harden his heart, so that God might establish the types demonstrated in the Passover and the Exodus, and the parting of the Red Sea. In so doing, His power and glory were made known to the nations. Think of Rahab's testimony:

> **Josh. 2:9** [Rahab] said to the men [spies]: "I know that the LORD has given you the land, that the terror of you has fallen on us, and that all the inhabitants of the land are fainthearted because of you.
> **10** For we have heard how the LORD dried up the water of the Red Sea for you when you came out of Egypt, and what you did to the two kings of the Amorites who *were* on the other side of the Jordan, Sihon and Og, whom you utterly destroyed.

God's power and glory were also known by the Philistines. When the Philistines stole the ark of the covenant, they placed it in the temple of their god Dagon, and the next morning, Dagon was face-down on the ground. So they propped Dagon upright again and the next day not only was Dagon face-down on the ground, but his hands and arms were broken off. In addition to this, God sent some type of tumorous plague to the people. The political leaders of the

Philistines rushed to their priests to know what they should do. The priests told them to send the ark back to Israel, along with a trespass offering and gold images, and then the Philistine priests admonished their nation's political leaders:

> **1 Sam. 6:6** Why then do you harden your hearts as the Egyptians and Pharaoh hardened their hearts? When He did mighty things among them, did they not let the people go, that they might depart?

EVEN HARD-HEARTED PHARAOH SAW GOD'S GLORY

God's purpose in Egypt also was to make His power and glory known.

> **Exod. 7:3** And I will harden Pharaoh's heart, and multiply My signs and My wonders in the land of Egypt.

Before God hardened Pharaoh's heart, the Exodus narrative reports that on several occasions Pharaoh hardened his own heart. Hodges concludes:

> It is unmistakable that all that God really does is to confirm and extend a process of hardening that Pharaoh himself had initiated ... The case of Pharaoh is instructive, since Pharaoh hardened his own heart before God hardened it. Paul would no doubt have said the same of Israel. Its hardness to the gospel of Jesus Christ was a process Israel itself began and which God has merely confirmed. This national hardness will continue "until the fullness of the Gentiles has come in" (Rom 11:25). But Paul's development of this theme also shows that God will still have mercy on any individual Israelite who believes.[2]

Paul anticipates another objection in v. 19:

> **Rom. 9:19** You will say to me then, "Why does He still find fault? For who has resisted His will?"

If God chooses not to show mercy to some, but instead, hardens their hearts, then how can God blame them for being hard-hearted? Paul thinks this question is impertinent, because we cannot possibly know God's purposes. Notice his response:

THE POTTER AND THE CLAY

> **Rom 9:20 But indeed, O man, who are you to reply against God? Will the thing formed say to him who formed** *it,* **"Why have you made me like this?"**
> **9:21 Does not the potter have power over the clay, from the same lump to make one vessel for honor and another for dishonor?**

How can anyone question God? It's like the creature complaining to the Creator, "Why did you make me this way?" Paul probably got this idea of the potter and the clay from Isaiah:

> **Isa. 45:9** Woe to him who strives with his Maker! ... Shall the clay say to him who forms it, "What are you making?

How audacious for clay to question the potter! The point is clear: how audacious for mere man to question sovereign God! Just like the potter decides what he is going to make out of the clay — whether an unblemished fancy vessel to be put on display or a lowly vessel with imperfections that is not going to be used for anything special — so God as Creator can decide how He fashions man.

Paul then expounds further on these two types of vessels:

TWO TYPES OF VESSELS

> **Rom. 9:22-24** *What* **if God, wanting to show** *His* **wrath and to make His power known, endured with much longsuffering the vessels of wrath prepared for destruction, and that He might**

> make known the riches of His glory on the vessels of mercy, which He had prepared beforehand for glory, *even* us whom He called, not of the Jews only, but also of the Gentiles?

If God wants to show His wrath and make His power known by hardening the heart of Pharaoh, then that is His prerogative! Paul has already warned his readers of God's wrath earlier in the book:

> **Rom. 1:18** For the wrath of God is revealed from heaven against all ungodliness and unrighteousness of men.

Pharaoh was a "vessel of wrath prepared for destruction." The word *destruction* does not mean Hell; it means "loss or ruin." It is referring to God's temporal judgment upon man. In other words, God used pagan Pharaoh's hard-heartedness to accomplish His purposes with respect to Israel, then destroyed him in the Red Sea. Meanwhile, Israel was shown God's mercy in the Red Sea.

VESSELS OF WRATH PREPARED FOR DESTRUCTION

But now the tables are turned. Because Israel has become hard-hearted toward God in unbelief, they have become His vessels of wrath, that His power might be made known. The first round of destruction (ruin) came when Rome conquered and demolished Jerusalem in AD 70, killing over one million Jews. Further destruction will be forthcoming during the tribulation. The Jewish people have brought God's wrath upon themselves. When writing to the church at Thessalonica, Paul said of the Jews:

> **1 Thess. 2:15-16** Who killed both the Lord Jesus and their own prophets, and have persecuted us; and they do not please God and are contrary to all men, forbidding us to speak to the Gentiles that they may be saved, so as always to fill up *the measure of* their sins; but wrath has come upon them to the uttermost.

Judgment begins "at the house of God," with His own people (1

Pet. 4:17). However, with respect to Israel, we know that judgment will result in national repentance and restoration when Jesus returns:

> **Zech. 12:10-11a** I will pour on the house of David and on the inhabitants of Jerusalem the Spirit of grace and supplication; then they will look on Me whom they pierced. Yes, they will mourn for Him as one mourns for *his* only *son*, and grieve for Him as one grieves for a firstborn. In that day there shall be a great mourning in Jerusalem.

Thus, God's purposes will be fulfilled. Dare we question God as to His purposes or even His methods? Zane Hodges writes:

> Paul is affirming that God "wishes" to do two things: (1) manifest "His wrath" and "His power" (v 22); and (2) manifest *the wealth of His glory* (v 23). The former He does with reference to "the vessels of wrath," while the latter is done *upon the vessels of mercy*. These vessels of mercy are identified in v 24 as both Jews and Gentiles ... Paul means by this that God's mercy has overleaped the boundaries of Israel itself and has gone out to the Gentile world ... The growing number of Gentile believers proves the wealth of His glory in terms of God's measureless mercy.[3]

VESSELS OF MERCY PREPARED FOR GLORY

Notice again vs. 23-24:

> **Rom. 9:23-24 That He might make known the riches of His glory on the vessels of mercy, which He had prepared beforehand for glory,** *even* **us whom He called, not of the Jews only, but also of the Gentiles?**

To whom is this referring? Paul's answer is clear: *even us whom He called*, that is, faithful believers of the church age. Remember back to Rom. 8:

Rom. 8:29-30 For whom He foreknew, He also predestined *to be* conformed to the image of His Son, that He might be the firstborn among many brethren. Moreover whom He predestined, these He also called; whom He called, these He also justified; and whom He justified, these He also glorified.

As pointed out in Chapter 20, these verses have nothing to do with salvation in the initial sense of regeneration. They are talking about God's calling of sons to glory out from among His children. *Sons to glory* are those Christians of the church whom Christ deems faithful to serve as His co-rulers. He is now working to conform them to the image of Christ, calling them, and justifying them (i.e., declaring them righteous in a *behavioral* sense). When they hear "Well done!" at the Bema Seat, they will be glorified, which means they will glow with some degree of light as part of their reward. These are the ones Paul refers to in Rom. 9:24 as *us whom He called*. Thus, we read with rejoicing that God will one day "make known the riches of His glory on the vessels of mercy, which He had prepared beforehand for glory, *even* us whom He called" — both Jews and Gentiles! This is only for those of the church of Jesus Christ who qualify. What about national Israel?

GOD'S GLORY ULTIMATELY MANIFESTED THROUGH ISRAEL ...

When Israel repents and becomes restored to fellowship at the end of the tribulation, God's glory will be manifest through the nation as they rule over the nations on Earth in the next age. That is made abundantly clear in the Old Testament prophets. This has been God's purpose all along — and what God purposes, He accomplishes! Hallelujah!

Paul then backs up this truth with three quotations from the Old Testament Scriptures. The first is from Hosea 2:23 and 1:10:

Rom. 9:25 As He says also in Hosea: *"I will call them My people, who were not My people, and her beloved, who was not beloved."*
9:26 *"And it shall come to pass in the place where it was*

said to them, 'You are not My people,' there they shall be called sons of the living God."*

It is important to remember the context of the book of Hosea. The ten tribes of the north had turned to idolatry. So God tells Hosea to marry a prostitute, symbolizing God's wife Israel, who had turned to harlotry. But the good news is that one day God's people will return and repent and be restored to fellowship, causing God to receive them back. Those who are not His people (due to idolatry) will again become His people, and they will be called sons of the living God.

... AND THROUGH THE CHURCH

Although this was a prophecy for Old Testament Israel, it will be fulfilled in the future by repentant and restored Israel. Remarkably, Paul also applies this prophecy to the Gentiles, for that is the context of his quote. Verse 24 refers to *even us whom He called* — that's Christians, the church of Jesus Christ — comprised not merely of Jews, but also of the Gentiles. Zane Hodges says:

> For Paul's purposes the words of Hosea sufficiently establish the principle that those at one time rejected as the people of God can be received by Him as His people. Since the vessels of mercy are composed of both Jews and Gentiles (vv 23-24), God's loving action in having mercy on them makes the principle exhibited in Hosea applicable to both.[4]

How marvelous! God has included us — church age believers who qualify — as vessels of mercy unto glory. A second quotation is found in vs. 27-29, taken from Isa. 10:22 and 1:9:

> **Rom. 9:27 Isaiah also cries out concerning Israel:**
> *"Though the number of the children of Israel be as the sand of the sea, the remnant will be saved.*
> **9:28** *For He will finish the work and cut it short in right-*

> *eousness, because the LORD will make a short work upon the earth."*
> 9:29 And as Isaiah said before: *"Unless the LORD of Sabaoth had left us a seed, we would have become like Sodom, and we would have been made like Gomorrah."*

SALVATION OF A REMNANT

Whereas Hosea prophesied to Israel; Isaiah prophesied to Judah, warning of coming destruction upon the nation. Isa. 10 seems to be referring to the coming tribulation, when millions of Jews will be killed by antichrist. Thankfully, God will cut the tribulation short, so that some Jews will survive. Jesus said:

> **Matt. 24:22** Unless those days were shortened, no flesh would be saved; but for the elect's sake those days will be shortened.

Isaiah speaks of a remnant being saved; otherwise, Israel would become like Sodom and Gomorrah, which were completely destroyed, leaving no remnant. Thus, God's saving of a remnant of Israelites is an act of His mercy. Hodges says:

> The chain of quotations has established the fact the God who sovereignly bestows mercy on whom He wishes (9:14-18) is acting now in a way consistent with Biblical revelation. As the Divine Potter, answerable to no one, He both postpones His ultimate judgment on the vessels of wrath while dealing mercifully with the vessels of mercy, both Jewish and Gentile (9:19-24).[5]

Before giving his final Old Testament quote, Paul pauses for some words of summary:

THE IRONY OF SINFUL GENTILES LIVING RIGHTEOUSLY

> **Rom. 9:30-31** What shall we say then? That Gentiles, who did not pursue righteousness, have attained

> to righteousness, even the righteousness of faith; but Israel, pursuing the law of righteousness, has not attained to the law of righteousness.
> 9:32 Why? Because *they* did not *seek it* by faith, but as it were, by the works of the law. For they stumbled at that stumbling stone.

Ironically, the Gentiles who were known for their sinful behavior have entered into righteous living, by depending on the provision of Jesus Christ. On the other hand, the Jews, who were known for behaving in accordance to the Mosaic law, have not entered into righteous living, because they have focused on observing the works of the law (legalism), that is, the Mosaic rituals, which cannot make one righteous. That has happened because "they stumbled at that stumbling stone," in other words, because they rejected Messiah.

Hodges doesn't like the term *stumbling stone*. He says it is too weak to convey the meaning of the original languages. Instead, he translates it "stone of collision." He quotes BDAG's definition, which is: "to cause to strike against something" and "to make contact with something in a bruising or violent way." Thus, the bottom line, according to Hodges is:

> Israel is the object of God's wrath, and the Gentiles of His mercy, because of Israel's rejection of Christ.[6]

We find Paul's third quotation, which is from Isa. 28:16, in v. 33:

> **Rom. 9:33 As it is written:** *"Behold, I lay in Zion a stumbling stone* [Hodges: stone of collision] *and rock of offense, and whoever believes on Him will not be put to shame."*

THE IMPORTANCE OF CONFESSING CHRIST

Israel collided with Jesus, who was their Messiah, though they didn't realize it. The result of the collision was the nation's unbelief and Messiah's death. Notice the last phrase of the verse: *whoever believes on Him will not be put to shame.* The verb *believes* is an active present participle, thus it is literally translated, "whoever *is believing* on Him will not be put to shame." Hodges says this is a command, not a statement. In other words, Paul is warning the believing Jews that despite Israel's "collision" with Messiah, they must continue on unashamed of Him.[7]

What an admonition for us all! As Christians, followers of our Lord Jesus Christ, we must continue depending on our Lord so we can confess Him before men. Jesus said:

> **Matt. 10:32-33** Whoever confesses Me before men, him I will also confess before My Father who is in heaven. But whoever denies Me before men, him I will also deny before My Father who is in heaven.

This has nothing to do with initial salvation. To confess Christ is to speak of Him and defend him in the presence of others, whether they are hostile regarding Christ or not. Those who faithfully confess Him will be rewarded. Those who cower in fear and refuse to confess Him (which is the equivalent of denying Him before men), will not be rewarded. Are you regularly confessing Christ?

CHAPTER 24
THE WORD OF FAITH IS NEAR YOU
ROMANS 10

Have you ever used the *Romans Road to Salvation* to witness to an unbeliever? It is a method of witnessing that uses verses from Romans (3:10, 23; 5:8; 6:23; 10:9, 13) to share the Gospel of Grace. I shared the details of this method in Chapter 5, if you need to review.

The Romans Road typically closes with Rom. 10:9, 13:

Rom. 10:9 If you confess with your mouth the Lord Jesus and believe in your heart that God has raised Him from the dead, you will be saved.

10:13 For *"whoever calls on the name of the LORD shall be saved."*

The person sharing the plan typically urges the sinner to pray to receive Christ, often suggesting the words to a prayer or encouraging the person to "repeat these words after me." There's one big problem.

THE PROBLEM WITH THE "ROMANS ROAD TO SALVATION" METHOD OF WITNESSING

As I said in Chapter 5, the book of Romans is not about *initial* salvation, which means that none of these verses are intended for leading an unbeliever to faith in Jesus Christ. In fact, the so-called *Romans Road to Salvation* misuses all of these verses. That is because the book of Romans is not written to unbelievers, telling them how to be regenerated; it is written to believers, telling them how to be sanctified.

I believe the *Romans Road to Salvation* method of witnessing does damage to Christianity in at least two ways:

1. The book of Romans is misinterpreted as evangelistic, thus the errors that came out of the Reformation are perpetuated.

2. Many are led to think that initial salvation is by confessing Christ, calling on Him, praying a prayer, which takes the emphasis off believing and puts it on *doing* something. Once that door is opened, it is a slippery slope downward.

What, then, does Paul mean when using the words *saved* (vs. 1, 9, 13) and *salvation* (v. 10)?

> **Rom. 10:1 Brethren, my heart's desire and prayer to God for Israel is that they may be saved.**

SALVATION AS USED IN ROM. 10

Is this being saved from Hell, as so many have interpreted? No! Salvation is not used in that sense of the word in the book of Romans. It is critical to remember the context. Romans was written during the period of re-offer of kingdom inheritance to national Israel. Jesus initially offered a special inheritance — inclusion in the heavenly New Jerusalem during the Messianic kingdom — for those who would repent and follow Him in discipleship. The Jewish leadership rejected Christ's offer, but God allowed the entire generation of Israelites living at the time to hear the offer of kingdom inheritance for another thirty years.

The nation ultimately rejected the offer, so Paul focused his attention on the Gentiles. Consequently, Jerusalem was destroyed by the Romans, as both Jesus and John had predicted. Since that time up to the present day national Israel continues in unbelief because "they stumbled at that stumbling stone" (9:32). They *collided* with Messiah (to use Hodges' term), who was to them a *rock of offense*. As a result,

God refers to Israel as "vessels of wrath prepared for destruction" (9:22). The destruction will come during the tribulation, when Satan and antichrist unleash their fury on Israel. Nevertheless, God will use the tribulation as a tool of judgment with the primary purpose of turning national Israel to repentance. In light of all this, and with heavy heart, Paul cries out:

> **Rom. 10:1 Brethren, my heart's desire and prayer to God for Israel is that they may be saved.**

Given the time-frame when he wrote Romans (probably around AD 56-57) — which was during the period when the apostles were re-offering kingdom inheritance — Paul is praying that the nation will accept the offer of kingdom inheritance and be delivered from temporal destruction. That is the salvation being discussed in ch. 10. It is important to keep that in mind throughout the exposition of this chapter. Look now at vs. 2-3:

ZEAL WITHOUT KNOWLEDGE VS. GOD'S RIGHTEOUSNESS

> **Rom. 10:2 For I bear them witness that they have a zeal for God, but not according to knowledge.
> 10:3 For they being ignorant of God's righteousness, and seeking to establish their own righteousness, have not submitted to the righteousness of God.**

Having zeal for God without knowledge is an apt description of Paul himself, before meeting Jesus on the road to Damascus. He zealously persecuted the church, for he did not realize Jesus was the Messiah. Paul now uses the same term to describe national Israel — zealous for Yahweh — offering sacrifices, following the letter of the Old Testament law, at least outwardly, and even persecuting Paul and the other apostles and the new Christians. Paul says they are ignorant of God's righteousness. Referring back to what he had said earlier in the epistle, Paul says:

> **Rom. 10:4** For Christ *is* the end of the law for righteousness to everyone who believes.

Perhaps this is a reminder to his audience — especially for the Jewish believers — of what he had written in Rom. 3-4. Living righteously and being justified by God is not through observing the Mosaic rituals. God wants His people to obey Him by faith, depending on His Son Jesus for the grace to live righteously.

The word *believes* in v. 4 is an active present participle, so it literally reads: "to everyone who *is believing.*" Jesus is the answer to living righteously! His Spirit dwells within believers, so that those who continue believing, depending on Jesus, are enabled with grace to obey God and live righteously.

> **Rom. 5:2** Through [Jesus] also we have access by faith into this grace in which we stand.

So many Christians miss these basic truths, both Jews and Gentiles. That was true in Paul's day, and it is true in ours.

THE MOSAIC LAW — ALL OR NOTHING

In v. 5 Paul points out how dire the problem is for the Jewish believers:

> **Rom. 10:5** For Moses writes about the righteousness which is of the law, *"The man who does those things shall live by them."*

This is a quote from Lev. 18:

> **Lev. 18:5** You shall therefore keep My statutes and My judgments, which if a man does, he shall live by them: I *am* the LORD.

The Mosaic law is structured in such a way that a person must keep all of it or else he has violated all of it.

> **Jas. 2:10** For whoever shall keep the whole law, and yet stumble in one *point*, he is guilty of all.

Nobody can keep the law perfectly, so no one can be made righteous by keeping it. What the Jews need — and, for that matter, what modern fundamentalists who are bound to rules need — is "the righteousness which is by faith." But Paul first needs to clear up some erroneous thinking.

JEWISH UNBELIEF VS. THE RIGHTEOUSNESS OF FAITH

> **Rom. 10:6-7 But the righteousness of faith speaks in this way,** *Do not say in your heart, "Who will ascend into heaven?"* **(that is, to bring Christ down** *from above***) or,** *"Who will descend into the abyss?"* **(that is, to bring Christ up from the dead).**

Zane Hodges explains why Paul speaks in this manner:

> The heart attitude, therefore, must not reflect the mind-set that Messiah (the Christ) had yet to come and needed to be brought down from heaven by someone. Naturally, in rejecting Jesus as God's Christ, Israel had adopted the attitude that Messiah was yet to appear. But in Paul's day, the view of many was that the coming of the Messiah could be hastened by Jewish obedience to the law.
>
> In addition, neither should one say in his heart that the Christ was still in Sheol (i.e., Hades). Paul's reference here to "the Abyss" is naturally construed as a reference to the abode of the departed, at least as understood by Pharisaic Judaism. (The Sadducees did not believe in resurrection: Luke 20:27.) In his exchanges with unbelieving Jews, Paul often must have heard the retort, "Well, if your Jesus is the Christ, He's a dead One!"
>
> Thus the two interrogatives presented here represent the two extremes of Jewish unbelief about Jesus. On the one hand, "Christ has not yet come; who can go and get Him?" and on the other, "Your Christ is dead; who can raise Him up?" But such attitudes, insists Paul, are not the message of the gospel that proclaims the right-

eousness which is by faith. In fact, they are the opposite of the truth that Paul preached.[1]

Paul sets the record straight:

THE WORD OF FAITH

> **Rom. 10:8 But what does it say?** *"The word is near you, in your mouth and in your heart"* **(that is, the word of faith which we preach):**

This verse has been greatly perverted by the charismatic Word of Faith movement. They teach that Christians can be healthy and wealthy if they think and speak words of faith — "name it and claim it" theology. That is *not* what Paul teaches in v. 8. Paul makes clear that Messiah has already come, and those who are believing Him consistently are living righteously — *that's* the word of faith message he preached.

It's not, "I name this and claim this in the name of Jesus, so it *has to happen!*" No, it's, "I am trusting Jesus to give me victory over sin and to help me live righteously in a manner that pleases Him" — *that's* the word of faith message!

Incidentally, Paul is no longer speaking to national Israel (as a group), as in v. 1. He is now speaking to individual Israelites, and we know that because he uses the singular for *you* and *your* in this verse, and continuing on into vs. 9-10.

IT IS NEAR — IN YOUR MOUTH AND HEART

Paul says that this word of faith message — living righteously by believing Jesus — *is near to you*. In fact, it is as close as being in your mouth and in your heart. He explains that in vs. 9-10:

> **Rom. 10:9 that if you confess with your mouth the Lord Jesus and believe in your heart that God has raised Him from the dead, you will be saved.**
> **10:10 For with the heart one believes unto right-**

eousness, and with the mouth confession is made unto salvation.

Verse 9 says you must *confess with your mouth the LORD Jesus*. Does that mean the Bible teaches Lordship salvation? Using verses such as this, Lordship salvation proponents say that to be saved one must recognize Jesus is not merely Savior, but Lord — master of all in your life. In other words, the prerequisites for discipleship — like denying self, taking up your cross, and following Him — are included as part of initial salvation. But that involves works!

While Lordship salvation is the logical conclusion of Calvinism's view of salvation, it is not biblical. Rom. 10:9-10 is not the way one's spirit is saved *initially*. It is the way one's soul is saved in an *ongoing* sense.

CONFESSING "LORD JESUS"

So what does it mean to *confess with your mouth the Lord Jesus*? The article *the* is not in the original. Thus it should read, confess with your mouth, "Lord Jesus!" Bob Wilkin writes:

> This is not someone telling another person, "Jesus is Lord." It is instead a direct appeal to the Lord Jesus for deliverance from the current wrath.[2]

Confessing "Lord Jesus" results in deliverance from God's wrath as defined in Rom. 1 — His judgment that leads to self-destruction.

Rom. 1:18 For the wrath of God is revealed from heaven against all ungodliness and unrighteousness of men.

God gives those who are sinning over to their ways. I like the way Hodges translates v. 10:

Rom. 10:10 (Hodges) *For with the heart He is believed for righteousness, but with the mouth He is confessed for deliverance.*[3]

A child of God who has not been living for Jesus cannot genuinely refer to Him as Lord (Master), because He is not Master of everything in *their* life, They need to get to the point where they are ready to submit to and confess Jesus as Lord, which means submitting to His prerequisites for discipleship. This is the same as "calling on the name of the Lord" in v. 13 — For *"whoever calls on the name of the LORD shall be saved."* John Niemela writes:

> Confessing, "Lord Jesus" (vv 9-10) equals calling upon His name (vv 13-14).[4]

Those who confess, "Lord Jesus!" are calling upon Him. They will find salvation in the sense of deliverance. If national Israel were to have confessed "Lord Jesus!" in Paul's day, the nation would have been delivered from destruction. Again, this is not a so-called salvation from Hell message! It is a sanctification unto reward message.

BELIEVING JESUS WAS RAISED FOR OUR JUSTIFICATION

In addition to confessing "Lord Jesus," God's children must believe in their heart that Jesus was raised from the dead. Why is this so important? Remember what Paul said in Rom. 4:

> **Rom. 4:25** [Jesus] was delivered up because of our offenses, and was raised because of our justification [i.e., righteous living].

The blood of Jesus on the cross is for *initial salvation and cleansing from sin*, but the resurrection of Jesus is for *ongoing salvation and victory over sin*. If you desire to embrace this word of faith message — living righteously by faith in Jesus, who is the Righteous One — then you must believe in your heart that the *resurrected* Jesus is able and willing to enable you to live righteously. Now look at v. 11:

> **Rom. 10:11 For the Scripture says, *"Whoever believes on Him will not be put to shame*** [i.e., ashamed].***"***

Again, the word *believes* is an active present participle, so it literally reads: "to everyone who *is believing*." Niemela says the last part of v. 11 should read: *"let him not be ashamed."*[5] Thus, a better translation is: *"Whoever is believing on Him, let him not be ashamed."*

CONFESSING CHRIST BEFORE MEN

Don't be ashamed of Jesus! In Paul's day the Jewish believers were intimidated by their countrymen who did not believe Jesus was Messiah, so they were reluctant to confess Christ before men, lest they face persecution. That's why Paul gives this admonition in v. 11, which is a quote from Isa. 28:16, (also quoted in 9:33).

This is the idea of confessing Christ unashamedly — telling others about Him, so that He will one day confess you before the Father. Those who deny Him will be denied in the presence of the Father. That doesn't mean they forfeit salvation (regeneration); it means they forfeit reward/inheritance. Confessing Christ before men is not required for becoming saved initially. Hodges says:

> Contrary to much contemporary theology, neither Paul nor the rest of the NT requires confession as a condition for receiving everlasting life (cf. Acts 16:31; Eph 2:8-9; 1 Tim 1:16). One should note especially John 12:42-43 where Johannine doctrine requires us to understand the non-confessing rulers as possessors of eternal life who lacked the courage of their convictions.[6]

Paul continues to add details to his argument in vs. 12-13:

CALLING UPON THE NAME OF THE LORD

> **Rom. 10:12 For there is no distinction between Jew and Greek, for the same Lord over all is rich to all who call upon Him.**
> **10:13 For *"whoever calls on the name of the LORD* shall be saved."**

This isn't praying a prayer to be saved initially. It is daily crying out to God for His strength and help to live the Christian life, which demonstrates humility. Anyone who calls on Him will be delivered — Jew or Gentile! Their soul will be saved! Arlen Chitwood says:

> Jews believing or not believing in relation to the re-offer of the kingdom are centrally in view throughout this section. The salvation spoken of has to do with ... salvation and life in the kingdom, not with eternal verities, for the Jews being dealt with during both the offer and re-offer of the kingdom ... were already saved (else there could have been no offer or re-offer of this kingdom).
>
> The salvation in Rom. 10:9, 10 was associated with calling upon the Lord in verses 12, 13 ... quoting a Messianic verse from Joel. And this is not at all in line with the way that a person is saved today; nor does it have to do with the same thing. One had to do with *Messianic values for individuals already saved (with the kingdom in view)*; the other has to do with *eternal values for unsaved individuals (with the kingdom ultimately in view)* ... Using Rom. 10:9, 10 when dealing with the unsaved could easily result in confusion.[7]

Look again at v. 13:

> **Rom. 10:13 For** *"whoever calls on the name of the LORD shall be saved."*

The verb *to call on* means "to appeal to or invoke."[8] This is not referring to a one-time confession; it is continual. We do this every Sunday when we come together for corporate worship — we *appeal to* or *invoke* the name of the Lord. Children of God should be calling upon the name of the Lord regularly and finding consistent deliverance.

ISRAEL'S FUTURE CALLING ON THE NAME OF JEHOVAH

Verse 13 is a direct quote from Joel 2, which is talking about the tribulation. Notice the original text:

> **Joel 2:30-32** And I will show wonders in the heavens and in the earth: blood and fire and pillars of smoke. The sun shall be turned

into darkness, and the moon into blood, before the coming of the great and awesome day of the LORD. <u>And it shall come to pass *that* whoever calls on the name of the LORD shall be saved.</u> For in Mount Zion and in Jerusalem there shall be deliverance, as the LORD has said, among the remnant whom the LORD calls. (underline mine)

If individual Jews will repent and turn to the Lord during the tribulation, Jesus will deliver them from the destruction and will include them amongst the remnant who are rescued. Paul uses this verse in a spiritual sense for the Jews of his generation to urge them to take up his gospel of kingdom inheritance (Rom. 1:16), aka *the righteousness of faith* (10:6), aka *the word of faith* (10:8). This principle applies to *anyone* who calls on Him, Jew or Gentile (v. 12).

FOR THOSE WHO ARE ALREADY BELIEVERS

To include verses like Rom. 10:13 in the so-called *Romans Road to Salvation* only muddies the soteriological waters! That's what the Reformation handed down to us. Christians need to reject it as error! Arlen Chitwood says:

> This was a deliverance for those who were already saved, not for individuals "dead in trespasses and sins."[9]

Hodges adds:

> Although the text of these verses (especially v 13) has been used innumerable times as though it referred to a cry for salvation from hell, in context the verses are no such thing. The "deliverance" ... is a deliverance from wrath.
>
> The concept of a one-time event of confession, used by many evangelists, is the product of an ill-conceived evangelistic use of Rom 10:9-13. The idea of a two-step "conversion," that is (1) faith in the heart, and (2) public acknowledgement of this (i.e., "I just accepted Christ," etc.), is quite far from Paul's thought here. Confessing "Lord Jesus" is what Christians do regularly and it is what marks them as believers in Jesus Christ.[10]

If there is any doubt that those who call on the Lord for salvation (i.e., deliverance) in this text are already saved, then look at v. 14a:

> **Rom. 10:14a How then shall they call on Him in whom they have not believed?**

You can't call on Jesus for deliverance if you have never believed on Him. Arlen Chitwood writes:

> *Believing* and *calling* in Rom. 10:13, 14 are not to be equated; nor are they to be thought of as two inseparable things which, in the end, result in eternal salvation. Romans 10:13 — "For whosoever shall call upon the name of the Lord shall be saved" — has been vastly misused over the years by well-meaning individuals in a "Roman's Road" type presentation of the salvation message.
>
> *Eternal salvation* is brought to pass *through believing alone* [v. 14; e.g., John 3:16; Acts 16:31] ... *on the Lord Jesus Christ* [a one-time event], after hearing the message from the one sent to deliver it ... *Calling*, on the other hand, *follows believing*. The person first *believes*, and only then does *he call*. The text is very clear concerning this order: "How then shall they call on him in whom they have not believed?" [v. 14a]. *Calling* [something which could be repeated time after time] has to do with a deliverance following salvation [brought to pass through believing].[11]

BEAUTIFUL FEET

The verse continues:

> **Rom. 10:14b And how shall they believe in Him of whom they have not heard? And how shall they hear without a preacher?**
> **10:15 And how shall they preach unless they are sent? As it is written:** *"How beautiful are the feet of those who preach the gospel of peace, who bring glad tidings of good things!"*

Before a person can call on Jesus for deliverance, they must have believed on Him. To have believed on Him, they must have heard about Him, and they must have heard about Him from a preacher, one who proclaims the good news about Him. The preacher must have been sent — *sent by God* is the implication. Paul then bursts out with another glorious quote from the Old Testament:

> **Isa. 52:7** How beautiful upon the mountains are the feet of him who brings good news, who proclaims peace, who brings glad tidings of good *things,* who proclaims salvation, who says to Zion, "Your God reigns!"

Isa. 52 is a millennial text. It is good news about Messiah coming to reign and those who go to spread the good news about it. The Isaiah passage concludes with this magnificent statement:

> **Isa. 52:10b** All the ends of the earth shall see the salvation of our God.

Arlen Chitwood comments:

> The contextual emphasis in Rom. 10:15 … has to do with *the saved*, not with the unsaved … This message of *peace* would have two facets — *the peace of God* now (having to do with the present aspect of salvation, the outworking of the saving of the soul), culminating in a future *peace* when *the Prince of Peace* is Himself present (having to do with the future aspect of salvation, when the salvation of the soul will be realized).[12]

ISRAEL DID NOT BELIEVE

Though the glorious good news of peace had been proclaimed to Israel, they did not believe.

> **Rom. 10:16** But they have not all obeyed the gospel. For Isaiah says, *"LORD,* **who has believed our report?"**

The Jews did not believe Paul's gospel of kingdom inheritance through faith-filled righteous living because they did not believe Jesus was the Messiah. Thus, Paul quotes the opening verses of Isa. 53, which should have instantly prodded the Jews into realizing that Isaiah was prophesying of Messiah's death. Nevertheless, the unbelieving Jews failed to believe the good news as proclaimed by God's preachers, so Paul adds:

Rom. 10:17 So then faith *comes* by hearing, and hearing by the word of God.

This translation is a bit misleading, because it emphasizes *hearing*, but in reality the two usages of hearing are from the same Greek word translated report in v. 16. Thayer says it is "a thing heard, specifically, the preaching."[13] Hodge prefers the *Jerusalem Bible's* translation of this verse:

As Isaiah said, Lord, how many believed what we proclaimed? So faith comes from what is preached, and what is preached comes from the word of Christ.[14]

This is a more accurate translation of the verse. Interestingly, *word* in this verse is not *logos* in Greek; it is *hrema*. *Logos* refers to the entirety of God's revelation to man — think of John 1:1:

John 1:1 In the beginning was the Word, and the Word was with God, and the Word was God.

That's not the Greek word used here. *Hrema* refers to specific statements, specific subject matter. It is also used twice in v. 8:

Rom. 10:8 *'The word is near you, in your mouth and in your heart'* (that is, the word of faith which we preach):

GOD'S PEOPLE ARE NOT TAKING HEED TO HIS WORD

Paul is emphasizing that the Jews need to listen to, pay attention to, the specific subject matter he is preaching to them as God's representative. He is the preacher proclaiming the truth they need to hear and to which they need to take heed. What a tragedy that children of God even today do not take heed to God's Word because they don't know it! Arlen Chitwood says:

> A major problem in Christendom today though is *an existing, widespread ignorance of the Word of God.* Christians simply do not know this Word. And the ability of these same Christians to exercise "faith" — to walk "by faith" — is, accordingly, adversely affected. Not knowing the Word of God, they simply cannot exercise faith, cannot walk by faith. That is, not knowing that which God has said, they cannot believe that which God has said. And this is particularly true when it comes to that which God has said relative to *the salvation of the soul.*
>
> Christians in general are so ill-versed in Scripture that they see only one thing when it comes to the salvation issue. They see *eternal salvation alone,* and they attempt to fit everything pertaining to salvation or deliverance into their framework of thinking in this one area.
>
> Christians *invariably* use the expression, "salvation of the soul," referring to eternal salvation. Scripture though *never* uses the expression in this manner. Scripture *always* uses the expression referring to present and future aspects of salvation, *never* to the past aspect of salvation.[15]

In v. 18 Paul demonstrates that Israel's problem was not that they had not heard. Quoting Ps. 19:4, he says:

Rom. 10:18 But I say, have they not heard? Yes indeed: *"Their sound has gone out to all the earth, and their words to the ends of the world."*

The Jews have heard the message! Paul has declared it everywhere he has traveled, so have the other apostles. The message has gone out to the ends of the populated world of their day. Tradition says Thomas preached in India, so the problem is not that they haven't heard; it's that they refuse to accept the truth.[16] That is the same problem with twenty-first century Christianity. Start talking to believers about kingdom inheritance, and they will brand you aberrant at best or heretical at worst. This leads Paul to v. 19:

> Rom. 10:19 But I say, did Israel not know? First Moses says: *"I will provoke you to jealousy by those who are not a nation, I will move you to anger by a foolish nation."*

PROVOKED TO JEALOUSY

Israel has heard the truth, but they have rejected it in large part out of anger and jealousy over the Gentiles' hearty reception of it (see Acts 13:45-50). Ironically, Moses had predicted Israel's jealousy in Deut. 32:21, which Paul quotes in v. 19. God provoked Israel to jealousy through the Gentile church of Jesus Christ, referred to as *those who are not a nation* and *a foolish* [ignorant] *nation*. Think of the signs performed in the book of Acts amongst the Gentiles and even in Gentile churches (e.g., Corinth). Arlen Chitwood writes:

> God was using those whom Israel considered *Gentile dogs* to manifest supernatural powers which naturally belonged to Israel *in order to provoke the nation to jealousy ... in a continuing effort to effect Israel's repentance ...* But the religious leaders in Israel would still have nothing to do with *the manifested supernatural signs* and *the message being proclaimed;* and the Jewish people, following their religious leaders, *continued in unbelief.* Accordingly, *the re-offer of the kingdom was eventually removed from the nation, with a corresponding cessation of miraculous signs.*[17]

God wanted to provoke Israel to jealousy in order to lead the nation to repentance. We will see that in the next chapter. We come now to the two final verses of the text:

Rom. 10:20 But Isaiah is very bold and says: *"I was found by those who did not seek Me; I was made manifest to those who did not ask for Me."*
10:21 But to Israel he says: *"All day long I have stretched out My hands to a disobedient and contrary people."*

Paul has already quoted from Moses, which characterizes the law. Now he quotes Isaiah (65:1-2), representing the prophets. Verse 20 is fulfilled by the Gentiles. The church of Jesus Christ, which is predominantly Gentile, found the Lord though they were not seeking Him. How gracious of God to give us the truth!

Verse 21 is fulfilled by Israel. They have remained in unbelief and disobedience, and they have not embraced the righteousness which is by faith. How tragic! For Paul says this word of faith is *near you* — it is *in your mouth and in your heart* (v. 8).

The application for believers today is clear. The same word of faith is near *you*. Knowing this, confess with your mouth, "LORD Jesus." He needs to become Lord (Master) of your life in all things. Believe in your heart that His resurrection enables your justification (i.e., righteous living). Don't be like Israel!

CHAPTER 25
ISRAEL'S TIME-OUT
ROMANS 11:1-15

What do you do with an incorrigible child? You have tried everything — corporal punishment, loss of privileges, grounding, positive reinforcement, negative reinforcement, letting them face the consequences of their decisions, etc. But nothing seems to work. The child is stubborn and hard-hearted and resistant! That sounds just like God's son, Israel. National Israel tested God in the wilderness, disobeyed His laws, turned to foreign alliances and idolatry, and rebelled against Him countless times through the centuries.

God disciplined His wayward children on numerous occasions — using famines, plagues, locusts, storms, defeat by enemies, captivity, dispersion, destruction of cities, etc. — all of the "curses" He promised to send for disobedience (see Deut. 28). Despite God's merciful discipline, Israel continued to rebel and stiff-arm God, and despite numerous preachers with "beautiful feet" being sent to proclaim the gospel of peace (10:15), the nation's leaders killed the prophets and even killed God's own Son! God's summary is given in 10:21:

> **Rom. 10:21** But to Israel he says: *"All day long I have stretched out My hands to a disobedient and contrary people."*

HAS GOD REJECTED ISRAEL?

This prompts Paul to ask:

> **Rom. 11:1a I say then, has God cast away His people?**

As will be seen later in the text, the implication of this question is: "Has God cast away His people *permanently*?" Zane Hodges writes:

> This question is relevant even today. Over the centuries of Christian history right up to the present day many have claimed in one way or another that Israel's special relationship to God is over. This is often softened into the concept of a new Israel which the largely Gentile Church supposedly fulfills. But Paul knows nothing of this. His concern here is not about a so called spiritual Israel, but about the real, physical nation that goes by that name. No suggestion of anything like a spiritual counterpart to Israel can be discovered anywhere in chaps. 9–11.[1]

Paul's answer to his opening question is given in the latter half of v. 1:

> **Rom. 11:1b Certainly not! For I also am an Israelite, of the seed of Abraham, *of* the tribe of Benjamin.**

Jan Bonda adds:

> Paul considers his own calling as an apostle a guarantee that God has not rejected His people! He, a persecutor of the church, had been called by Jesus to be His servant – irresistibly. For Paul this is proof that God will not give up on His people. He will do with all what He did with him.[2]

God might feel like obliterating Israel, as He nearly did during Moses' day, but Moses interceded then, and Paul intercedes here:

> **Rom. 9:3** For I could wish that I myself were accursed from Christ for my brethren, my countrymen according to the flesh.
>
> **10:1** Brethren, my heart's desire and prayer to God for Israel is that they may be saved.

GOD'S CALLING IS IRREVOCABLE

We can adamantly say that God has not cast off His people *permanently*, on the basis of Rom. 11:29:

> **Rom. 11:29** For the gifts and the calling of God *are* irrevocable.

God has made promises to Israel that He will fulfill through Israel! Nothing can keep God from fulfilling His Word, not even His incorrigible child. Thankfully, God's arsenal of discipline has not been exhausted. The nation is presently experiencing a "time-out" during this present age of the church. His final disciplinary technique at the end of the age will bring Israel to repentance.

During the course of this chapter and the next, I hope to answer three questions:

1. What does Israel's time-out mean *for Israel*?
2. What does Israel's time-out mean *for the Gentiles*?
3. What will happen after Israel's time-out?

1. WHAT DOES ISRAEL'S TIME-OUT MEAN FOR ISRAEL?

> **Rom. 11:2a God has not cast away His people whom He foreknew.**

God has not cast away Israel *permanently*, nor will He! James Dunn writes:

> Just as the choice of Jacob and rejection of Esau was without regard to their future conduct (9:10–13), so Israel's status as God's people remains unaffected by Israel's latest and most serious failure.[3]

Nevertheless, God has set aside His people *for a time*, while He works to call out another people for His name, all the while disciplining His son Israel, to bring the nation to repentance.

> **Rom. 11:2b-3** Do you not know what the Scripture says of Elijah, how he pleads with God against Israel, saying, *"LORD, they have killed Your prophets and torn down Your altars, and I alone am left, and they seek my life"*?
> **11:4** But what does the divine response say to him? *"I have reserved for Myself seven thousand men who have not bowed the knee to Baal."*

As an encouragement, Paul recalls the Old Testament account of Elijah, who was being chased by Jezebel after the triumphant victory of calling fire down from heaven on Mt. Carmel. Elijah felt very alone and afraid. In fact, he felt as if he were the only one taking a stand for God. However, God reminded him that seven thousand others were standing strong also — a remnant.

GOD HAS PRESERVED A REMNANT

Paul's point in the ensuing verses is that, in like manner, God has preserved many Israelites who are living for Jesus. They are the ones who have embraced the *word of faith* message that Paul has been proclaiming, the gospel of kingdom inheritance. Incidentally, Paul is not talking about matters of initial salvation — as if the remnant are regenerated Israelites and all the others are not. Israel is a regenerate nation at the point in history in which Paul is writing. The same had been true when Elijah prophesied to Israel. That is important to remember, for it shapes one's interpretation of this text, the *grace/works* discussion in v. 6, and the *salvation* in vs. 11 and 26, as we shall see.

> **Rom. 11:5** Even so then, at this present time there is a remnant according to the election of grace.

THE ELECTION OF GRACE – FOR SERVICE

Notice the phrase at the end of v. 5: *the election of grace.* This does not refer to initial salvation. Calvinists believe God elects some to salvation which, by default, means He has elected all the others to damnation. Here is an important interpretation principle that will keep you falling into that theological sinkhole: *election* in the Scriptures is to *service*, not to eternal life (regeneration). God doesn't elect some to be saved and condemn all others. But He does elect some to service — to become sons to glory — and His election is based on foreknowledge. Rom. 8:29 says:

> **Rom. 8:29** For whom He foreknew, He also predestined *to be* conformed to the image of His Son, that He might be the firstborn among many brethren.

Election is God's choosing and setting aside for rigorous training, those He knows are choosing to follow Jesus in discipleship. Many Jews in the church at Rome had not only embraced Jesus as the Messiah, they were also on the pathway of sanctification unto reward — *they* were the remnant according to the election of grace.

> **Rom. 11:6 And if by grace, then it is no longer of works [of the law]; otherwise grace is no longer grace. But if it is of works [of the law], it is no longer grace; otherwise work is no longer work.**

Other Jewish believers had embraced Jesus as Messiah, but continued to observe the Mosaic rituals, thinking that would sanctify and make them righteous before God. Paul condemned *works of the law* in Rom. 3-4, emphasizing that God wants His children to depend on His Son Jesus for daily victory over sin and righteous behavior. Thus it is important to interpret v. 6 in light of Rom. 4, not in light of Eph. 2:8-9, which has no bearing on this verse.

LEGALISM NULLIFIES GRACE LIVING

Those who thought they were entitled to grace because they were keeping the Mosaic rituals put the cart before the horse, so to speak — and they even had the wrong horse! Dunn writes:

> What Paul objects to is "works" understood as a qualification for God's favor simply because it is they which qualify for membership of the covenant people and which sustain that identity as God's elect. It is this *reduction* of God's election to matters of ethnic and ritual identity which Paul sees as the fatal misunderstanding and abandonment of God's grace and of the election of grace.[4]

In ch. 4 Paul had said:

> **Rom. 4:4** Now to him who works [i.e., does works of the law – see Rom. 3:20, 28], the wages are not counted as grace but as debt.
> **4:5** But to him who does not work [i.e., do works of the law] but believes on Him who justifies the ungodly, his faith is accounted for righteousness, (emphases added)

According to 5:2, we access God's grace by faith, and so Paul uses Abraham as an example in ch. 4, emphasizing that he did works (long before the law ever existed) *by faith*. In other words, Abraham accessed God's grace by faith and lived accordingly, not according to some system of entitlement, and God counted it to him for righteousness. That is, God considered Abraham righteous because he obeyed in faith. Merely keeping the works of the law doesn't please God. Rom. 11:6 must be interpreted in that context.

Paul is writing to the Jewish believers and emphasizing that God has graciously chosen them to live as Christ's disciples — *they* are the remnant! Accordingly, they must stop living legalistically and start accessing God's grace by faith to live in a manner pleasing to God (Rom. 5:2). Ironically, those who are legalistic spurn God's grace, even though they think they are earning His favor. Legalistic living nullifies grace-living.

Paul sums up this part of his argument in v. 7:

> **Rom. 11:7** What then? Israel has not obtained what it seeks; but the elect have obtained it, and the rest were blinded.

Despite keeping the Mosaic rituals, Israel has not received God's grace, to which the nation believes it is entitled. On the other hand, the elect have obtained His grace, because they have trusted God for the grace to live righteously. All the rest live in blindness.

NATIONAL BLINDNESS

Paul then quotes two Old Testament prophecies referring to Israel's blindness:

> **Rom. 11:8** Just as it is written: *"God has given them a spirit of stupor, eyes that they should not see and ears that they should not hear, to this very day."*

This is a paraphrase of a passage from Isaiah:

> **Isa. 29:10,13** For the LORD has poured out on you the spirit of deep sleep, and has closed your eyes ... Inasmuch as these people draw near with their mouths and honor Me with their lips, but have removed their hearts far from Me, and their fear toward Me is taught by the commandment of men.

God has allowed Israel to pursue its own way, giving them over to stupor (slumber), blindness and deafness. Interestingly, Jesus gives a similar description to the church at Laodicea in Rev. 3

> **Rev. 3:17** You say, "I am rich, have become wealthy, and have need of nothing"—and do not know that you are wretched, miserable, poor, blind, and naked—

Paul then quotes from Psalm 69:

> **Rom. 11:9** David says: *"Let their table become a snare*

> *and a trap, a stumbling block and a recompense to them.*
> **11:10** *Let their eyes be darkened, so that they do not see, and bow down their back always."*

Regarding v. 9, Hodges says:

> In Paul's mind their table would most likely be a reference to the special provisions and blessings God had granted to the nation (enumerated in 9:4-5). Their very sense of privilege and blessing (an undoubted source of Jewish pride) had lured them into a feeling of "worthiness" that motivated them to vainly seek righteousness by means of the law (11:7; 10:3). But this vain search for law-based righteousness was a snare as well as a trap into which they had fallen; their search should have convicted them of their sinfulness and led them to the righteousness of God (Rom 3:19-22).[5]

Consequently, in v. 10 Paul essentially repeats what he had said earlier — *let their eyes be darkened* — which seems to be referring to spiritual blindness. The latter half of the verse portrays the image of a man hunched over due to a great burden. In Israel's case, it is the spiritual burden of pride and legalism, which was characteristic of the Pharisees and held the nation back from repentance.

2. WHAT DOES ISRAEL'S TIME-OUT MEAN FOR THE GENTILES?

> **Rom. 11:11** I say then, have they stumbled that they should fall? Certainly not! But through their fall, to provoke them to jealousy, salvation *has come* to the Gentiles.

Paul is asking what is likely on the minds of some of his audience. Does Israel's stumbling mean they are going to fall apart completely as a nation? Paul's answer: Certainly not!

But through their fall. This second usage of the word *fall* is a different Greek word than the one used earlier in the verse. The NASB correctly translates it, *through their transgression.* In other words, as a result of Israel's transgression, *salvation has come to the Gentiles.*

We must not automatically jump to the conclusion that this is solely a soteriological matter. Our Reformation baggage teaches us to think that way. Salvation in that sense has always been available to the Gentiles through Israel. Paul's focus here is on the specific salvation that had been offered to Israel and rejected by them. What kind of salvation is that?

KINGDOM INHERITANCE GIVEN TO THE GENTILE CHURCH

To answer the question, it is important to remember back to the first usage of the words *gospel* and *salvation* in the epistle:

> **Rom. 1:16**a For I am not ashamed of the gospel of Christ, for it is the power of God to salvation for everyone who believes [literally, *to everyone who is believing*].

In Chapter 5 we learned that Paul is writing to believers – thus, this *salvation* is not the initial salvation of one's spirit (referred to briefly in Rom. 8:16). Rather, this is the good news of kingdom inheritance. *Salvation* in this sense is twofold: a) ongoing salvation of the soul — i.e., sanctification unto reward (e.g., James 1:21; Matt. 16:24-27); and b) deliverance from God's temporal wrath, because those whose souls are being saved are living righteously. Arlen Chitwood writes:

> "Salvation" coming to the Gentiles as a result of Israel's "fall" has nothing to do with eternal salvation [but] with the same thing Israel relinquished — *salvation in relation to the proffered kingdom.* And "Gentiles" is used in this passage the same way Paul previously used the word in the first chapter of this book, *referring to saved Gentiles, those forming the Church* (v. 16).
>
> The reason for the very existence of the Church, or the fact that the "salvation" referenced in Rom. 11:11 can even be realized by Christians, has to do with that referred to as Israel's "fall." Israel rejected the proffered kingdom and crucified the One making the

offer. The kingdom was then taken from Israel (Matt. 21:43), and an entirely new entity — *the one new man* "in Christ," — was called into existence to be the recipient of that which Israel rejected (I Peter 2:9-11).[6]

ISRAEL PROVOKED TO JEALOUSY

Paul says in v. 11 that this *salvation* coming to the Gentiles is designed *to provoke [Israel] to jealousy* — how so? A classic example of this is found in Acts 13:

> **Acts 13:45** But when the Jews saw the multitudes, they were filled with envy; and contradicting and blaspheming, they opposed the things spoken by Paul.
> 46 Then Paul and Barnabas grew bold and said, "It was necessary that the word of God should be spoken to you first; but since you reject it, and judge yourselves unworthy of everlasting life, behold, we turn to the Gentiles.
> 47 For so the Lord has commanded us: *"I have set you as a light to the Gentiles, that you should be for salvation to the ends of the earth."*
> 48 Now when the Gentiles heard this, they were glad and glorified the word of the Lord. And as many as had been appointed to eternal life believed.
> 49 And the word of the Lord was being spread throughout all the region.
> 50 But the Jews stirred up the devout and prominent women and the chief men of the city, raised up persecution against Paul and Barnabas, and expelled them from their region.

The Jews were provoked to jealousy by the preaching of the gospel of the kingdom to Gentiles. The jealousy will likely intensify during the tribulation, when multitudes of Gentiles embrace Messiah and the gospel of the kingdom, as the 144,000 Jewish evangelists proclaim that message globally. Paul then makes a remarkable statement:

Rom. 11:12 Now if their fall *is* riches for the world,

and their failure riches for the Gentiles, how much more their fullness!

RICHES FOR THE GENTILES

The word *fall* is the same Greek word as the second usage in v. 11, meaning "transgression." The word *failure* is new in Romans, meaning "diminished or defeated." Thus, Israel's transgression and temporary time-out has resulted in *riches for the Gentiles*. The storm cloud of Israel's transgression has a silver lining!

The Gentile world has actually been enriched by Israel's time-out, for Gentiles are now receiving the Gospel of grace and the gospel of kingdom inheritance — in this present age! The Holy Spirit is seeking out sons to glory from His predominantly Gentile church. If that is the glorious result of Israel's stumbling, *how much more* if Israel were to be restored to fellowship with the Lord by embracing His Messiah! Incidentally, that *will happen* by the end of this age, when Jesus returns the second time. The Millennium to follow will be a glorious age indeed, for Israel will be God's priestly nation to all the nations of the world. Jan Bonda says:

> The issue is nothing less than the promise to Abraham that through his posterity all nations of the earth would be blessed. Abraham will be the inheritor of the world (Rom. 4:13)! This blessing has no limits! — it goes far beyond the riches the church has received.
>
> The greater riches that were promised by the prophets are not the salvation of *some* people, called by God from the nations, while the vast majority will remain doomed. No, the promise is for *all* humanity ... These riches will not come until "all Israel" is saved ... As long as only a fraction of Israel serves its Messiah, there can be no salvation for all the nations.[7]

Paul now addresses the Gentiles, referring to himself as *an apostle to the Gentiles* — which is, indeed, what God had called him to be (see Acts 9:15).

Rom. 11:13-14 For I speak to you Gentiles; inasmuch

> as I am an apostle to the Gentiles, I magnify my ministry, if by any means I may provoke to jealousy *those who are* my flesh and save some of them.

He desires to leverage his ministry so as to provoke Jews to jealousy, so that some will receive the gospel of kingdom inheritance and experience deliverance from God's wrath through righteous living. Hodges says: "His goal is that the Jews should say, 'We want that too.'"[8]

> Rom. 11:15 For if their being cast away *is* the reconciling of the world, what *will* their acceptance *be* but life from the dead?

RECONCILING OF THE WORLD

Paul says something similar to what he had said in v. 12, but here he uses different terminology. The phrase *being cast away* means "rejection." Hodges translates it "throwing aside."[9] In other words, Israel's temporary being cast to the side has resulted in *the reconciling of the world*. Hodges adds:

> Reconciliation is inherently a two-party process, but the first step was taken at the cross where God reconciled the world to Himself by imputing their sins to Christ (2 Cor 5:19). Therefore the world is no longer estranged from God by an unbridgeable gulf of sin. As a result, the believer can experience personal reconciliation to God by faith (2 Cor 5:20). Thus the whole world has been reconciled as a result of Israel's fall.
>
> In the process of rejecting Messiah and crucifying Him, Israel precipitated her own throwing aside. But the result of this tragic loss of opportunity and privilege was the reconciling of the entire world. In the cross, Israel's supreme sin becomes God's supreme act of reconciling love (5:8) to all mankind.[10]

LIFE FROM THE DEAD

In light of this glorious news for mankind following Israel's temporary *rejection*, Paul wonders out loud in the latter half of v. 15 if Israel's *acceptance* will result in *life from the dead?* Of course, he knows it will! What does he mean by *life from the dead?*

Paul is obviously speaking of resurrection, at least the resurrection of believers, which will occur when Israel is restored to fellowship with Jehovah. He already referred to this glorious day in Rom. 8:

> **Rom. 8:19-21** For the earnest expectation of the creation eagerly waits for the revealing of the sons of God. For the creation was subjected to futility, not willingly, but because of Him who subjected *it* in hope; because the creation itself also will be delivered from the bondage of corruption into the glorious liberty of the children of God.

This will happen when Israel embraces Messiah and repents at His second coming. The nation's repentance will result in *life from the dead* — how so? Not only will church-age believers be resurrected, so will the Jewish people from all ages (Ezek. 37). Israel will then be promoted to rule over the nations — pointing people to Jesus their Messiah.

The sons to glory will ascend to their assigned places of rulership in New Jerusalem. When God's three firstborn sons (Jesus, Israel, and the sons to glory) step into their assigned roles, there will be a tremendous spiritual life from the dead, as multitudes are turned to Messiah, and that will continue throughout the entire Millennium! Hodges refers to this as "a resurrection of the world itself."[11]

In this sense we are beneficiaries of Israel's time-out, which was all planned by God before the foundation of the world. Bonda writes:

> In Romans 5:18-19 (and 1 Cor. 15:20-28) we read that all humanity, since Adam, will be saved through what God did for humankind in Christ. In Romans 8:19-21 we are informed about the role of God's

children in this process of redemption. But now we hear that God will not do that without the Jews. The salvation of all peoples — full "riches for the Gentiles" and "life from the dead" — will not come about before the Jewish people have accepted Jesus as their Messiah.[12]

PREPARING THROUGH DISCIPLESHIP

Jesus told His disciples about this glorious coming era and how we as God's children should prepare for it:

> **Matt. 19:28** So Jesus said to them, "Assuredly I say to you, that in the regeneration, when the Son of Man sits on the throne of His glory, you who have followed Me will also sit on twelve thrones, judging the twelve tribes of Israel.
>
> **29** And everyone who has left houses or brothers or sisters or father or mother or wife or children or lands, for My name's sake, shall receive a hundredfold, and inherit eternal life.

The word *regeneration* in v. 28 means "rebirth or restoration." Christ's Messianic kingdom will truly be a world resurrection, a rebirth, a time of reconciling and restoring for all mankind.

Jesus promises that those who have paid a price to follow Him in discipleship *now* will receive abundant reward and inherit the life *for that age*. What a glorious prospect! Are you on that pathway of reward?

CHAPTER 26
ISRAEL WILL BE SAVED AND ALL MANKIND TOO

ROMANS 11:16-36

Israel has been cast aside by God for a so-called "time-out," as a result of the nation's disobedience in rejecting Messiah and His offer of kingdom inheritance. As seen in the previous chapter, the time-out is temporary, not permanent — lasting throughout the duration of the church age.

PROPHETIC FORESHORTENING

God prophesied of this in the Old Testament, but the prophets did not fully understand what it all meant, because of *prophetic foreshortening* — which is the tendency to view events in the distant future and the near future as close together in time. In other words, the prophets could see something glorious coming for Israel, the Messianic kingdom, but they thought it was imminent. What they did not realize is that Messiah would come a first time to die on the cross for mankind and be resurrected, then return a second time to launch His kingdom.

The two thousand years between Christ's first and second coming would be Israel's time-out for rejecting the Messiah and His kingdom offer. During the two millennia God would extend the offer of kingdom inheritance to the Church, *the one new man in Christ* (see Eph. 2:15), comprised of both Jews and Gentiles who have believed Christ's promise of eternal (age-lasting) life. Near the end of the two thousand-year period, the final seven years would be a time of tribulation to bring national Israel to repentance. The prophets were largely oblivious of these details. However, Hosea — whether he realized it or not — prophesied of the time frame for Israel's time-out:

AFTER TWO DAYS ... ON THE THIRD DAY

God says to the prophet:

> **Hos. 5:15** I will return again to My place till they acknowledge their offense. Then they will seek My face; in their affliction they will earnestly seek Me.

From the book of Daniel, we know this "affliction" is Daniel's seventieth week, a period of seven years, known as the tribulation, which completes Jewish history, culminating in the nation's repentance.

Hosea speaks of Israel's return to the Lord at the end of the time-out:

> **Hos. 6:1-2** Come, and let us return to the LORD; for He has torn, but He will heal us; He has stricken, but He will bind us up. After two days He will revive us; on the third day He will raise us up, that we may live in His sight.

Peter gives the key to interpreting these "days":

> **2 Pet. 3:8** Beloved, do not forget this one thing, that with the Lord one day *is* as a thousand years, and a thousand years as one day.

The *two days* in Hosea's prophecy refer to two thousand years, and the *third day* is the thousand-year-long Messianic kingdom that follows, with Israel restored and placed as ruler over all the nations on Earth.

ISRAEL'S TIME-OUT AND THE BENEFITS FOR GENTILES

Paul develops the theme of Israel's present disobedience and future repentance, and the effect on the Gentiles:

> **Rom. 11:16 For if the firstfruit *is* holy, the lump *is* also *holy;* and if the root *is* holy, so *are* the branches.**
> **11:17-18 And if some of the branches were broken off, and you, being a wild olive tree, were grafted in among them, and with them became a partaker of the root and fatness of the olive tree, do not boast against the branches. But if you do boast, *remember that* you do not support the root, but the root supports you.**

Paul uses the metaphor of an olive tree to describe Israel. But he starts with the metaphor of a *lump of dough* — which is what the word *lump* means in v. 16.[1] The *lump* represents the entirety of Israel. God makes clear that, at her core, Israel remains holy, for the nation is the elect of God, despite her disobedience in rejecting Messiah.

The *firstfruit* in the opening illustration is likely the remnant — those Jews who have embraced Jesus as Messiah. They are also holy and will be raptured with the church, several years before national Israel's repentance. Hodges says:

> The believing remnant should be construed as a kind of *first fruits* which prefigure the future transformation of the entire *batch of dough*, that is, of the entire nation. For ultimately "*all* Israel will be delivered" (11:26, emphasis added). The holy status that now pertains to the first fruits will someday pertain to the complete batch of dough.[2]

THE OLIVE TREE

In the latter half of v. 16, Paul changes metaphors to an olive tree and its branches. The root of the tree is *holy* — again, referring to national Israel overall — which means the branches are holy. But there's a problem – some of the branches have been broken off, referring to Israel's national rejection of Jesus as Messiah. Nevertheless, branches of a *wild* olive tree — representing believing Gentiles — have been grafted into the tree. Paul warns the Gentiles not to boast about their spiritual windfall, since it is the Israelite tree and roots that are the source of their spiritual vitality.

Keep in mind the ethnic hostility between the Jewish believers and Gentile believers in the church at Rome. Some of the Greeks were gloating in Israel's downfall, thinking it was permanent. But Paul reminds them that Israel will rise again, and the holy roots are evidence of that fact. The roots are likely a reference to Abraham, whom Paul has already used as an illustration of righteous living by faith in ch. 4. Without Israel, and without the righteous legacy of father Abraham, they would not have the life God has given them. In Gal. 3 Paul said:

> **Gal. 3:28** There is neither Jew nor Greek, there is neither slave nor free, there is neither male nor female; for you are all one in Christ Jesus.
>
> **29** And if you *are* Christ's, then you are Abraham's seed, and heirs according to the promise.

Zane Hodges writes:

> With these two vivid metaphors Paul manages to look both forward and backward. The metaphor of the first fruits points to a future reality, while the metaphor of the root points to the past, that is, to the nation's origin. However viewed, whether in terms of its future destiny or in terms of its beginning, Israel is holy.[3]

Rom. 11:19 You will say then, "Branches were broken off that I might be grafted in."

11:20 Well *said.* Because of unbelief they were broken off, and you stand by faith. Do not be haughty, but fear.
11:21 For if God did not spare the natural branches, He may not spare you either.

BRANCHES BROKEN OFF AND OTHERS GRAFTED IN

Israel's branches were broken off because of their *unbelief.* Gentiles have been grafted in because of their *faith.* So Paul urges Gentiles to be humble and grateful, seeing God has graciously allowed you to be engrafted into Israel's tree, so to speak. Needless to say, this illustration should have quashed any thinking on the part of the Gentiles that Israel's demise was permanent. Paul warns the Gentiles not to be arrogant, but fear, for if God didn't spare Israel, He may not spare Gentiles either. The implication: "Keep standing in faith!" Zane Hodges says:

> A case can be made that this change in Gentile responsiveness is already far advanced. Today the Gentile world largely rejects the gospel *in the form in which it was preached by Paul and by the Lord Jesus Christ Himself.* That is not the same as saying that Christendom has disappeared. It has not, but its message is no longer really the message that Paul proudly preached (Rom 1:16-17).
>
> As a matter of fact, Jesus prophesied this degeneration in the parables of Matt 13 ... The truth of God, like three measures of wheat flour, is now fully mixed with the leaven of false doctrine (Matt 13:33; cf. Matt 16:12). Gentile failure is thus more and more evident as time passes.[4] (italics added)

The *gospel of kingdom inheritance* and the *salvation of the soul* is rarely preached any more, particularly since the Reformation.

As Gentiles, we should regularly stop to think about all the wonderful blessings that have been extended to us through Israel. We have a personal relationship with Jesus, the Jewish Messiah. His Holy Spirit lives within us. We have the Holy Scriptures — imagine life without a Bible! — and we have a glorious future, because God has promised Israel a glorious future. All of this was part of His plan from before the foundation of the world. How marvelous!

Paul's warning gets stiffer in vs. 22-23:

GENTILES WARNED OF BEING CUT OFF LIKE ISRAEL

> **Rom. 11:22 Therefore consider the goodness and severity of God: on those who fell, severity; but toward you, goodness, if you continue in *His* goodness. Otherwise you also will be cut off.**
> **11:23 And they also, if they do not continue in unbelief, will be grafted in, for God is able to graft them in again.**

Notice the word *severity* — it means "a sharp, abrupt cutting off." Paul essentially says to the Gentiles: "God has been good to *you* and severe in cutting off Israel. But the tables will be turned, and you will find yourselves cut off abruptly if you do not continue in faith." Indeed, this will happen when the rapture occurs, ending the church age, and multitudes of Gentile believers stand before Jesus in judgment, naked and ashamed, struggling to give an account for their behavior.

Gentile coldness toward the gospel of kingdom inheritance signals the fulfillment of what Jesus prophesied in His parable — the loaf is nearly leavened (see Matt. 13:33). Zane Hodges says:

> Paul obviously knew that this warning would be ignored (as it already has been) and that the ancient promises to his nation would truly come to pass. Today it is only a matter of time before this prophecy catches up with Gentile self-satisfaction and pride.[5]

Consequently, just as Israel's time-out is temporary, so the Gentiles' being grafted into the olive tree is temporary. Gentile faith has almost entirely lapsed — as evidenced by wide-scale rejection of the kingdom inheritance offer. We are near the end of the two thousand years, the rapture is soon to occur, and the tribulation about to begin. Thus, Paul's warning to the Gentiles is about to become the fulfillment of prophecy.

> **Rom. 11:24 For if you were cut out of the olive tree which is wild by nature, and were grafted contrary to nature into a cultivated olive tree, how much more will these, who *are* natural *branches*, be grafted into their own olive tree?**

ISRAEL TO BE RE-GRAFTED

Seeing that Gentiles were cut out of a wild olive tree and grafted into Israel's cultivated olive tree (which is not the natural order of grafting), *how much more will Israel* — the natural branches — be re-grafted into their own tree. Indeed, when the tribulation begins, the ones who will carry the message of kingdom inheritance around the world will be the 144,000 Jewish preachers that God has called to spread this message, *not* Gentiles. The day is coming when Israel will be grafted back into the olive tree!

> **Rom. 11:25 For I do not desire, brethren, that you should be ignorant of this mystery, lest you should be wise in your own opinion, that blindness in part has happened to Israel until the fullness of the Gentiles has come in.**

Bonda writes:

> Paul refers to a mystery. He summarizes its content. First, there is the hardening of part of Israel. Then, there is the coming in of the "fullness" of the Gentiles. Finally, there is the salvation of all Israel. This fully agrees with the imagery of the olive tree. The hardening of part of Israel is the cutting off of part of the branches. The coming in of the fullness of the Gentiles is the grafting of the wild shoots. And the salvation of all Israel is the grafting in of the branches that had been cut off.[6]

All of this was a mystery until revealed by Paul and could not be fathomed by the Gentiles. Because of Israel's rejection of Messiah, the Gentile believers thought God was finished with Israel and that going forward, they — the Gentiles exclusively — would be God's people through Jesus. The re-grafting of Israel back into its own national tree was a mystery in the Old Testament and, therefore, to the first century church, until Paul gave this new revelation in Rom. 9-11.

THE FULLNESS OF THE GENTILES

The prophets foresaw Israel's ascension as head of the nations, but they did not see Israel's setting aside, being broken off as branches for two thousand years while the Gentiles were to be given the opportunity to embrace the kingdom inheritance message. They also did not know about Israel's two-millennia-long spiritual blindness.

Paul wants the church at Rome to understand that Israel will be returning, re-grafted back into its own olive tree. That will occur *when the fullness of the Gentiles has come in.* I have heard two incorrect views on the meaning of this phrase:

1. Some a-millennialists take millennial passages in the Old Testament — such as Isa. 2:1-4, about Gentile nations flocking to Zion to worship Jesus — as the fulfillment of Gentile grafting in, at least those who are "elected" to be saved. This is the view of replacement theology. But that is a misinterpretation of millennial texts, for God promised Abraham that *all* the families of the earth would be blessed *through him* (i.e., through Israel), *not* through the Gentiles. Paul also said that all Israel will be saved (not merely so-called elect Gentile surrogates).

2. Many dispensationalists say this phrase — *when the fullness of the Gentiles has come in* — is referring to the end of the church age, when all have been saved who are going to be saved, and by "saved" they mean "regenerated." Then the rapture of the church takes place. This has led some to believe there will be a great evangelistic harvest just before Jesus returns, but I can't find any Scripture to support this.

THE END OF THE SPIRIT'S SEARCH FOR A BRIDE

I personally believe, in light of the previous verses, that the phrase — *when the fullness of the Gentiles has come in* — is referring to the end of the Holy Spirit's search for, and calling out of, the *sons to glory* — those saints who are faithful and therefore chosen to be Christ's rulers in the next age. This is typified in the Old Testament by Abraham's servant procuring the Gentile bride for Isaac. Once the bride was found, the search ended, and the bride was wed to her husband. So it will be at the end of this age of the church. When God has found the bride for His Son, the fullness of the Gentiles will have come in, and the rapture will occur. Arlen Chitwood explains:

> "The fulness of the Gentiles" (Rom. 11:25) ... is an expression referring to a work of God among the Gentiles ... This activity involves God turning His attention to the Gentiles "to take out of them a people for his name" (Acts 15:14).
>
> God brings "the fulness of the Gentiles" to pass during the present dispensation through placing believing Gentiles together in the same body with believing Jews, forming the one new man "in Christ" (cf. Eph. 2:12-15; 3:1-6). During the present dispensation, the Spirit of God is in the world searching for a bride for God's Son who will reign as consort queen with Him during the Messianic Era. And the bride is being taken from the one new man "in Christ," made up mainly of individuals removed from the Gentiles rather than from the Jews (though individuals removed from the Jews are included).
>
> God's removal of "a people for his name," from among the Gentiles, is for purposes involving the government of the earth ... to exercise supremacy over the nations during the coming age.[7]

ISRAEL REMAINS IN BLINDNESS

Until the fullness of the Gentiles comes in, Israel remains in blindness. Remember back to the two disciples on the road to Emmaus, on the very day of Christ's resurrection. Their eyes were blinded to the Old Testament prophecies, and they were dismayed at Christ's crucifixion. Though they had heard of the empty tomb, they thought the worst, not believing that He had risen. Then Jesus anonymously joined them on their journey and taught them from the Old Testament law and prophets while walking along with them. When they finally arrived at their home, Jesus prayed and broke the bread. Only at that point were their eyes opened, they understood the Scriptures, and they realized instantly that they had been with Jesus. What was the cause of their blindness?

> **Luke 24:25** Then He said to them, "O foolish ones, and slow of heart to believe in all that the prophets have spoken!"

They failed to believe the Old Testament Scriptures, and that is national Israel's problem today, as well.

ALL ISRAEL WILL BE SAVED

When Jesus returns the second time at the close of the tribulation, the eyes of the Jews will be opened, and they will recognize Him as Messiah.

> **Zech. 12:10-11** I will pour on the house of David and on the inhabitants of Jerusalem the Spirit of grace and supplication; then they will look on Me whom they pierced. Yes, they will mourn for Him as one mourns for *his* only *son,* and grieve for Him as one grieves for a firstborn. In that day there shall be a great mourning in Jerusalem.

Thus Paul, quoting Isa. 59:20-21 and 27:9 says:

> **Rom. 11:26-27 And so all Israel will be saved, as it is written:** *'The Deliverer will come out of Zion, and He will turn away ungodliness from Jacob; for this is My covenant with them, when I take away their sins."*

This *salvation* in v. 26 is national deliverance from Israel's enemies, including antichrist, at the close of the tribulation — as well as deliverance from God's wrath because "ungodliness" is being turned away from Jacob (Israel). Bonda says:

Those who were the objects of His wrath (Rom. 9:22) will become the objects of His mercy (11:31-32).[8]

Israel will be healed from blindness, the nation will embrace Jesus as Messiah and will repent of her sins, confessing that Jesus is LORD (see 10:9-13). Consequently, Israel will be restored to fellowship with Jehovah, and the New Covenant will be launched, which includes forgiveness of sins.

ISRAELITES RESURRECTED FROM ALL OF HISTORY

I personally believe this statement, *all Israel will be saved,* refers to Israelites from all of history, who will be resurrected according to Ezek. 37, the valley of dry bones prophecy. Every Israelite who has ever lived will be restored to fellowship and become part of the new covenant. Otherwise, this statement, *"All Israel will be saved"* makes no sense. Bonda says:

> The only argument adduced against this view is that the dead are excluded from this number. But this exclusion wreaks havoc with the interpretation of Romans 11:26a. Here the faulty exegesis in our tradition of Romans 5:12-21 takes its toll. It denies that God's redemption in Christ includes all generations since Adam, while this is precisely the point Paul wants to make. If we grasp that, then we know that if Israel will be saved, this will include all Israelites who have died.[9]

Bonda quotes another commentator named Stroter as saying:

> Restricting salvation to the last generation 'would be a purely arbitrary distinction between equally guilty generations of the same people.' For that reason, 'this salvation must extend as far into the past as the judgment of the national hardening.'[10]

Think about it; for God to save only the last generation of Israelites would not be merciful to all the Israelites who were judged before that time.

REPLACEMENT THEOLOGY AND ITS IMPACT ON THE SALVATION OF ALL

Tragically, as discussed in previous chapters, the doctrine that national Israel will return to favor with God was trounced in the Reformation. Today, there are countless millions in Protestant churches who believe in replacement theology, the teaching that the Church has replaced Israel in a spiritual sense. That doctrine is completely contrary to what Paul teaches in Romans 11, and it has serious ramifications for the salvation of all men. Bonda claims:

> The teaching that Israel has been replaced by the church as the people of God has, from the beginning, dominated — and derailed — Christendom. For when the church no longer anticipated the salvation of all Israel, she changed her thinking about God. This was inevitable: The God who drops His own people because of its disobedience and chooses another people is not the kind of God who will save a disobedient world. He becomes a God who wants to save only a few from the mass of humanity.
>
> Thus the doctrine of election could find acceptance. The wonderful expectation described by Paul that the coming of Christ and of God's children would set creation free, disappeared. This had been the theme of the hymns of praise of the early church. When there is hope that Israel — disobedient Israel — will be saved, there is hope that the world will be saved. That joy, however, has been smothered. The hope for the world has lost its foundation.
>
> The church, which had substituted herself for Israel, operated with a shortened expectation of the future ... The revelation of the children of God was not to be the beginning of the saving kingly rule of Christ but its end. He would come, so the church taught, not to save the lost world but to condemn the world. Ever since, the church has been perplexed about the prayer, *Thy kingdom come!*[11]

That is profound! The future is glorious! But Paul returns to the present state of Israel:

Rom. 11:28 Concerning the gospel *they are* enemies

for your sake, but concerning the election *they
are* beloved for the sake of the fathers.
**11:29 For the gifts and the calling of God *are*
irrevocable.**

Though the future is bright for Israel, they are presently enemies of the gospel. Paul is referring to the gospel of kingdom inheritance. Nevertheless, *they are beloved for the sake of the fathers*, that is, the patriarchs — Abraham, Isaac, and Jacob. God loved those men and called Israel through their lineage. Thus the Gentiles need to remember that while Israel is presently in opposition to the gospel, they are the apple of God's eye. We read in v. 29 that His gifts (listed in 9:4-5) and calling upon this special nation, are irrevocable. **God has a plan for Israel, and He will fulfill it!**

GOD WILL HAVE MERCY ON ALL MANKIND

What are the ramifications of God's plan for Israel? First, God will have mercy on all mankind.

> **Rom. 11:30-31 For as you were once disobedient to God, yet have now obtained mercy through their disobedience, even so these also have now been disobedient, that through the mercy shown you they also may obtain mercy.
> 11:32 For God has committed them all to disobedience, that He might have mercy on all.**

11:30-31. Incidentally, the KJV translates the words *disobedient* and *disobedience* as *unbelief*, but *disobedience* is more accurate. Hodges agrees. Thayer says the Greek word means *"disobedience, obstinacy, and in the N.T. particularly, obstinate opposition to the divine will.*[12] Here's Paul's point (my paraphrase):

> Just as you Gentiles were once disobedient to God, but you have obtained God's mercy because Israel became disobedient, so Israel's disobedience to God will one day lead to God's mercy being

bestowed upon them. For God has committed *all* — both Jews and Gentiles — to disobedience so He might bestow mercy on all mankind.

11:32. BDAG says the word translated *committed* is the idea of being "imprisoned in disobedience" or "given over to disobedience."[13] In Luke 5:6 the word is translated *caught*, referring to fish caught in a net. So Paul is teaching here that God has allowed all men to be caught in the net of their own disobedience — both Jews and Gentiles — so He might show His mercy to all mankind — including all those who have died! He is going to resurrect all men and lead "them back to obedience and to be merciful to them."[14]

That's a glorious truth! To quote Bonda again:

> Romans 11:32 is the finale of Paul's unfolding of the gospel, in which he summarizes his entire argument: All people have become disobedient, and all will find mercy with God. This is confirmed by the song of praise that immediately follows … This praise comprises all of creation, and ends with the words: "To Him are all things" (v. 36). From the beginning of this letter the apostle emphasized that God wants to save all people without distinction (Rom. 3:23-24) …
>
> The story does not end with God's mercy toward Israel. For what God did for Israel is only the beginning of what he will do for all nations. Then the prophecies will be fulfilled: He will forever destroy death and He will wipe away the tears from all faces (Isa. 25:8). This is the mercy toward all who have been disobedient as described by Paul in Romans 11:32.[15]

GOD'S WAYS ARE INSCRUTABLE!

What are the ramifications of God's plan for Israel? Second, man will praise Him. Certainly, that will happen in the future, as the whole world will bow in universal praise (Rev. 5:13). But we should praise God *now*, as Paul does, for His riches and wisdom and knowledge and inscrutability! His ways and purposes are far above us, yet He ordered these things regarding mankind before the foundation of the world, and He is carrying out His purposes.

> **Rom. 11:33 Oh, the depth of the riches both of the wisdom and knowledge of God! How unsearchable *are* His judgments and His ways past finding out!**
> **11:34 *"For who has known the mind of the LORD? Or who has become His counselor?"***
> **11:35 *"Or who has first given to Him and it shall be repaid to him?"***

Verse 34 is a quote from Isa. 40:13, and v. 35 is a quote from Job 41:11. Zane Hodges says:

> Paul is moved by the profundity of a divine wisdom that can rise so far above the tragedy and evil of human disobedience and unbelief. And precisely because the divine plan was drawn from the wealth of God's wisdom and knowledge, it was previously a "mystery" (v 25). It was therefore utterly unknowable apart from being revealed to men.[16]

> The "mystery" of Israel's hardening (v 25) was God's secret (*"Who indeed has known the mind of the Lord?"*) and was in no way a result of human "counsel" or "advice" (*"Or who has been His counselor?"*). At the same time, God's plans for Israel do not flow from any merit on Israel's part, as though they had given Him something He needed to repay (*"Or who has given first to Him, so that it shall be paid back to him?"*). God's actions toward His ancient people, as well as toward the Gentiles, are pure and simple products of His mercy.[17]

Paul closes with a triumphant verse of praise:

> **Rom. 11:36 For of Him and through Him and to Him *are* all things, to whom *be* glory forever. Amen.**

Some refer to this as a doxology. Hodges points out that in the Greek of Paul's day, the term "all things" referred to the universe.[18]

Thus, Paul is moved by God being the *source* and the *facilitator* and the *recipient* of all things in the universe. Here's why Paul sings the doxology, so to speak, in the words of Bonda:

> The olive tree in its fullness is greater and richer than before: It is the tree with all the original branches and the numerous new branches that have been grafted in.[19]

Accordingly, God receives all the glory! Amen! Is *your* life glorifying Him?

CHAPTER 27
METAMORPHOSIS CULMINATING IN GLORY
ROMANS 12:1-2

Paul has finally completed the heavy doctrinal sections of his epistle. Keep in mind that he writes to believers — both Jewish and Gentile — in the church at Rome, which is characterized by division and disunity. He shares with them the *gospel* (good news) of kingdom inheritance and the *salvation* of the soul, which sanctifies and unifies believers, ultimately leading to reward. He emphasizes that God justifies those who are living righteously. A simple overview of the epistle's themes in the first eleven chapters could be stated as follows:

- Rom. 1 — Paul condemns *licentious* living, warning that continuing in sinfulness leads to a downward spiral of self-destruction, which is the revealing of God's wrath.
- Rom. 2-5 — He condemns *legalistic* living, warning that keeping the Mosaic rituals (works of the law) does not please God, but rather, what pleases the Lord is living righteously, by continued faith in Jesus.
- Rom. 6-8 — He teaches how to live the Christ-life of victory, which leads to becoming a son to glory.
- Rom. 9-11 — He announces that Israel has been cast aside for a time, until the fullness of the Gentiles has come in (i.e., until the Holy Spirit has called out a bride for Jesus),

after which Israel will be saved and will lead all the families of the earth to be saved as well.

After laying this important doctrinal foundation, Paul begins to make practical applications to the Christian life, starting in ch. 12, which will continue to the end of the epistle. After the heavy doctrinal section (ch. 1-11), the practical application section of the epistle (ch. 12-16) is refreshing, but also convicting.

"WHERE THE RUBBER MEETS THE ROAD"

> Rom. 12:1 I beseech you therefore, brethren, by the mercies of God, that you present your bodies a living sacrifice, holy, acceptable to God, *which is your reasonable service.*

The word *therefore* means "accordingly." It's as if Paul is saying, "It all boils down to this — this is where the rubber meets the road." That is, based on everything he has said in the preceding eleven chapters — and especially in ch. 11 — the apostle now addresses a challenge to *the brethren*. I have mentioned it numerous times in this book, but it is absolutely critical to grasp: Paul is not writing to unbelievers, urging them to be saved initially (i.e., regenerated). He is writing to believers, urging them to be saved in an ongoing sense (i.e., sanctified). The word *beseech* is used in that context. It is the idea of urging someone to do something. To paraphrase the first phrase of v. 1: *I urge you, children of God, in light of all I have just written.*

Before getting to what he wants them to do, Paul inserts another important little phrase: *by the mercies of God.* If Rom. 12 is not kept in its proper context, this phrase may seem out of place. So it is important to recall what Paul has just talked about in ch. 11.

Incidentally, that is the beauty of preaching through books of the Bible over and above topical preaching. There is certainly a place for occasional topical preaching, but when a preacher favors topical preaching, he tends to preach his favorite subjects, rather than the whole counsel of God. The other danger is taking things out of context. By studying and preaching through entire books, we are forced to see the entire context.

THE MERCIES OF GOD

Remember the immediate context.

> **Rom. 11:30-31** For as you were once disobedient to God, yet have now obtained mercy through their disobedience, even so these also have now been disobedient, that through the mercy shown you they also may obtain mercy.
>
> **11:32** For God has committed them all to disobedience, that He might have mercy on all.

Paul is speaking to the Gentiles at this point, and he reminds them that while they had previously been disobedient, they have obtained God's mercy because of Israel's disobedience. In other words, Israel's temporarily being cast aside by God has resulted in Gentiles receiving not only the gospel of grace, but also the gospel of kingdom inheritance. Israel's disobedience to God will one day lead to His mercy being bestowed upon the nation when they ultimately repent at the end of the coming tribulation. Then Paul makes this remarkable statement in 11:32 (my paraphrase):

> God has allowed all men to be caught in the net of their own disobedience — both Jews and Gentiles — so He might show His mercy to all mankind, including all those who have died. He is going to resurrect all men and lead them back to obedience.

PRESENTING YOUR BODY

In light of this marvelous truth, Paul urges believers in 12:1 to *present your bodies a living sacrifice*. He stresses the importance of living righteously — in light of God's goal of mercifully leading all men to obedience — and in making his point, Paul uses a metaphor: *present your body a living sacrifice*. The KJV sometimes translates *present* as *yield*, as in Rom. 6:13:

> **Rom. 6:13 (KJV)** Neither <u>yield</u> ye your members *as* instruments of unrighteousness unto sin: but <u>yield</u> yourselves unto God, as those that are alive from the dead, and your members *as* instruments of righteousness unto God. (underline added)

Thus, to present your body is to yield yourself to God's control. Arlen Chitwood writes:

> The word "present" has to do with a one-time act to be performed at the beginning of the pilgrim walk, never to be repeated. As the Old Testament priest placed the sacrifice upon the altar and left it there, the New Testament priest (a Christian) is called upon to do the same with his body. The body is to be placed upon the altar through a one-time act, and the body is then to remain upon the altar in a continuous state of sacrifice, never to be removed.[1]

Under the Old Testament sacrificial system, animals were offered on the altar to God as the atonement for man's sins. Vincent says the word *present* "is the technical term for presenting the Levitical victims and offerings ... The offerer placed his offering so as to face the Most Holy Place, thus bringing it before the Lord."[2] It was a bloody mess, resulting in the death of a living creature, signifying the horrible price of sin. But thankfully, since Jesus died as the Lamb of God, once for all, we no longer offer animal sacrifices.

A LIVING SACRIFICE

Now we are to offer ourselves as a *living* sacrifice. Vincent says: "Living, in contrast with the *slain* Levitical offerings."[3] In other words, we are to offer ourselves back to Him. This beautiful metaphor pictures obedience to God. Just as the little lamb went obediently to the slaughter, so you as a child of God must willingly and obediently place your own life on the altar — in a living sense — not to die physically, but to die to self — and to live righteously! Jesus essentially said the same thing when He challenged His disciples to deny self, take up their cross, and follow Him. Paul said, "I die daily" (1 Cor. 15:31). Zane Hodges says:

When believers present their bodies as a sacrifice, it is in fact the deeds of the body that are put to death, but the body itself is living because it is alive with the very life of God. From that perspective, this is truly the sacrifice of a living body—not merely "alive" in the physical sense—but above all "alive" in a spiritual sense. The entire life of Christian obedience to God, as empowered by the indwelling Spirit, is therefore a superlative act of sacrifice.[4]

When we offer ourselves as a living sacrifice, our obedience is considered by God to be *holy* (consecrated, set apart), and it is *acceptable* to Him. That means God is in full agreement with our obedience; it is well-pleasing to Him.

YOUR REASONABLE SERVICE

To live in this manner — as *a living sacrifice, holy, acceptable to God* — is your *reasonable service*. The word *reasonable* is from the Greek word *logikos*, from which we get our English word *logic*. Thus, for you to live obediently, righteously, is only logical, considering God's mercy upon your life.

What does this imply about a believer who does *not* offer him or her self as a sacrifice? Their lifestyle is *not* holy or acceptable to God and, consequently, they are *not* justified in His sight. Keep in mind from our earlier studies in Romans that justification is not *positional*, based on some supposed legal transaction that occurs at initial salvation. It is *conditional*, based on one's behavior.

Think about your *reasonable service* to God. He has redeemed you, by paying your sin penalty. He has given you eternal (age-lasting) life. He has given you the provision for living righteously, the Holy Spirit. If you do not live obediently, as a living sacrifice, then you are spurning His grace and mercy, and that way of living doesn't make any sense at all!

One of the problems with a *living* sacrifice is that it has the tendency to keep getting off the altar. God wants us to remain there, continually yielded to Him, holy and acceptable in His sight. But many repeatedly make the mistake of refusing to yield, which will have serious ramifications at the Judgment Seat of Christ!

In v. 2 Paul gives some practical help for remaining on the altar:

DON'T BE CONFORMED TO THE SPIRIT OF THE AGE

Rom. 12:2a Do not be conformed to this world.

When I was a pre-teen, my mom bought a poster for my bedroom, which was a color drawing of the world with a man scrunched up inside. At the top of the poster was a paraphrase of the first part of this verse: *Don't let the world squeeze you into its mold.* I'll never forget that poster and the scriptural idea it conveyed, as it helped my thinking as a young man. But there is one small detail that needs to be clarified.

The word *world* is a mistranslation from the Greek word *aion*, which should have been translated *age*. In this particular context, the idea is *the philosophy of the age*. Trench defines *aion* (for this context) as:

> All that floating mass of thoughts, opinions, maxims, speculations, hopes, impulses, aims, aspirations, at any time current in the world ... which constitute a most real and effective power, being the moral, or immoral atmosphere which at every moment of our lives we inhale, again inevitably to exhale,—all this is included in the *aiōn* (age), which is, as Bengel has expressed it, the subtle informing spirit of the *Kosmos* or world of men who are living alienated and apart from God.[5]

AVOID THE ZEITGEIST

The Germans have a word that sums it up well: *zeitgeist*, which essentially translates, *the spirit of the age*. According to the dictionary, *zeitgeist* is "the defining spirit or mood of a particular period of history as shown by the ideas and beliefs of the time."[6] When I mention the zeitgeist of the 1960s, most — who are of my generation or older —immediately think of drugs, sex, rock-n-roll, hippies, and bell-bottom pants. Every age has its own spirit, which is Satanic humanism repackaged for the particular era. In the present era it is new age philosophy, which is merely ancient, pagan philosophy dressed in modern garments.

Paul tells us *not* to be *conformed to* — i.e., *fashioned by or patterned after* — the spirit of the age. Don't let it shape you. The apostle gives this warning because he knows it is the very thing the soul gravitates toward, keeping believers from becoming and remaining living sacrifices.

Seeing that we all have a natural bent toward the *zeitgeist*, how can we avoid it? The latter half of v. 2 provides the answer:

TRANSFORMED THROUGH MIND RENEWAL

> **Rom 12:2b Be transformed by the renewing of your mind, that you may prove what *is* that good and acceptable and perfect will of God.**

Notice the word *transformed*. It is the Greek word *metamorphoo*, which means "to change inwardly in fundamental character or condition, be changed."[7] It is the Greek word used for the *transfiguration* of Jesus. Our English word *metamorphosis* comes from this Greek word — which describes the process of an ugly caterpillar spinning a cocoon and emerging a beautiful butterfly or moth a few weeks later.

God wants His children *not* to be shaped by the spirit of the age, but rather, to experience a complete spiritual metamorphosis or transformation. Incidentally, the command to *be transformed* is in the present tense, which implies that it needs to be continual (*keep being transformed*).

Continual transformation occurs through *renewing the mind*, which is also in the present tense — *keep being transformed by continually renewing your mind*. Mind renewal is the idea of "renovating" one's thoughts. For example, replacing impure thoughts with pure thoughts, replacing incorrect doctrine with correct doctrine, replacing wrong philosophies with right philosophies.

In Phil. 4:8, Paul commands that we *think on these things* — that which is *true, honorable, just, pure, lovely, of good reputation, virtuous,* and *praiseworthy*. Choices must be made to replace the spirit of the age in the soul with the Spirit of Christ. To that end, you must fill your mind with God's Word, as you submit to the Holy Spirit, for they are the *agents* of renewal and metamorphosis.

> **Jas. 1:21** Lay aside all filthiness and overflow of wickedness, and receive with meekness the implanted word, which is able to save your souls.

The *implanted Word* is the Holy Spirit of God who takes the *written Word* and breathes life upon it in your innermost being. That is why it is important to saturate yourself in God's Word — by reading, studying, memorizing, and meditating upon it. Then God will do the renewing and transforming work in your life, for you are incapable of doing that. Arlen Chitwood says:

> The reception of the Word of God is able to bring about the salvation of one's soul because it is this Word which the Spirit of God uses as He effects the metamorphosis of Rom. 12:2.[8]

APPROVING GOD'S WILL

When your mind is being renewed, and you are thereby experiencing an inward metamorphosis, you will *prove what is that good and acceptable and perfect will of God*. I used to think this means that when my mind is being renewed, I will understand God's perfect will for those important decisions in my life, such as: Where should I go to college? Whom should I marry? What career should I pursue? Where should I go to church? — and a host of other particular decisions in life. But now I don't think that is what Paul is talking about, especially in this context.

The apostle is writing to believers who are characterized by division and disunity. He emphasizes the salvation of the soul, which is what they desperately need. In that context, what is the will of God? The question can be answered from one of Paul's other epistles:

> **1 Thess. 4:3** For this is the will of God, your sanctification.

God's will is that His children keep cooperating with Him in the ongoing sanctification process — the saving of the soul — which requires continued choices to live obediently. When Christians are living in this manner, they are proving God's will. What does that mean? Greek expert Kenneth Wuest answers this question:

> "Prove" is ... "to put to the test for the purpose of approving, and finding that the thing tested meets the specifications laid down, to put one's approval upon it." As a result of the Spirit's control of the mental processes of the saint, the latter is enabled to put his life to the test for the purpose of approving it, the specifications being that it conform to the Word of God, and thus, experiencing what obedience is to the Word, and finding out what it feels like to have the Word saturate and control the life, he sees that it really is the Word of God and puts his approval upon it.[9]

When children of God are living uprightly, they experience firsthand that God's will is truly *good and acceptable and perfect*, able to bring saints to maturity. Zane Hodges explains further:

> Doing God's will results in an experiential demonstration of its excellence. This is akin to our colloquial phrase, "Try it, you'll like it!" ... Paul is saying that when we actually perform the will of God in our lives, we will discover for ourselves that His will is *good and pleasing and perfect*.[10]

INWARD TRANSFORMATION RESULTS IN OUTWARD TRANSFORMATION

Only those Christians who are experiencing this *inward* metamorphosis on a consistent basis will be transformed *outwardly* when they meet Jesus. Paul speaks further about this in another epistle:

> **Phil. 3:17** Brethren, join in following my example, and note those who so walk, as you have us for a pattern.
>
> **18** For many walk, of whom I have told you often, and now tell you even weeping, *that they are* the enemies of the cross of Christ:

Paul warns believers to walk (live) in a manner consistent with the apostles and others who were living similarly, for they were patterns or examples of Christlike behavior. In contrast, many believers were not living righteously, and this broke Paul's heart, to the point that he shed tears over them. He refers to them as *enemies of the cross of Christ*. The epistle to the Hebrews describes believers living like this as those who: "trampled the Son of God underfoot, counted the blood of the covenant by which he was sanctified a common thing, and insulted the Spirit of grace" (Heb. 10:29). The Hebrews passage warns that believers who live in this manner will suffer "much worse punishment" than those who rejected the Mosaic law.

In Phil. 3 Paul describes their future verdict at the Judgment Seat of Christ:

> **Phil. 3:19** whose end *is* destruction, whose god *is their* belly, and *whose* glory *is* in their shame—who set their mind on earthly things.

Instead of experiencing God's righteous deliverance in this age, they are self-destructing, experiencing God's wrath. When they meet Jesus, their glory will be *in their shame*. In other words, they will not be glorified with garments of light, as Adam and Eve presumably had before they fell and became "naked and ashamed." These worldly Christians will, instead, be ashamed, for they will not have garments of light that are essential for co-rulership with Jesus in the Millennium. They will not be rewarded, because they *set their mind on earthly things* (v. 19), conforming to the spirit of the age, rather than being transformed inwardly by mind renewal.

"HEAVENLY" CITIZENSHIP

Paul explains what will happen at the Judgment Seat of Christ for those who continue to submit to metamorphosis of the soul internally by having their mind renewed consistently through the Word of God:

> **Phil. 3:20** For our citizenship is in heaven, from which we also eagerly wait for the Savior, the Lord Jesus Christ,

Those who are living obediently have citizenship in heaven — that is, they will be rewarded with inclusion in New Jerusalem, the heavenly ruling realm of the Messianic kingdom. Jesus will glorify them, making them suited for serving in His presence in the bridal city of reward.

> **Phil. 3:21** who will transform our lowly body that it may be conformed to His glorious body, according to the working by which He is able even to subdue all things to Himself.

The phrase *our lowly body* literally translates, "the body of our humiliation," referring to the post-Fall non-glorified body, that has been corrupted by sin. Those who live righteously — who have chosen *not* to be shaped by the spirit of the age, but have instead experienced inner metamorphosis by renewing their mind in God's Word — their body of humiliation will be *transformed*. Incidentally, the word *transformed* (Greek, *metaschematizo*) in Phil. 1:21 is not the same as *metamorphoo* in Rom. 12:2, but it is a similar word with a slightly different meaning. It means "to change the form of."[11]

What will *the body of humiliation* be changed into? A body like Christ's body of glory!

A BODY OF GLORY LIKE CHRIST'S

So here's the point: Those Christians who are presently undergoing metamorphosis in their spiritual lives will be given a body of glory like Christ's at His Judgment Seat. They will shine with some degree of His brightness. In light of this glorious promise of glorification for those who live righteously, Paul admonishes:

> **Phil. 4:1** Therefore, my beloved and longed-for brethren, my joy and crown, so stand fast in the Lord, beloved.

Arlen Chitwood writes:

The word "change" in Phil. 3:21 (referring to changing our body of humiliation) is a translation of the Greek word *metaschematizo*, which refers to *an outward change*. An outward change though would necessitate *a previous inward change*, described by the Greek word *metamorphoo* (Rom. 12:1, 2 [translated, "transformed"]). Christians who allow the Spirit to perform a present inward change in their lives will one day realize the corresponding outward change, finding themselves *enswathed in Glory*, with their bodies "fashioned like unto" *Christ's body of Glory* (Phil. 3:21).[12]

The Scriptures are clear that this must begin *now* if you want to be glorified for the next age. My life verse is 2 Cor. 4:18, but my second favorite verse is:

2 Cor. 3:18 But we all, with unveiled face, beholding [reflecting] as in a mirror the glory of the Lord, are being transformed into the same image from glory to glory, just as by the Spirit of the Lord.

If you are presently living in such a manner that the glory of Christ is being reflected by your life, then you are being transformed (experiencing inward metamorphosis from glory to glory). You are literally metamorphosing into the image of Jesus Christ — becoming more and more like Him. This is describing an upward spiral, as you move on to greater and greater degrees of glory internally. But this is not of you, for the Holy Spirit does this work of transforming, as you submit to His leadership by faith.

Those who are being conformed in greater and greater measure to the image of Christ will one day be glorified in His presence (Rom. 8:29-30). Are you on the pathway of metamorphosis culminating in glory?

CHAPTER 28
GET OFF YOUR HIGH HORSE
ROMANS 12:3-8

The behavior of God's children is atrocious! Multitudes of believers are self-focused, living for themselves and for the here and now, accompanied by a sense of pride that elevates self above others. Then there is the matter of continued sinning, often without remorse and with no desire for change. Christianity is rife with these problems, which has led to a systemic spiritual crisis within the church of Jesus Christ.

FALLING SHORT OF THE GOAL FOR THE CHURCH

How can local churches expect to reach the goal, as given in Eph. 4:13-16?

> **Eph. 4:13** Till we all come to the unity of the faith and of the knowledge of the Son of God, to a perfect man, to the measure of the stature of the fullness of Christ;
> **14a** that we should no longer be children, tossed to and fro and carried about with every wind of doctrine ...
> **15** but, speaking the truth in love, may grow up in all things into Him who is the head—Christ—
> **16** from whom the whole body, joined and knit together by what every joint supplies, according to the effective working by which

every part does its share, causes growth of the body for the edifying of itself in love.

Does that sound like a description of the church of Jesus Christ in our age? Not hardly! In fact, typically, that kind of maturity and selflessness is not even found in *local* churches, much less in the broader, *universal* church of those who are *in Christ*! Nevertheless, what we are experiencing in Christianity today is nothing new. Paul wrote the epistle to the believers at Rome, because the church was plagued with division and disunity.

The church is not an *organization*, but an *organism*, so the fault lies squarely with the individual believers at Rome, who were living licentiously (in the case of the Gentiles) and legalistically (in the case of the Jews). The bottom line: there were many carnal Christians in the church at Rome who were causing the church to have some very serious spiritual problems. The church certainly was not coming to the unity of the faith, to a greater knowledge of Christ, to a perfect (mature) body, to the measure of the stature of the fullness of Christ! Ironically, the first century problem is still with us in the twenty-first century, and now more intense than ever!

To that end, Paul gives several rules in chs. 12-13 for a well-ordered life and church — teaching how God's children should behave like disciples of Jesus. It is important to remember that all disciples are believers, but not all believers are disciples. Disciples are those believers who determine, by God's grace, to deny self, take up their cross, and follow Jesus.

LEGALISM AND MAN-MADE RULES

Seeing that I am referring to these as *rules* for a well-ordered life and church, there could be some who charge me with legalism. So let me clarify up front. *Legalism* is the ritualistic observance of man-made rules (e.g., the Pharisees' rabbinical traditions and modern fundamentalism's "standards") or laws that have been nullified by God (e.g., the Mosaic rituals). The rules are based on *preferences* and the focus is *outward*.

In Paul's day the problem was typically with the Jews, who were swayed by the Judaizers — those who taught that sanctification is by keeping the Mosaic law. In our day, the problem is typically with the fundamentalists, who insist that certain standards must be kept for holiness, even though the Bible doesn't specify. For example, legalists insist that you have to wear the right clothes (and they get to dictate which clothes are right and which are wrong) and fix your hair in their prescribed manner. They insist that you have to listen to the kind of music and watch the kind of television programs they have approved. All others are verboten. They like to tell you where you can and cannot go. If you are seeking a life mate, you must follow their model of courtship. In many cases, they even mandate that you must use a particular version of the Bible (virtually always the KJV) or else you have a corrupted Bible. This is not an exhaustive list, but representative. The icing on the cake is that they look down upon those who do not live according to their rules. Their legalistic system is full of pride, just like the first century Pharisees. The emphasis is *outward*, even though they try to insist that it must come from the heart.

OBEDIENCE AND SPIRITUAL RULES

In contradistinction to legalism, *obedience* is faith-filled, Spirit-enabled observance of God-given spiritual rules, as mandated by the Scriptures, not matters of preference mandated by man; the focus is *inward*.

Paul has already written three chapters (chs. 6-8) on the importance of living by faith, through the grace and power of the Holy Spirit, rather than in the flesh. So when I mention *rules* for a well-ordered life and church, I am not talking about man-made rules and the fleshly effort that is expended in carrying them out. The rules given by Paul in Romans are provided in the context of choosing to obey, by faith, through the enabling power of God's Spirit, our provision for living righteously. These rules are essentially an expanded version of the law of Christ. In other words, these are the details as to how Jesus wants us to live. This chapter will examine only the first rule. The remaining rules will be covered in the next chapter.

RULE #1: GET OFF YOUR HIGH HORSE AND BECOME A TEAM PLAYER!

Forgive me for being a bit colloquial, but I find that some folks understand better when using vernacular with which they are familiar.

> Rom. 12:3 For I say, through the grace given to me, to everyone who is among you, not to think *of himself* more highly than he ought to think, but to think soberly, as God has dealt to each one a measure of faith.
> 12:4-5 For as we have many members in one body, but all the members do not have the same function, so we, *being* many, are one body in Christ, and individually members of one another.

In America, because of the way our nation was founded, and because of our constitutional ideals, we are taught to be rugged individualists — independent spirits — people who march to the beat of our own drum. Because of our capitalistic economy, we also tend to be competitive. But that's the spirit of the age, which can very quickly corrupt our spirituality within the church. The way the church of Jesus Christ should function is entirely different from the way American culture functions. Perhaps one of the reasons American Christians struggle spiritually is because they bring the spirit of the age into the church.

A BODY WITH COOPERATING MEMBERS

The biblical metaphor used in the Scriptures to describe how the church should function is not a competition, but a human body, with each of its members cooperating, working together for the good of the overall body. To that end, God has given spiritual gifts to every believer so the body can profit overall. Robert Govett comments:

> Certain special powers were communicated to each of the members, in order that each might be in part dependent on others. It was not

God's design that each saint should possess every gift, and be required for every use; but He bestows various gifts, suited to the perfections of the body.[1]

Paul gives a beautiful description of the body of Christ in 1 Cor. 12:

> **1 Cor. 12:24b-25** God composed the body, having given greater honor to that *part* which lacks it, that there should be no schism in the body, but *that* the members should have the same care for one another.
> **26** And if one member suffers, all the members suffer with *it;* or if one member is honored, all the members rejoice with *it.*
> **27** Now you are the body of Christ, and members individually.

W.H. Griffith Thomas (1861-1924) said:

> Three great thoughts are thus emphasized, or at least suggested in these words: Unity, Diversity, and Harmony. And it is only when these three are realized and blended that the Church of Christ can live its true life and do its proper work.[2]

Thus, it's time for Christians to get off their high horses, humble themselves, and become team players, recognizing that the *body overall* is the focus, not the individual members.

I love the illustration Paul uses in 1 Cor. 12. He wants to know if the whole body were an eye, then how would it hear? If it were an ear, then how would it smell? I picture a huge eyeball rolling into the church auditorium on Sunday morning. That's brother so-and-so who thinks he is God's gift to the church, because he thinks he is like an eyeball — all important to the church. Then sister so-and-so hops into church like a huge ear. She also thinks of herself as being important. But Paul says:

IT'S NOT ABOUT YOU; IT'S ABOUT THE BODY

> **1 Cor. 12:14** The body is not one member but many.

It's not about *you*; it's about *the body*. In Rom. 12:3 Paul essentially says (my paraphrase), "Stop thinking of yourself as better than others — get serious! — and recognize that God has given you a measure of faith (aka *spiritual gifts*) for you to use to make the team better, more harmonious. If you don't get off your high horse, the church will have a measure of division and disunity." Griffith Thomas emphasizes the catastrophe that results when believers march to the beat of their own drum:

> Each Christian ... is only a part of the great whole, and unless his opinion of himself agrees with God's opinion of him his life will inevitably result in failure.[3]

Handley Moule (1841-1920), in his commentary on Romans, writes:

> The one Lord distributes the one faith-power into many hearts, "measuring" it out to each, so that the many, individually believing in the One, may not collide and fight but lovingly cooperate in many kinds of service, the result of their "like precious faith" (2 Pet. 1:2) conditioned by the variety of their lives.[4]

A "MINI-SERMON" ON RECEIVING CORRECTION

Allow me to interject a parenthetical thought. I am a pastor of 27 years (as of this writing) and need to "preach" a bit at this juncture. Because we are to function as a unified body and not have division among us, we must sometimes correct one another, and we are to be open to receiving correction.

Throughout my pastoral tenure, I have had to confront people about how they are living or about decisions they are making that are having a negative effect on their spiritual lives. That is part of my job description as a pastor. I don't particularly enjoy it, but I do it because it is critically important, and I love the folks in my congregation and care about their spiritual growth. More often than not, church members either ignore what I have to say or bristle when I confront them, which I always do lovingly. In fact, church members have left churches that I have pastored through the years, because of my pastoral confrontation of something that definitely needed spiritual attention.

There used to be a day when people would respect the wisdom and insight of their pastor, and they would seriously consider what he had to say, as long as he shared it in love and not with a "lording it over the flock" attitude. Nowadays, for whatever reason, the default mode seems to be for people to get angry and defensive. I want to cry out to them, "Hey, I'm on the same team! I'm not against you; I'm for you! I want you to move on in maturity, but that's not going to happen unless you get off your high horse and address this problem."

Of course, I never say that, because nowadays, pastors have to be consummate diplomats, overly cautious, "tip-toeing through the tulips," so to speak, so as not to set people on edge. It ought not to be that way. So many are thin-skinned and don't want to be corrected.

BIBLICAL ADMONITIONS ABOUT RECEIVING CORRECTION

The book of Proverbs has a great deal to say about receiving correction. For example (emphasis added):

Prov. 12:1b He who hates **correction** *is* stupid.

13:18a Poverty and shame *will come* to him who disdains **correction**, but he who regards a rebuke will be honored.

15:5b He who receives **correction** is prudent.

15:10b He who hates **correction** will die.

16:22 The **correction** of fools *is* folly.

I hate to be blunt, but according to the book of Proverbs, many Christians are stupid and foolish, because they refuse to accept correction. Frankly, sometimes knowing what a person's reaction will be, I refrain from confronting them, because correcting fools is futile. That is very unfortunate, for if you disdain correction, you are hurting yourself and your church.

Christians need to be open to correction — not merely by the pastor, but by other brothers and sisters in Christ. Those who get angry and bristle and threaten to leave the church are revealing the ugly, prideful condition of their heart.

> **Prov. 13:10 (KJV)** Only by pride comes contention.

In other words, the only reason you bristle and become contentious is because of your pride. That's why Paul essentially says, "Get off your high horse and become a team player." Notice these verses again:

> **Rom. 12:4-5** For as we have many members in one body, but all the members do not have the same function, so we, *being* many, are one body in Christ, and individually members of one another.

THE IMPORTANCE OF EXERCISING SPIRITUAL GIFTS

Recognizing this truth, exercise the spiritual gifts God has given you so the body can function in a unified and cohesive manner.

> **Rom. 12:6-8** Having then gifts differing according to the grace that is given to us, *let us use them:* if prophecy, *let us prophesy* in proportion to our faith; or ministry, *let us use it* in *our* ministering; he who teaches, in teaching; he who exhorts, in exhortation; he who gives, with liberality; he who leads, with diligence; he who shows mercy, with cheerfulness.

Every child of God has one or more spiritual gifts. The word *gifts* in v. 6 comes from the Greek word *charisma,* which are given by God's *grace* (Greek, *charis*). Thayer says:

[*Gifts* (Greek, *charisma*)] denote extraordinary powers, distinguishing certain Christians and enabling them to serve the church of Christ, the reception of which is due to the power of divine grace operating in their souls by *the Holy Spirit.*[5]

SPIRITUAL GIFTS TESTS – A PERSONAL TESTIMONY

Some Christian ministries publish *Spiritual Gifts Tests*, hoping that Christians will take the test and determine their spiritual gifts. Though they are well-meaning, I personally think those tests merely determine one's personality traits, the way God made you with your own unique personality. Spiritual gifts are entirely different. They are the God-given abilities to do what you are unable to do, what your personality cannot accomplish on its own. God gifts you, not for your own personal benefit, but so you can exercise your gifts in the context of the local church, thereby being a blessing to the body.

I distinctly remember, many years ago, shortly after the Lord called me to be a pastor, going to my wise old pastor with a grave concern. Though I had no doubt about my calling, I feared that I did not have the gift of a pastor, mentioned in Eph. 4:11, and my spiritual gift test results confirmed it. I had the "gift" of speaking and even teaching, but not pastoring, and that caused me great consternation. My pastor was rather relaxed about the whole conversation and calmly said, "Oh, don't worry about that. God will give you what you need when you need it!"

Leaving his office, I was scared to death. How could I be a good pastor to people? And how could my pastor treat this so lightly! Sure enough, when I later became a pastor, I learned quickly that God intervened and gave the grace to do what was needed *at the very moment it was needed*. Spiritual gifts tests only revealed my natural abilities to speak and teach, not the God-given ability to pastor. I now realize that spiritual gifts are God's enablement to do what we are unable to do in our strength or ability. Throughout the years I have repeatedly sought the Lord's help to be a good pastor, and I believe He has helped in every situation.

Carnal (fleshly) Christians — those who are not led by the Spirit — are unable to exercise their gifts, because they are not surrendered to the Holy Spirit. They are not using their gifts for the benefit of the local church and, depending on how long they have been living in carnality, they may *never* have exercised their gifts. In fact, some may not even know what their gifts are. What a tragedy! God intends spiritual gifts to be used to benefit and prosper the church toward its goal of unity and maturity in Christ-likeness.

According to both Paul and Peter, the gifts fall into two main categories, and although some are more visible than others, they are *all equally important.*

1. *Speaking* gifts — prophecy (preaching), teaching
2. *Serving* gifts — ministry, exhortation, giving, leading, showing mercy, etc.

SPEAKING GIFTS

Prophecy. In Rom. 12 Paul mentions the gift of *prophecy*, which is preaching. Thayer says that, in this context, the word refers to "the endowment and speech of the Christian teachers."[6] Vine says it is "forth-telling … the telling forth of the mind of the Lord."[7] Wm. Barclay says:

> It is only rarely that prophecy in the New Testament has to do with foretelling the future; it usually has to do with *forthtelling* the word of God.[8]

IN PROPORTION TO FAITH

Paul says the preacher should exercise his gift "in proportion to faith" (v. 6). Commentators point out the two possible ways in which this could be interpreted. First, in Greek there is an article before *faith — the faith.* BDAG says this could be defined as "in agreement with" the faith.[9] In support of this position, Hodges writes:

> The possibility was all too real that individuals claiming prophetic inspiration might express ideas that ran counter to true Christian

doctrine. The true prophet does what Paul enjoins here: he prophesies in agreement with the faith.[10]

A second, alternate position is taken by Vine regarding the preacher exercising the gift of prophecy *in proportion to faith*. He says:

> It is a warning against going beyond what God has given and faith receives. This meaning ... is in keeping with the context ... That there is a definite article before "faith" in the original does not necessarily afford an intimation that the faith, the body of Christian doctrine, is here in view. The presence of the definite article is due to the fact that faith is an abstract noun.[11]

So Hodges claims that the preacher is bound to say what is consistent with "the faith," the body of teaching found in the New Testament, whereas Vine claims the preacher is bound to say only what God authorizes him to say, which he must take by faith and go no further. By way of application, it seems that God could allow some preachers to say more than others on a certain matter, but only if God has given him liberty to do so, and providing the preacher steps out by faith.

In support of this alternate position, Wm. Newell (1868-1956), in his classic commentary on Romans, goes into an interesting discussion — quoting Darby (1800-1882) — emphasizing that while there is no new revelation in our era, a "prophet" could be led by God to preach truth which is in the Word of God but has been lost, so it is new to the audiences to whom the prophet is addressing. In that sense he is functioning as a biblical prophet.[12] If Newell is correct, then could this apply to those preachers who are preaching kingdom inheritance, which has been largely lost to modern audiences?

Teaching. The other speaking gift Paul mentions is *teaching* in v. 7. Whereas preaching is general proclamation of the Word of God, teaching seems to be focused instruction in the doctrines of the Word and how they apply to life. This gift is for helping others understand the Bible. Aquila and Priscilla had this gift and taught Apollos. Those are the *speaking* gifts — preaching and teaching.

SERVING GIFTS

Ministry. In the category of serving gifts, Paul first mentions *ministry*. This is general service, a willingness to serve as needed in the church. *Ministry* is translated from the Greek word *diakonia*, from which we get our English word *deacons*. But other members of the body (who are not in the office of deacon) may also have the gift, including women. Alva McClain says of deacons:

> [The deacons] are really the closest assistants to the pastor, to help him in every duty and to help the church. It should be a place of service, not a position of power.[13]

Exhorting and Giving. Next, Paul mentions *exhorting*, which is the gift of encouraging others to live uprightly, followed by *giving*, which is to be done with liberality. God gifts some with the ability to make more money than others, not so they can spend it all on themselves, but so they can be a blessing in the local church.

Incidentally, whether you have the gift of giving or not, ALL Christians are to be giving! Hodges says:

> The fact that the giver should give with generosity is therefore best understood as applicable to *all* who give. Giving is a general Christian responsibility ... The model of Jesus Christ Himself is the inspiration for true Christian generosity (cf. 2 Cor 8:9).[14]

> **2 Cor. 9:7** *So let* each one *give* as he purposes in his heart, not grudgingly or of necessity; for God loves a cheerful giver.

WHAT ABOUT TITHING?

I have discovered that in the retreat away from tithing — which was mandated under the Mosaic law and, therefore, is not a mandate for our church age — many Christians hardly give at all. They have gone from one extreme to the other, but that is not the spirit of the New Testament. Should not New Testament-era Christians, who have so much more than Old Testament believers, give all the more? We should be like the liberated Ebenezer Scrooge, *after* his awakening — giving generously, *hilariously* is the idea of the Greek word (with great joy and merriment) — not begrudgingly, like the pre-awakened Scrooge. Avoid the polar extremes — legalism on the one end, and licentiousness leading to neglect on the other. Find the right balance according to God's Word. While tithing is not biblically mandated for Christians, it is a good starting point for giving, nonetheless — and quite easy to calculate too.

Leading. Another spiritual gift that Paul mentions is *leading*. This certainly applies to pastors, but it could apply to others as well, those who are not in an official capacity or office. Maybe it means you will lead church projects to help the pastor. Leading must be done with *diligence,* which implies consistent effort, but also includes the idea of *speed.* In other words, not lackadaisical or dilly-dallying, but getting the job done.

Showing Mercy. Finally, some are gifted to show *mercy*, having a great heart of compassion for others — above and beyond. This could include having a heart for the needy or recovery-type ministries in the church. This kind of ministry can be discouraging at times, so remain cheerful, because those to whom you are ministering need love and encouragement.

PETER'S TEACHING ABOUT GIFTS

Peter also talks about the gifts, and he also divides them into the two general categories:

> **1 Pet. 4:10** As each one has received a gift, minister it to one another, as good stewards of the manifold grace of God.
>
> **11** If anyone speaks, *let him speak* as the oracles of God. If anyone ministers, *let him do it* as with the ability which God supplies, that in all things God may be glorified through Jesus Christ, to whom belong the glory and the dominion forever and ever. Amen.

No matter what your spiritual gift, you are to "minister it to one another." Again, spiritual gifts are not for *your* benefit; they are for the benefit of *others,* for the *church overall.*

God wants you to be a good steward of His manifold grace, which is His divine enablement. But in this context, it is a reference to spiritual gifts — the ability to do things that do not come naturally to you. His grace is *manifold*, that is, variegated. In other words, God's grace is diverse and comes in many different forms. Notice that Peter categorizes all spiritual gifts into two groups, just like Paul:

1. Ministry = helps, administration, giving, mercy, hospitality, etc.
2. Speaking = preaching, teaching, evangelist, pastor-teacher

How do we exercise good stewardship in the use of these gifts? Notice the two "if ... as" statements in v. 11. *If* you have a *ministry* gift, then you are to serve *as* of the ability (enablement) which God supplies. *If* you have a *speaking* gift, then you are to speak *as* the oracles of God, that is, as if God Himself were speaking, for we are proclaiming His Word.

Christ is glorified when the minister is ministering according to the ability (or enablement) that God gives and when the preacher is preaching as the oracles of God. Are you using your God-bestowed spiritual gifts? If not, it's time to get off your high horse and become a team player!

CHAPTER 29
RULES FOR REVOLUTIONIZING HOME AND CHURCH
ROMANS 12:9-21

We are now well into the practical application section of the book of Romans. In Rom. 12-13 Paul shares several rules for a well-ordered life and church. The rules in these chapters are about obedience — spiritual rules that God gives as further expansion on the law of Christ found in Matt. 22:37-40. God expects His children to live according to these rules. In the previous chapter the first one was given, from 12:3-8.

Rule #1: Get off your high horse and become a team player! In this chapter thirteen additional rules for Christian living will be given. The second one is found in v. 9:

Rom. 12:9a *Let* **love** *be* **without hypocrisy.**

RULE #2: MAKE SURE YOUR LOVE IS GENUINE.

The word *love* here is *agape*, which means *"the quality of warm regard for and interest in another, esteem, affection, regard, love."*[1] A detailed description of *agape* love is given in 1 Cor. 13, which you can study on your own.

This rule implies that love can be put-on, hypocritical. But put-on love is false at worst or impure at best. Moody called it "Talking cream and living skim milk."² Paul later says in Rom. 13:10 that "love is the fulfillment of the law." Isn't that exactly what Jesus said?

In Matt. 22, when a lawyer asked Jesus, "Which is the great commandment in the law?" — Jesus replied:

> **Matt. 22:37** *You shall love the LORD YOUR GOD WITH ALL YOUR HEART, WITH ALL YOUR SOUL, AND WITH ALL YOUR MIND.*
> **38** This is *the* first and great commandment.
> **39** And *the* second *is* like it: *You shall love your neighbor as yourself.*
> **40** On these two commandments hang all the Law and the Prophets.

In other words, those who are truly loving are fulfilling the spirit of the entire Old Testament, including the Mosaic law! In 1 Cor. 13:13 Paul said:

> **1 Cor. 13:13** Now abide faith, hope, love, these three; but the greatest of these *is* love.

Showing genuine love toward God and man is, by far, the greatest thing you can do in life; it is the ultimate virtue in the Christian life. However, love can be faked; you can act as if you love someone when you really don't. Barclay says:

> There must be no hypocrisy, no play-acting, no ulterior motive. There is such a thing as cupboard love [a British idiom for greedy love], which gives affection with one eye on the gain which may result. There is such a thing as a selfish love, whose aim is to get far more than it is to give. Christian love is cleansed of self; it is a pure outgoing of the heart to others.³

As Barclay suggests, Christians sometimes have impure motives for demonstrating love toward others. Perhaps insincere love is shown for "political" reasons — that is, what the believer can get out of it. Maybe Christians who know they should love others, nevertheless, attempt to do so out of their own strength and flesh, but it is not energized by the Holy Spirit and, therefore, is hypocritical love.

That kind of hypocrisy can actually deaden others spiritually, rather than enliven. Peter says:

> **1 Pet. 1:22** Since you have purified your souls in obeying the truth through the Spirit in sincere love of the brethren, love one another fervently with a pure heart.

Notice the only way that Christians can show genuine, sincere love to others is through the Holy Spirit. Paul emphasizes this same truth early in the epistle:

> **Rom. 5:5b** The love of God has been poured out in our hearts by the Holy Spirit who was given to us.

The fruit of the Spirit is love (Gal. 5:22). A third rule for Christian living is given in the latter half of v. 9:

> **Rom. 12:9b Abhor what is evil. Cling to what is good.**

RULE #3: DETEST EVIL AND HOLD ON TO WHAT IS GOOD.

The Greek word translated *abhor* is a strong verb and conveys the idea of *hatred*. *Hate evil and embrace good* might be another way of saying this. Evil runs rampant in our culture, so we must be especially vigilant to despise it. Barclay says:

> Our one security against sin lies in our being shocked by it. It was Thomas Carlyle who said that what we need is to see the infinite beauty of holiness and the infinite damnability of sin.[4]

Don't merely hate the consequences of sin; hate sin itself. If you are unsure what is sinful and evil, then ask yourself this question: What would God think of it?

Many Christians violate this rule by not moving themselves away from evil friends or evil entertainment or evil literature. Instead of detesting it and purging it from their lives, they become comfortable with sin around them, eventually tolerating it in some cases and welcoming it in other cases. God commands that we detest it, for He is holy and He wants us to be holy (1 Pet. 1:16). Then embrace that which is good. This requires daily choices to think on things that are true, honorable, just, pure, lovely, of good reputation, things that are virtuous and praiseworthy — think on these things (Phil. 4:8)! A fourth rule for Christian living is found in v. 10:

> Rom. 12:10 *Be* **kindly affectionate to one another with brotherly love, in honor giving preference to one another;**

RULE #4: SHOW STRONG AFFECTION TO BRETHREN IN CHRIST.

The phrase *kindly affectionate* comes from a Greek root word that conveys the idea of love within a family. The problem in our age is the overwhelming presence of dysfunctional families, even amongst Christians. As a result, people don't understand this terminology, because they haven't experienced it in their homes. But imagine a loving, harmonious family of blood relatives. That is what your relationship with your brothers and sisters should be like in the church. Literally, your church family should be as close to you as your blood relatives. This is emphasized by the next term used, *brotherly love*, which is translated from the Greek word *philadelphia*, meaning, "the love which Christians cherish for each other as brethren."[5]

In other words, don't be superficial with your brothers and sisters in Christ, but truly value them, putting their preferences above your own. The last phrase of this verse, *in honor giving preference to one another*, conveys the idea of leading the way in showing honor. Hodges says, "the believer is encouraged to be a 'presenter' of honor, rather than a recipient."[6] Is that how you treat other Christians?

If you presently are upset with another church member or if you have animosity in your heart toward someone in your family, then you are unable to fulfill this command. You must reconcile with your brother or sister and move forward in victory, showing strong affection to your Christian brethren.

A MINI-SERMON ON TAKING DOWN "WALLS"

I would like to put in a parenthesis here before moving on to the next point. Many Christians have an invisible wall that they have erected around themselves. You can't see it, but it's there. The purpose of the wall is to keep others from getting too close. Maybe you put up walls out of fear of getting hurt, or it could be because you don't want others to know "the real you." Whatever the reason, it has to go if the church of Jesus Christ is going to fulfill its mission to come to the unity of the faith, to maturity in Christ-likeness.

The walls must come down! Believers must become transparent. Yes, by being transparent others will see "the true you," which is always a risk, but it's a risk worth taking with people who love one another.

If others are also being transparent, you will see "the true them" as they see the "the real you." Then, if we can all learn to receive correction from one another, as mentioned in "the mini-sermon" of the previous chapter, then we are on the road to close fellowship and spiritual growth and maturity within the body of Christ. If you are going to obey the Lord by demonstrating strong affection to your brethren in Christ, then the walls must come down. A fifth rule for Christian living is found in v. 11:

> **Rom. 12:11 not lagging in diligence, fervent in spirit, serving the Lord;**

RULE #5: DON'T BE LAZY ABOUT YOUR SERVICE FOR THE LORD.

Prioritize service for the Lord, and particularly within the local church, for that has been the context all along. Don't drag your feet; don't hesitate; don't dilly-dally; don't be a spiritual "couch potato." Get busy serving the Lord with diligence, having a fervency of spirit. Be zealous for God and for His people and for His work. Have a fire in your soul that drives you to want to be a help and blessing in the church. People like this are contagious; others want to be around them.

Incidentally, to be zealous, you don't have to be in your 20's, 30's, or 40's. Those in their 60's, 70's and 80's can be zealous too, because zeal is rooted in the soul. Arlen Chitwood is 91 years old, and he's still writing and re-writing books, despite his eyesight being greatly constrained. Granted, the older we get, the less physical capabilities we have, but the point is that if your soul is on fire for God, you can accomplish much for the Lord!

Assuming you still have a mind that can function, then talk to people about the Lord, take them out to lunch, send them an email or card, talk with them on the phone. If you are retired, then you have even more time to serve the Lord. A sixth rule for Christian living is given in v. 12:

> **Rom. 12:12 rejoicing in hope, patient in tribulation, continuing steadfastly in prayer;**

RULE #6: REJOICE WHILE ENDURING THE TRIALS OF LIFE.

God wants you to persevere in obedience and faithfulness, come what may — that is, despite the hardships and frustrations and any persecution you might face. Choose to rejoice in the Lord as the habit of your life.

> **1 Pet. 4:13** Rejoice to the extent that you partake of Christ's sufferings, that when His glory is revealed, you may also be glad with exceeding joy.
> **Jas. 1:2-3** My brethren, count it all joy when you fall into various trials, knowing that the testing of your faith produces patience.
> **4** But let patience have *its* perfect work, that you may be perfect and complete, lacking nothing.

All of God's children experience trials, but the key is how we respond. Those who choose to rejoice while persevering amidst trials will be so much happier and will have an infectious spirit that others want. Think of Paul and Silas in prison and the Philippian jailor ultimately being saved.

"Grumps" and "cranks" are those who have made a habit of complaining and griping throughout life instead of rejoicing. As they grow older, they often display an outwardly bitter and irritable spirit, conveying the attitude that they were "shafted" in life. Nobody wants to be around them. Their Judgment Seat verdict will likely not be "Well done!", but "wicked and lazy servant."

Incidentally, Paul shares *how* we can rejoice in persevering at the end of v. 12: through prayer. Those who remain *steadfast* (i.e., *persevere*) in prayer will persevere in their trials.

One final note on v. 12. Our *rejoicing* is to be *in hope* — i.e., confidently expecting that a brighter future is ahead for those who persevere — knowing that God will give reward and glory for those who maintain a joyful spirit amidst trials. A seventh rule for Christian living is given in v. 13:

> **Rom. 12:13 distributing to the needs of the saints, given to hospitality.**

RULE #7: CHOOSE TO BE GIVING AND HOSPITABLE TO OTHERS.

All Christians should be concerned about the needs of other Christians, and doing their best to help to meet those needs. We don't want to see other members of our body suffer. Going one step further, God wants you to be hospitable (entertaining guests, even strangers at times).

Are you hospitable? When was the last time you had someone else from church over to your house for dinner, or for coffee and dessert, or out to a restaurant to share a meal together? Part of the problem is that our culture is so busy that few make time for fellowship with other Christians. That's awful! Our lives need to be restructured so we can all enjoy being with other Christians from time to time.

When inviting others over, don't focus on your home; that is not what is important. Also, don't overemphasize the food — it doesn't have to be perfect or gourmet, just simple food shared in love. Invite someone you don't know very well. Imagine how close we could get with one another if we were to regularly fellowship with others in our church family. Peter reminds:

> **1 Pet. 4:9** *Be* hospitable to one another without grumbling.

Barclay says: "A home can never be happy when it is selfish. Christianity is the religion of the open hand, the open heart and the open door."[7] Paul shares an eighth rule for Christian living in v. 14:

> **Rom. 12:14 Bless those who persecute you; bless and do not curse.**

RULE #8: BLESS THOSE WHO PERSECUTE YOU.

This is especially difficult, especially when other believers are the ones doing the persecuting. When people persecute by wrongly accusing or saying evil things about you, the natural tendency is to want to blast them. However, God wants us to wish them well and pray for them, don't wish them evil or (worse yet) do something evil to them.

Remember the spirit of Jesus on the cross, when He prayed, "Father, forgive them, for they know not what they do." When Paul wrote this, was he thinking of Stephen, who essentially prayed the same prayer and had the same attitude? Yet it was Saul of Tarsus who consented to Stephen's death. How convicting! A ninth rule for Christian living is found in v. 15:

> **Rom. 12:15 Rejoice with those who rejoice, and weep with those who weep.**

RULE #9: EMPATHIZE WITH YOUR BROTHERS/SISTERS IN CHRIST.

To *sympathize* is to feel or express pity and sorrow for someone else's misfortune, but to *empathize* is to actually put yourself in their shoes, understanding and actually sharing their feelings. In so doing, you actually *feel* their pain, and your heart mourns with them. This can only happen if you are in close connection with your brothers and sisters in Christ. If you're not closely related, you will never feel their pain.

Maybe a brother or sister is hurting from the loss of a loved one or experiencing a tremendous financial hardship, such as loss of their job. Perhaps they are being persecuted by someone. Whatever the case, you are to share their pain.

On the flip side, rejoice with them when they are rejoicing, which some commentators claim is more difficult.

> **Eccl. 3:1** To everything *there is* a season, a time for every purpose under heaven:
> **4** A time to weep, and a time to laugh; a time to mourn, and a time to dance;

Paul admonishes that we experience these joys and sorrows of life *together*, not alone. Think of how Jesus responded to Mary and Martha after Lazarus had died, even knowing that their sorrow would soon turn to rejoicing after Lazarus was raised. A tenth rule for Christian living is given in v. 16:

> **Rom. 12:16 Be of the same mind toward one another** [Hodges: "Have the same aspirations for each other"]. **Do not set your mind on high things, but associate with the humble. Do not be wise in your own opinion.**

RULE #10: BE HUMBLE AND RELATE TO OTHERS.

Hodges writes:

> To *have the same aspirations for each other* instructs us to desire that others should experience what we ourselves would like to experience. This contrasts sharply with what often actually happens in a church, where one's own ambition is to "get ahead" of others.[8]

This means you cannot set your mind on high and lofty things. You must choose to be humble and on the same page as your other brothers and sisters in Christ, not wise in your own opinion — that is, wise in your own eyes — for there is pridefulness in that. The eleventh rule is found in v. 17:

Rom. 12:17 Repay no one evil for evil. Have regard for good things in the sight of all men.

RULE #11: DO TO OTHERS AS YOU WOULD HAVE THEM DO TO YOU.

Is this not the golden rule? Jesus initially shared this law in the Sermon on the Mount:

> **Matt. 7:12** Therefore, whatever you want men to do to you, do also to them, for this is the Law and the Prophets.

The negative version of the Golden Rule is sometimes called the Silver Rule: Do not do to others what you would not have them do to you. Barclay said this form of the rule "is not an essentially religious rule at all. It is simply a common-sense statement without which no social intercourse at all would be possible."[9] In fact, societal laws are in large part based on this principle.

Though Jesus did not teach the so-called Silver Rule, it is often how Christians apply His Golden Rule — by softening it. Hodges says:

> The impulse to get even is intrinsic to our sinful nature, and rationalizations for retributive actions are easy to come by. Paul knows this, of course, so he emphasizes that such actions are not justified toward anyone at all.[10]

Thus, Paul goes the extra mile. He says that believers should not pay back those who have done them wrong with wrongdoing in return. Rather, give back good for evil. A twelfth rule for Christian living is given in v. 18:

Rom. 12:18 If it is possible, as much as depends on you, live peaceably with all men.

RULE #12: DO YOUR BEST TO BE AT PEACE WITH OTHERS.

It is not always possible to be at peace with others, even other Christians. The reason is that others may have no desire to reconcile or come to terms of peace, and you can't force the issue. That is why Paul conditions being at peace with others with the admonition — *if it is possible, as much as depends on you*. In other words, make sure to do your part to restore the peace. Confess your fault in the animosity, whatever it is. Make apologies. Seek to restore the friendship; be forgiving. Hodges says: The Christian attitude should be, "I, for my part, have no hostility against him/her."[11] Much is at stake. If the hostility is between brothers or sisters in Christ, then division and disunity has been brought into the church.

Nevertheless, being at peace with others is a "two-way street." The other party has to agree to forgive and move forward in peace, and they need to confess their faults in the process. But if they are unwilling, there is nothing you can do about that. Remember the classic verse from Proverbs:

> **Prov. 13:10a** (KJV) Only by pride cometh contention.

The thirteenth rule is given in v. 19, which is a quote from Deut. 32:35:

> **Rom. 12:19** Beloved, do not avenge yourselves, but *rather* give place to wrath; for it is written, *"Vengeance is Mine, I will repay,"* says the Lord.

RULE #13: DON'T SEEK REVENGE.

Throughout life you will surely be insulted and treated poorly by others and perhaps even hurt in some way, likely even by other Christians. God wants you to know that He will take care of injustices. In fact, He will *repay*, which means "to pay back" those who hurt you. Hollywood movies and television programs are largely built around the principle of seeking revenge. The offended party typically seeks to "settle the score," a principle that pervades our unbelieving culture.

Paul says, "Not you, Christian!" You are not to seek revenge; that is God's responsibility. Stay out of it and let God work. Do not attempt to take on God's role. Hodges says:

> Our own ill-considered or inappropriate revenge can short-circuit what God would otherwise do Himself.[12]

The fourteenth rule is found in vs. 20-21, which is a quote from Prov. 25:21-22:

> **Rom. 12:20 Therefore** *"If your enemy is hungry, feed him; if he is thirsty, give him a drink; for in so doing you will heap coals of fire on his head."*
> **12:21 Do not be overcome by evil, but overcome evil with good.**

RULE #14: TREAT ENEMIES WITH KINDNESS.

Barclay writes:

> To treat people with kindness rather than vengeance is the way to move them. Vengeance may break the spirit; but kindness will break people's hearts. 'If we are kind to our enemies,' says Paul, 'it will heap coals of fire on their heads.' That means not that it will store up further punishment for them but that it will move them to burning shame.[13]

Is Barclay correct? Will kindness toward our enemies "move them to burning shame?" I don't think that is what typically happens in the "real world." Not to mention, that doesn't seem to be the meaning of "heaping coals of fire on their heads." Instead, I prefer Hodge's understanding:

> To perform such kindness to one's foe is to "heap coals of fire on his head" and thus to augment divine wrath against him. Some people

may feel that it is totally inappropriate for Christians even to think of God's vengeance as a substitute for their own. But Scripture gives no support to this humanistic idea. The God of the Bible is a God of justice and His providence ordains that "whatever a man sows, that will he also reap" (Gal 6:7).[14]

Barclay thinks by doing good to an enemy, you will bring conviction upon him to the point of shame. While Hodges thinks by doing good to an enemy, you will invoke God's wrath upon the evildoer. I personally think the latter interpretation is more accurate. But either way, your duty is to be kind and do good to enemies, not evil. God wants you to be overcome with good, not evil.

Are you obeying God's rules?

1. Get off your high horse and become a team player.
2. Make sure your love is genuine.
3. Detest evil and hold on to what is good.
4. Show strong affection to brethren in Christ.
5. Don't be lazy about your service for the Lord.
6. Rejoice in persevering while enduring the trials of life.
7. Choose to be giving and hospitable to others.
8. Bless those who persecute you.
9. Empathize with your brothers/sisters in Christ.
10. Be humble and relate to others.
11. Do to others as you would have them do to you.
12. Do your best to be at peace with others.
13. Don't seek revenge.
14. Treat enemies with kindness.

If believers were to live like this, division and disunity would instantly disappear in Christian homes and churches. May God help us!

CHAPTER 30
OBEYING GOVERNMENT AND LOVING MANKIND
ROMANS 13

I started my college years as a freshman at the Univ. of Ill. at Chicago. My major at that time was pre-law. The liberal professor of my political science class included as required reading, Saul Alinsky's *Rules for Radicals*. That is the book hailed by Hillary Clinton and Barak Obama as formative in their political careers. Alinsky dedicated his book, in part, *to Lucifer,* whom he calls:

> The very first radical known to man who rebelled against the establishment and did it so effectively that he at least won his own kingdom."[1]

Following is the opening paragraph:

> What follows is for those who want to change the world from what it is to what they believe it should be. *The Prince* was written by Machiavelli for the Haves on how to hold power. *Rules for Radicals* is written for the Have-Nots on how to take it away.[2]

In the next paragraph Alinsky says, "This means revolution."[3] In contrast to Alinsky's *Rules for Radicals*, the apostle Paul writes:

Rom. 13:1 Let every soul be subject to the governing

authorities. **For there is no authority except from God, and the authorities that exist are appointed by God.**

We have before us two dramatically different philosophies as to our relationship to government – God's and Satan's — for even as Alinsky admits, Satan was the first radical, rebel and revolutionary. Satan has been working throughout history to overthrow God's sovereignty and destroy His Messiah and those who are preparing as sons to glory. One of his methods is to convince Christians to become revolutionaries, to disobey God-ordained government.

STRUGGLING TO KNOW HOW TO APPLY ROM. 13

Many American Christians struggle to know how they should understand and apply Rom. 13, and that is because our form of government — a constitutional republic — opens the door to challenge government. Further muddying the waters is that many Christians think our nation was founded as a Christian nation, but it was not. Some of our key founders — for example, Ben Franklin and Thomas Jefferson — were deists and did not believe the Bible to be the Word of God. Many of the other founders were freemasons — for example, George Washington — a very prominent, high-level mason who had a skewed view of the Bible and was united with what I believe is a Satanic brotherhood or fraternity, freemasonry. If you're surprised by any of this, do some research. The facts are readily available.

Nevertheless, many within our nation and even our early government were Christians, and there certainly was a greater degree of morality than we find today. But it is important to understand that America has never been a so-called Christian nation.

In addition, our form of government, though it is quite good — for it recognizes the inalienable, God-given rights of all mankind — is not a perfect government by any means. It is man-made. Some may be surprised to learn that the Bible does not mandate a form of government for the Gentile rulers of the world. It seems to leave that for mankind to figure out, recognizing full well that man is going to make a mess of things. In fact, God sometimes has to intervene when man's governmental mess treads on His sovereign will. Think of the Tower of Babel, the book of Esther, and Psalm 2, for some quick examples. The ultimate governmental mess will come during the tribulation — antichrist's one-world government, that God will destroy.

THE BEST FORM OF GOVERNMENT

The best form of government is a monarchy, led by a righteous king, for that will characterize the millennial kingdom. Throughout world history we read of numerous monarchies, some of which were led by righteous kings, but they were short-lived and faced tremendous opposition from opponents. However, we know Christ's coming Messianic government will be a glorious reign of righteousness for a thousand years — a time of peace and prosperity. Could it be that carnal Christians, who do not learn to submit to governmental rulers in this age, will have difficulty submitting to Christ's rule "with a rod of iron" in the age to come?

Of course, we believe God, and so we want to obey His Word. Thus we must learn how to apply the principles of Rom. 13 in our Christian lives.

> **Rom. 13:1 Let every soul be subject to the governing authorities. For there is no authority except from God, and the authorities that exist are appointed by God.**

What does this mean? Does this apply when murderous men like Hitler or Stalin or Mao or Pol Pot are in power? Are we to accept whatever the brutal dictators heap upon us? Rom. 13 raises numerous questions.

SUBJECT TO WHOM?

God has ordained three institutions, not merely two: the home, the church, and government. But what is the government? Who or what is our rightful authority, and to whom are we commanded to be subject?

Some American Christians think the U.S. constitution is our lawful government, thus we are not bound to submit to leaders, per se, but solely to the constitution, the law of the land. But God makes clear that we are to submit to the *authorities;* i.e., people! Verse 3 refers to *rulers* — again, people! — whether they abide by the constitution or not. In other lands, the form of government could be a monarchy or a dictatorship, but regardless, we are to submit to the *rulers* of our government. Remember that Nero was emperor when Paul wrote this, yet Nero became a despotic maniac. God puts people like this in power from time to time, and He has His purposes. Zane Hodges says the Greek makes clear that:

> God does not merely *allow* certain men to rule, He *arranges* it.[4]

Though it may be difficult to accept, God makes very clear that we are to submit to (that is the meaning of *be subject to*) the governing authorities, including rulers who are hostile to Christians. Thankfully, in our country, because we still have a republic form of government, we still get to elect our leaders, at least in theory.

WHAT CHRISTIANS CAN DO TO CHANGE GOVERNMENT

There are things we can do as Christians in America to reshape the government and its policies, at least to some degree:

- We can (and should) vote.
- We can voice our objections through proper channels, typically through our elected representatives.
- We can also pursue legal options if the rulers get out of line and violate the laws of the land. Our constitution allows for this.
- Most importantly, we can pray! — and we are commanded to do so in 1 Tim. 2:1-3:

> **1 Tim. 2:1-2** Therefore I exhort first of all that supplications, prayers, intercessions, and giving of thanks be made for all men, for kings and all who are in authority, that we may lead a quiet and peaceable life in all godliness and reverence.
> **3** For this is good and acceptable in the sight of God our Savior,

If the above means are not successful in changing the laws or removing oppressive leaders, we are, nonetheless, obligated to submit to our rulers and obey them, even if they are out of line. Commentator James Stifler (1839-1902) shares some thought-provoking comments about Rom. 13:

> Within this limit it does not forbid teaching and agitation for better government if these do not lead to resistance, but under this principle it is hard to see how a Christian can lead in a rebellion. Paul's words are unmistakable, and yet there stand Cromwell and Washington![5]

WEIGHTY QUESTIONS

Was the American War for Independence within the spirit of Rom. 13 or a violation of it? What about the infamous French Revolution? And what about Oliver Cromwell's beheading of King Charles in the English Civil War? Is "civil disobedience" an appropriate tactic for Christians to utilize in light of Rom. 13? I cannot delve into a discussion of these questions, lest I get off track, but I would encourage the reader to ponder questions such as these. Stifler goes on to say:

> Civil government has its source in God, and all constituted power is appointed and ordained by him. The cruel abuses in governments ... do not invalidate their divine charter any more than the abuses of marriage rob it of its sacredness. Any government is preferable to anarchy, just as poorly enforced marriage laws are better than none. Man abuses all God's gifts.[6]

OBEYING GOD RATHER THAN MEN

While we are to submit to governmental authorities, the Bible gives an exception: "We ought to obey God rather than men" (Acts 5:29).

If the government orders us not to confess Christ, we must confess Christ nonetheless. For this is a biblical mandate. If the government orders us to worship the king or idols of some sort or to stop praying, we must disobey like Shadrach, Meshach, Abednego and Daniel.

If the government is killing people, we must do our best to save people. Think of the midwives sparing the babies that Pharaoh had ordered to be killed, and of Moses' mother's efforts to save him. Think of Queen Esther and Mordecai plotting to save the Jews from destruction, even behind the king's back.

By way of modern example, think of women in China who have refused to abort their second child, despite the government's one-child mandate — and the many Christians who saved Jews during the Holocaust. Other examples could be given, but the point has been made.

Now here's a thorny question: Was is right for Dietrich Bonhoeffer, a Lutheran pastor and theologian, to attempt to assassinate Adolf Hitler? Considering Hitler's dastardly deeds, feelings may drive some to exclaim, "Way to go Dietrich!" But wasn't even Adolf Hitler appointed by God? To be sure, God did not ordain Hitler's actions, but God ordained his rulership.

In case you are not aware, Bonhoeffer was not successful, and he was ultimately executed for his actions, even after the war had officially ended. Is that not what God warns about in v. 2? Those who resist bring judgment upon themselves. Some claim Bonhoeffer's assassination attempt was justified as a Christian, because it happened during a time of war. Yes, but Bonhoeffer was not a citizen or soldier of the allied nations, he was a *German* citizen, so he attempted to murder the ruler of his own nation. This is a sticky wicket indeed!

THE PRICE OF DISOBEDIENCE

If you disobey the government, you must be prepared to pay the price, which could result in fines, imprisonment, persecution, or even death. When Peter and the other apostles said, "We ought to obey God rather than men," they were beaten and threatened, and they had already been imprisoned. The bottom line is that God orders you to obey the governing authorities, whom He has ordained, unless the government's decrees violate God's commands. Hodges says:

> In modern "democracies" there is a temptation to categorize laws as good or bad, where the latter category furnishes justification for disobedience. But unless the law runs counter to a direct divine command, there is no Biblical authorization to disobey it. On the contrary, this passage commands obedience. Moreover, Paul warns that the failure to submit to this authority entails consequences.[7]

Christians may not like this, but it is what God commands, and we must remember how this must have gone over with the first century Jews in particular. Stifler writes:

> Only a few years before, the Jews in Rome had rebelled and were expelled ... Priscilla and Aquila among them ... He knew that Jews everywhere disputed the authority of Rome, and that they held the fanatical doctrine, sometimes appearing sporadically in more modern church history, that God's child is directly responsible to God alone and that the king's authority is a usurpation.
> That a Gentile prince could have divine authority was a doctrine hard for a Jew to accept, especially when that authority was exercised over him. If Paul was hated for this teaching, as he must have been, by the Jewish nation, Titus [the Roman emperor] gave him a thorough vindication twelve years later. The disregard of this verse was the Jews' national ruin.[8]

Notice what Stifler is saying. The Jews hated Rome and resisted Rome's authority, but their opposition to the Roman government ultimately resulted in the destruction of Jerusalem (AD 70), which was the price they paid for disobedience. Thus, we read in v. 2 a serious warning:

> **Rom. 13:2 Therefore whoever resists the authority resists the ordinance of God, and those who resist will bring judgment on themselves.**

RULERS – A TERROR TO THOSE WHO DO EVIL

Those who disobey government rulers at any level — federal, state, or local — are resisting God's ordained authorities, and will face consequences by the rulers. Paul continues in vs. 3-4:

> **Rom. 13:3 For rulers are not a terror to good works, but to evil. Do you want to be unafraid of the authority? Do what is good, and you will have praise from the same.**
> **13:4 For he is God's minister to you for good. But if you do evil, be afraid; for he does not bear the sword in vain; for he is God's minister, an avenger to *execute* wrath on him who practices evil.**

For the most part, rulers won't bother you if you are obeying and doing what is right. Although you might be nervous about the police officer who is driving behind you, there is no need to fear if your vehicle registration is up to date and you are obeying the motor vehicle laws. The FBI is probably not going to knock down your door if you are obeying the laws of the land and not ranting and raving about guns or violence or making aggressive political statements on the internet. But if you are disobedient or if there is a warrant out for your arrest, you ought to be scared to death, for you are an evildoer, and the authorities will be coming after you.

Government does not bear the sword in vain. In other words, they have the authority, which is God-given — whether they recognize His ultimate authority or not — to punish, all the way up to capital punishment, if necessary. Notice in v. 4 that God refers to governmental authorities as *God's minister* — the Greek word is *diakonos*, which means servant — the word from which we get *deacon*. They are God's minister, "an avenger to *execute* wrath on him who practices evil." So live righteously, obeying the laws of the land, and you will have nothing to fear from government authorities. Paul continues the admonition in v. 5:

MOTIVATIONS FOR OBEYING GOVERNMENT AUTHORITIES

> **Rom. 13:5 Therefore *you* must be subject, not only because of wrath but also for conscience' sake.**

The apostle gives two motivations for obeying government:

1. The wrath of the government upon lawbreakers.
2. A violated conscience for disobedience.

In fact, Paul goes one step further:

> **Rom. 13:6 For because of this you also pay taxes, for they are God's ministers attending continually to this very thing.**
> **13:7 Render therefore to all their due: taxes to whom taxes *are due*, customs to whom customs, fear to whom fear, honor to whom honor.**

Nobody likes taxes, but God says to pay them nonetheless. Jesus paid his taxes — He rendered to Caesar the things that are Caesar's. We may not like how the government *uses* our taxes, but there are right and proper ways of correcting that, and it's not by refusing to pay your taxes!

Give fear to whom it is due and honor (respect) to whom it is due. Respect the authority of the governmental leaders, not just at the highest levels, but all the way down to the level of local police officers and sheriff's deputies. You may not like their attitude or their methods, but you must honor their position of God-given authority. There is absolutely no place for Christians resisting arrest or mouthing off at police officers.

LOVE ALL MANKIND

Paul then takes the opportunity to broaden his admonition from government authorities to all mankind (including unbelievers).

> **Rom. 13:8 Owe no one anything except to love one another, for he who loves another has fulfilled the law.**

This does *not* mean "don't have a mortgage or loans or credit cards." It means "keep current on your payments" — and, in the broader context of the text, it is keeping current on taxes.

In the second half of the verse, God commands that you have but one outstanding debt — a debt to mankind — a continual obligation to love one another. Then Paul adds, "he who loves others fulfills the law." That is especially important for his Jewish audience to hear, for they had been focused on keeping the Mosaic rituals for sanctification. Paul has condemned this, focusing instead on the importance of submitting to the Holy Spirit, by faith, for the grace to be victorious over sin and self. Now he tells them that to love others is to fulfill the Mosaic law. Loving others is selfless; it is the law of Christ. Those who live in this manner please the Lord and will hear "Well done!" when they meet Him in judgment.

LOVE YOUR NEIGHBOR AS YOURSELF

Paul goes one step further and teaches that love-living doesn't merely fulfill the Mosaic rituals, it also fulfills "the righteous requirements of the law" (a term he used previously in the epistle). By way of example, Paul lists several of the ten commandments.

> **Rom. 13:9 For the commandments, "You shall not commit adultery," "You shall not murder," "You shall not steal," "You shall not bear false witness," "You shall**

> *not covet,"* and if *there is* any other commandment, are *all* summed up in this saying, namely, *"You shall love your neighbor as yourself."*

A child of God who is truly loving others will not be committing adultery or murdering (even inwardly, in the heart) or stealing or lying or coveting (lusting). Paul teaches that all the commands are summed up in this one: *Love your neighbor as yourself*. This applies to our love, not merely toward other Christians, but to all mankind. Paul makes the point again for emphasis:

> **Rom. 13:10 Love does no harm to a neighbor; therefore love *is* the fulfillment of the law.**

Love never hurts anyone, and that is why love fulfills "the righteous requirements of the law." Incidentally, this kind of *agape* love is not about *feelings*; it's about *actions*. Bob Wilkin says:

> While believers are no longer under the law of Moses (Rom 7:6; Gal 4:5-7, 10-11, 21-31), they ultimately fulfill it since the commands of the NT likewise center on love for one's neighbor. A by-product of Christians heeding the law of Christ (Gal 6:2), is meeting the moral standards of the law of Moses, even without knowing the law of Moses.[9]

WAKE UP, CHRISTIAN!

In closing the chapter, Paul warns the believers:

> **Rom. 13:11 And *do* this, knowing the time, that now *it is* high time to awake out of sleep; for now our salvation *is* nearer than when we *first* believed.**

Wake up, Christian! Shake off your spiritual slumber! Your *salvation* is nearer that when you believed. The word *salvation* in Romans is not used to refer to *initial* salvation, that is, regeneration — the point at which you first believed on Jesus and received eternal (age-lasting) life. Rather, *salvation* in Romans refers to *ongoing* salvation — *soul-salvation* — sanctification unto maturity, so the believer can hear "Well done!" at the Judgment Seat of Christ.

That salvation is now nearer that when you believed. The next thing on the agenda for believers is the rapture, immediately followed by the Judgment Seat, which determines whether or not one's soul has been saved. If the soul has been saved, abundant reward will be given, in the form of:

1. Crowns, symbolizing authority to rule
2. White robes of righteousness, symbolizing purity
3. Glorification — glowing in some degree, sharing in Christ's glory
4. Inclusion in the New Jerusalem, the heavenly city of reward
5. Ruling as Christ's bride and co-regent in the Millennium

If the soul has *not* been saved in this life, the child of God will be naked and ashamed, relegated to the relative darkness outside New Jerusalem, which is the earthly realm of the kingdom. So wake up Christian, for there is much at stake!

ARMOR OF LIGHT

> **Rom. 13:12 The night is far spent, the day is at hand. Therefore let us cast off the works of darkness, and let us put on the armor of light.**
> **13:13 Let us walk properly, as in the day, not in revelry and drunkenness, not in lewdness and lust, not in strife and envy.**
> **13:14 But put on the Lord Jesus Christ, and make no provision for the flesh, to *fulfill its* lusts.**

Works of darkness will result in negative reward at the Bema, so by God's grace, cast them off! Put on, by appropriating God's grace through faith (Rom. 5:2), armor of light. Could this armor of light represent the glory that will be bestowed on those who live righteously now?

Walk properly, that is, live in an honorable manner, pleasing the Lord — not in revelry (carousing) and drunkenness (controlled by something other than the Holy Spirit, including illicit drugs), not in lewdness (sexual immorality) and lust (sensuality), not in strife (fighting, contention) and envy. Rather, put on Jesus Christ. Let *Him* be your provision to live righteously. Don't give way to your flesh.

There is much at stake regarding these behavioral decisions! Your salvation is near! The reckoning regarding your the salvation of your soul will be here before you know it, and you want to be ready! Are you ready?

CHAPTER 31
EVERY KNEE SHALL BOW
ROMANS 14

In Rom. 14 *stronger* Christians are instructed to receive and accommodate *weaker* brethren out of love. Who are the *weaker* brethren in this text? Who are the *stronger* ones? *Stronger* Christians are those who recognize they are free in Christ, not to live licentiously, but in the sense that they are not bound by the rituals of the Old Testament law or by laws of man's devising. *Weaker* brethren are those who still feel bound by rules in some degree.

THE MODERN FUNDAMENTALIST MOVEMENT ...

Ironically, many in the modern fundamentalist movement *think* of themselves as stronger Christians, because they hold to so many rules. They view all others as weaker. The same was true of the Pharisees in Christ's day — but that is upside down! However, even if we correct their erroneous view and recognize that they are the weaker brethren, we cannot use this text as justification for accommodating their legalism in the church of Jesus Christ. As we shall see, Paul is *not* teaching that we should accommodate legalism in the church! If there's any doubt, study the book of Galatians.

That being said, I need to clarify something very important from the beginning of this chapter. I have come to the conclusion in the past fifteen-plus years that the modern fundamentalist *movement* is largely characterized by *weak* Christians led by *weak* pastors. In contrast, *historic* fundamentalism was — and still is — characterized by many *strong* Christians led by *strong* pastors.

If a pastor is unabashedly committed to the truths of the Bible, properly interpreted — and nothing else! — he will lead his congregation as a good shepherd into paths of truth and righteousness. However, if a pastor is committed to legalistic separational standards, he will lead his congregation as a bad shepherd into error and frequent stumbling over matters that are not biblical. In the latter case, the pastor is weak, for he is not grounded upon Scripture alone, and his congregation will also be weak.

Ironically, both pastor and church will *think* they are stronger than others, for they have what they like to refer to as "strong convictions." Some pastors refer to their standards as "higher" and those of others as "lesser" or "lower," thinking they are right and others are wrong. Those like this often tend to condescend to and separate from others who do not hold to their convictions and standards.

A THROWBACK TO FIRST CENTURY PHARISAISM

Can you see through this problem? Those who are weak *think* they are strong, because they hold to many rules. But, in reality, they are weak, because the rules are not God's laws — *the law of Christ* — they are man's rules — *preferences* that they have elevated to the level of truth. The Pharisees were like this, and notice what Jesus said about them:

> **Mark 7:6** [Jesus] answered and said to them, "Well did Isaiah prophesy of you hypocrites, as it is written: *'This people honors Me with their lips, but their heart is far from Me.*
>
> *7 And in vain they worship Me, teaching as doctrines the commandments of men.'*
>
> *8* For laying aside the commandment of God, you hold the tradition of men" ...

9 He said to them, *"All too* well you reject the commandment of God, that you may keep your tradition.

13a making the word of God of no effect through your tradition which you have handed down.

The modern fundamentalist *movement* is largely guilty of the same error. They have established traditions — which they call "separational standards" — and they equate these man-made "standards" with commands of God, though they are merely man's preferential dictates. Their "standards" are focused on matters such as clothing, music, hair styles, Bible versions, entertainment choices, etc.

God's Word does not speak directly to these matters and gives Christians liberty to make choices, keeping within biblical commands and principles. Granted, we must make wise choices, for we are called to live in holiness. But by pushing the pastor's or the church's convictions on the church members, and implying that those convictions are necessary for spirituality, the wrong message is sent. Jesus makes clear, that in so doing, they are nullifying God's Word by promoting their own commands. They think this makes them more spiritual than others who do not hold to their standards and whom they patronize.

STRENGTH OR WEAKNESS?

Is this strength or weakness? In God's eyes, it is weakness, thus fundamentalist churches which have succumbed to the ways of the modern *movement* typically have weak pastors and weak church members. If Jesus condemned this type of legalistic behavior, then should we expect Paul to encourage first century believers to accommodate it? No, that is not what Paul is doing in this text, which is frequently misinterpreted and misapplied.

Paul condemned legalistic living in the earlier chapters of this epistle. He made very clear to the Jews that continuing in the Mosaic rituals does not make one righteous. Observing circumcision, dietary laws, feast days and sabbaths does not guarantee that one is righteous before God. Christians — both Jewish and Gentile — must depend on Jesus, by faith, to live righteously. So if anyone is against legalism, Paul certainly is. There is *no way* that he would tell modern Christians to accommodate it in the church of Jesus Christ. Legalism *destroys* churches! Incidentally, so does license! Thus, we cannot apply Rom. 14 to the modern fundamentalist *movement*, nor are we to accommodate their legalistic error in the church. Paul is dealing with something quite different in the first century church at Rome, as we shall see.

THE JEWISH DILEMMA

At the time of Paul's writing of Romans — probably around AD 56 or 57 — the church of Jesus Christ had become well-established, and Jews and Gentiles were becoming the one new man in Christ (Eph. 2:15). But there were still some bumps and snags along the way, resulting in division and disunity, and that is why Paul wrote the epistle to the church at Rome.

One of the issues he takes up here in Rom. 14 is that the Jewish believers in particular are having a difficult time assimilating to the new environment of the church. Now that they are Christians, are they to stop observing feast days? Are they to abandon their Jewish diets? Is the Sabbath to be ignored?

Perhaps they understand from Paul's earlier chapters in Romans that these things do not make them righteous before God. They must trust Jesus by faith to live righteously. But are they to abandon these markers of their Jewish identity? Or are they to remain distinct in the culture by continuing to honor the Lord in this manner? After all, God had called Israel to be His nation of priests in the culture, and Paul is writing before the nation's destruction.

THE WEAKNESS OF JEWISH BELIEVERS

I take the position (and several commentators do as well) that Paul describes some of the *Jewish believers* as weak, for they are having difficulty letting go of their observance of the Old Testament law entirely. That means Paul considers the Gentiles to be strong, for they have assimilated well, and we can sympathize with this. Their former lifestyle was pagan and licentious, but they had forsaken all this to follow Christ subsequent to their initial salvation. They have no divine connection to laws or observances in their past.

The Jews, on the other hand, have always been God's people — observing their feast days and sabbaths, which are in some cases memorials of past events, and in other cases, types of future events. Their diet identifies them as Jews in the culture. Shouldn't they keep doing these things, even though these things do not make them holy? Jan Bonda adds some additional detail to the Jewish reasoning:

> What value did the weak attach to these Jewish customs? We should first of all note that God himself had given the Jewish dietary laws ("kosher" food) and the Jewish festivals to Israel to keep them focused on his service. The weekly Sabbath was the most prominent among these festivals. These customs kept them separate from the nations and prevented them from falling back into paganism. Jesus himself had observed these commandments, and so had the early Jerusalem church.
>
> But they were not obligatory for the Gentiles who accepted the gospel. For one was not saved by keeping those commandments but through faith in Jesus. But the Jews who believed in Jesus saw no reason to break with these customs. The situation was similar with regard to the proselytes, worshipers of God from the Gentiles who had accepted Judaism. They had become attached to these Jewish customs.[1]

THE JEWISH DIET AND OBSERVANCE OF SPECIAL DAYS

Paul identifies the weak Jews and proselytes by their customs:

> **Rom. 14:2 For one believes he may eat all things, but he who is weak eats *only* vegetables.**

Some claim the Jews had become vegetarian because they weren't able to get kosher meats in the Roman marketplace; so much of that meat had been offered to idols. Bonda says:

Abandoning these customs under pressure from the strong might carry the danger of relapsing into paganism. Paul warns against this: "Do not let what you eat cause the ruin of one for whom Christ died." And: "Do not, for the sake of food, destroy the work of God." (Rom. 14:15, 20).[2]

Many Jews also kept up observance of special days.

> **Rom. 14:5 One person esteems *one* day above another; another esteems every day *alike*. Let each be fully convinced in his own mind.**
> **14:6a He who observes the day, observes *it* to the Lord; and he who does not observe the day, to the Lord he does not observe *it*.**
> **14:6b He who eats, eats to the Lord, for he gives God thanks; and he who does not eat, to the Lord he does not eat, and gives God thanks.**

Those Jews in the Roman church who continue to hold to certain aspects of the law, Paul considers to be weak, because they are not completely free from Judaism, in contrast to the stronger Gentile believers, who have made a clean break with their past.

CONTINUED OBSERVANCE IS NOT FORBIDDEN

14:6a. These Jews continue to observe sabbath days and feast days. If someone is going to do this, Paul says, they must be fully persuaded in their own mind that this pleases the Lord, and they must observe it *as unto the Lord*.

14:6b. The same applies to dietary restrictions, which must be observed *as unto the Lord* and not for any other reason. Those who do not observe days or limit their diet must also carry out their beliefs *as unto the Lord*.

Interestingly, Paul doesn't blast the Jews and tell them to get rid of all vestiges of Jewishness, because that is all they have ever known, and to do so would injure their conscience and thereby hurt their faith. Not to mention, Paul recognizes that they remain God's people, distinct from the nations. Keep in mind that Paul writes this epistle more than a decade prior to Israel's destruction by Rome in AD 70.

A SPIRIT OF ACCEPTANCE

Rather than condemning, Paul urges a spirit of acceptance in the church:

> **Rom. 14:1 Receive one who is weak in the faith, *but* not to disputes over doubtful things.**

Paul urges the Gentiles to receive those Jewish believers who are weak in the faith, thinking they must continue to observe the hallmarks of their Jewishness. Zane Hodges says:

> Evidently, sometimes in the Roman churches a certain pseudo-acceptance was extended to the weak. But its real intent was to convert them to the opinions of those stronger in the faith. Paul makes clear here that this is not the kind of acceptance he has in mind. Disputes over such matters revealed that true Christian acceptance had not occurred ... Paul is warning against such debates, especially at the Lord's Table.[3]

Further instructions are given in vs. 3-4:

> **Rom. 14:3 Let not him who eats despise him who does not eat, and let not him who does not eat judge him who eats; for God has received him.**
> **14:4 Who are you to judge another's servant? To his own master he stands or falls. Indeed, he will be made to stand, for God is able to make him stand.**

THE ADMONITION WORKS BOTH DIRECTIONS

Adding to the problem within the church is that the Jews think the Gentiles are too liberal; they need to limit their behavior. Although the Gentiles (those who can eat anything) are not to despise the Jews for not eating certain foods, the Jews (those who restrict their diets) are not to judge the Gentiles for eating whatever they want — for God has accepted them!

14:4. We are all God's servants, so we must let Him be the judge of His own servants. He decides whether they stand (i.e., are approved by Him) or fall (i.e., are disapproved by Him). Indeed, He enables men to stand and be approved, so don't underestimate your brethren. Have mutual respect for the beliefs of one another.

Despite being Jewish and a former Pharisee, Paul himself has freedom in Christ:

> **Rom. 14:14 I know and am convinced by the Lord Jesus that *there is* nothing unclean of itself; but to him who considers anything to be unclean, to him *it is* unclean.**
> **14:15 Yet if your brother is grieved because of *your* food, you are no longer walking in love. Do not destroy with your food the one for whom Christ died.**

Hodges comments:

> Paul wants to make clear that what is involved here is not concurrence in some fashion with the unjustified scruples of the weak. The concern for the sensitivities of others that he urges does not involve submission to their principles. To make this point he starts with himself.[4]

DON'T DESTROY YOUR CHRISTIAN BRETHREN

Paul is free in Christ to eat whatever he pleases. Thus, he identifies with the strong, and he knows "there is nothing unclean of itself." He is not, of course, referring to matters of morality, but matters of Jewish identity. Nevertheless, he realizes that some of his believing Jewish brethren have not gotten to that same point of freedom. Therefore, those who are strong must be careful not to ignore the sensitivities of the weak, for to do so would be tantamount to not walking in love. Paul tells the Gentiles: "Don't destroy these Jewish believers; Christ died for them too!"

> **Rom. 14:16 Therefore do not let your good be spoken of as evil;**

He reminds the Gentiles that the Jewish Christians are their brethren whom they must not grieve by enjoying freedoms in their presence. They wouldn't want their good (their freedom in Christ) to be evil spoken of — i.e., become the subject of scorn — simply because they are not willing to curb it for others. Furthermore, the Messianic kingdom is not about eating and drinking.

THE SPIRITUAL FOCUS OF THE KINGDOM

> **Rom. 14:17 for the kingdom of God is not eating and drinking, but righteousness and peace and joy in the Holy Spirit.**

Hodges asks:

> Is Paul speaking, as many commentators suggest ... of *the present experience* of God's kingdom?
> The kingdom is not yet. Christ is not ruling and His kingdom is not currently in effect (John 18:36; Acts 1:7; Heb. 12:2; Rev. 3:21). His kingdom will come when He returns to earth after the Tribulation.[5]

In this verse Paul emphasizes that food and dietary restrictions will not be the focus in the Millennium. The focus will be on righteousness and peace and joy — as if to say, have that focus *now*, for it honors the Lord! In the words of the songwriter, this is a "foretaste of glory divine."[6]

Now don't worry (those of you who like to eat). There will be food in the Millennium, for it starts with the Marriage Supper of the Lamb, which will indubitably be quite a feast. Incidentally, believers must qualify to be at that Supper. Merely being a child of God is not sufficient qualification, as Jesus taught in the parable of the man with the improper wedding garment (Matt. 22:1-14).

> Rom. 14:18 For he who serves Christ in these things *is* acceptable to God and approved by men.
> 14:19 Therefore let us pursue the things *which make* for peace and the things by which one may edify another.

Do what is necessary to keep peace with your brethren, living in righteousness and joy and peace. Serve the Lord by edifying others. Those who do will be accepted by God and even by other believers.

WHATEVER IS NOT FROM FAITH IS SIN

> Rom. 14:20 Do not destroy the work of God for the sake of food. All things indeed *are* pure, but *it is* evil for the man who eats with offense.
> 14:21 *It is* good neither to eat meat nor drink wine nor *do anything* by which your brother stumbles or is offended or is made weak.
> 14:22 Do you have faith? Have *it* to yourself before God. Happy *is* he who does not condemn himself in what he approves.
> 14:23 But he who doubts is condemned if he eats, because *he does* not *eat* from faith; for whatever *is* not from faith is sin.

In the final analysis, Paul urges the believers not to destroy the church (e.g., cause church splits) over food. Humble yourself, refrain from eating certain things in the presence of your Jewish brethren in order to protect them from violating their consciences and stumbling. Because if they can't eat something in good faith toward the Lord, then they are condemning themselves, for whatever is not driven by faith is sinful. Hodges says:

The way in which we live the Christian life is by living out what God has impressed upon us from His Word (Rom 12:2; 2 Cor 3:18). If our actions are not by faith, that is, if our actions contradict what we believe the Scriptures teach, then they are sinful actions, not godly ones.[7]

Why is this admonition in Rom. 14 so important? And how does it have application today? Why doesn't Paul merely tell the Jews to "shape up" and stop clinging to their dietary restrictions and sabbaths and feast days? Why does he instead put pressure on the Gentiles to accept the Jews and to accommodate their customs? Why does he tell the Jews not to judge the Gentiles for living freely? These are important questions. The answer spans from vs. 7-13, which I have saved for last.

REMEMBER: THE JUDGMENT SEAT OF CHRIST IS COMING

> **Rom. 14:7 For none of us lives to himself, and no one dies to himself.**
> **14:8 For if we live, we live to the Lord; and if we die, we die to the Lord. Therefore, whether we live or die, we are the Lord's.**

If you are God's child, then you belong to the Lord while living; after death, you still belong to the Lord. Death doesn't end your relationship with him.

> **Rom. 14:9 For to this end Christ died and rose and lived again, that He might be Lord of both the dead and the living.**

Christ died for all mankind, and He arose and lives again. Thus, He is Lord of both the living and the dead. This implies that the dead are accountable to Him also. All mankind will stand before Him in judgment. That being the case, Paul drops v. 10 like a bomb:

> **Rom. 14:10 But why do you judge your brother? Or**

why do you show contempt for your brother? For we shall all stand before the judgment seat of Christ.

Paul is essentially saying (my paraphrase):

Jewish believers, why do you judge your Gentile brethren for eating what they want and not celebrating certain days as special? Gentile believers, why do you look down upon your Jewish brethren for holding to a special diet that has been their hallmark for centuries and for observing feast days and sabbaths as they have done for countless generations? Remember, we are all going to stand before the Judgment Seat of Christ and give an account for our lives. So you'd better treat your brothers and sisters in Christ honorably!

ALL MANKIND WILL BOW AND CONFESS JESUS AS LORD

Paul then broadens the circle to include *all mankind*, not merely children of God:

Rom. 14:11 For it is written: *"As I live, says the LORD, EVERY knee shall bow to Me, and EVERY tongue shall confess to God."* (emphasis mine)

Rom. 14:11 quotes Isa. 45:23, which refers to *all mankind*, not merely believers:

Isa. 45:22 "Look to Me, and be saved, ALL you ends of the earth! For I *am* God, and *there is* no other.
23 I have sworn by Myself; the word has gone out of My mouth *in* righteousness, and shall not return, that to Me EVERY knee shall bow, EVERY tongue shall take an oath.
24b To Him *men* shall come, and all shall be ashamed who are incensed against Him. (emphasis mine)

Notice that God is speaking to *all mankind*. He calls *all* to Him to be saved (delivered). Then God predicts that *every* knee will bow and *every* tongue will confess that He is Lord. This is the ultimate salvation of all mankind through Jesus Christ.

Opponents of universal reconciliation claim that this bowing of the knee and confessing with the mouth that Jesus is Lord will be forced upon all mankind, but it does not mean that all will be saved. However, Thomas Talbott writes:

> [Paul] chose a verb that throughout the Septuagint implies not only confession, but the offer of praise and thanksgiving as well ... [which] can only come from the heart.[8]

Notice in Isa. 45:24: "all shall be ashamed who are incensed against Him." How will they become ashamed? By spending time in the lake of fire and brimstone, which is not merely for punishment, but also for remedial purposes, to bring all mankind to the point of being ashamed in God's presence. *All* will confess Him as Lord (i.e., Master). I can imagine sinners crying out, "Lord, you were right; I was wrong. I lived wickedly though I should have lived righteously. I now humble myself before you and bow in obedience, confessing that you are now my Lord, giving you praise for your great mercy!"

This truth of Scripture — that *every* knee will bow and *every* tongue will confess — is mentioned three times in Scripture — Isa. 45:23; Rom. 14:11; Phil. 2:10-11.

> **Phil. 2:9-11** Therefore God also has highly exalted Him and given Him the name which is above every name, that at the name of Jesus EVERY knee should bow, of those in heaven, and of those on earth, and of those under the earth, and *that* EVERY tongue should confess that Jesus Christ *is* Lord, to the glory of God the Father. (emphasis mine)

THOSE IN HEAVEN AND ON EARTH AND UNDER THE EARTH

Notice who will bow: those in heaven and those on earth and those under the earth. YLT translates: "of heavenlies, and earthlies, and what are under the earth." Those in the "heavenlies" are the supernatural realm, both good and evil. Those in the "earthlies" are living mankind. Those "under the earth" are the dead and perhaps also the demonic realm. *Every* knee will bow; *every* tongue will confess. Paul already confirmed this universal salvation in Jesus Christ earlier in Romans:

> **Rom. 5:18** Through one man's offense *judgment* came to all men, resulting in condemnation, even so through one Man's righteous act *the free gift came* to ALL men, resulting in justification of life.

If words have meaning, then *every* means *every* and *all* means *all*! In my opinion, those who hold to eternal conscious torment short-change God's love and mercy and justice — and even His Word!

Notice the culmination of this glorious salvation of all men, found in the book of Revelation:

> **Rev. 5:13** EVERY creature which is in heaven and on the earth and under the earth and such as are in the sea, and all that are in them, I heard saying: "Blessing and honor and glory and power *be* to Him who sits on the throne, and to the Lamb, forever and ever!" (emphasis mine)

Again, *every* means *every*! Back in Rom. 14, Paul includes a warning in v. 12:

JUDGMENT DAY IS COMING!

> **Rom. 14:12 So then each of us shall give account of himself to God.**

Believers will be resurrected and judged at the Judgment Seat (Bema) of Christ *before* the Millennium. Unbelievers will be resurrected and judged at the Great White Throne Judgment *after* the Millennium. A day of reckoning is coming for all mankind.

Let's make this personal. *You* will stand before God in judgment, and *you* will give an account for how you lived. Your reward will either be positive or negative.

2 Cor. 5:10 For we must all appear before the judgment seat of Christ, that each one may receive the things *done* in the body, according to what he has done, whether good or bad.

11 Knowing, therefore, the terror of the Lord, we persuade men.

In this context, Paul is not saying, "Go out and convince the lost to be saved (regenerated), knowing the terror of the Lord." Rather, he is saying, "Go out and convince believers that they need to be ready to meet Jesus in judgment and give a good account!"

Because of the Reformation, Christians are largely being taught the erroneous doctrine that *all* children of God will be rewarded at Christ's Bema Seat, but that is not correct. Only the good (righteous) and faithful (persevering in faith) will hear "Well done!" (see Matt. 25:21, 23). All others will be naked and ashamed, relegated to the darkness outside New Jerusalem, which will be the earthly realm of the kingdom. In light of this truth, Paul concludes in v. 13:

> **Rom. 14:13 Therefore let us not judge one another anymore, but rather resolve this, not to put a stumbling block or a cause to fall in *our* brother's way.**

Hodges says: "We are neither to 'trip up' *our brother*, nor cause him to be 'ensnared.'"[9] Let God judge your brethren, or else you will be judged!

In closing, I must ask an important question: Why is it so important that the Jews and Gentiles get along in harmony in the church of Jesus Christ? Paul answers that gloriously in ch. 15, which will be discussed in the next chapter, but let's have a sneak preview — look at 15:10:

> **Rom. 15:10** Again he says: *"Rejoice, O Gentiles, with His people!"*

This is a quote from Deut. 32:43, and it is a prophetic reference to the Messianic kingdom. In other words, Paul urges the Jews and Gentiles to accept each other — both weak and strong — to picture the harmonious Messianic reign, in which the Gentiles will join the

Jews in rejoicing and praising the Messianic king, glorifying God for His mercy (Rom. 15:9). That future unity of worship should characterize Christ's church *now*! Those who have that spirit of love toward their Christian brethren in this age will be rewarded to co-rule with Him as His bride in the next age. Do you have that spirit of love toward your Christian brethren?

CHAPTER 32
GLORIFYING GOD WITH ONE MIND AND VOICE
ROMANS 15

One day, after all mankind has been resurrected, *every* knee will bow and *every* tongue will confess that Jesus Christ is Lord, to the glory of God the Father. The result of that bowing and confessing will be universal worship of the Lamb of God. Again, I quote the marvelous passage from Revelation:

> **Rev. 5:13** EVERY creature which is in heaven and on the earth and under the earth and such as are in the sea, and all that are in them, I heard saying: "Blessing and honor and glory and power *be* to Him who sits on the throne, and to the Lamb, forever and ever!" (emphasis mine)

God will be worshipped universally throughout the ages by every human being who has ever lived on planet Earth. That is an indisputable truth of Scripture. But that is not the case in our present age, not even within the church of Jesus Christ. It is certainly not the case in the church at Rome to whom Paul is writing.

A PERENNIAL PROBLEM WITHIN THE CHURCH

The major obstacle standing in the way of glorifying God in the church at Rome is division and disunity, and that also continues to be a problem in the modern church. Believers are on different pages, so to speak, and they cannot seem to put aside their differences and move forward in unity for the cause of Christ and for the sake of the gospel. The problem is epidemic.

The particular problem in Rome in Paul's day was that the Jewish believers were finding it difficult to let go of their Jewish identifiers — observing the feast days and sabbaths and dietary restrictions. The Gentiles did not have this problem, for they were never subject to any law. They found it easier to enjoy their freedom in Christ — that is, freedom to *obey* Him — as opposed to the Jews, who felt compelled to continue living as Jews, distinct in the culture. Instead of receiving one another, division had resulted in disunity.

Jan Bonda helps us to understand what a significant problem this was in the church:

> Just imagine: a church in which some observe the Sabbath in honor of the Lord, while some feel that this day has no special significance; a church in which some refrain from eating certain things to honor the Lord, while others do not refrain from eating certain things in honor of the Lord! That was the situation (Rom. 14:6). One group does in honor of the Lord what the other group refuses to do in honor of the same Lord. How can the members there "live in harmony with one another," and "with one voice glorify" God, as Paul writes in 15:5-6?[1]

Thus, Paul reiterates what he taught in ch. 14:

Rom. 15:1 We then who are strong ought to bear with the scruples of the weak, and not to please ourselves.

APPLICATION FOR MODERN BELIEVERS AND CHURCHES

By way of application, are you willing to forego certain behaviors and activities while in the presence of others who are weaker, so as not to cause them to stumble? Zane Hodges comments:

Of course, this injunction has general application well beyond the issue of eating and drinking. This is a great principle for marriage, sports teams, work, driving, neighborhoods, and all of life.) While there is nothing wrong with believers enjoying the things God has given us to enjoy (cf. 1 Tim 6:17), we must not stubbornly do so while knowingly injuring other believers in our church.[2]

Incidentally, how does this apply in the modern church? We know that Paul was writing specifically about the problem of those Jewish believers who saw the need to continue observing certain aspects of the Mosaic law in order to honor the Lord, but could this have other applications? Hodges' follow-up comment is helpful:

> What Paul has in mind is situations where the weaker brother is directly present; that is, any time we are breaking bread together. We are not enjoined to live in fear that our *private actions* will hurt the weaker brother. We should simply make sure that we do not flaunt our liberty.[3]

GOD COMMANDS MUTUAL ACCEPTANCE

However, this is not merely to be one way! Paul urges *mutual acceptance*, which is a "two-way street."

> **Rom. 14:3** Let not him who eats despise him who does not eat, and let not him who does not eat judge him who eats; for God has received him.

So those who are *weak* — who cannot do in good conscience what those who are *strong* can do — must not get offended by the freedom of the strong, as long as it doesn't violate God's moral laws. Choices like these — "on both sides of the aisle," so to speak — must be made lovingly, not begrudgingly. When genuine love is the spirit of believers, harmony and unity will flourish within the church of Jesus Christ, bringing the body into greater maturity and conformity to Christ.

Paul summarizes what should be the spirit of believers within the church of Jesus Christ:

> **Rom. 15:2 Let each of us please *his* neighbor for *his* good, leading to edification.**

Are you willing to do what is necessary to please your brothers and sisters in Christ for their good, for the purpose of building them up? Sadly, many Christians do not have this goal, and so they end up breaking apart relationships in the church rather than building up.

MOTIVATIONS FOR PLEASING OUR CHRISTIAN BRETHREN

Three motivations are given in the text for pleasing our Christian brethren:

1. THE EXAMPLE OF JESUS

> **Rom. 15:3 For even Christ did not please Himself; but as it is written, *"The reproaches of those who reproached You fell on Me."***

Jesus did not live to please Himself, but to please the Father. The latter half of this verse is a quote from Psalm 69:9b, but what does it mean? When Jesus was on Earth, He was despised and rejected by the Jewish people. They were actually reproaching God Himself, but Jesus — the incarnation of God on Earth — bore the brunt of it. Knowing this, we should be willing to please others over and above ourselves. A second motivation is given for pleasing our Christian brethren:

2. THE HOPE OF FUTURE REWARD

> **Rom. 15:4 For whatever things were written before were written for our learning, that we through**

> the patience and comfort of the Scriptures might
> have hope.

The *things written before* certainly include the Old Testament and very likely the New Testament epistles already written — at least James and Galatians, perhaps more. The Old Testament prophets spoke of the coming Messianic kingdom, which Jesus did not launch at His first coming.

Thus, those who believe Jesus to be the Messiah, long for His return and the establishment of His kingdom. Many believers desire to be considered worthy of ruling as His bride and co-regents in the kingdom. This hope, Paul says, should motivate us as believers to live peaceably with other believers. Our verdict at the Judgment Seat is at stake, as Paul has already pointed out Rom. 14:

> **Rom. 14:10** But why do you judge your brother? Or why do you show contempt for your brother? For we shall all stand before the judgment seat of Christ.

A third motivation is given in the text for pleasing our Christian brethren:

3. THE PROSPECT OF GLORIFYING GOD

> **Rom. 15:5-6** Now may the God of patience and
> comfort grant you to be like-minded toward one
> another, according to Christ Jesus, that you may
> with one mind *and* one mouth [voice] glorify the
> God and Father of our Lord Jesus Christ.
> **15:7** Therefore receive one another, just as Christ
> also received us, to the glory of God.

When weaker brethren and stronger brethren have a healthy respect for one another and receive one another as Paul admonishes, then they are like-minded and glorify God together. Of course, the opposite is also true. When believers are at odds with other believers in their local church, and not receiving one another in a spirit of love, there is not a spirit of unity and harmony and like-mindedness, and God is not being glorified. That is tragic, especially in light of future, universal glory that will be given to God. Rev. 5:13 was already quoted above.

God wants believers to glorify Him *now* through their unified voices. Those who do, will be rewarded. The Holman Christian Standard Bible translates these verses:

> **Rom. 15:5-6 (HCSB)** Now may the God who gives endurance and encouragement allow you to live in harmony with one another, according to the command of Christ Jesus, so that you may glorify the God and Father of our Lord Jesus Christ with a united mind and voice.

So, as Paul says in v. 7, we need to receive one another as Jesus received all of us, so we can glorify Him. What a motivation!

GLORIOUS PROPHECIES FROM THE OLD TESTAMENT

Paul continues with a series of marvelous quotations from the prophecies of the Old Testament. The first is quoted from Psalm 18:49, which King David sang as praise to the Lord, after God had delivered from all of his enemies.

> **Rom. 15:8-9 Now I say that Jesus Christ has become a servant to the circumcision for the truth of God, to confirm the promises *made* to the fathers, and that the Gentiles might glorify God for *His* mercy, as it is written: *"For this reason I will confess to You among the Gentiles, and sing to Your name."***

Paul says the Messiah came to confirm the promises made to your forefathers, so that the Gentiles might share in the blessings of those promises, glorifying God for His great mercy. The next two quotations are found in vs. 10-11, which quote Deut. 32:43 and Ps. 117:1, respectively.

> Rom. 15:10 And again he says: *"Rejoice, O Gentiles, with His people!"*
> 15:11 And again: *"Praise the LORD, all you Gentiles! Laud Him, all you peoples!"*

How magnificent! Jews and Gentiles rejoicing and glorifying God together! These quotations and their original sources in the Old Testament are obviously referring to the coming Messianic kingdom. One final quotation is given in v. 12, which quotes Isa. 11:10.

> Rom. 15:12 And again, Isaiah says: *"There shall be a root of Jesse; and He who shall rise to reign over the Gentiles, in Him the Gentiles shall hope."*

This passage is also Messianic, about the wolf and lamb dwelling peaceably. A glorious utopian age is coming! Jesus — the root of Jesse, which is another way of saying "a descendant of David" — will reign over the Gentiles, and in Him they will hope. Indeed, we are presently longing for His return. It will be a glorious age indeed!

UNIVERSAL PRAISE BEGINS NOW, IN THE CHURCH

Bonda writes about the importance of present Jewish-Gentile relations in the church as key to future unity:

> Paul viewed the church of Jews and Gentiles as the beachhead to God's future. That future was, "Rejoice, O Gentiles, with his people," and: "Let all the peoples praise him" (15:10-11). The church was a beginning of this future: There, already, the Gentiles *rejoiced together with his people.*
>
> If this venture were to end in failure, if in the church the non-Jewish members could not praise him together with the Jewish members, then this praise of God by all nations together with his people Israel would never come about. This is Paul's motive when he writes, "Welcome one another, therefore, just as Christ has welcomed you, for the glory of God."[4]

Do you see what Bonda is saying? God wants the Gentile believers to receive the Jewish believers, *as Jews*. Their unique identification as God's chosen people — as seen through their dietary restrictions and observance of special days — distinguishes them from the Gentiles. The Jews, however, must not expect the Gentile believers to become Jewish in their identity. The two groups must receive one another in a spirit of love and sensitivity.

Through this show of love and harmony between the two nationalistic groups, the church of Jesus Christ will be portraying the glorious coming Messianic kingdom, in which Jews and Gentiles will praise God together as one people under Messiah. If the church fails in this by segregating themselves, then the picture that God intends to convey by the church will not be portrayed to the world. Thus, Paul prays for the church:

FILLED WITH JOY, PEACE, FAITH, AND HOPE

> **Rom. 15:13 Now may the God of hope fill you with all joy and peace in believing, that you may abound in hope by the power of the Holy Spirit.**

Paul wants the believers at Rome to be filled with joy and peace as they believe God about the importance of accepting one another. If they will do so, in the power of the Holy Spirit, they will abound in *hope* — that is, they will confidently expect a glorious future kingdom of Jews and Gentiles dwelling together peaceably. Bonda continues:

> This blessing involves a mandate: "Welcome one another." Jews and non-Jews in the church must accept each other as Christ has accepted them: the Jews as Jewish and the Gentiles as Gentile. As long as the church refuses to do this, she will not be filled with this hope for the world of which Paul speaks.[5]

Paul carried out his ministry to the churches with their end goal in sight:

> Rom. 15:14 Now I myself am confident concerning you, my brethren, that you also are full of goodness, filled with all knowledge, able also to admonish one another.
> 15:15 Nevertheless, brethren, I have written more boldly to you on *some* points, as reminding you, because of the grace given to me by God,
> 15:16 that I might be a minister of Jesus Christ to the Gentiles, ministering the gospel of God, that the offering of the Gentiles might be acceptable, sanctified by the Holy Spirit.
> 15:17 Therefore I have reason to glory in Christ Jesus in the things *which pertain* to God.
> 15:18 For I will not dare to speak of any of those things which Christ has not accomplished through me, in word and deed, to make the Gentiles obedient—
> 15:19 in mighty signs and wonders, by the power of the Spirit of God, so that from Jerusalem and round about to Illyricum I have fully preached the gospel of Christ.
> 15:20 And so I have made it my aim to preach the gospel, not where Christ was named, lest I should build on another man's foundation,
> 15:21 but as it is written: *"To whom He was not announced, they shall see; and those who have not heard shall understand."*

Paul starts by commending the church in v. 14, and referring to them as "full of goodness." He also compliments them as being "able also to admonish (warn, reprove) one another." Interestingly, this word is used in view of the Judgment Seat of Christ (v. 10). Only *spiritual* believers are able to do this.

HOW PAUL MINISTERED TO ACHIEVE THE GOAL

The apostle continues by mentioning at least three ways in which he ministered:

1. He preached the gospel of Christ (v. 19) — also known as "the gospel of God" in v. 16 — which is the gospel of kingdom inheritance.
2. He helped the Gentiles become obedient (v. 18) and sanctified by the Holy Spirit (v. 16), so that they might be acceptable to God (justified in a behavioral sense).
3. He helped the Gentiles see the debt of gratitude they owe to the Jews for becoming "partakers of their spiritual things" (v. 27).

By teaching these things, Paul hoped to bring the Gentiles to spiritual maturity, so they would receive the Jews and portray to the world the unity amongst believers, and the ultimate unity in Christ's Messianic kingdom. He preached and taught and ministered these things starting at Jerusalem and round about to Illyricum. We know from the book of Acts that he ministered on his missionary journeys throughout Asia Minor and even Greece. But apparently, he went as far as Illyricum, though we don't read anything about this in the book of Acts.

Illyricum is the southern part of eastern Europe, separated from Italy by the Adriatic Sea. Today, this includes the countries Slovenia, Serbia, Croatia, Bosnia, Albania, Macedonia. Whether Paul actually traveled there to minister or perhaps ministered to people from these regions who were living in Asia Minor and Greece, we don't know.

Paul said he ministered the gospel everywhere where Christ was not already named. This may mean where Christ was not readily being confessed, which is normal protocol for missionaries. Perhaps that's why he had not yet gone to Rome, because the gospel was already well-established in that region and the church of Jesus Christ had already formed.

ON THE WAY TO SPAIN

Paul then expressed his desire to visit them in Rome on his way to Spain.

> **Rom. 15:22 For this reason I also have been much hindered from coming to you.**
> **15:23 But now no longer having a place in these parts, and having a great desire these many years to come to you,**
> **15:24 whenever I journey to Spain, I shall come to you. For I hope to see you on my journey, and to be helped on my way there by you, if first I may enjoy your** *company* **for a while.**

Paul hopes they will support him financially on his planned journey to Spain. However, he never mention this in his introduction in ch. 1, because he knows they are not spiritually ready to help him. They have division and disunity in their midst due to ethnic prejudices. The Greeks — i.e., the cultured Gentiles who consider themselves Greco-Roman — look down upon the Jews and upon the barbarians (the primitive Gentiles in the far reaches of the Roman empire; in Spain, for instance).

Paul is hopeful that now that they have read his letter, they will change their attitudes and accept his mission to Spain, even to the extent of supporting him. But before traveling to Rome to visit with them, he must first go to Jerusalem. He shares the reason for going to Jerusalem so that they will pray for him and appreciate the Jewish people all the more.

THE EXAMPLE OF THE MACEDONIAN AND ACHAEAN BELIEVERS

To motivate the Roman Christians, Paul uses the believers of Macedonia and Achaia as examples:

> **Rom. 15:25 But now I am going to Jerusalem to minister to the saints.**

15:26 For it pleased those from Macedonia and Achaia to make a certain contribution for the poor among the saints who are in Jerusalem.
15:27 It pleased them indeed, and they are their debtors. For if the Gentiles have been partakers of their spiritual things, their duty is also to minister to them in material things.
15:28 Therefore, when I have performed this and have sealed to them this fruit, I shall go by way of you to Spain.
15:29 But I know that when I come to you, I shall come in the fullness of the blessing of the gospel of Christ.
15:30 Now I beg you, brethren, through the Lord Jesus Christ, and through the love of the Spirit, that you strive together with me in prayers to God for me,
15:31 that I may be delivered from those in Judea who do not believe, and that my service for Jerusalem may be acceptable to the saints,
15:32 that I may come to you with joy by the will of God, and may be refreshed together with you.

The Gentiles in these regions of Greece have collected a substantial offering for the Jewish believers in Jerusalem who are suffering in poverty. Paul says it pleased the Gentiles to do this (v. 27), for they feel as if they owe a spiritual debt to the Jews for bringing them Messiah. So the least they can do is pay back the debt in small measure through a material (i.e., monetary) gift to help their brethren.

After delivering the offering to the Jerusalem church, Paul expects to visit the Roman Christians. We know from our historical vantage point that Paul's life is threatened in Jerusalem by the Jews who want to kill him. For his own protection, the Romans arrest Paul and put him on trial, and then he appeals to the Caesar. So he does eventually make it to Rome, but not on his timetable and not freely. He arrives under arrest and under guard by the Romans, and he is kept under house arrest in Rome while awaiting trial. Of course, Paul doesn't know any of this when he is writing the epistle to the Romans, because it hasn't happened yet. We know, because we have the advantage of reading the book of Acts and seeing the end of the story.

One thing is clear from v. 31. The apostle expects trouble in Jerusalem from those Jews who do not believe Jesus is Messiah, so he urges the Roman Christians to pray for his Jerusalem ministry, that the Jews will be receptive.

THE TRAGEDY IN JERUSALEM

Upon arriving in Jerusalem, Paul delivers the offering and meets with the elders of the church to give an account of the Gentile ministry.

> **Acts 21:19** When he had greeted them [i.e., James and the elders of the Jerusalem church], he told in detail those things which God had done among the Gentiles through his ministry.
>
> **20** And when they heard *it*, they glorified the Lord. And they said to him, "You see, brother, how many myriads of Jews there are who have believed, and they are all zealous for the law;
>
> **21** but they have been informed about you that you teach all the Jews who are among the Gentiles to forsake Moses, saying that they ought not to circumcise *their* children nor to walk according to the customs."

James and the Jerusalem church elders put pressure on Paul to demonstrate his solidarity with the Jews by accompanying four Jewish men to the temple to conclude their temporary Nazirite vows. The sponsor would not only show support but also pay their expenses. Here's what James and the elders ask of Paul:

> **Acts 21:24** Take them and be purified with them, and pay their expenses so that they may shave *their* heads, and that all may know that those things of which they were informed concerning you are nothing, but *that* you yourself also walk orderly and keep the law.

Paul should not have agreed to this, but he does. While he is at the temple, Jews from Asia (who had persecuted him there) cause an uproar and are going to kill him. But at just the right moment, the Roman soldiers rush in and take him into custody for his own safety.

THE POTENTIAL IMPACT ON THE ROMAN CHURCH

Bonda explains how Paul anticipated a potential crisis in Jerusalem before arriving there, and the profound impact such a crisis would have on Jewish-Gentile relations in Rome. Thus, he seeks the sincere prayers of the brethren in Rome:

> Many in Jerusalem had grave misgivings with regard to Paul's work among the Gentiles. The story of what happened when he arrived illustrates this: Thousands of Jews have come to believe, and "all are zealous for the law." They feared that Paul's work would result in churches that would relinquish the tie with the Jewish people and its service to God (Acts 21:20-21).
>
> Precisely the behavior of the strong [Gentile believers] in Rome was apt to strengthen those doubts. As a result the Jerusalem church might refuse to accept the tangible proof of fellowship ([the offering from Macedonia] Rom. 15:31). <u>Thus these Gentile churches — God's beachhead to the nations — would be detached from Israel, the people through which God seeks to bring about his saving plan for all humanity.</u> The church in Rome had to be aware of what was at stake![6] (underline added).

The mission to Jerusalem is critical! Paul desperately needs the prayers of the Roman believers, because he knows there is tension arising from the legalistic Jews who insist the Gentiles must become Jewish proselytes if they are to be righteous before God. There is no other way to be sanctified, they claim. This legalism and divisiveness would destroy the unity God desires between Jewish believers and the Gentile believers. Furthermore, it would rob God of the glory that is due to Him, and it would rob the world of the beautiful picture of what God intends to accomplish in the Millennium.

Consequently, Paul's goal is to *unite* Jew and Gentile in Christ and, to that end, he urges the strong to accept the weak and the weak not to judge the strong. If they will unite in this matter then, as Paul says in v. 6, they will "with one mind and one mouth [voice] glorify ... God." Moreover, they will picture in advance — as Paul says in vs. 9-12 — the glorious unity of Jews and Gentiles in the coming Messianic kingdom.

THE CHURCH'S PROGRESS THROUGH THE CENTURIES

How has the church progressed in this goal throughout the centuries? In one word, *miserably*. There are two reasons for this.

First, as we have already seen, the Judaizers put tremendous pressure on Christians, insisting that to live righteously and become sanctified unto reward, they must keep the Old Testament rituals. Paul taught vigorously against this, as we have seen in Galatians and in the earlier chapters of Romans.

Continuing to observe the markers of Jewishness to honor the Lord is one thing, which the Gentiles could accept, but requiring it of Gentiles as a requirement for sanctification (soul-salvation) is legalism, which Paul condemned.

Second, the church has progressed miserably in its goal, because — at the other end of the spectrum — the Gentile believers were repulsed by the aggressiveness and viciousness of these Judaizers who were trying to make them Jewish. This prompted the Gentile Christians to further segregate themselves from their Jewish brethren. Consequently, the churches did not become unified, but more divided.

In fact, the division so intensified during the early centuries of the church, to the point that the Jewish believers started their own Messianic congregations, segregated from their Gentile brethren — and the Gentiles were glad to let them go their separate ways. That is why today only a very tiny percentage of churches are comprised of Jewish believers. Most of the Jewish believers have formed Messianic congregations, which are very Jewish by nature, geared to the Jewish dietary restrictions and observance of sabbaths and feast days. Gentiles are welcome, but they are essentially viewed as the weaker brethren, which seems to be the opposite of what Paul intended for the church.

INCREASED ANIMOSITY

On the Gentile side of things, animosity toward the Jews increased through the early centuries. Bonda writes:

> After two centuries the church in Rome had become a church which fiercely opposed the Jews of the synagogue. The replacement doctrine, the teaching of the substitution of the church for Israel, had taken hold. The vast majority of Jews had rejected their Messiah, and that had sealed the fate of the Jewish people. Jerusalem was destroyed, and its temple was no more. God no longer needed them.
>
> A new people replaced the former people. The church grew, and Christianity became the official religion of the empire. The victory of the Christian faith was ample proof that the God of Israel was now the God of the church and no longer the God of the Jews. The pride of the Gentiles had persisted and done its work. The Gentile Christians wanted distance: Christians had nothing to do with Jews![7]

THE HIJACKING OF THE REFORMATION

Bonda quotes a Jewish Christian scholar, Jacob Jocz, as saying:

> The church of history has shown herself to be the greatest enemy of the Jewish people. The church has, therefore, been the first and foremost stumbling block in Jewish appreciation of Jesus.[8]

The Reformation did not change any of this. In fact, as noted in Chapter 21 of this book, it fueled the fires, as Martin Luther was avowedly antisemitic, holding to replacement theology, and so was Calvin after him. Satan hijacked the Reformation! The irony is that today, Reformation theology pervades the church of Jesus Christ, including churches that claim no Reformation or Protestant heritage. Many doctrines that are readily taught as orthodox today are actually heretical. But Satan has spun it the other direction, so that those who teach biblical doctrines are the ones branded as heretics.

I urgently call Christianity to remove Reformation glasses and start viewing the New Testament biblically rather than theologically! My prayer is that churches everywhere will have the spirit of Rom. 15:6 — that we might "with one mind and one voice glorify ... God" — and as v. 33 says, may "the God of peace be with [us] all." To that I join Paul in a hearty "Amen!."

CHAPTER 33
CRUSHING THE DEVIL
ROMANS 16:1-24

How do you kill a venomous snake? Experts say you must crush its head. During my childhood years, I remember visiting one of our family friends on his ranch in Tennessee. I was especially intrigued by a six ft. long rattlesnake skin which was mounted on the wall of his family room. He told me that he was putting up a fence on his property when a rattlesnake struck at him, but missed. Our friend instantly grabbed a metal pipe and crushed the head of the serpent. He had the snake skin mounted as a demonstration of his victory.

An evangelist friend of mine used to travel throughout Southeast Asia in ministry. Years ago, he told my family an interesting story around the dinner table. On one of his journeys to rural India, he heard a dog barking outside of his hotel window. He looked out the window and noticed a king cobra striking down at the dog. The dog dodged it every time.

Interestingly, cobras do not coil and strike; they stand and strike, and they typically stand about one-third of their total body length. So an eighteen ft. king cobra stands about six ft. tall and can look a man in the eye. How terrifying! Further, the hood on king cobras can be almost as wide as a human head.

My friend watched as an Indian man snuck up behind the cobra and whacked the snake on its back, just below the head, with a large stick. Instantly, the snake fell dead. That is how you kill venomous snakes, though I don't recommend that you try that at home.

Interestingly, the Bible uses the imagery of a snake and sometimes even a dragon to refer to Satan. Thus, we picture in our minds a hideous creature that is highly venomous and destructive. He has already been disarmed and rendered powerless by Christ, and because of that truth we are promised that Satan will be trampled under our feet shortly.

> **Rom. 16:20a And the God of peace will crush Satan under your feet shortly.**

However, before expositing the end of the chapter, we must start at the beginning:

> **Rom. 16:1 I commend to you Phoebe our sister, who is a servant of the church in Cenchrea,**
> **16:2 that you may receive her in the Lord in a manner worthy of the saints, and assist her in whatever business she has need of you; for indeed she has been a helper of many and of myself also.**
> **16:3 Greet Priscilla and Aquila, my fellow workers in Christ Jesus,**
> **16:4 who risked their own necks for my life, to whom not only I give thanks, but also all the churches of the Gentiles.**
> **16:5 Likewise *greet* the church that is in their house. Greet my beloved Epaenetus, who is the firstfruits of Achaia to Christ.**
> **16:6 Greet Mary, who labored much for us.**
> **16:7 Greet Andronicus and Junia, my countrymen and my fellow prisoners, who are of note among the apostles, who also were in Christ before me.**

GREETINGS TO THE BRETHREN

The passage continues in this fashion, down through v. 16.

If I were to write the church that I formerly pastored in Pennsylvania, I would include a few paragraphs to greet all the dear people that I once knew so well and ministered to over the course of eleven years. I would probably recall some of the endearing memories we had with those folks, as Paul does here. Granted, the apostle had not pastored the church at Rome. In fact, as of the time of writing, he had not even travelled there yet. But many of the folks he met along his missionary journeys — and to whom he ministered — were there in Rome, for one reason or another. He greets twenty-six individuals.

John Niemela, in the *Introduction* to Zane Hodge's commentary on Romans says:

> Paul greets fifteen distinct groups of believers in Rom 16:3-15. Each use of... "greet" distinguishes an autonomous assembly.
>
> The first church mentioned met in a home: "Greet Pricilla and Aquila...[and] the church that is in their house" (Rom 16:3-5). None of the others listed are specifically said to meet in a house. Probably most or all of the other fourteen listed churches met in tiny tenement rooms (about 10 feet by 10 feet). Hence, these are referred to as *tenement churches* (in contrast with larger *house churches*).
>
> Though Paul had not been to Rome, he was acquainted with a host of people there, having met (during his various missionary journeys) many of those he mentions.[1]

AVOIDING THOSE CAUSING DIVISIONS AND OFFENSES

After these endearing greetings, Paul admonishes the church:

> **Rom. 16:17 Now I urge you, brethren, note those who cause divisions and offenses, contrary to the doctrine which you learned, and avoid them.**

Paul urges the believers to *note* those who cause divisions and offenses. *To note* is "to pay attention to; to watch closely."[2] In colloquial English, we might say, "Keep an eye on that person."

We are to keep an eye on those who cause divisions and offenses contrary to the doctrine (teaching) we have received from God's Word. This would include individuals who persist in sinning in some fashion, so that their behavior is disruptive; it causes distractions and division in the church.

Further, we are commanded to *avoid* them. *To avoid* is "to turn away from" and "shun."[3] This is essential in church discipline cases, and here's why:

> **Rom. 16:18 For those who are such do not serve our Lord Jesus Christ, but their own belly, and by smooth words and flattering speech deceive the hearts of the simple.**
> **16:19 For your obedience has become known to all. Therefore I am glad on your behalf; but I want you to be wise in what is good, and simple concerning evil.**

The apostle commends the believers at Rome for living obediently, but he wants them to remain wise in things that are good and simple in things that are evil. Paul doesn't want them to stumble and fall prey to similar patterns of sinning. To that end, they should shun those members who are living in sinfulness and, presumably, are under church discipline.

SHUNNING THOSE WHO WALK IRRESPONSIBLY

Another similar passage is found in 2 Thess. 3:

> **2 Thess. 3:6** But we command you, brethren, in the name of our Lord Jesus Christ, that you withdraw from every brother who walks disorderly and not according to the tradition which he received from us.

A person who walks *disorderly* is one whose behavior is "irresponsible."[4] Paul makes two comments about them:

> **Rom. 16:18a** Those who are such do not serve our Lord Jesus Christ, but their own belly.

1. They are self-seeking, out to satisfy their own desires, driven by their *soul* rather than their *spirit* (and God's Spirit). Paul spoke of fleshly believers of this nature in Phil. 3:

> **Phil. 3:18-19** For many walk, of whom I have told you often, and now tell you even weeping, *that they are* the enemies of the cross of Christ: whose end *is* destruction, whose god *is their* belly, and *whose* glory *is* in their shame—who set their mind on earthly things.

What a tragedy! Yet there are people like this from time to time in the church of Jesus Christ. Paul makes a second comment about them:

> **Rom. 16:18b** by smooth words and flattering speech deceive the hearts of the simple.

2. They are hypocritical, putting on a polished outward act, thereby deceiving undiscerning believers. In other words, whether they do it intentionally or not, they "schmooze" other believers into thinking they are good and spiritual, when in reality they are not. In fact, church members are often surprised when a person like this becomes the object of church discipline.

A WONDERFUL PROMISE

Amidst the warning to avoid people of this nature, who are actually being used as tools of Satan, Paul inserts a wonderful promise:

> **Rom. 16:20a** And the God of peace will crush Satan under your feet shortly.

The Bible says that Satan is an angel, created by God, very powerful, but not omnipotent like God. Early in his angelic career Satan rebelled against God. He had been created as a bright star, but he let his power and glory go to his head and pridefully considered himself the equal of God. As a result of this willful defiance of God, Satan was cast out of heaven. Jesus said, "I beheld Satan as lightning fall from heaven" (Luke 10:18).

Satan took one-third of the holy angels with him, and they forever after became known as fallen angels. His mission is to oppose God and destroy the work of Christ, to trip Christians up and cause them to stumble so they will be ineffective for Christ, to blind unbelievers so they will not see the truth of the gospel, and to walk around as a roaring lion seeking whom he may devour.

He is a liar and the father of all lies, a murderer from the beginning, a deceiver, a counterfeiter, and an accuser. Satan is highly effective and very powerful. Even Michael, the great archangel of God, dared not to bring a reviling accusation against him but said, "the Lord rebuke you" (Jude 9). Needless to say, we are up against a formidable foe.

SATAN RENDERED POWERLESS

Nevertheless, we have before us a promise of victory: v. 20 "the God of peace will crush Satan under your feet shortly." This verse is post-crucifixion and post-resurrection. In other words, the truth of this verse is made possible by the cross and the subsequent raising of Christ from the dead. There is great power there.

One of Christ's objectives in coming to earth was to destroy the devil.

> **1 John 3:8** For this purpose the Son of God was manifested, that He might destroy the works of the devil.

Did Christ accomplish this? Oh yes, the writer to the Hebrews said:

> **Heb. 2:14** He destroyed him who had the power of death, that is, the devil,

The word *destroyed* means "to make powerless."[5] It does *not* mean "to annihilate." As a spirit being, Satan is still very powerful when compared with mere humans. But when believers exercise their position of authority in Christ, the demon world shudders.

THREE PARADOXES IN ROM. 16:20

While Rom. 16:20 is a beautiful promise, it contains some paradoxical statements. The first is found in the statement, *the God of peace shall bruise*. Doesn't it seem odd that someone so peaceful would do something so hostile?

PARADOX #1: ENEMIES MUST BE CONQUERED FOR PEACE TO PREVAIL.

There must be war before there can be peace; that's a paradox, for it sounds rather hostile!

> **1 Cor. 15:24** Then *comes* the end, when He delivers the kingdom to God the Father, when He puts an end to all rule and all authority and power.
> 25 For He must reign till He has put all enemies under His feet.
> 26 The last enemy *that* will be destroyed *is* death.

The glorious day is coming when all enemies will be subjected and God will be all in all. That will come after the Millennium, after Satan is finally defeated, at which time Jesus will turn over the kingdom to the Father.

In Solomon's day there was peace across the promised land, but only because his father David had finished off the enemies of Israel. Enemies are a threat to peace. Of course, the great enemy of Christianity and the peace that Christ offers is Satan, along with his entire echelon of fallen angels and demons.

- He is the great disturber of the peace.

- He produces conflict, fighting and warfare.
- He is the source of hatred and murder.
- He promotes revolution and rebellion.
- He works to drive wedges between people.
- He promotes discord and disunity amongst church members and within homes.
- He delights when Christians are living in sin and have broken fellowship with God.

RIGHTEOUSNESS AND PEACE

In order to have peace in your personal life, Satan must be bruised. Christ bruised him *positionally* on the cross of Calvary, but we must bruise Him *practically* each day of our Christian lives, by defeating sin through the enabling power of the Holy Spirit. Sin is a deterrent to peace. Peace only co-exists with righteousness.

Isa. 57:21 *"There is* no peace," says my God, "for the wicked."

Ps. 85:10 Mercy and truth have met together; righteousness and peace have kissed.

Isa. 32:17 The work of righteousness will be peace, and the effect of righteousness, quietness and assurance forever.

Jas. 3:18 Now the fruit of righteousness is sown in peace by those who make peace.

Rom. 14:17 for the kingdom of God is not eating and drinking, but righteousness and peace and joy in the Holy Spirit.

Just as righteousness and peace are inseparable, so unrighteousness and turmoil are connected. Peace characterizes God's kingdom; turmoil characterizes Satan and the world system over which he presides. Jesus said:

John 14:27 Peace I leave with you, My peace I give to you; not as the world gives do I give to you.

Jesus also prayed to the Father: "Your kingdom come. Your will be done on earth as *it is* in heaven" (Matt. 6:10). Is there peace in heaven? Yes! — But only because there is righteousness. Is it God's will that there be peace on earth? Yes! But the unrighteousness of man (including the unrighteous lifestyle of believers) is holding it back.

To get victory over Satan, believers must get victory over their sinning through the power of the Holy Spirit who dwells within. The enemies of the cross of Christ must be defeated in a practical sense. We must stop being ignorant of Satan's devices and start resisting the devil so that he flees from us.

A second paradoxical statement is found in the phrase: *God will crush Satan ... under **your** feet* (16:20). Doesn't it seem odd that we, mere mortals, are to crush Satan (who is supernatural)?

PARADOX #2: GOD CRUSHES, USING OUR FEET!

The word *crush* means "to trample; to break in pieces, shatter."[6] By implication, it means "to win the victory over." Jesus used a synonym for this word in Luke's Gospel:

> **Luke 10:19** Behold, I give you the authority to trample on serpents and scorpions, and over all the power of the enemy, and nothing shall by any means hurt you.
>
> **20** Nevertheless do not rejoice in this, that the spirits are subject to you, but rather rejoice because your names are written in heaven.

By extension, as disciples of Christ, we have been given authority by Christ to trample on serpents and scorpions. This is a metaphor, for Jesus clarifies: *over all the power of the enemy*. In Luke 10:20 Jesus refers to *spirits* (i.e., the spirit world), so this passage is obviously referring to the trampling of Satan and his host.

THE POWER OF CHRIST TO DEFEAT SATAN

How can we, mere humans, possibly trample the foe? The quick answer is through Christ who strengthens us. But a deeper answer is given, starting in Phil. 2:

> **Phil. 2:5-7** Let this mind be in you which was also in Christ Jesus, who, being in the form of God, did not consider it robbery to be equal with God, but made Himself of no reputation, taking the form of a bondservant, *and* coming in the likeness of men.
>
> **8** And being found in appearance as a man, He humbled Himself and became obedient to *the point of* death, even the death of the cross.
>
> **9-11** Therefore God also has highly exalted Him and given Him the name which is above every name, that at the name of Jesus every knee should bow, of those in heaven, and of those on earth, and of those under the earth, and *that* every tongue should confess that Jesus Christ *is* Lord, to the glory of God the Father.

Jesus was rewarded by God for completing the work of redemption, by being exalted and given authority over all things. Paul expands this thought to include authority over Satan's realm.

> **Eph. 1:19-22** and what *is* the exceeding greatness of His power toward us who believe, according to the working of His mighty power which He worked in Christ when He raised Him from the dead and seated *Him* at His right hand in the heavenly *places,* far above all principality and power and might and dominion, and every name that is named, not only in this age but also in that which is to come. And He put all *things* under His feet, and gave Him *to be* head over all *things* to the church,

Christ is now seated in a position of authority at the right hand of the Father. He is far above all principality and power and might and dominion — an obvious reference to the spirit world. In other words, the spirit world, including Satan, has been placed in subjection to Christ. Remarkably, He delegates authority over the spirit world to His children!

DELEGATED AUTHORITY

> **Eph. 2:5** even when we were dead in trespasses, made us alive together with Christ (by grace you have been saved),
> **6** and raised *us* up together, and made *us* sit together in the heavenly *places* in Christ Jesus,

Not only are we made alive in Christ through initial salvation (regeneration), we are also seated together with Him in the heavenlies, which implies that we share in His authority over the spirit world. John MacMillan (1873-1956) said:

> The believer, who is fully conscious of divine Power behind him, and of his own authority thereby, can face the enemy without fear or hesitation.[7]

When we do battle against Satan and the hosts of darkness, we do so in Jesus' name, possessing his authority and power. Since Jesus has already been given the victory over Satan and the forces of darkness, we too share in that victory. We must simply claim it by faith.

We are enabled by Christ to trample the devil when we are appropriating our "throne-seat authority" — the truth of Eph. 2:5-6. Paul gives more details in Eph. 3:

> **Eph. 3:10** to the intent that now the manifold wisdom of God might be made known by the church to the principalities and powers in the heavenly *places*,
> **11** according to the eternal purpose which He accomplished in Christ Jesus our Lord,
> **12** in whom we have boldness and access with confidence through faith in Him.

APPROPRIATING THE POWER

We trample the devil in large part by preaching the unsearchable riches of Christ with great boldness and power that we receive by depending on Jesus. This is what happened to Peter on the Day of

Pentecost. He preached with such power and authority that three thousand Jews repented, and the devil was soundly defeated! John MacMillan asks:

> Why, then, is there not more manifest progress? Because a head is wholly dependent upon its body for the carrying out of its plan. All the members of its body must be subservient, that through their coordinated ministry may be accomplished what is purposed. The Lord Jesus ... is hindered in his mighty plans and working, because His body has failed to appreciate the deep meaning of His exaltation and to respond to the gracious impulses which He is consciously sending for its quickening.[8]

The qualification for possessing this authority is given in Eph. 1:

Eph. 1:19 and what *is* the exceeding greatness of His power toward us who believe,

Notice the phrase: *us who believe*. This does not mean *those who are saved*. It is an active present participle in Greek and means *those who are believing*. Have you been believing that God wants to give you abundant life and victory, and that He wants to prepare you for the Bema? Or are you living in unbelief? Without faith it is impossible to please God. Without faith, you are not possessing your rightful authority in Christ. Without faith, you are not trampling the devil. Without faith, you are not an obedient Christian. What a tragedy!

A third paradoxical statement is found in one word — *God ... will crush Satan ... shortly* (16:20). The word *shortly* means "quickly" or "soon," as in a brief space of time. Doesn't it seem odd that something written nearly two thousand years ago claims that it will happen *shortly*?

PARADOX #3: THE PROMISE TRANSCENDS TIME BUT GIVES A TIMETABLE FOR FULFILLMENT.

This promise was written by the Apostle Paul who was inspired by the Holy Spirit, and it was written in the first century AD. It applied to the church at Rome, and yet it applies to the church in the twenty-first century — and to every believer of every era of the church age — because it is a promise that transcends time. Nevertheless, the promise also gives a timetable for fulfillment, which is *shortly* — "soon!"

Some commentators claim this promise applied exclusively to the church at Rome, because according to v. 17, they had been experiencing divisions in the church. Thus, Paul writes to encourage them that Satan will be defeated in this division shortly. Other commentators claim this promise will be exclusively fulfilled in the future, when Christ returns the second time with the saints as His army to defeat Satan. But what these commentators are missing is that this promise also has a present-day fulfillment. All throughout the church age, God promises to crush Satan under the feet of the saints (see Luke 10:19-20).

Why, then, are we not seeing this happening widespread? Why is it that Satan seems to be gaining ground? Because believers are not recognizing their authority as seated with Christ, and they are not claiming the promise. Furthermore, many do not see this as a promise for today. They either relegate it to the first century or to the second coming. God says the promise is for today – soon! quickly! God's will is that we crush the devil through spiritual warfare now, in the power of Jesus Christ. Do you believe Him?

St. Andrew of Crete (660-732) wrote a poem entitled, *The Power of Evil*.

> Christian, dost thou see them
> On the holy ground,
> How the powers of darkness
> Rage thy steps around?
> Christian, up and smite them,
> Counting gain but loss;

In the strength that cometh
By the holy cross.

Christian, dost thou feel them,
How they work within,
Striving, tempting, luring,
Goading into sin?
Christian, never tremble;
Never be downcast;
Gird thee for the battle,
Thou shalt win at last.

Christian, dost thou hear them,
How they speak thee fair?
"Always fast and vigil,
Always watch and prayer?"
Christian, answer boldly;
"While I breathe, I pray!"
Peace shall follow battle.
Right shall end in day.

Well I know thy trouble,
O my servant true;
Thou art very weary,
I was weary, too;
But that toil shall make thee
Some day all Mine own.
And the end of sorrow
Shall be near My throne.[9]

CHAPTER 34
THE FELLOWSHIP OF THE MYSTERY
ROMANS 16:25-27

In closing this great epistle, Paul adds one long sentence at the end of ch. 16:

> **Rom. 16:25-27 Now to Him who is able to establish you according to my gospel and the preaching of Jesus Christ, according to the revelation of the mystery kept secret since the world began but now made manifest, and by the prophetic Scriptures made known to all nations, according to the commandment of the everlasting God, for obedience to the faith—to God, alone wise,** *be* **glory through Jesus Christ forever. Amen.**

Many commentators refer to this as the benediction, which is the bestowing of a blessing, typically at the end of something — a religious service, for example, or in this case, at the end of the epistle of Romans.

The benediction starts out, "Now to Him who is able to establish you." *Him* is obviously referring to God. Paul claims that God is able to *establish* you. To establish is *"to strengthen, make firm."*[1] God is able to strengthen and make firm those who are His children. But notice that Paul says He is *able* to establish (strengthen). Why didn't Paul say that God *strengthens*. In other words, why doesn't God simply come right out and do the work of strengthening? The word *able* implies that He has the wherewithal to make it happen, but He doesn't do it automatically. Why is that?

Sanctification is not automatic. It requires cooperation with God (see Phil. 2:12-13). Yet not all Christians have chosen to cooperate with God in the sanctification process. Those who do not cooperate with Him are not strengthened and established in the faith. Nevertheless, His intent is to strengthen those who choose to participate in His purposes (Rom. 8:28).

WHAT GOD USES TO STRENGTHEN BELIEVERS

What, specifically, does God use to strengthen believers? From the above text, three things are listed:

- *my gospel and the preaching of Jesus Christ*
- *the revelation of the mystery kept secret since the world began but now made manifest*
- *the prophetic Scriptures made known to all nations ... for obedience to the faith*

Each of these things will be examined in greater detail.

THE PREACHING OF CHRIST

The preaching of Jesus Christ, His exclusive message to Israel, can be summed up in one verse:

Matt. 4:17 From that time Jesus began to preach and to say, "Repent, for the kingdom of heaven is at hand."

Repentance is a change of mind that precipitates a change of behavior. That is the way the word is used in the Scriptures. The Jewish people of Christ's day needed to repent of their sins and get right with Jehovah God in the spirit of 2 Chron. 7:14. That applied to both legalistic sinners (the Pharisees) and licentious sinners (the tax collectors and harlots).

THE OFFER OF KINGDOM INHERITANCE

Jesus called on His people to repent in light of the *kingdom of the heavens*, which was at hand. To summarize from previous chapters in this book, Jesus was offering inheritance in heavenly New Jerusalem, the ruling realm of the coming Messianic kingdom — if the nation were to repent. In the Old Testament the Jews had been promised rulership over the nations on Earth in the Messianic kingdom. They will receive that regardless, once the nation repents at Christ's second coming, for it had been promised. But Christ was offering something more, something greater and grander.

Tragically, national Israel did not accept Christ's offer. So He took the offer away from Israel and began offering it to a new entity — the predominantly Gentile church.

> **Matt. 21:43** Therefore I say to you, the kingdom of God will be taken from you and given to a nation bearing the fruits of it.

Just as Israel had to qualify by humbling themselves, praying, seeking God's face, and turning from their wicked ways (2 Chron. 7:14), so believers of the church age must essentially qualify in the same manner — by denying self, taking up their cross, and following Jesus. To paraphrase: living righteously by faith, confessing Christ, and persevering amidst trials and persecutions. Those who meet these qualifications will inherit a place of rulership as Christ's bride and co-ruler in New Jerusalem.

This was the nature of the *gospel* preached by Christ. It is known as the *gospel of the kingdom* (see Matt. 4:23; 9:35; 24:14; Mark 1:14). Unfortunately, when most Christians hear the word *gospel*, they automatically think of the message of being saved from Hell and going to Heaven when they die. But that is not the gospel that Jesus preached. Incidentally, the *gospel of the kingdom* involves works, for it is a sanctification message, good news for people who are already believers. This is salvation of the soul in preparation for the Judgment Seat of Christ.

PAUL'S GOSPEL

When Paul uses the term *my gospel*, he is referring to the good news regarding present-tense salvation, soul-salvation or sanctification, the gospel of kingdom inheritance. But in what sense was it *his*? Didn't Jesus preach it and Peter too? What about the other disciples of Jesus? Yes, they all preached it, but what was unique about Paul's ministry was that he was chosen as God's apostle *to the Gentiles*.

> **Acts 9:15** The Lord said to him (Ananias), "Go, for he (Paul) is a chosen vessel of Mine to bear My name before Gentiles, kings, and the children of Israel."

Paul's gospel was unique, first of all, because it was primarily focused on the Gentiles. But the second reason Paul's gospel was unique is because he was the apostle that God chose to give further revelation about the church of Jesus Christ. Notice the next phrase in Rom. 16:25: *according to the revelation of the mystery kept secret since the world began but now made manifest.*

The phrase *since the world began* in Greek is *chronos aionios*, which literally translates "the time when the ages began." Thus, throughout the ages, some truth was kept hidden (a mystery) until Paul could reveal it. He revealed it mostly in the book of Ephesians, where three major mysteries are made manifest:

1. THE MYSTERY OF THE ONE NEW MAN IN CHRIST

> **Eph 2:11** (HCSB) So then, remember that at one time you were Gentiles in the flesh—called "the uncircumcised" by those called "the circumcised," which is done in the flesh by human hands.
>
> **12** At that time you were without the Messiah, excluded from the citizenship of Israel, and foreigners to the covenants of the promise, without hope and without God in the world.

13 But now in Christ Jesus, you who were far away have been brought near by the blood of the Messiah.

14-15 For He is our peace, who made both groups one and tore down the dividing wall of hostility. In His flesh, He made of no effect the law consisting of commands and expressed in regulations, so that He might create in Himself one new man from the two, resulting in peace.

16 He did this so that He might reconcile both to God in one body through the cross and put the hostility to death by it.

What a marvelous truth! Because of Christ's death, Gentiles are brought into Israel's blessings, including salvation by grace (initial salvation). Furthermore, the ritual aspects of the Mosaic law have been abolished, so that Jews and Gentiles are now one in Christ, forming the church, which is His body.

2. THE MYSTERY OF KINGDOM INHERITANCE FOR GENTILES

Eph. 3:1-2 (HCSB) For this reason, I, Paul, the prisoner of Christ Jesus on behalf of you Gentiles—you have heard, haven't you, about the administration of God's grace that He gave to me for you?

3 The mystery was made known to me by revelation, as I have briefly written above.

4 By reading this you are able to understand my insight about the mystery of the Messiah.

5 This was not made known to people in other generations as it is now revealed to His holy apostles and prophets by the Spirit:

6 The Gentiles are co-heirs, members of the same body, and partners of the promise in Christ Jesus through the gospel.

7 I was made a servant of this gospel by the gift of God's grace that was given to me by the working of His power.

8-9 This grace was given to me—the least of all the saints—to proclaim to the Gentiles the incalculable riches of the Messiah, and to shed light for all about the administration of the mystery hidden for ages in God who created all things.

10 This is so God's multi-faceted wisdom may now be made

known through the church to the rulers and authorities in the heavens.

11 This is according to His eternal purpose accomplished in the Messiah, Jesus our Lord.

This must have been glorious for the Gentiles to hear and shocking for the Jews. Jesus took the kingdom inheritance offer from Israel and began offering it to the predominantly Gentile church. Again, this is the gospel of the kingdom message, the good news of kingdom inheritance. Those who are *in Christ* — both Jews and Gentiles — can qualify to become His bride and co-rulers in the Messianic kingdom. This is *the fellowship of the mystery* that Paul wants all men to see. Incidentally, it is also what we should desire all believers to see in our era of the church age.

3. THE MYSTERY OF UNITY IN THE FAITH AS A BODY

Eph. 4:11-13 (HCSB) And He personally gave some to be apostles, some prophets, some evangelists, some pastors and teachers, for the training of the saints in the work of ministry, to build up the body of Christ, until we all reach unity in the faith and in the knowledge of God's Son, growing into a mature man with a stature measured by Christ's fullness.

14 Then we will no longer be little children, tossed by the waves and blown around by every wind of teaching, by human cunning with cleverness in the techniques of deceit.

15 But speaking the truth in love, let us grow in every way into Him who is the head —Christ.

16 From Him the whole body, fitted and knit together by every supporting ligament, promotes the growth of the body for building up itself in love by the proper working of each individual part.

Not only are Gentiles included with Jews in the body of Christ as *one new man*. Not only are Gentiles now being offered the privilege of kingdom inheritance if they will meet the qualifications. But now, through men God has gifted for the local church, Gentiles can become equipped to do the work of the ministry so that the body of Christ is edified. The ultimate goal is becoming unified together (as a body) in Christ-likeness, *to the measure of the stature of the fullness of Christ*. The pathway involves growing together in knowledge of Christ and increasing in spiritual maturity.

Incidentally, it seems Jesus will not merely judge individual believers at His Bema seat, He will also judge local churches bodies. As evidence for corporate judgment, God has given us this text in Eph. 4 and the letters to the seven *churches* in Rev. 2-3. Also, Paul said to the church at Corinth:

> **2 Cor. 4:14** knowing that He who raised up the Lord Jesus will also raise us up with Jesus, and will present *us* with you.

Those *churches* that do not take seriously the matter of division and disunity in the congregation will be judged by Jesus and may incur negative reward. That is a frightening prospect. So not only should we be preparing to meet Jesus *as individual believers*, we should also be preparing to meet Him *as churches*. As daunting as it seems, the goal is attainable through Christ, and Paul has revealed this as another aspect of the mystery.

THE PROPHETIC SCRIPTURES MADE KNOWN TO ALL NATIONS

Notice again the phrase in Rom. 16:26: *the prophetic Scriptures made known to all nations*. The Old Testament prophets repeatedly refer to the Gentile nations as coming to Jehovah in the Messianic kingdom. Paul proclaimed these truths to show that God's purposes include the Gentiles, and to demonstrate His salvation of all mankind, including the offer of soul-salvation and kingdom inheritance promises for church age saints.

All that Paul preached was *according to the commandment of the everlasting God*. God commanded that Paul preach these truths *for obedience to the faith*. When Christians understand and apply these truths, they are obeying God and thereby loving Him, and He is being glorified. Those who do so *now* will be rewarded and glorified *then*.

Verse 27 closes the epistle to the Romans with an ascription of praise to *God, alone wise, be glory through Jesus Christ forever. Amen.* May He truly be glorified in His faithful children!

ADDENDUM 1: ETERNAL IS NOT FOREVER

Adapted from the author's book: The Savior of All Men

If you were to survey a large group of Christians and ask them, "Where will the saved spend eternity?" — the overwhelming majority would say, "in Heaven." If you were to ask that same group, "Where will the unsaved spend eternity?" the overwhelming majority would say, "in Hell." I would have given those same answers for most of my life. However, from my studies of the Scriptures in recent years, I have to say that both answers are technically incorrect. I now have a new understanding of Heaven and Hell based on what God's Word actually teaches.

ETERNAL LIFE – THE MEANS TO AN END

If you have believed on Jesus for the gift of eternal life, then you possess eternal life. But have you ever deeply considered the question: *What is eternal life?* Is it an end in itself? Or is it the means to an end?

The traditional understanding is that eternal life is an end in itself, somewhat like a ticket to heaven — you either have it or you don't. Some consider it a "get-out-of-Hell-free-card." But neither of these understandings is correct. However, the Scriptures teach that eternal life is the *means* to an end.

Here's where the rub comes in. Since the time of the Reformation, Christians have been led to believe that eternal life is endless life in Heaven and eternal condemnation is endless life in Hell. That is due to an unfortunate mistranslation in most English Bibles.

The word *eternal* in the New Testament is translated from the Greek adjective *aionios*, which is derived from the noun *aion*. But here's the problem: *aion* means "age" or "eon." Its adjective *aionios* means "age-lasting," "age-during," or "for the age." The same is true in the Old Testament of the Hebrew adjective *olam* which was translated *aionios* in the Septuagint. In contrast, the English adjectives *eternal*, *everlasting*, and *forever* mean "unending" or "perpetual." Do you see the problem? English Bible versions have muddied the waters by translating the Greek adjective *aionios* and the Hebrew adjective *olam* as *eternal*, *everlasting*, or *forever*, which is incorrect.[1]

WHERE DID WE GET OFF THE PATH?

How did our English Bible versions drift so far from the correct meaning? Several scholarly books have been written on the subject, but only a summary can be provided here. The general consensus is that — despite the correct meanings of *aion* and *aionios* understood by Jesus and the writers of Scripture — something happened in the early centuries of the church that skewed the definitions for later generations of Christians.

The early fifth century church leader known as Augustine (AD 354-430) admittedly could not read Greek. Latin was his native language. Thus, he was compelled to study Scripture, using Jerome's recently translated Latin Vulgate (published in 382).

The Vulgate is known to have many translation errors, not the least of which was the translation of the Greek word *aionios* as *aeternus*, which is Latin for *eternal*. Augustine popularized the use of *aionios* as meaning eternal, though that's incorrect. During the centuries known as the Middle Ages, the Roman Catholic church popularized the meaning further, until it became the established lexical definition. By the time of the Reformers — who hailed Augustine as a theological hero — *aionios* was being unquestionably translated *eternal*. Of course, our modern English Bibles are products of the Reformation, including the revered King James Version (originally published in 1611). The unfortunate consequence is that generations of Bible readers have assumed eternal life is unending life, despite the attempts of several Bible scholars to set the record straight.

THE CORRECT MEANING OF AION AND AIONIOS

Marvin R. Vincent (1834-1922) was a Presbyterian minister and an esteemed professor of New Testament exegesis at Union Theological Seminary. He is well known for his *Word Studies in the New Testament*, a multi-volume set which is often found in the libraries of pastors and professors.

Vincent wrote an extensive note at 2 Thess. 1:9 in his *Word Studies* as to the correct meaning of the Greek adjective *aionios*. A few of the pertinent paragraphs will be quoted below:

> *Aion*, transliterated *eon*, is a period of time of longer or shorter duration, having a beginning and an end, and complete in itself ... The word always carries the notion of *time*, and not of *eternity*. It always means a period of time ... It does not mean something endless or everlasting.
>
> The adjective *aionios* in like manner carries the idea of time. Neither the noun nor the adjective, in themselves, carry the sense of *endless* or *everlasting* ... *Aionios* means *enduring through or pertaining to a period of time*. Both the noun and the adjective are applied to limited periods.
>
> *Zoe aionios*, *eternal life*, which occurs 42 times in N.T. ... is not endless life, but life pertaining to a certain age or eon, or continuing during that eon ... Life may be endless. The life in union with Christ is endless, but the fact is not expressed by *aionios*.
>
> Thus, while *aionios* carries the idea of time, though not of *endlessness*, there belongs to it also, more or less, a sense of *quality*. Its character is ethical rather than mathematical. The deepest significance of

the life beyond time lies, not in endlessness, but in the moral quality of the eon into which the life passes.[2]

Vincent is not the only scholar who makes this point. Many others do as well, including several modern Greek experts.

We should not allow Augustine, the Roman Catholic Church, and the Reformers to hijack the correct understanding of the adjective *aionios* and the term, *zoe aionios, eternal life*. Unfortunately, Reformation theology has pervaded much of our thinking in the last few hundred years, and especially so with the meaning of the words, *eternal* and *everlasting*. That is why it is so important to study the original meaning of those words at the time the Bible was written. Correct interpretation is critically important to rightly dividing the Word of God.

NOT QUANTITY BUT QUALITY

Thus, the best translation for the Greek noun *aion* is "age" and for the Greek adjective *aionios* is "age-lasting" or "age-during." YLT translates the term *zoe aionios* (*eternal life* in the KJV) as *life age-during*. Rotherham's Emphasized Bible (1902) translates it *life age-abiding*. Weymouth New Testament (1903) translates it *life for the ages*. Concordant Literal New Testament (1926) translates it *life eonian*. N.T. Wright calls it "the life of God's coming age."

Thanks to the Reformation we are programmed to think that eternal life is a ticket to heaven where we will dwell forever and ever, endlessly, and there is nothing else we need to do now to prepare for that eternal, blissful state. That is erroneous!

Nevertheless, Christians should not be alarmed by the correct translation of *aionios* as "age-during," for we will live forever! Although the Greek term *zoe aionios* — incorrectly translated *eternal life* — means "age-during life," *not* "unending life," the apostle Paul uses different words to convey the idea of unending life for believers.

> **1 Cor. 15:51-52** Behold, I tell you a mystery: We shall not all sleep, but we shall all be changed—in a moment, in the twinkling of an eye,

at the last trumpet. For the trumpet will sound, and the dead will be raised incorruptible, and we shall be changed.

53 For this corruptible must put on incorruption, and this mortal must put on immortality.

The word *incorruption* means "unending existence," and *immortality* means "deathlessness."³ Thus, God's children will live forever.

However, *zoe aionios*, or *age-lasting life*, is not about *quantity* of life, living forever in Heaven. It is about *quality* of life, here and now, that leads to inheritance in the coming kingdom. In other words, eternal life (as correctly translated as *age-during life*) is exclusively offered in our age, giving the guarantee of life in the next. If eternal life is *appropriated* in this life, it will result in quality of life now, with the hope of quality of life in the age to come, in the form of inheritance.

Granted, the term is used once in the Old Testament, in Dan. 12:2, but the context is referring to the close of the Tribulation, when deceased Israelites are resurrected to be judged. The faithful ones will be rewarded with age-lasting (millennial) life, while the unfaithful will be disinherited to experience age-lasting shame and contempt, a reference to the darkness outside. For Israelites, this negative reward could possibly result in exclusion from the promised land during the Millennium. Eternal life as a present possession, however, is unique to our age, having been offered only since the time of Christ.

THE BENEFITS OF ETERNAL LIFE

What happens when a person believes on Jesus for eternal life?

John 5:24 He who hears My word and believes in Him who sent Me has everlasting life, and shall not come into judgment, but has passed from death into life.

Here we find two benefits of age-lasting life:

1. THE BELIEVER INSTANTANEOUSLY PASSES FROM DEATH TO LIFE.

Our minds are geared to think that this means our future destiny changes from Hell to Heaven. But that's not actually what this means. It means you are no longer separated from God — for death is separation from God. As a believer you are now in vital communion with God.

What happens when believers do not appropriate their age-lasting life? They fall back into spiritual deadness! That's why, in this verse, John actually uses a present active participle in Greek to convey the verbs *hears* and *believes*. Literal translations bring out the essence of the participle in their translations. For instance:

> **John 5:24** (YLT) He who is hearing my word, and is believing Him who sent me, hath life age-during, and to judgment he doth not come, but hath passed out of the death to the life.

The use of the participle doesn't mean you can lose your eternal life if you stop hearing and believing, for you have believed on Jesus for eternal life, and have received His unconditional gift. But it means if you do not continue depending on Him in your Christian life, then you will dry up and wither, like the branches in John 15 that do not continue abiding in the vine. In other words, you will not be in vital communion with Christ. This is demonstrated from other Scripture passages, as well:

> **Jas. 1:15** When desire has conceived, it gives birth to sin; and sin, when it is full-grown, brings forth death. (*the idea of spiritual deadness*) — parenthesis mine

> **Rom. 8:6** For to be carnally minded is death, but to be spiritually minded is life and peace.

> **Rom. 8:13** For if you live according to the flesh you will die; but if by the Spirit you put to death the deeds of the body, you will live.

Those believers who do not appropriate their eternal life end up spiritually dead, having lost vitality. They will not be rewarded by Jesus.

THE DUALISM OF ETERNAL LIFE

Interestingly, *eternal life* has a dual meaning, depending on context, not merely singular. In that respect, it is much like the word *salvation*. Context dictates whether the word *salvation* is referring to *initial* salvation (regeneration) that occurred in the past, or *ongoing* salvation (sanctification) — sometimes called "soul salvation" or "saving of the soul" — that is occurring in the present for those believers who are cooperating with God, with a view to future reward.

In like manner, eternal life is a *gift* that one receives from God upon belief in Jesus for His life. The *gift* is bestowed when one initially believes and is saved (regenerated). But the gift keeps on giving! As the child of God continues to believe Jesus for daily grace to live the Christian life victoriously, their soul is progressively saved (sanctified) so that they are earning the reward of eternal life, which is based on Spirit-enabled works. This does not happen automatically, but only to the extent the believer cooperates with God in the sanctification process.

ETERNAL LIFE INVOLVING WORKS

The terms *eternal life* and *everlasting life* are used a total of forty-five times in the New Testament. Surprisingly, twenty-five of the forty-five usages refer to the *gift* of eternal life, speaking of how it is received by faith. But the remaining twenty usages (about 45%) speak of eternal life as involving *works*. Following are some examples of verses in this latter category:

> **Rom. 2:6-7** God ... will render to each one according to his deeds: eternal life to those who by patient continuance in doing good seek for glory, honor, and immortality.

Rom. 6:22 But now having been set free from sin, and having become slaves of God, you have your fruit to holiness, and the end, everlasting life.

John 6:27 Do not labor for the food which perishes, but for the food which endures to everlasting life, which the Son of Man will give you, because God the Father has set His seal on Him.

Gal. 6:7-8 Do not be deceived, God is not mocked; for whatever a man sows, that he will also reap. For he who sows to his flesh will of the flesh reap corruption, but he who sows to the Spirit will of the Spirit reap everlasting life.

1 Tim. 6:12 Fight the good fight of faith, lay hold on eternal life, to which you were also called and have confessed the good confession in the presence of many witnesses.

John 12:25 He who loves his life will lose it, and he who hates his life in this world will keep it for eternal life.

INHERITING ETERNAL LIFE (LIFE FOR THE AGE)

Also consider the rich young ruler. He comes to Jesus and asks, "Sir, what must I do to inherit eternal life [*life for the age*, referring to the Messianic kingdom age]?" Jesus tells him to obey the law, naming several of the Ten Commandments. The man assures Jesus that he has been obedient. But then Jesus tells the ruler he is missing one thing: He must sell everything and give the proceeds to the poor. Then he will inherit eternal life. This eternal life is according to works.

Because of verses like these — showing eternal life to be according to works — some religious groups (such as Roman Catholicism) have arrived at the conclusion that salvation is by faith *plus* works. They see many Bible verses indicating that eternal life is by faith, yet many others indicating that eternal life is according to works. In a desire to be consistent, they have made the assumption that *both* are required for salvation and have, consequently, arrived at a faith-plus-works salvation doctrine. I believe this is an interpretation error.

Ironically, Calvinist "perseverance" doctrine — despite its Reformation mantra of "faith alone" — makes a similar error, teaching that those who are true believers will essentially live in a righteous manner, otherwise, they were never truly saved. Both religious belief systems (Roman Catholicism and Reformation-based Calvinism) essentially synthesize salvation and sanctification, making them inseparable. That results in a misinterpretation of Scripture.

The key to correct interpretation is distinguishing between the *gift* of eternal life and the *reward* of eternal life. The *gift* of eternal (age-lasting) life is free to those who believe.

> **Eph. 2:8-9** For by grace you have been saved through faith, and that not of yourselves; it is the gift of God, not of works, lest anyone should boast.

If you have believed, then you have passed from death to life, which is commonly called salvation (in the sense of regeneration or initial salvation of one's spirit).

The *reward* of eternal (age-lasting) life is earned by those who do good works *after* salvation. That is commonly called sanctification or discipleship or soul salvation, which leads to reward.

If you are appropriating your age-lasting life now, then you are spiritually alive and one day will enjoy His kingdom to the fullest. If you are not appropriating your age-lasting life, then you are spiritually dead and will not enjoy the blessings of kingdom life (though you will be *in* the kingdom). Instead, you will have regrets, for you will not receive the inheritance of ruling with Christ in the New Jerusalem.

A second benefit of age-lasting life is seen in John 5:24:

2. THE BELIEVER HAS IMMUNITY FROM JUDGMENT AT THE GREAT WHITE THRONE.

Does this mean Christians will not be judged at the Judgment Seat of Christ? No! It simply means they will not be judged with unbelievers at the Great White Throne.

> **John 5:28-29** Do not marvel at this; for the hour is coming in which all who are in the graves will hear His voice and come forth—those who have done good, to the resurrection of life, and those who have done evil, to the resurrection of condemnation.

Jesus will raise *everyone* on Earth to face Him in judgment. The Bible speaks of two general resurrections:

1. The resurrection of *life* for believers to face Jesus at the Judgment Seat of Christ. This resurrection occurs *before* the Millennium.

2. The resurrection of *condemnation* for unbelievers to face Jesus at the Great White Throne. This resurrection occurs *after* the Millennium.

Believers have immunity from the Great White Throne Judgment that unbelievers will experience, thus, believers will appear at the first judgment, the Judgment Seat of Christ. Nevertheless, the first judgment is also a judgment!

At the Judgment Seat of Christ, the fire will try every man's work of what sort (quality) it is (1 Cor. 3:13). Most Christians think the Judgment Seat is all positive — the dispensing of rewards. But what is often missed is that many will be recompensed for *bad* behavior.

> **2 Cor. 5:10** For we must all appear before the judgment seat of Christ, that each one may receive the things done in the body, according to what he has done, whether good or bad.

> **Col. 3:23-25** And whatever you do, do it heartily, as to the Lord and not to men, knowing that from the Lord you will receive the reward of the inheritance; for you serve the Lord Christ. But he who does wrong will be repaid for what he has done, and there is no partiality.

Thankfully, believers have immunity from the Great White Throne Judgment, but we know conclusively that all believers will meet Jesus in judgment at the Judgment Seat of Christ.

WHAT IS ETERNAL LIFE?

Anyone who believes on Jesus for eternal (age-lasting) life, receives His marvelous gift of regeneration, the indwelling presence of His Holy Spirit, and the guarantee of resurrection prior to the Millennium. There are other glorious benefits, but we will leave it at that for now. Again, eternal (age-lasting) life is not a ticket to Heaven. What, then, is the purpose for this life? Here is my definition:

Eternal life is the provision of Jesus within believers as the means by which they can live righteously and thereby qualify for age-lasting (millennial) inheritance.

LIKE A DIMMER SWITCH

Perhaps I could illustrate as follows. Eternal (age-lasting) life is like a dimmer switch. The switch must first be turned on so there is power to the light fixture, resulting in some light. Even though the light is quite dim and minuscule, it demonstrates, nonetheless, that the light fixture is connected to power. But it is only as the dimmer switch is increased that light shines more brightly.

Eternal life (life for the ages) is like that. When you believe on Jesus for eternal life, you are connected to the power source and with that come a couple of tremendous benefits. First, you pass from death to life and, second, you are given immunity from the Great White Throne Judgment. Indeed, you will be resurrected *before* the Millennium to meet Jesus at the Judgment Seat of Christ. 1 Cor. 15 makes that quite clear.

Before the light can grow brighter, you must draw upon your age-lasting life, then the dimmer switch can be increased so the light shines brighter. To the extent you continue to draw upon His life, your light will continue to grow brighter, and you will reflect to others the glory of Christ through your life, in increasing measure. Perhaps that is why Jesus said,

Matt. 5:16 Let your light so shine before men, that they may see your good works and glorify your Father in heaven.

Are you living out your age-lasting life? Is your light growing brighter? Or are you becoming dim and spiritually dead?

Eternal (age-lasting) life is really *not* about getting a ticket to Heaven and living endlessly. It is about getting the life of Jesus *now*, accessing that life, and thereby qualifying to live in the coming kingdom age as a co-ruler with Jesus Christ.

NOT HEAVEN, BUT EARTH

Most Christians think that believers will live forever in Heaven. But that is not correct; in fact, we never go to Heaven, in the sense of the third Heaven, where God dwells. (See Chapters 5-7 in my book, *The Savior of All Men*, for a more detailed explanation).

Faithful saints will dwell with Jesus in the New Jerusalem, which will be a glorious place that will hover over the earth during the Millennium (see Rev. 21-22). Unfaithful saints will be excluded from that place and will dwell on Earth, in the darkness outside the bright New Jerusalem.

Following the Millennium, and some time after the age of Satan's rebellion that Jesus puts down, God will create a new heaven (universe) and new earth (2 Pet. 3:10), where man will dwell perpetually. In fact, Rev. 21:2-3 speak of God descending to Earth to live together with man. So, technically, we will *not* spend eternity in Heaven — we will always dwell on Earth (or, if qualified, in the New Jerusalem).

A NEW LOOK AT HELL

How does this corrected translation of the word *eternal* (as *age-lasting*) change our concept of Hell? Notice the underlined words in these familiar verses:

John 3:16 For God so loved the world that He gave His only begotten Son, that whoever believes in Him should not <u>perish</u> but have everlasting life.

John 3:18 He who believes in Him is not <u>condemned</u>; but he who does not believe is <u>condemned</u> already, because he has not believed in the name of the only begotten Son of God.

Most Christians assume that the word *perish* means "to go to Hell." They think the word *condemned* means "consigned to Hell," and *everlasting* means "forever" or "unending." Therefore, they conclude that, after this life, believers go to Heaven, where they live forever and unbelievers go to Hell, where they burn forever. But this is incorrect.

The correct definition of *perish* is "to be destroyed; to be put to death, to die; to be lost, to stray."[4] The word does *not* convey the idea of going to Hell. To *condemn* is "to separate; to make a distinction between; to exercise judgment upon."[5] Once again, the word does not convey the idea of going to Hell. Of course, we've already seen that the words *eternal* and *everlasting* are a mistranslation. They actually mean "age-lasting," or "age-during."

An overwhelming majority of evangelical Christians believe the doctrine of eternal conscious torment, which teaches that unbelievers will burn forever and ever in the lake of fire. I don't see that doctrine as biblical and have written an entire book on the subject.[6] How does understanding the correct meaning of the word *eternal* shape one's understanding of Hell? Notice the following verses that refer either to eternal or everlasting punishment or fire (emphases mine):

> **Matt. 18:8** If your hand or foot causes you to sin, cut it off and cast it from you. It is better for you to enter into life lame or maimed, rather than having two hands or two feet, to be cast into the <u>everlasting [age-lasting] fire</u>.

> **Matt. 25:41** Then He will also say to those on the left hand, "Depart from Me, you cursed, into the <u>everlasting [age-lasting] fire</u> prepared for the devil and his angels."

Matt. 25:46 These will go away into <u>everlasting (age-lasting) punishment</u>, but the righteous into eternal [age-lasting] life.

Mark 3:29 He who blasphemes against the Holy Spirit never has forgiveness, but is subject to <u>eternal [age-lasting] condemnation</u> —

2 Thess. 1:9 Who shall be punished with <u>everlasting [age-lasting] destruction</u> from the presence of the Lord, and from the glory of his power;

Heb. 6:1-2 Therefore, leaving the discussion of the elementary principles of Christ, let us go on to perfection, not laying again the foundation of repentance from dead works and of faith toward God, of the doctrine of baptisms, of laying on of hands, of resurrection of the dead, and of <u>eternal [age-lasting] judgment</u>.

Mark 3:29 refers to what is commonly called "the unpardonable sin," which is not a Bible term, but refers to the uniquely Jewish sin of attributing Christ's mighty works to the devil or demons and not to God. That sin against the Holy Spirit will not be forgiven for the millennial age. Rather, those who commit that sin will suffer some sort of age-lasting punishment. The Jewish leadership were primarily the ones guilty of this sin, and it led the nation into unbelief, as they rejected the Messiah. As a result, Jesus took the kingdom offer away from Israel and now offers it to the church (see Matt. 21:43).

What can we conclude about these verses that refer to some form of future judgment or punishment? The use of the adjective *aionios*, translated *eternal* or *everlasting*, specifies that the judgment or punishment is only for a period of time — it could be a very long time, but it is limited in duration, nonetheless, and apparently remedial in nature.

ADDITIONAL RESOURCES

Much more could be said about the correct translation of the Greek adjective *aionios* as "age-lasting" or "for the age," but space does not permit. This Addendum is merely intended as an introduction to this important subject. The reader is encouraged to research further. The following materials are helpful:

Hanson, John Wesley, *The Greek Word Aion—Aonios: Translated Everlasting—Eternal in the Holy Bible Shown to Denote Limited Duration*, Forest City, NC: HollyPublishing, 2020), originally published 1875.

Keizer, Heleen M. "Eternity Revisited: A Study of the Greek Word Aion," *Philosophia Reformata* 65 (2000) 53–71.

Keizer, Heleen M., *Life Time Entirety: A Study of Aion in Greek Literature and Philosophy, the Septuagint and Philo*, doctoral dissertation, self-published, 1999.

Ramelli, Ilaria L.E. and David Konstan, *Terms for Eternity: Aionios and Aidios in Classical and Christian Texts*, Piscataway, NJ: Gorgias Press, 2013.

ADDENDUM 2: FOUR DEGREES OF SALVATION

Why does God sometimes make audacious statements in the Bible that "mess up" our theology? Of course, I say that tongue-in-cheek, but I remember when I read a verse of Scripture many years ago, and it arrested my attention as never before:

1 Tim. 4:10 For to this *end* we both labor and suffer reproach, because we trust in the living God, who is *the* Savior of all men, especially of those who believe.

Then more Scriptures began to trouble me:

1 John 4:14 We have seen and testify that the Father has sent the Son *as* Savior of the world.

John 1:29 John saw Jesus coming toward him, and said, "Behold! The Lamb of God who takes away the sin of the world!"

John 4:42 We know that this is indeed the Christ, the Savior of the world.

THE ERROR OF INTERPRETING THROUGH THE LENS OF ONE'S THEOLOGY

The tendency of modern Christians is to interpret the Bible through one's theological grid — whether learned in church or Bible college or seminary, or all of the above. Of course, God's Word is not the problem. The problem is traditional theology — the lenses through which we typically view Scripture. Doctrines that have been perpetuated from the time of the Reformation are the real culprit.

Jesus died for *all mankind*, not merely for the elect, as Calvinism teaches. The verses above are merely a representative sampling of the scope of His atonement. The Scriptures do *not* support the doctrine of limited atonement, but rather, *un*-limited atonement. However, the verses quoted above say something much more profound!

Not only did Christ *die* for all men, He is the *Savior* (the rescuer or deliverer) of *all men*. He takes away the sin of the *whole world* — not *potentially*, as some like to suggest, but *de facto*, in actuality. That's what these verses are saying, even though theological systems want to interpret them otherwise. Thus, in some sense, God has already saved *everyone*, and He has *especially* saved those who believe (1 Tim. 4:10). What does that mean?

ESPECIALLY THOSE WHO BELIEVE

As the title of this Addendum implies, I believe the Scriptures teach at least *four degrees* of salvation. Notice again the wording of the verse that initially caught my attention:

> **1 Tim. 4:10** The living God ... is *the* Savior of all men, especially of those who believe.

In the context of this passage, Paul is emphasizing the importance of being a good minister of Jesus Christ (v. 6). So those who *believe*, contextually, are those who believe *on Jesus* — those who have believed His promise of eternal (age-lasting) life and have thereby been regenerated as children of God.

Why does Paul include the word *especially*? Strong says the adverb *especially* (Greek, *malista*) means "most of all" or "in the greatest degree," being the superlative use of a basic adverb (Greek, *mala*), meaning *very*.[1] Thayer says it means, "chiefly, most of all, above all."[2] The BDAG lexicon adds, "to an unusual degree."[3] Thus, those who believe Jesus Christ for eternal (age-lasting) life are saved in a greater degree than those who do not believe Him for eternal life. Logically, that suggests that there are *degrees* of salvation. I believe at least four degrees are taught in the Scriptures.

When stating each of the degrees, I will first indicate what it is salvation *from* and then indicate to whom it applies.

FIRST DEGREE SALVATION — FROM THE PENALTY OF SIN, FOR ALL MANKIND

Mankind has two problems: sin (singular) and sins (plural). Understanding the distinction is critical. Sin (singular) is a natural inclination to commit sins (plural), which put us at enmity with God. Sin (singular) spread to all mankind from our common ancestor (Adam):

> **Rom. 5:12** Through one man sin entered the world, and death through sin, and thus death spread to all men, because all sinned—

Death — separation from God — is the penalty for sin (singular), and the implication is that, apart from some radical solution on God's part, death would be never-ending separation from God. But — thanks be to God! — Jesus has delivered all mankind from sin (singular) and death by His redemption.

> **2 Tim. 1:10** Our Savior Jesus Christ ... has abolished death and brought life and immortality to light through the gospel,

> **Heb. 2:14-15** Inasmuch then as the children have partaken of flesh and blood, He Himself likewise shared in the same, that through death He might destroy him who had the power of death, that is, the devil, and release those who through fear of death were all their lifetime subject to bondage.

John the Baptist emphasized that Jesus is the Lamb of God who takes away the sin (singular) *of the world* (John 1:29). The Lamb of God imagery implies that He paid the penalty for sin (singular) by His blood atonement. Consequently, no one will experience never-ending separation from God — all mankind will be resurrected! That is why Jesus is called the Savior of the world (John 4:42) and the Savior of all men (1 Tim. 4:10). He has already saved each and every person from their sin penalty, whether individuals realize it or not.

Incidentally, this is why we know that babies and young children that die will not be condemned. They have not yet knowingly committed sins (plural), and their sin (singular) penalty has already been paid for by Jesus, who is the Savior of all men, including babies and young children.

AS IN ADAM, SO IN CHRIST

We see this truth taught in Rom. 5 also (as noted in Chapter 13):

> **Rom. 5:18** Therefore, as through one man's offense judgment came to all men, resulting in condemnation, even so through one Man's righteous act the free gift came to all men, resulting in justification of life.
>
> 19 For as by one man's disobedience many were made sinners, so also by one Man's obedience many will be made righteous.

The word *made* in v. 19 means "designated" or "constituted."[4] As a result of Adam's sin, *many* — that is, *all mankind* — were designated sinners, *because all sinned* (Rom. 5:12). Consequently, *judgment came to all men, resulting in condemnation* (v. 18). From Rom. 5:12 we know this judgment/condemnation is the sentence of *death* — never-ending separation from God. However, because of Christ's righteous action on the cross, salvation in the first degree — the payment of sin's penalty — has been given to *all mankind*. What a gift! This marvelous truth is also clearly stated in other passages of Scripture:

> **1 Cor. 15:22** For as in Adam all die, even so in Christ all shall be made alive.

> **2 Cor. 5:19** God was in Christ reconciling the world to Himself, not imputing their trespasses to them.

God has already reconciled the entire world to Himself through Christ. Because Jesus paid mankind's sin penalty, *all* humans have been reconciled to God (from God's perspective) and can, therefore, believe God and choose to live righteously. Indeed, *all* will be resurrected and will be judged for their works.

Incidentally, this truth negates the first point of Calvinism's T-U-L-I-P acrostic — *total depravity* — which Calvinists essentially define as *total inability*, suggesting that mankind cannot possibly believe God and live righteously. However, God's expectation has always been for man to believe Him and live uprightly, back to the very beginning of time. This is made possible because Jesus has already saved mankind from the penalty of sin (singular).

What good is salvation in the first degree? It makes possible salvation in the second degree.

SECOND DEGREE SALVATION — FROM THE WRATH OF GOD, FOR ALL WHO LIVE RIGHTEOUSLY

As glorious as salvation in the first degree is, mankind still has a problem. Because *all* have the natural inclination to sin (singular), *all* commit sins (plural), which keeps man from reconciling with God (from man's perspective).

Sins (plural) are the individual lawless behaviors that are committed by *all* mankind. Yet Yahweh is righteous and demands that *all* believe Him and live righteously. Those who obey are declared *justified* in His sight (not *positionally* or *legally*, but in a *behavioral* sense, at any given point in time).

> **Acts 17:30-31** God ... commands all men everywhere to repent [Repent of what? Sins!], because He has appointed a day on which He will judge the world in righteousness by the Man whom He has ordained.

Paul didn't say this to a Baptist church congregation; he said it to the pagan idolaters at Athens! Furthermore, he didn't urge them to believe on Jesus for eternal (age-lasting) life (third degree salvation). He urged them to repent of sins and live uprightly, because a day of reckoning is coming for all men. Because God has saved all mankind from the penalty of sin (singular), He commands all to believe Him and live righteously, not committing sins. Thus, man *can* choose to believe God and live righteously — and thereby please God — otherwise, God could not expect it of mankind.

Traditional theology that came out of the Reformation says that all mankind has the stigma of original sin. Consequently, man *cannot* live righteously, in any degree. In support of this, they often quote Rom. 3:10-18, which starts out, *There is none righteous, no not one.* Some will also quote Isa. 64:6, *All our righteousnesses are as filthy rags.*

The Isa. 64:6 argument can be eliminated from the discussion, because to quote it in this context is a misuse of the text. Isa. 64 is talking about Israel needing revival because although they were sacrificing and offering incense, they were going about it in the wrong way and continuing in their sinfulness, thinking their sacrifices were sufficient to make God happy, so that text doesn't apply here. In Rom. 3:10ff Paul is making the point that: "This is what the law says to those who are under the law," because no one can keep the law perfectly.

SCRIPTURAL EXAMPLES:

God said of Noah and Job:

> **Gen. 6:9b** Noah was a just man, perfect in his generations. Noah walked with God.

> **Job 1:1** Job ... was blameless and upright, and one who feared God and shunned evil.

These men were Gentiles, who knew nothing of Christ or His salvation, and although they surely committed some sins (for there is none righteous); they, nevertheless, pleased God by their choices to believe Him and live righteously. In the New Testament God said of Cornelius (before Peter told him of initial salvation in Jesus Christ):

> **Acts 10:1-2** There was a certain man in Caesarea called Cornelius, a centurion ... a devout *man* and one who feared God with all his household, who gave alms generously to the people, and prayed to God always.

Peter said of Cornelius:

> **Acts 10:34-35** In truth I perceive that God shows no partiality. But in every nation whoever fears Him and works righteousness is accepted by Him.

So it is quite possible for those who have not believed Christ's promise of eternal (age-lasting) life, both Jews and Gentiles, to believe God and live righteously — not perfectly, of course, but to a great degree, so that God is pleased with their lifestyle. Incidentally, that is also true of the multitudes today in this world — people who do not know of Jesus or His salvation in the sense of regeneration and, therefore, do not possess eternal (age-lasting) life. Nevertheless, they *can* possess a lesser degree of salvation because they believe God and live uprightly. In fact, they can be saved from the wrath of God.

> **Rom. 1:18** For the wrath of God is revealed from heaven against all ungodliness and unrighteousness of men, who suppress the truth in unrighteousness,

NO CONDEMNATION FOR THOSE WHO LIVE RIGHTEOUSLY

The wrath of God was not upon Noah and his family, but upon all the other peoples on earth, whom God killed in the flood. The wrath of God was not upon Job, but upon Job's three friends who criticized him. The wrath of God was not upon Cornelius; in fact, God sent Peter to bring Cornelius greater revelation so that he could obtain a higher degree of salvation! These people were all accepted by God and, consequently, were saved from His wrath. Lot could also be added. He was saved from God's wrath upon Sodom, because he was righteous (i.e., he *lived* righteously — see 2 Peter 2:6-8).

When all of these people meet Jesus in judgment, they will *not* be cast into the lake of fire, for they have been accepted by God, saved in the second degree because of their righteous living, driven by believing God. Nevertheless, some object to this view by quoting Rev 20:15, *Anyone not found written in the Book of Life was cast into the lake of fire.* They assume that being written in the Book of Life means having believed on Jesus for eternal (age-lasting) life. But that is a mere assumption — and an incorrect one — that has been perpetuated through the centuries. The Book of Life lists the names of those who have *lived righteously* – that is easily demonstrated by looking at all the passages in the Scriptures that mention the Book of Life.

I find it curious that every one of the judgments in the Scriptures is based on *works* (i.e., deeds, whether sinful or righteous):

- Judgment Seat of Christ (1 Cor. 3:13-15)
- Sheep and Goats Judgment (Matt. 25:34-36)
- Jewish Judgment Seat (Ezek. 20:34-38)
- Great White Throne Judgment (Rev. 20:12)

Those who believe in God and live righteously — even though they may not have a right understanding of who God is — are accepted by Him. They will *not* be cast into the lake of fire, but will instantly bow the knee and confess that Jesus Christ is Lord, to the glory of God the Father (Phil. 2:9-11). In that sense, they will be saved from the wrath of God.

Those who ignore God's command to repent and live righteously will be punished for their sins (plural) at the Great White Throne Judgment, and will spend time in the lake of fire. Isa. 13:11, *I will punish the world for its evil, and the wicked for their iniquity.*

FOUR SUPPORTING EVIDENCES:

Anyone who believes God and lives uprightly is accepted by Him and "saved" from His wrath. The examples of Noah, Lot, Job, and Cornelius have already been shared. Following are four supporting evidences that explain why this is feasible:

1. Solomon said in Eccl. 3:11 that God has put eternity in the hearts of all men. Man has been made in God's image and, therefore, has been given an inherent sense of something much bigger and grander than the mere here and now. The Hebrew word for *eternity* in this verse is *olam*. This word refers to the ages in God's plan. Though man doesn't know the details, he suspects there is life even after death, and a utopian age to come. That should prompt him to seek God.

2. In Rom. 1:20 Paul points out that all men can see the invisible God's attributes in His works of creation, even His eternal power and glory, so that they are without excuse. The tendency of traditionalists is to assume this means man is without excuse to believe on Jesus for eternal (age-lasting) life, but that is not Paul's point in Rom. 1. His point is that *all* mankind is without excuse to believe in God and live righteously.

3. When Jesus died, He also paid the price for sins (plural) for the whole world. The parentheses are my own in the following verses:

> **Heb. 9:27-28** As it is appointed for men to die once, but after this the judgment, so Christ was offered once to bear the sins (plural) of many.

> **1 Pet. 3:18** Christ also suffered once for sins (plural), the just for the unjust, that He might bring us to God.

> **1 John 2:2** He Himself is the propitiation for our sins (plural), and not for ours only but also for the whole world.

Because Christ's death is the propitiation for the sins of the whole world, He has already provided the means of forgiveness for sins (plural), when one repents and lives righteously. Therefore, all men have no excuse for not believing in God and living righteously.

4. All men have a conscience. Paul makes this clear in Rom. 2:

> **Rom. 2:14-16** For when Gentiles, who do not have the law, by nature do the things in the law, these, although not having the law, are a law to themselves, who show the work of the law written in their hearts, their conscience also bearing witness, and between themselves their thoughts accusing or else excusing them) in the day when God will judge the secrets of men by Jesus Christ, according to my gospel.

Since all men have a God-given conscience, the entire creation knows the difference between right and wrong, even Gentiles who were never privileged to have the Mosaic law. That being the case, all mankind is without excuse to live righteously.

SPARED FROM THE LAKE OF FIRE

If a person believes in God, repents, and lives righteously, to the best of his or her knowledge, it seems likely that God will give that person greater understanding and perhaps greater revelation, maybe even about His Son Jesus Christ and the eternal life He offers. But even if that never happens, all are without excuse, nonetheless. They will give an account at the Great White Throne, and Jesus will judge their works.

Those who believe in God and live righteously, even if they don't have all their doctrine straight, or don't know about the person of Jesus, will not be cast into the lake of fire. On the other hand, those who snub God's command to repent and choose not to live righteously, will be subject to God's wrath in this present age, and they will be consigned to the lake of fire for a period of refining and purging, until they are ready to bow the knee in humble submission to King Jesus.

Keep in mind that those appearing at the Great White Throne will have already been judged for not believing on Jesus for eternal (age-lasting) life, by being left in the grave during the entire Millennium. What a tremendous loss! They will miss an entire age of glory!

Whose names will be found written in the Book of Life at the Great White Throne? Those who fear God and live righteously — they will avoid the lake of fire.

THIRD DEGREE SALVATION — FROM THE POWER OF SIN, FOR ALL WHO BELIEVE CHRIST'S PROMISE OF ETERNAL (AGE-DURING) LIFE

This is the degree of salvation with which we are most familiar. In fact, most Christians think it is the *only* degree of salvation. This is believing on Jesus for the *gift* of eternal (age-lasting) life, which is millennial life (John 3:16; 3:18; 5:24; 6:47; 11:25-26). These are the "especially those who believe" in 1 Tim. 4:10 — *God ... is the Savior of all men, especially of those who believe.* This degree of salvation is received by God's grace, when man simply believes Christ's promise of eternal (age-lasting) life:

> **Eph 2:8-9** For by grace you have been saved through faith, and that not of yourselves; *it is* the gift of God, not of works, lest anyone should boast.

This degree of salvation results in regeneration.

> **Titus 3:5** not by works of righteousness which we have done, but according to His mercy He saved us, through the washing of regeneration and renewing of the Holy Spirit.

NOT OF WORKS

This degree of salvation is not of works; therefore, repentance is not required. When John the Baptist and Jesus, and later the disciples, proclaimed, "Repent, for the kingdom of heaven is at hand," they were not preaching a message of initial salvation by grace, through faith. They were calling the Jews — who were already believers in an Old Testament sense — to turn from their ways (repent) and return to fellowship with Yahweh, in the spirit of 2 Chron. 7:14.

When we believed on Jesus for eternal (age-lasting) life, we were regenerated and all our past sins were forgiven. Consequently, we passed from death to life, so that we are assured of resurrection before the Millennium. We have been given the provision to live righteously, for the Righteous One lives within. His name is Holy Spirit. Righteous living is the purpose for eternal life (life for the age), so that we can qualify to become His millennial bride and co-regents. It's not about Heaven vs. Hell!

Incidentally, being saved in this sense does not mean we are positionally or perpetually justified (as the Reformers taught and which is erroneously being taught by most evangelicals today). We must continually confess sins (by claiming 1 John 1:9 — the New Testament equivalent of the Old Testament sacrificial system) and appropriate our provision for living righteously.

SAVED FROM THE POWER OF SIN

Salvation in the third degree is salvation from the *power* of sin!

> **Rom. 6:4** Therefore we were buried with Him through baptism into death, that just as Christ was raised from the dead by the glory of the Father, even so we also should walk in newness of life.
>
> **5** For if we have been united together in the likeness of His death, certainly we also shall be *in the likeness* of *His* resurrection, knowing this, that our old man was crucified with *Him*, that the body of sin might be done away with, that we should no longer be slaves of sin.
>
> **7** For he who has died has been freed from sin.

As discussed at length in Chapter 14, our old man was crucified with Christ. Consequently, we no longer have to be sin's slaves; we are free from sin. We have a new Master, Jesus Christ, who gives victory over sin when we cooperate with Him.

> **2 Cor. 5:17** Therefore, if anyone *is* in Christ, *he is* a new creation; old things have passed away; behold, all things have become new.

Do you now see why He is the Savior of ALL men, but *especially* of those who believe? As believers in Christ, we have been given so much! All of our past sins have been forgiven, and we have been freed from sin's power going forward. When we sin, we can claim the promise of 1 Jn. 1:9. We have life for the age — the millennial age — which means we will be resurrected to live in that age. We have the Holy Spirit living within, to enable us to live righteously.

> **2 Cor. 5:15** He died for all, that those who live should live no longer for themselves, but for Him who died for them and rose again.

> **Rom. 12:1** I beseech you therefore, brethren, by the mercies of God, that you present your bodies a living sacrifice, holy, acceptable to God, *which is* your reasonable service.

Jesus is *especially* the Savior of those who have believed on Him. This means we have a stewardship responsibility to live righteously, and if we will, then we can experience the fourth degree of salvation.

FOURTH DEGREE SALVATION — FROM DISINHERITANCE, FOR ALL BELIEVERS WHO QUALIFY

God wants all mankind to live righteously. He *especially* expects this of those who have believed Him for eternal (age-lasting) life, because we have a special provision for living righteously — Jesus living within! When we appropriate our provision and live righteously, victorious over sinning, then our *soul* is being saved. James talks about this:

> **Jas. 1:21** Therefore lay aside all filthiness and overflow of wickedness, and receive with meekness the implanted word, which is able to save your souls.

James is talking to believers; he says so numerous times in the book. So this is obviously a higher degree of salvation — *soul* salvation.

> **1 Cor. 1:18** For the message of the cross is foolishness to those who are perishing, but to us who are being saved it is the power of God.

SOUL-SALVATION NOT AUTOMATIC

Jesus taught that the soul is being saved when believers are denying self, taking up their crosses, and following Him. This is sanctification of the mind, will, and emotions (the soul) that leads to reward (see Matt. 16:24-27). The saving of the soul is *not* automatic, despite the fact that multitudes of churches and Christian schools and Bible colleges and seminaries teach that it is — claiming that all believers will be rewarded, which is also essentially what the Pharisees taught.

Most Christians today think that because they are *in Christ*, they have all the rights and privileges of an inheritor, but Paul clarifies:

> **Rom. 8:16-17** The Spirit Himself bears witness with our spirit that we are children of God, and if children, then heirs—heirs of God and joint heirs with Christ, if indeed we suffer with *Him*, that we may also be glorified together.

All believers are children of God and, therefore, His heirs, but only those who suffer with Jesus (by denying self, taking up their crosses, and following Him) are joint-heirs with Christ who stand to be glorified with Him (to become His bride and co-rulers).

THE WEDDING GARMENT — WHITE ROBES OF RIGHTEOUSNESS

It is quite common in Christianity to assume that all believers comprise the bride of Christ and, therefore, all will be rewarded, at least in some degree, and all will rule with Jesus in the coming kingdom. Consequently, the Judgment Seat of Christ is presumed essentially to be an awards ceremony — but that is not correct! The purpose of the Judgment Seat is for determining who qualifies to become Christ's bride and co-rulers in the coming Messianic kingdom. His bride will be those who have the wedding clothes of righteousness — not Christ's righteousness, but our own righteous living:

> **Rev. 19:7** Let us be glad and rejoice and give Him glory, for the marriage of the Lamb has come, and His wife has made herself ready.

8 And to her it was granted to be arrayed in fine linen, clean and bright, for the fine linen is the righteous acts of the saints.

You are making your own wedding garment by how you are living here and now. If you are living selfishly, your garment will be defiled. Just as the man at the wedding supper who did not have on the appropriate wedding clothes was removed (Matt. 22:1-14), so you will be disinherited and removed from Christ's presence. You will not qualify to be His bride and co-ruler in the kingdom.

Those who qualify with pure white wedding garments — based on righteous living — will rule with Him in New Jerusalem, which will hover over the earth and will serve as the ruling headquarters for the kingdom (Rev. 21-22). Those who do not qualify will be disinherited and excluded and consigned to another realm of the kingdom — the outer darkness. New Jerusalem is intensely bright because Jesus is the light of it, thus metaphorically and relatively speaking, Earth is the outer darkness, literally, the darkness outside. Christianity has wrongly assumed the outer darkness to be Hell, but that is not correct Scripturally.

THE PROSPECT OF NEGATIVE REWARD

Negative reward is a biblical doctrine! In other words, those who do not live righteously will be recompensed for their bad behavior; it will not be overlooked.

> **Col. 3:23-24** And whatever you do, do it heartily, as to the Lord and not to men, knowing that from the Lord you will receive the reward of the inheritance; for you serve the Lord Christ.
>
> **25** But he who does wrong will be repaid for what he has done, and there is no partiality.

The fire at the Judgment Seat is a terrifying prospect (see 1 Cor. 3:11-15), which will consume works of inferior quality (fleshly works or works done in our own strength or from wrong motivations). They will be burned up, and many will have nothing left.

1 Cor. 3:14-15 If anyone's work which he has built on *it* endures, he will receive a reward. If anyone's work is burned, he will **suffer loss**; but he himself will be saved, yet so as through fire. (emphasis mine)

The doctrine of negative reward (suffering loss) has been largely ignored in Christianity, due to the Reformation's incorrect teaching regarding the doctrine of justification.

THE PARABLE OF THE TALENTS

What happens to the good and faithful servant in Christ's parable of the talents (Matt. 25:14-30)? He hears:

Matt. 25:21, 23 Well *done,* good and faithful servant; you have been faithful over a few things, I will make you ruler over many things. Enter into the joy of your lord.

What happens to the unfaithful servant? He hears:

Matt. 25:26, 30 You wicked and lazy servant ... Cast the unprofitable servant into the outer darkness. There will be weeping and gnashing of teeth.

Notice, they are both *servants*. Unbelievers are never called *servants*.

Weeping and gnashing of teeth is an oriental idiom for conscious regret. Those believers who are consigned to Earth during the Millennium will weep and regret the fact that they did not live for Jesus here and *now* and thereby qualify to rule with Him *then*.

GOD'S PURPOSE IN SENDING JESUS TO DIE

2 Cor. 5 explains the glorious purpose of God in sending Jesus to die for the sins of mankind. It isn't to save people so they can go to Heaven when they die and not have to go to Hell (as is commonly taught). God's purpose is spelled out in 2 Cor. 5:

2 Cor. 5:21 For He (God the Father) made Him (Jesus Christ the Son) who knew no sin *to be* sin for us, that we might become the righteousness of God in Him.

2 Cor. 5:15 He died for all, that those who live should live no longer for themselves, but for Him who died for them and rose again.

God wants mankind to live righteously, *especially* His children (those who have believed). A life lived in this manner will be rewarded with crowns and glorification at the Judgment Seat of Christ, welcomed as His co-ruler. Is that how you are living? Or will you be disinherited?

If you want to know the qualifications for kingdom inheritance, study the Sermon on the Mount (Matt. 5-7). If you want to know how you can *fulfill* the qualifications, study the Christ life of victory (Rom. 6-8).

I trust God's four degrees of salvation are now clear:

FIRST DEGREE SALVATION — From the *penalty* of sin, for all mankind

SECOND DEGREE SALVATION — From the wrath of God, for all who live righteously

THIRD DEGREE SALVATION — From the *power* of sin, for all who believe Christ's promise of eternal (age-during) life

FOURTH DEGREE SALVATION — From disinheritance, for all believers who qualify

ENDNOTES

1. WHAT ARE REFORMATION GLASSES?

1. https://en.wikipedia.org/wiki/Free_grace_theology (accessed 4/12/24)
2. https://en.wikipedia.org/wiki/Protestantism_by_country (Accessed 4/10/24)
3. https://web.archive.org/web/20170525141543/http://www.gordonconwell.edu/resources/documents/1IBMR2015.pdf (accessed 4/10/24)

2. JUSTIFIED BY FAITH-FILLED WORKS PART 1

1. Watchman Nee, *The Spiritual Man* (Richmond, VA: Christian Fellowship Publishers, 1968).
2. Clarence Larkin, *Dispensational Truth* (Glenside, PA: Rev. Clarence Larkin Est., 1920), pp. 98-99. Modern reprints are available.
3. Pastor Todd Tjepkema, private email correspondence dated 7/26/24, used with permission.

4. JUSTIFIED BY FAITH-FILLED WORKS PART 3

1. Robert E. Van Voorst, *Eerdmans Dictionary of the Bible*, s.v. "JUDAIZING," 747.

5. THE ROMANS ROAD TO SALVATION MISNOMER

1. Zane C. Hodges, *Romans: Deliverance From Wrath* (Corinth, TX: Grace Evangelical Society, 2013), Introduction by John Niemela, pp. 14-15.
2. Arlen Chitwood, *Message in the Gospels, Acts, Epistles* (Cottonwood, AZ: The Lamp Broadcast, 2018), pp. 92-93.
3. Hodges, p. 29.
4. Ibid., p. 18.

6. EXCHANGING GLORY FOR SHAME

1. Arlen Chitwood, *Salvation in Romans* (Cottonwood, AZ: The Lamp Broadcast, undated pamphlet), p. 2.
2. The word "Christian" is used consistently throughout this book to refer to those who are "in Christ," having believed on Him for eternal life, *not* to those who identify with nominal Christianity.
3. Chitwood, p. 1.
4. Jan Bonda, *The One Purpose of God: An Answer to the Doctrine of Eternal Punishment* (Grand Rapids, MI: Wm. B. Eerdman's Publ. Co., 1998), p. 76.

5. Zane C. Hodges, *Romans: Deliverance From Wrath* (Corinth, TX: Grace Evangelical Society, 2013), p. 40.

7. ETERNAL LIFE FOR DOING GOOD?

1. The term *eternal life* is used several times in this chapter. In every case, it should be translated *age-lasting life*, though to avoid redundancy, I may not indicate that each time.
2. *Robert Govett on Romans* (Hayesville, NC: Schoettle Publ. Co., 2010), p. 18.
3. *A Greek–English Lexicon of the New Testament and Other Early Christian Literature*, 3rd ed. (BDAG), Accordance electronic edition, s.v. "ἔργον," 390.
4. Govett, pp. 22-23.
5. Arlen Chitwood, private email correspondence, dated 8/2/24, used with permission.

8. THE RIGHTEOUS REQUIREMENTS OF THE LAW

1. James D.G. Dunn, *Romans 1-8*, Word Biblical Commentary, vol. 38a (Grand Rapids: Zondervan, 1988), pp. 125-26.
2. Ibid., pp. 126-27.
3. Ibid., p. 127.
4. Ibid., p. 127.
5. Ibid., pp. 127-28.

9. THE MYSTERY OF THE ORACLES

1. https://www.oxfordreference.com/display/10.1093/oi/authority.20110803100252605 (accessed 5/20/24).
2. James D.G. Dunn, *Romans 1-8*, Word Biblical Commentary, vol. 38a (Grand Rapids: Zondervan, 1988), pp. 138-39.
3. Ibid., p. 138.
4. Ibid., p. 139.
5. Ibid., p. 142.
6. Ibid., p. 157.
7. Ibid., p. 148.
8. Ibid., p. 158.
9. Ibid., p. 158.

10. SOUL-SALVATION BY GRACE THROUGH FAITH

1. James D.G. Dunn, *Romans 1-8*, Word Biblical Commentary, vol. 38a (Grand Rapids: Zondervan, 1988), p. 177.
2. Ibid., p. 178.
3. J.N. Young, *Young's Literal Translation of the Holy Bible*, 1898, public domain.
4. Dunn, p. 178.
5. Ibid.

6. Ibid., p. 179.
7. Ibid., p. 180.
8. Ibid., pp. 181-82.
9. Ibid., p. 182.
10. Arlen Chitwood, *The Acts Period* (Cottonwood, AZ, 2020), p. 217

11. HIS RESURRECTION FOR OUR RIGHTEOUS LIVING

1. Joseph Henry Thayer, *Thayer's Greek-English Lexicon on the New Testament* (Accordance Electronic edition), "logizomai"
2. *Strong's Greek Dictionary of the New Testament* (Accordance Electronic edition), "logizomai"
3. *Apple Dictionary*, ver. 2.3.0, "impute"
4. James D.G. Dunn, *Romans 1-8, Word Biblical Commentary*, vol. 38a (Grand Rapids: Zondervan, 1988), p. 232.
5. Ibid.
6. Ibid., pp. 232-33.
7. Ibid., p. 233.
8. Arlen Chitwood, *Judgment Seat of Christ* (Cottonwood, AZ: The Lamp Broadcast, 2011), p. 214.
9. Dunn, p. 235.
10. Ibid., p. 240.
11. Footnote in Zane C. Hodges, *Romans: Deliverance From Wrath* (Corinth, TX: Grace Evangelical Society, 2013), p. 129.

12. REJOICING IN HOPE OF GLORY

1. James D.G. Dunn, *Romans 1-8, Word Biblical Commentary*, vol. 38a (Grand Rapids: Zondervan, 1988), p. 262.
2. Ibid., p. 262.
3. Marvin R. Vincent, *Word Studies in the New Testament*, Accordance electronic ed. 2004), paragraph 12688.
4. Zane C. Hodges, *Romans: Deliverance From Wrath* (Corinth, TX: Grace Evangelical Society, 2013), Note by John Niemela, p. 133.
5. Ibid., p. 133.
6. Ibid. Note by Niemela, p. 133.
7. A. T. Robertson, *Word Pictures in the New Testament*, Accordance electronic ed. (Altamonte Springs: OakTree Software, 2001), paragraph 4686.
8. Dunn, p. 264.
9. Hodges, p. 136.
10. Dunn, p. 265.
11. Ibid., p. 268.
12. Hodges, pp. 184-85.
13. Dunn, pp. 268-69.

13. GRACE WINS!

1. Jan Bonds, *The One Purpose of God: An Answer to the Doctrine of Eternal Punishment* (Grand Rapids: Wm. B. Eerdmans Publ. Co, 1998), pp. 100-101.
2. Ibid., p. 101.
3. Ibid.
4. Zane C. Hodges, *Romans: Deliverance From Wrath* (Corinth, TX: Grace Evangelical Society, 2013), p. 146.
5. James D.G. Dunn, *Romans 1-8, Word Biblical Commentary*, vol. 38a (Grand Rapids: Zondervan, 1988), p. 291.
6. Ibid., pp. 293-94.
7. Hodges, pp. 147-48.
8. Dunn, p. 292.
9. Hodges, pp. 152-53.
10. Ibid., quoting Moulton, p. 153.
11. Ibid., p. 154.
12. Ibid., p. 156, note by Bob Wilkin.
13. Dunn, p. 299.
14. Hodges, p. 160.
15. Ibid.

14. BURIED IN DEATH, RISEN IN LIFE

1. George Duffield, "Stand Up, Stand Up for Jesus," 1858.
2. William R. Newell, *Romans: Verse-by-Verse* (Chicago: Moody Press, 1938), p. 201.
3. John A. Witmer, *Romans* (*The Bible Knowledge Commentary*; eds. John F. Walvoord and Roy B. Zuck; Accordance electronic ed. 2 vols.; Wheaton: Victor Books, 1983), 2:460-61.
4. Rene A. Lopez, *Romans, The Grace NT Commentary*; ed. Robert N. Wilkin (Denton, TX: Grace Evangelical Society, 2010), vol. 2, p. 651.
5. Witmer, 2:461-62.
6. Ibid.
7. Alva McClain, *Romans: The Gospel of God's Grace* (Chicago: Moody Press, 1973), p. 144.
8. Zane C. Hodges, *Romans: Deliverance From Wrath* (Corinth, TX: Grace Evangelical Society, 2013), p. 171.
9. McClain, p. 144.
10. Marvin R. Vincent, *Word Studies in the New Testament*, Accordance electronic ed. 2004), paragraph 12787.
11. McClain, p. 145.
12. Vincent, paragraph 12794.
13. James D.G. Dunn, *Romans 1-8, Word Biblical Commentary*, vol. 38a (Grand Rapids: Zondervan, 1988), p. 351.
14. William Harrison, *Romans: Peace for All Through Christ* (Self-published, 2020), p. 83.

15. WHO'S YOUR MASTER?

1. Zane C. Hodges, *Romans: Deliverance From Wrath* (Corinth, TX: Grace Evangelical Society, 2013), p. 178.
2. Ibid., p. 177.
3. *Robert Govett on Romans* (Hayesville, NC: Schoettle Publ. Co., 2010), p. 226.
4. William R. Newell, *Romans: Verse-by-Verse* (Chicago: Moody Press, 1938), p. 241-42.
5. Hodges, p. 179.
6. William Harrison, *Romans: Peace for All Through Christ* (Self-published, 2020), p. 84-85.
7. Hodges, p. 180.
8. Retired U.S. Army Chaplain Rev. John M. Sweigart, "Eternal Life: Gift or Reward?" (unpublished paper, 7-11-17).
9. John Piper, "Will We Be Finally 'Saved' by Faith Alone?" March 2, 2018, https://www.desiringgod.org/interviews/will-we-be-finally-saved-by-faith-alone (accessed 2/8/24).
10. Dale Taliaferro, study notes on Romans 6, dated June 20, 2018.

16. THE DEADENING EFFECTS OF LEGALISM

1. Zane C. Hodges, *Romans: Deliverance From Wrath* (Corinth, TX: Grace Evangelical Society, 2013), p. 185.
2. Ibid., p. 188.
3. Ibid. p. 189.
4. Ibid. Footnote by Robert N. Wilkins
5. Ibid. p. 191.

17. HOW TO HAVE VICTORY OVER SINNING

1. Watchman Nee, *The Normal Christian Life* (London: Witness and Testimony Publishers, 1957), p. 9.
2. Ibid.
3. Zane C. Hodges, *Romans: Deliverance From Wrath* (Corinth, TX: Grace Evangelical Society, 2013), p. 206.
4. Ibid., p. 207.
5. Ibid. Footnote by Robert N. Wilkin.
6. Ibid.
7. Ibid. Footnote by Robert N. Wilkin.
8. Ibid., pp. 153, quoting Moulton and Milligan.
9. Ibid., p. 206.
10. Ibid., p. 207, footnote by John Niemela.
11. Charles Trumbull, *Victory in Christ* (Fort Washington, PA: CLC Publications, 2019, originally published by The Sunday School Times, 1959).
12. Hodges, p. 211.
13. Ibid., pp. 212-13.

14. Ibid., pp. 213-14.
15. Ibid. Footnote by Robert N. Wilkin, pp. 216-17.
16. Ibid., p. 218.

18. THE REVEALING OF GOD'S GLORIFIED SONS

1. W.H. Griffith Thomas, *Commentary on Romans* (Grand Rapids: Kregel Publications, 1974), p. 213.
2. Zane C. Hodges, *Romans: Deliverance From Wrath* (Corinth, TX: Grace Evangelical Society, 2013), p. 222-23.
3. Ibid., Note by John Niemela, p. 222.
4. Ibid., Note by John Niemela, p. 223.
5. *Robert Govett on Romans* (Hayesville, NC: Schoettle Publ. Co., 2010), p. 318.
6. Arlen Chitwood, *God's Firstborn Sons* (Cottonwood, AZ: The Lamp Broadcast, 2013), p. 29.
7. Hodges, p. 221.
8. Ron Hamilton, *I'm Adopted* (Greenville, SC: Majesty Music, 1987).
9. Ibid., p. 225.
10. G.H. Lang, *Firstborn Sons* (Hayesville, NC: Schoettle Publ. Co., 1984), p. 123.
11. G.H. Lang, *World Chaos: Its Root and Remedy* (London: Paternoster Press, 1948), p. 65.

19. BIRTH OF A NEW AGE

1. Galt MacDermot, Gerome Ragni, and James Rado, "Aquarius/Let the Sunshine In" (BMG Rights Management, Sony/ATV Music Publishing LLC, Warner Chappell Music, Inc., 1969).
2. Billy Davis, Bill Backer, Roger Cook, and Roger Greenaway, "I'd Like to Teach the World to Sing" (EMI April Music Inc. o/b/o Shada Music Inc., 1971).
3. Frank E Manuel and Fritzie P. Manuel, *Utopian Thoughts in the Western World* (Cambridge, Mass.: Harvard Univ. Press, 1979).
4. Arlen Chitwood, *The Time of the End*, vol. 1 (Cottonwood, AZ: The Lamp Broadcast, revised 2024, originally published in 2011), pp. 274-75.
5. Ibid., pp. 119-120.
6. G.H. Lang, *World Chaos: Its Root and Remedy* (London: Paternoster Press, 1948), p. 250.
7. Arlen Chitwood, *The Study of Scripture* (Cottonwood, AZ: The Lamp Broadcast, 2011), p. 272.
8. Arlen Chitwood, *The Time of the End*, vol. 2 (Cottonwood, AZ: The Lamp Broadcast, revised 2024, originally published in 2011), p. 31.
9. Ibid., pp. 316-17.
10. Ibid., p. 109.
11. Arlen Chitwood, *By Faith* (Cottonwood, AZ: The Lamp Broadcast, 2012), pp. 347-48.

20. PROMISES FOR FIRSTBORN SONS

1. Zane C. Hodges, *Romans: Deliverance From Wrath* (Corinth, TX: Grace Evangelical Society, 2013), p. 233.
2. Ibid, pp. 233-34.
3. G.H. Lang, *World Chaos: Its Root and Remedy* (London: Paternoster Press, 1948), pp.63-4.
4. Hodges, p. 240.
5. Ibid., note by Bob Wilkin, p. 241.
6. G. Campbell Morgan, *The Parables of the Kingdom* (New York: Fleming Revell, 1907), p. 184.
7. Lang, pp.64.
8. Hodges, p. 248.

21. HAS ISRAEL BEEN REPLACED?

1. https://ccjr.us/dialogika-resources/primary-texts-from-the-history-of-the-relationship/luther-1543, accessed 7/22/24, from the Council of Centers on Jewish-Christian Relations, MARTIN LUTHER, "On the Jews and Their Lies" (1543), Parts 11-13 [Martin H. Bertram, translator, *Luther's Works* (Philadelphia: Fortress Press, 1971)]
2. Ibid.
3. https://en.wikipedia.org/wiki/On_the_Jews_and_Their_Lies, accessed 7/22/24.
4. Ibid., quoting Marc H. Ellis, "Hitler and the Holocaust, Christian Anti-Semitism" Archived 2007-07-10 at the Wayback Machine, Baylor University Center for American and Jewish Studies, Spring 2004, slide 14. Also see "Nuremberg Trial Proceedings" Archived 2006-03-21 at the Wayback Machine, Vol. 12, p. 318, Avalon Project, Yale Law School, April 19, 1946.
5. Walter L. Wilson, *A Dictionary of Bible Types* (Peabody, Mass: Hendrickson Publ., 1999, originally published in 1957 by Eerdman's), p. 254.
6. Jan Bonda, *The One Purpose of God: An Answer to the Doctrine of Eternal Punishment* (Grand Rapids, MI: Wm. B. Eerdman's Publ. Co., 1998), pp. 131-32.
7. http://www.messianicassociation.org/ezine17-at.replacement-theology.htm, a publication of the Association of Messianic Congregations, accessed 7/22/24.
8. Bonda, p. 131.
9. Arlen Chitwood, *Salvation Message* (Cottonwood, AZ: Lamp Broadcast, 2021), p. 74.
10. Bonda, pp. 62-63.
11. Ibid., p. 131

22. ISRAEL'S FUTURE RESTORATION AND GLOBAL IMPACT

1. Henry M. Morris, *The Genesis Record* (Grand Rapids: Baker Book House, 1976), pp. 39-40.
2. Arlen Chitwood, *God's Firstborn Sons* (Cottonwood, AZ: Lamp Broadcast, 2004, revised 2013), pp. 13-15.

3. Chitwood, booklet entitled, "Salvation in the O.T., N.T.", pp. 1-2.
4. Chitwood, *God's Firstborn Sons*, pp. 19-20.
5. Zane C. Hodges, *Romans: Deliverance From Wrath* (Corinth, TX: Grace Evangelical Society, 2013), p. 262.
6. Jan Bonda, *The One Purpose of God: An Answer to the Doctrine of Eternal Punishment* (Grand Rapids, MI: Wm. B. Eerdman's Publ. Co., 1998), p. 141.
7. Hodges, p. 263.
8. Hodges, p. 266.
9. Bonda, p. 140.
10. Rene A. Lopez, *Romans, The Grace NT Commentary*; ed. Robert N. Wilkin (Denton, TX: Grace Evangelical Society, 2010), vol. 2, p. 671.
11. Bonda, pp. 143-45.
12. Hodges, p. 269.

23. VESSELS OF MERCY PREPARED FOR GLORY

1. Zane C. Hodges, *Romans: Deliverance From Wrath* (Corinth, TX: Grace Evangelical Society, 2013), p. 270-71.
2. Ibid., pp. 273-74.
3. Ibid., pp. 279-80.
4. Ibid., p. 282.
5. Ibid., p. 285.
6. Ibid., pp. 285-87.
7. Ibid., p. 288.

24. THE WORD OF FAITH IS NEAR YOU

1. Zane C. Hodges, *Romans: Deliverance From Wrath* (Corinth, TX: Grace Evangelical Society, 2013), p. 296-97.
2. Ibid., p. 299. Footnote by Bob Wilkin.
3. Ibid., p. 299.
4. Ibid., p. 299, Footnote by John Niemela.
5. Ibid., p. 302 Footnote by John Niemela.
6. Ibid., p. 302-03.
7. Arlen Chitwood, *Message in the Gospels, Acts, Epistles* (Cottonwood, AZ: Lamp Broadcast, 2018), pp. 191-92.
8. *Strong's Greek Dictionary of the New Testament* (Accordance Electronic edition), "epikaleomai"
9. Chitwood, *Had Ye Believed Moses*, 1999, revised in 2013, p. 48.
10. Hodges, pp. 303-304.
11. Chitwood, *Search for the Bride*, 2001, revised in 2012, pp. 82-83.
12. Chitwood, *Judgment Seat of Christ*, 1986, revised in 2011, p. 67.
13. Joseph Henry Thayer, *Thayer's Greek-English Lexicon on the New Testament* (Accordance Electronic edition), "akoē"
14. Hodges, p. 310, quoting the *Jerusalem Bible*.
15. Chitwood, *Had Ye Believed Moses*, pp. 114-15.
16. Hodges, p. 311.

17. Chitwood, *Signs in John's Gospel*, 2007, revised 2012, pp. 31-32.

25. ISRAEL'S TIME-OUT

1. Zane C. Hodges, *Romans: Deliverance From Wrath* (Corinth, TX: Grace Evangelical Society, 2013), p. 318.
2. Jan Bonda, *The One Purpose of God: An Answer to the Doctrine of Eternal Punishment* (Grand Rapids, MI: Wm. B. Eerdman's Publ. Co., 1998), p. 157.
3. James D.G. Dunn, *Romans 1-8*, Word Biblical Commentary, vol. 38a (Grand Rapids: Zondervan, 1988), p. 645.
4. Ibid., p. 647.
5. Hodges, p. 326.
6. Arlen Chitwood, *Had Ye Believed Moses* (Cottonwood, AZ: Lamp Broadcast, 1999, revised in 2013), p. 74.
7. Bonda, p. 161.
8. Hodges, p. 330.
9. Ibid., p. 331
10. Ibid.
11. Ibid.
12. Bonda, p. 163.

26. ISRAEL WILL BE SAVED AND ALL MANKIND TOO

1. *Strong's Greek Dictionary of the New Testament* (Accordance Electronic edition), "phurama"
2. Zane C. Hodges, *Romans: Deliverance From Wrath* (Corinth, TX: Grace Evangelical Society, 2013), p. 332.
3. Ibid., p. 332.
4. Ibid., pp. 336-37.
5. Ibid., p. 338.
6. Jan Bonda, *The One Purpose of God: An Answer to the Doctrine of Eternal Punishment* (Grand Rapids, MI: Wm. B. Eerdman's Publ. Co., 1998), p. 170.
7. Arlen Chitwood, *Judgment Seat of Christ* (Cottonwood, AZ: Lamp Broadcast, 1986, revised 2011), pp. 210-11.
8. Bonda, p. 171.
9. Bonda, p. 184.
10. Bonda, p. 185.
11. Bonda, pp. 171-72.
12. Joseph Henry Thayer, *Thayer's Greek-English Lexicon on the New Testament* (Accordance Electronic edition), "apeitheia"
13. *A Greek–English Lexicon of the New Testament and Other Early Christian Literature*, 3rd ed. (BDAG), Accordance electronic edition, s.v. "συγκλείω," 952.
14. Bonda, p. 193.
15. Ibid., pp. 192-93.
16. Hodges, p. 349.
17. Ibid., pp. 350-51.
18. Ibid., p. 351.

19. Bonda, p. 178.

27. METAMORPHOSIS CULMINATING IN GLORY

1. Arlen Chitwood, *Salvation of the Soul* (Cottonwood, AZ: Lamp Broadcast, 1983, revised 2011), p. 31.
2. Marvin R. Vincent, *Word Studies in the New Testament*, Accordance electronic ed. 2004), paragraph 13351.
3. Ibid.
4. Zane C. Hodges, *Romans: Deliverance From Wrath* (Corinth, TX: Grace Evangelical Society, 2013), p. 357.
5. Kenneth S. Wuest, *Mark — Romans — Galatians—Ephesians and Colossians, vol. 1 of Wuest's Word Studies from the Greek New Testament*, quoting Trench. Accordance electronic ed. (Grand Rapids: Eerdman's, 1973), 206.
6. *Apple Dictionary*, ver. 2.3.0, "zeitgeist"
7. *A Greek–English Lexicon of the New Testament and Other Early Christian Literature*, 3rd ed. (BDAG), Accordance electronic edition, s.v. "μεταμορφόω," 639.
8. Arlen Chitwood, *Run to Win* (Cottonwood, AZ: Lamp Broadcast, 1990, revised 2012), p. 24.
9. Wuest, p. 208.
10. Hodges, p. 360.
11. BDAG, s.v. "μετασχηματίζω," p. 641.
12. Arlen Chitwood, *By Faith* (Cottonwood, AZ: Lamp Broadcast, 1982, revised 2012), p. 348.

28. GET OFF YOUR HIGH HORSE

1. *Robert Govett on Romans* (Hayesville, NC: Schoettle Publ. Co., 2010), p. 484.
2. W.H. Griffith Thomas, *Commentary on Romans* (Grand Rapids: Kregel Publications, 1974), p. 333.
3. Ibid., p. 332.
4. H.C.G. Moule, edited by Philip Hillyer, *The Epistle to the Romans* (Fort Washington, PA: CLC Publications, 2001, originally published in 1958), p. 263.
5. Joseph Henry Thayer, *Thayer's Greek-English Lexicon on the New Testament* (Accordance Electronic edition), s.v. "charisma," par. 9870.
6. Ibid., s.v. "profeteia," par. 8192.
7. W.E. Vine, *The Epistle to the Romans* (London: Oliphants Ltd., 1948), p. 179.
8. William Barclay, *The Letter to the Romans, The New Daily Study Bible*, Accordance electronic ed. (Louisville: Westminster John Knox Press, 2002), 190.
9. *A Greek–English Lexicon of the New Testament and Other Early Christian Literature*, 3rd ed. (BDAG), Accordance electronic edition, s.v. "ἀναλογία," 67.
10. Zane C. Hodges, *Romans: Deliverance From Wrath* (Corinth, TX: Grace Evangelical Society, 2013), p. 366.
11. Vine, p. 179.
12. William R. Newell, *Romans: Verse-by-Verse* (Chicago: Moody Press, 1938), pp. 463-65.

13. Alva McClain, *Romans: The Gospel of God's Grace* (Chicago: Moody Press, 1973), p. 211.
14. Hodges, p. 367.

29. RULES FOR REVOLUTIONIZING HOME AND CHURCH

1. *A Greek-English Lexicon of the New Testament and Other Early Christian Literature*, 3rd ed. (BDAG), Accordance electronic edition, s.v. "ἀγάπη," p. 6.
2. William R. Newell, *Romans: Verse-by-Verse* (Chicago: Moody Press, 1938), pp. 469.
3. William Barclay, *The Letter to the Romans, The New Daily Study Bible*, Accordance electronic ed. (Louisville: Westminster John Knox Press, 2002), 193.
4. Ibid. p. 192.
5. BDAG, s.v. "φιλαδελφία," p. 869.
6. Zane C. Hodges, *Romans: Deliverance From Wrath* (Corinth, TX: Grace Evangelical Society, 2013), p. 370.
7. Barclay, p. 197.
8. Hodges, p. 374.
9. Barclay, pp. 317.
10. Hodges, p. 376.
11. Ibid., p. 377.
12. Ibid.
13. Barclay, pp. 200-01.
14. Hodges, p. 378.

30. OBEYING GOVERNMENT AND LOVING MANKIND

1. Saul Alinsky, *Rules for Radicals* (New York: Random House, 1971), dedication page.
2. Ibid., p. 1.
3. Ibid.
4. Zane C. Hodges, *Romans: Deliverance From Wrath* (Corinth, TX: Grace Evangelical Society, 2013), p. 383.
5. James M. Stifler, *The Epistle to the Romans* (New York: Fleming H. Revell Co, 1897), p. 230. Stifler's commentary was later published by Moody Press (1983).
6. Ibid.
7. Hodges, p. 384.
8. Stifler, pp. 230-31.
9. Hodges, p. 392, note by Bob Wilkin.

31. EVERY KNEE SHALL BOW

1. Jan Bonds, *The One Purpose of God: An Answer to the Doctrine of Eternal Punishment* (Grand Rapids: Wm. B. Eerdmans Publ. Co, 1998), pp. 240-41.
2. Ibid., p. 241.
3. Zane C. Hodges, *Romans: Deliverance From Wrath* (Corinth, TX: Grace Evangelical Society, 2013), p. 401.

4. Ibid., p. 413.
5. Ibid., p. 415.
6. From the hymn "Blessed Assurance," written by Fanny Crosby and Phoebe Knapp in 1873.
7. Ibid., p. 418.
8. Thomas Talbott, "Christ Victorious," in *Universal Salvation? The Current Debate*, ed. Robin A. Parry and Christian H. Partridge (Grand Rapids: Eerdmans Publ., 2004), 23.
9. Hodges, p. 413.

32. GLORIFYING GOD WITH ONE MIND AND VOICE

1. Jan Bonds, *The One Purpose of God: An Answer to the Doctrine of Eternal Punishment* (Grand Rapids: Wm. B. Eerdmans Publ. Co, 1998), p. 242.
2. Zane C. Hodges, *Romans: Deliverance From Wrath* (Corinth, TX: Grace Evangelical Society, 2013), p. 424.
3. Ibid.
4. Bonda, p. 243.
5. Ibid., p. 255.
6. Ibid., p. 244.
7. Ibid., pp. 244-45.
8. Ibid., p. 246.

33. CRUSHING THE DEVIL

1. Zane C. Hodges, *Romans: Deliverance From Wrath* (Corinth, TX: Grace Evangelical Society, 2013), pp. 15-16, note by John Niemela.
2. *Strong's Greek Dictionary of the New Testament* (Accordance Electronic edition), "skopeo"
3. Joseph Henry Thayer, *Thayer's Greek-English Lexicon on the New Testament* (Accordance Electronic edition), "ekklinō"
4. *A Greek–English Lexicon of the New Testament and Other Early Christian Literature*, 3rd ed. (BDAG), Accordance electronic edition, s.v. "ἀτάκτως," p. 148.
5. Ibid., s.v., "καταργέω," p. 525.
6. Thayer, s.v., "suntribō."
7. John A. MacMillan, *The Authority of the Believer* (Camp Hill, PA: Wing Spread Publ., 2007, originally published in 1932), p. 5.
8. Ibid., pp. 21-22.
9. Ibid., pp. 173-74.

34. THE FELLOWSHIP OF THE MYSTERY

1. Joseph Henry Thayer, *Thayer's Greek-English Lexicon on the New Testament* (Accordance Electronic edition), "stērizō"

ADDENDUM 1: ETERNAL IS NOT FOREVER

1. I will confine my comments going forward to the Greek adjective *aionios*, though the same principle applies to the Hebrew word *olam*.
2. Marvin R. Vincent, *Word Studies in the New Testament*, Accordance electronic ed. (2004), paragraph 16341ff. Additional Note on 2 Thess. 1:9.
3. *Strong's Greek Dictionary of the New Testament* (Accordance Electronic edition), "phthartos" and "athanasia"
4. William D. Mounce, *Mounce Greek Dictionary*, Accordance electronic ed. (Altamonte Springs: OakTree Software, 2006), s.v. "apollymi," paragraph 1915.
5. Ibid, s.v. "krino," paragraph 8710.
6. James S. Hollandsworth, *The Savior of All Men* (Forest City, NC: HollyPublishing, 2022).

ADDENDUM 2: FOUR DEGREES OF SALVATION

1. *Strong's Greek Dictionary of the New Testament* (Accordance Electronic edition), "malista"
2. Joseph Henry Thayer, *Thayer's Greek-English Lexicon on the New Testament* (Accordance Electronic edition), "malista"
3. *A Greek–English Lexicon of the New Testament and Other Early Christian Literature*, 3rd ed. *(BDAG)*, Accordance electronic edition, s.v. "μάλιστα," 613.
4. *Strong's*, "kathistemi"

ALSO BY JAMES S. HOLLANDSWORTH

Available on Amazon:

The End of the Pilgrimage: Your Judgment Seat Verdict and How it Determines Your Place in His Kingdom (2015)

Christ Magnified: Glorifying Jesus by Your Life (2015)

Keys for Inheriting the Kingdom: Unlocking the Parables of Jesus (2017)

The Savior of All Men: God's Plan to Reconcile All Through Jesus Christ (2022)

The Kingdom According to Jesus (Volume One): The Lamb of God and His Offer of Kingdom Inheritance (2023)

The Kingdom According to Jesus (Volume Two): The Sermon on the Mount and the Qualifications for Kingdom Inheritance (2023)

Made in the USA
Columbia, SC
28 September 2024

43021795R00303